Quiet Water

Canoe Guide

New York

BEST PADDLING LAKES AND PONDS
FOR CANOE AND KAYAK

John Hayes and Alex Wilson

APPALACHIAN MOUNTAIN CLUB BOOKS
BOSTON, MASSACHUSETTS

Cover Photograph: Moss Lake by Eric Dresser
All photographs by the author unless otherwise noted.
Cartographer: Ian Duncan
Book & Cover Design: Carol Bast Tyler

Distributed by the Globe Pequot Press, Inc., Old Saybrook, CT.

Library of Congress Cataloging-in-Publication Data
Hayes, John.
    Quiet water canoe guide, New York : best paddling lakes and ponds for canoe and kayak / John Hayes and Alex Wilson.
        p.   cm.
    Includes index.
    ISBN 1-878239-51-1 (alk. paper)
    1. Canoe and canoing—New York (State)—Guidebooks. 2. Lakes—New York (State)—Guidebooks. 3. Ponds—New York (State)—Guidebooks. 4. New York (State)—Guidebooks. I. Wilson, Alex, 1955- . II. Title.
GV776.N7H39   1996
917.47—dc20
                                                                    96-11297
                                                                          CIP

The paper used in this publication meets the minimum requirements of the American National Standard for Information Sciences—Permanence of Paper for Printed Library Materials, ANSI Z39.48–1984.∞

**Due to changes in conditions,
use of the information in this book
is at the sole risk of the user.**

Printed on recycled paper using soy-based inks.

Printed in the United States of America.

10 9 8 7 6 5 4 3 2 1   96 97 98 99 00 01

Contents

Nature Essays

Foreword

LET'S GET ONE THING STRAIGHT. If as a paddler you have a yen for exploits on the Upper Hudson and the Colorado's Grand Canyon, if the more challenging the waters the better you are satisfied, if, in short, heroism is your aim, this book is not for you. It is a book not for heroes who seek to dominate the natural world but for pilgrims who seek it humbly for understanding and harmony.

Quiet Water Canoe Guide: New York is a handbook of natural history as well as a practical guide to getting there. It will open your eyes to the richness of perception that awaits the casual paddler on New York State's lakes, ponds, and flatwater streams. The authors are competent guides. Alex Wilson is a naturalist and writer of two other quietwater guidebooks. John Hayes is a professor of biochemistry and environmental science and a leader of natural-history field trips. You may not have their luck of spotting four bald eagles at once, adults and fledglings, at a nest on Deer River Flow. But there is a good chance that they will draw your attention to cavorting river otters; to the spectacular flight of the peregrine falcon; to damselflies leaping off the landing pads of floating vegetation as your boat glides by; to the intricate mechanism by which carnivorous plants—sundew, pitcher, and bladderwort—feed on insects. And in the forever-wild forests of the Adirondacks and Catskills they will assist in transporting you back to an early time on this continent.

Quiet water has its rewards.

—Paul Jamieson
Writer with Donald Morris of
Adirondack Canoe Waters: North Flow

Acknowledgments

WE ARE INDEBTED to many individuals for helping in the creation of this book. First and foremost, we thank our families, Joanne, Andrew, and Stefanie Hayes, and Jerelyn, Lillian, and Frances Wilson. Thanks for joining us on occasional trips and putting up with too many weekends away during the paddling season and too many long evenings as we worked on the book.

For providing us with suggestions of bodies of water to visit, we thank Mary Ellen Jones of the Nissequogue River Canoe Club, Bill Marosz of the Whalers of Suffolk County, Diana Dreeben of Peconic Paddler, Dave Cilley of the St. Regis Canoe Outfitters, Beth Tickner of Tickner's Adirondack Canoe outfitters, Larry MacIntosh of Wildwater Outfitters, John Kowalski of the Canal View Cafe in Sylvan Beach, Jonathan and Nancy Fairbanks, Hudson Barton, Steve Bluestone, and Diane Arndt.

For putting up weary paddlers we thank John and Phyllis Conley, Stanley and Irma Selengut, Sandra Pell and Sherman Taishoff, Ellin Randel, Jonathan Ortlip, Kim and Dan Woodbury, and Lee Gratwick. For paddling companionship we thank Sally Andrews, Ian Duncan, Philip Demay, Lee and Lucy Gratwick, and Jill Hulme. Also, a special thanks to Dick Forrestal for mechanical assistance with Alex's car during a visit to Long Island.

For information on wildlife, we thank biologists Pete Nye, Bob Miller, and Michael Mathews with the Bureau of Wildlife at the New York State Department of Environmental Conservation and Bob Engel of Marlboro College.

Thank you to Ian Duncan for his fine computer cartographic work, to Marrin Robinson for the pen-and-ink wildlife illustrations, to Mark Lamoureux for photographic printing, to Nadav Malin for assistance with mapping and computer files, and to Gordon Hardy and his superb staff at the Appalachian Mountain Club, who consistently put up with sliding deadlines yet always seem able to deliver a book right on schedule.

Finally, on behalf of all paddlers who enjoy canoeing the Adirondack's wild rivers and lakes, we offer a heartfelt thanks to Paul Jamieson, coauthor of *Adirondack Canoe Waters: North Flow,* who reviewed and commented on portions of our manuscript. Over the past fifty years, Paul has probably done more than anyone else to promote canoeing in the Adirondacks—not only in showing others where to paddle, but also in working to ensure public access to these waters.

Introduction

NEW YORK offers some of the finest paddling in the eastern United States. Indeed, when most of us in the Northeast think about canoeing, it is the lakes, ponds, and rivers of New York's Adirondack Park that first come to mind. While few places in the state surpass the wildness of lakes and meandering flows of the Adirondacks, New York offers many other outstanding paddling destinations. From the tidal estuaries of Long Island, to the historic Erie Canal in the central part of the state, to the wild and marshy inlet creeks of Lake Ontario, there's tremendous paddling near and far—places just right for a several-day expedition or a half day of paddling near home.

This guide will help you find peace and quiet on the water. It will lead you to places where you can watch wood ducks swim through the early morning mist, where you can see old-growth white pines towering above crystal-clear ponds and imagine what our forests looked like centuries ago, where you can listen to the haunting wail of the loon as afternoon settles into dusk.

With quiet-water paddling, you don't need to carry around rapids or arrange complex drop-off and pickup logistics. You don't need a lot of fancy equipment and high-tech gear—though a light canoe makes it a lot easier if you plan to portage into New York's more out-of-the-way places. Among our most important gear on these paddling trips are binoculars and field guides to the fauna and flora.

Being avid paddlers, we have logged thousands of miles by car and hundreds of miles by canoe and kayak, searching for the best lakes and ponds to paddle. Some trips proved fruitless, as the pond we sought turned out to be inaccessible, off-limits to boating, ringed with cabins, or chock-full of speedboats. Some efforts yielded big surprises—when a place that looked uninteresting or inaccessible turned out to be a real gem.

This guide not only will lead you to a body of water but will explain why you might want to visit it. We hope it will simplify your research, so that you can spend your valuable time paddling, instead of driving around for hours trying to find an elusive or nonexistent access.

How We Selected These Lakes and Ponds

This guide includes only a small percentage of the several thousand lakes and ponds in New York. We started our selection process with some definite likes and dislikes when it comes to paddling: pretty scenery; limited development; few motorboats and Jet-skis; a varied shoreline with lots of coves and inlets to explore; and interesting plants, animals, and geological formations.

We included a variety of types of water as well: big lakes for when you really want to exercise your muscles over miles of paddling and small protected ponds that are just right when you have limited time, your children lack the patience for extended outings, or weather conditions preclude paddling the big lakes. To make the book useful to as many people as possible, we paid particular attention to lakes and ponds in more populated regions of the state. This is not only a book for vacationers planning a weeklong trip hundreds of miles from home but also a guide for the New York City business executive wanting to do some paddling on her afternoon off, or a Rochester family with a free Saturday morning and a sense of adventure.

When we took on this project, both of us were familiar with the Adirondacks, but we knew we'd be exploring mostly new places. Finding the best would take some work. We contacted friends and friends of friends—anyone who shared our interest in quiet-water canoeing— asking for suggestions. We studied DeLorme's excellent *New York Atlas and Gazetteer* and the superb canoeing guides from the Adirondack Mountain Club. We filled our files with information from the Department of Environmental Conservation, including their four-volume *Morphometric Atlas of Selected Lakes,* and we spent many days poring over the U.S. Geological Survey (USGS) 7.5-minute topographic maps of the state—all 850-plus.

We compiled an initial list of several hundred lakes, ponds, streams, and tidal estuaries for consideration. We paddled those that looked good from the boat access. In all, we found approximately 175 suitable for inclusion in the book's 86 sections. Some entries, such as the St. Regis Canoe Area, Beaver River Canoe Route, and Harriman State Park, include a number of different lakes, ponds, and streams.

We have by no means included all the very best places. During the course of our research, we constantly discovered new places—either through someone's tip, a reexamination of the maps, or just coincidence. Many dozens of other lakes and ponds around the state really should be in a guide like this. That's what future editions are for. If anyone has suggestions of other lakes and ponds that we should include, please pass them along to us (John Hayes or Alex Wilson, c/o AMC Books, 5 Joy Street, Boston, MA 02108). Also, please bring to our attention inaccuracies, suggestions for improvements, and clarifications to make future editions better.

Do We Really Want to Tell People about the Best Places?

Throughout this project, many people asked us how we could, in good conscience, tell others about our favorite hidden lakes and ponds—the more remote, pristine places, still unspoiled by too many people. After all, increased visitation would make these places less idyllic. That has indeed been a difficult issue for us—one we've spent many an hour grappling with as we paddled along.

We believe that by getting more people out enjoying these places—people who value wild remote areas—support will build for greater protection of these waters. For many lakes and ponds, protection will mean purchase of fragile surrounding areas by the state, local governments, or private organizations such as The Nature Conservancy to prevent further development. On other bodies of water, the best form of protection is restriction of high-speed boating.

We hope you will help protect some of our most treasured water resources. For many of the lakes and ponds in New York, the most vocal users right now are water-skiers and users of personal watercraft (Jet-skis), people who have the greatest impact on these delicate environments. The policy makers need to hear from low-impact users as well. We hope that when we update this guide in a few years, we'll be able to report that some of these lakes and ponds have more protection than they do today, thus preserving quiet waters for years to come.

Safety First

Your attraction to quiet water might result from having small children or not liking dangerous places—such as raging whitewater on rivers in the spring—or not wanting to concentrate too much on your paddling skills. So you turn to lakes and ponds, envisioning tranquil paddling on mirror-smooth water reflecting the surrounding hills.

You certainly will find these places, including the idyllic, mist-filled, mirror-smooth surfaces of quiet ponds at daybreak. But if you spend appreciable time paddling on New York's lakes, ponds, and estuaries, you will also encounter quite dangerous conditions. Strong winds can arise quickly, turning tranquil lakes into raging, whitecapped inland seas. On big lakes, strong winds can whip up two- to three-foot waves in no time—waves big enough to swamp a canoe. If you capsize in cold water far from shore, hypothermia can set in quickly. Along New York's coast, tidal rivers and estuaries often have swift currents—in some places faster than you can paddle against. If not approached with proper caution, these places can be very dangerous.

New York regulations require personal flotation devices, or PFDs, to be carried in all canoes and kayaks for every person in the boat (see further discussion of PFDs in the equipment section on page xiii). We recommend that everyone *wear* PFDs at all times on the water. Children under 12 years of age are required to wear PFDs on New York waters. With children in the boat, you too should wear a PFD so that if the boat capsizes you can help the children. A foam- or kapok-filled PFD will also keep you warmer in cold water.

If you don't normally paddle wearing a PFD, at least don it in windy conditions, when you're crossing large lakes, or when you may encounter substantial motorboat wakes. It may make you a little hotter, it may interfere with your paddling. But it could save your life.

Also, in the name of safety, be ready to change your plans. If you've just driven four hours to reach a particular Adirondack lake and it's blowing a gale, be ready to find a more protected body of water, or go hiking instead. We've made it a point to include in this guide small ponds and streams near some of the larger, better-known lakes for just this reason. Even if the weather forecast promises a beautiful sunny day with no wind, by afternoon it could be blowing a gale and pouring.

On some waters described in this guide, particularly the shallow, marshy ones, waterfowl-hunting season brings a big influx of activity. Avoid these areas during waterfowl-hunting season, especially if you see blinds and decoys in the water. To find out the hunting-season dates, contact the New York State Department of Environmental Conservation, Division of Fish and Wildlife, at 518-457-3521 or ask at a local sporting goods store.

Starting out Right: Equipment Selection

For quiet-water canoeing, you don't really need a whole lot of fancy, high-tech gear. Most any canoe will do, as long as it isn't a high-performance racing model or a tippy whitewater model. If you're new to canoeing, try to borrow a canoe before buying one. With a little experience, you'll be better able to select the right one.

Look for a stable canoe. Manufacturers often refer to both the initial stability and the secondary stability of their boats. A canoe with good initial stability and poor secondary stability will be unlikely to begin tipping, but once it starts to tip it may keep going (this is the case with some older aluminum canoes). Look for a model that does pretty well with both initial and secondary stability. The best canoe for lake and pond canoeing has a keel or shallow-V hull and fairly flat keel line to help it track in a straight line, even in a breeze. Whitewater canoes, on the other hand, have rounded bottoms and what's called rocker (a curve to the bottom from front to back) to provide maneuverability.

If you like out-of-the-way lakes and ponds, especially those requiring carries, try to stretch your budget to afford a Kevlar® canoe. Kevlar is a strong carbon fiber somewhat like fiberglass but much lighter. Our rugged, high-capacity, 18' 4" Mad River Lamoille canoe weighs just 60 pounds, and our solo 15' 9" Mad River Independence weighs less than 40 pounds. If you plan to canoe by yourself, you should consider a solo canoe, in which you sit (or kneel) close to the center of the boat. A well-designed solo canoe is far easier to paddle than a two-seater used solo.

Another solo paddling option is the sea kayak. These touring boats are rapidly increasing in popularity. Their long, narrow design, low profile to the wind, and two-bladed paddling style make them faster and more efficient to paddle than canoes, and we have used them on many of our trips. Kevlar sea kayaks are quite expensive, but they per-

Sally Andrews paddles a sea kayak as she explores a wooded shore.

form extremely well in rough water, particularly if equipped with a foot-operated rudder. To keep from taking on water in rough seas, a spray skirt is generally required.

A padded portage yoke in place of the center thwart on a canoe is essential if you plan on much carrying. If your yoke isn't padded, wear a life vest with padded shoulders for the carry. Attach a rope—called a "painter"—to the bow so you can secure the canoe when you stop for lunch, line it up or down a stream, and—if the need ever arises—grab onto it in an emergency. Both of us have embarrassing stories to tell about not using a painter—wind moves Kevlar boats where you don't want them to go!

Choose light and comfortable paddles. Our favorite for canoeing is a relatively short (50-inch), bent-shaft paddle that is handmade in West Danby, New York (Hilltop Paddles). Laminated from various woods, the paddle has a special synthetic tip to protect the tip of the blade. Bent-shaft paddles allow more efficient paddling, because the downward force of the paddle is more directly converted into forward thrust. However, straight-shaft paddles also work well, and we used them for years. Always carry at least one spare paddle per group, particularly on longer trips, in case a porcupine eats one.

As mentioned above, PFDs are a must—both by common sense and by law. The best life preserver is Coast Guard–approved Type I, II, or III. A floating cushion (Type IV PFD) is less effective than a life vest you wear. A good PFD keeps a person's face above water, even if he or she loses consciousness. There must be one PFD in the boat for each occupant, according to New York law, and children under 12 must wear their PFDs. With children, it is extremely important that the PFD be the right size so that it won't slip off. Adult PFDs are not acceptable for children. Although New York law does not require PFDs to be worn at all times by adults, we strongly recommend that you do so, especially when paddling with children.

As for clothing, plan for the unexpected—especially on longer trips. Even with a sunny day forecast, a shower can appear by afternoon. On trips of more than a few hours, we bring along a small stuff sack with rain gear. On day-long or longer trips, we also carry dry clothes. Along with rain coming up unexpectedly, temperatures can drop quickly, especially in the spring or fall—when you can avoid crowds. Lightweight nylon or polypropylene clothing dries more quickly than cotton, and wool still retards heat loss when wet. Remember that heads lose heat faster than torsos—bring a hat. Finally, even though you may be

Insist that life vests (PFDs) be worn by children. We recommend that everyone wear a life vest at all times when paddling.

plenty warm from paddling, children may be getting cold while just sitting in the bottom of the boat. Watch for signs of their discomfort.

Paddling Technique

As with equipment selection, canoeing technique is a lot more critical with whitewater canoeing than it is with quiet-water paddling. On a quiet pond, does it matter if you use the proper J-stroke, or if you know the sweep stroke, the draw, or the reverse J? No. Learning some of these strokes, however, can make a day of paddling more relaxing and enjoyable. We watch lots of novices zigzagging along, frantically switching sides while shouting orders back and forth. People have told us about marriage counseling sessions devoted to paddling technique.

Paddling doesn't have to be so difficult. If you want to learn canoeing techniques, buy a book or participate in a canoeing workshop, such as those offered by the Appalachian Mountain Club, equipment retailers, and canoe manufacturers. Among the books we recommend on canoeing are *Beyond the Paddle* by Garret Conover (Tilbury

House, 1991); *The Complete Wilderness Paddler* by Davidson and Gugge (Vintage, 1983); *The New Wilderness Canoeing and Camping* by Cliff Jacobson (ICS Books, 1986); and *Pole, Paddle & Portage* by Bill Riviere (Little, Brown & Co., 1969). For kayaking, good books include *The Essential Sea Kayaker* by David Seidman (Ragged Mountain Press, 1992) and *Derek C. Hutchinson's Guide to Sea Kayaking,* Second Edition, by Derek Hutchinson (Globe Pequot Press, 1990).

If you're a novice paddler, we suggest starting out on small ponds. Practice paddling into the wind, with the wind, and across it. On a warm day close to shore, you might even want to practice capsizing. That sounds odd, but intentionally tipping your canoe or kayak will give you an idea of its limits and how easily it can tip over (refer to the previous discussion of initial and secondary stability). You might also try to get back into a boat when you're away from shore. With two people, you should be able to right the canoe, getting most of the water out (keep a bailer *fastened* to a thwart). Getting back in is another story. . . . Good luck.

Public Access and Camping in New York

We have tried to list only public access locations for all of the lakes and ponds included here, but that doesn't mean the surrounding lands are public as well. Most bodies of water described in this book are bounded in part by private property. Do not launch your boat on private land without first asking permission, and do not get out just anywhere along the shore—particularly on land posted as private. Never camp on posted land. Disputes between recreational users of land and private property owners have sometimes gotten tense, particularly in some areas of Adirondack Park. Cooperation will help keep bodies of water open to paddlers.

Fortunately, within Adirondack Park and throughout the state, several million acres of public lands and many hundreds of bodies of water remain open for all of us to enjoy. The state also maintains several hundred campgrounds and camping areas for our enjoyment. Campgrounds charge modest fees, and some camping areas—particularly in Adirondack and Catskill Parks—are free. Because fragile vegetation around lakes and ponds can suffer damage easily from heavy use, we recommend camping in designated areas only.

Other Lodging Options

Along with camping, there are often options for other nearby lodging. For information, check your local bookstore or library for guides to bed-and-breakfasts or country inns, many of which can be found near the lakes and ponds in this guide. You might also want to contact local Chambers of Commerce for listings, as well as for names of area restaurants and attractions.

Bring the Kids Along

Quiet-water canoeing is a great activity to do with kids—but take adequate safety precautions. Maintain flexibility in your plans in case of adverse weather, and always make it a rule to wear life preservers in the canoe.

When canoeing with kids, try to make it fun. If parents argue about who should paddle where or when, or yell about rocks ahead, that will affect the kids. Try to keep calm. Your kids will do better, and you'll have a better time. On long paddling excursions, set up a cozy place where young children can sleep. After the initial excitement of paddling fades, the gently rolling canoe often puts children to sleep, especially near the end of a long day.

Respect for the Outdoors

Lakes and ponds can easily suffer from recreational use. Protecting them requires our careful attention. Even a low-impact pastime such as canoeing or kayaking can have a substantial effect on fragile marsh habitat. Carrying canoes on the Adirondack carry trails can damage plants and erode narrow trails, particularly in the spring and when using portage carts. Our wetlands are extremely important ecosystems and home to many rare and endangered species. An unaware paddler can disturb nesting loons and eagles, rare turtles, and fragile bog orchids. Please use care as you enjoy these waters.

You can go even further than the old adage, "Take only photographs, leave only footprints." On the most pristine of our lakes and ponds, we make it a habit to carry along a trash bag and pick up the leavings of less thoughtful individuals. If each of us does the same, we will enjoy more attractive places to paddle. While motorboaters tend to have a bad reputation when it comes to leaving trash, we want paddlers to have the opposite reputation—which could come in handy when some of us seek greater paddling access on some of New York's more remote lakes. To learn more about how to enjoy a wild area without damaging it, see the excellent book *Soft Paths* by Hampton and Cole (Stackpole Books, 1988).

What You'll See

Wetland ecosystems are diverse and exciting—by far the richest ecosystems accessible to us. In New York, you can visit everything from saltwater tidal marshes to deep, crystal-clear, mountain ponds to unique bog environments. You'll have the opportunity to observe hundreds of species of birds; dozens of species of mammals, turtles, and snakes; and literally thousands of plants. Some of these species are quite rare and exciting to discover—such as a delicate bog orchid or a family of otters. But even ordinary plants and animals offer a storehouse of information, leading to exciting discoveries and providing hours of enjoyable observation.

We've picked out and described a few interesting plants and animals you might encounter on New York's lakes and ponds. You will find these write-ups—and accompanying pen-and-ink illustrations by Marrin Robinson—interspersed in the lake and pond descriptions. By learning a little more about these species, you'll find them all the more fun to observe—well, maybe not the blackflies and mosquitoes . . . .

Have a Great Time

Our goal with this guide is to help you enjoy and appreciate the out-of-doors. We hope you will enjoy using this book as much as we enjoyed researching and writing it. Let us know what you like or dislike about the places we've described, and tell us about any others you think should be included.

Finally, this guide should not limit the areas you visit. Other lakes and ponds—literally thousands more in New York—offer excellent quiet-water canoeing. Buy some maps and explore. You'll find, as we did, that some ponds have no public access. Others bristle with summer homes. But many gems—not included in this guide—offer hours of paddling pleasure on hidden beaver ponds, quiet meandering channels of slow-moving streams, old millponds with ruins of long-abandoned mills, bird-filled estuaries. You can reveal these wonderful secrets, or keep them to yourself. And that's as it should be.

John Hayes
Alex Wilson
February 1996

How to Use This Book

FOR EACH LAKE or pond included in this book, we provide a short description and map. Most maps show the roads or highways that provide access to the body of water, as well as boat-launch sites. Some launch sites have boat ramps suitable for trailered motorboats as well as canoes, but many require a carry to the water—we do not distinguish between these types of launch sites on the maps.

The maps and descriptions included in this guide are designed to accompany road maps. If unfamiliar with your destination, you should also use a good highway map or the DeLorme Mapping Company's *New York Atlas and Gazetteer.* We have keyed each lake to this atlas, which divides the state into 80 10" x 15" maps. These detailed, 1:150,000-scale maps include most—but not all—boat-access locations, road names, campgrounds, parks, and other pertinent information. For more detail and information on topography, marsh areas, etc., refer to the 7.5-minute, 1:24,000-scale USGS topographic maps that we list at the beginning of each section.

Finally, while we call this a canoeing guide, the information applies equally well to sea kayaking. In fact, on the estuaries and big lakes, sea kayaking is often preferred over canoeing, because the lower profile of kayaks presents less surface area to the wind and—with a spray skirt—kayaks keep water out. We hope that whatever boat you choose, you will be careful and enjoy many hours of quiet-water paddling on the lakes and ponds of New York. Happy paddling!

Map Legend

⌒	Tent site
◀	Lean-to
⊓	Picnic area
Å	State or federal campground
Å	Private campground
⌣	Boat access
P	Parking area
⣤	Marsh
☼	Peak
Interstate highway	══════
State highway	━━━━━
Paved road	▪▬▪▬▪▬
Less-traveled road	─────
Rough dirt road	═ ═ ═ ═ ═
Foot path	─ ─ ─ ─ ─
River	═══→═══
Stream	───←───

} arrow indicates direction of flow

Locator Map

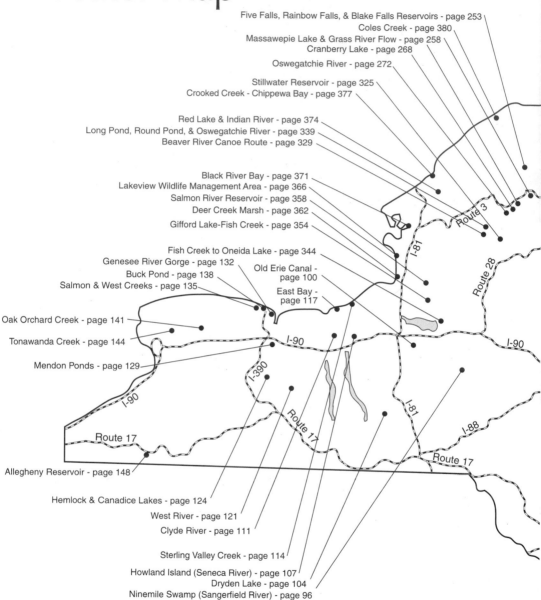

Five Falls, Rainbow Falls, & Blake Falls Reservoirs - page 253
Coles Creek - page 380
Massawepie Lake & Grass River Flow - page 258
Cranberry Lake - page 268
Oswegatchie River - page 272
Stillwater Reservoir - page 325
Crooked Creek - Chippewa Bay - page 377

Red Lake & Indian River - page 374
Long Pond, Round Pond, & Oswegatchie River - page 339
Beaver River Canoe Route - page 329

Black River Bay - page 371
Lakeview Wildlife Management Area - page 366
Salmon River Reservoir - page 358
Deer Creek Marsh - page 362
Gifford Lake-Fish Creek - page 354

Fish Creek to Oneida Lake - page 344
Genesee River Gorge - page 132
Buck Pond - page 138
Salmon & West Creeks - page 135

Old Erie Canal - page 100

East Bay - page 117

Oak Orchard Creek - page 141
Tonawanda Creek - page 144
Mendon Ponds - page 129

Allegheny Reservoir - page 148

Hemlock & Canadice Lakes - page 124
West River - page 121
Clyde River - page 111
Sterling Valley Creek - page 114
Howland Island (Seneca River) - page 107
Dryden Lake - page 104
Ninemile Swamp (Sangerfield River) - page 96

Route 3
I-81
Route 28
Route 17
I-90
I-390
I-88

N

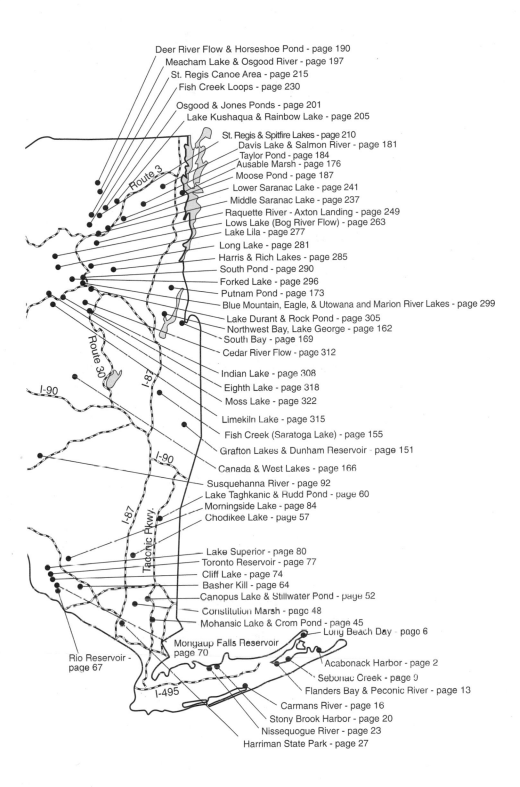

Route 3

Route 30

I-87

I-90

I-90

I-87

Taconic Pkwy.

I-495

Southern
New York

Acabonack Harbor
East Hampton, Long Island

MAPS
> **New York Atlas:** Map 29
> **USGS Quadrangle:** Gardiners Island West

INFORMATION
> **Area:** Tidal, 390 acres (high tide)
> **Shellfish and fish species:** Scallop, whelk, razor clam, striped bass
> **Canoe rentals and transportation:** Canoe and kayak rentals available at Main Beach Surf & Sport, Montauk Highway, P.O. Box 1359, Wainscott, NY 11975; 516- 537-2716 (also instruction and tours)
> **Parking permit:** Town of East Hampton; 516-324-4143
> **Information on trails:** The Nature Conservancy, South Fork–Shelter Island Chapter, P.O. Box 5125, East Hampton, NY 11937; 516-329-7689
> **Camping:** Hither Hills State Park, Montauk; 516-668-2461. Ccdar Point County Park; 516-852-7620.

Acabonack Harbor and East Harbor extend roughly two miles north to south but offer eight miles of shoreline to explore, including two principal islands. While there is some development here, the whole area has a wild feel to it and is rich with fauna and flora.

One might suspect that all salt marshes are pretty much the same. Not true. At Acabonack Harbor you will find a dramatically different salt marsh ecosystem than at Sebonac Creek, for example. While tall *Spartina alternifolia* dominates most of the estuaries described in this guide, the much shorter *Spartina patens* dominates Acabonack Harbor.

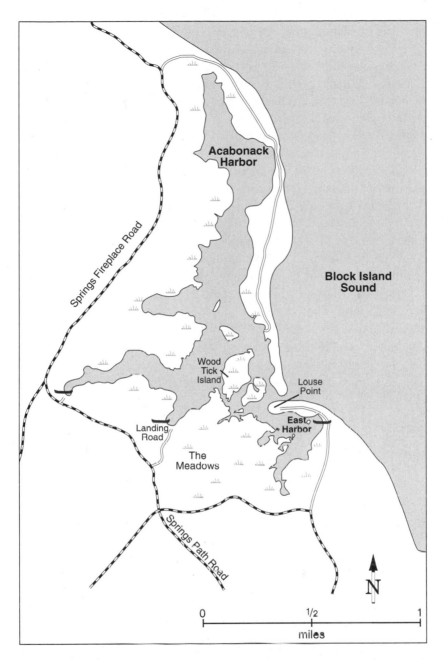

Acabonack
Harbor

Block Island
Sound

Springs Fireplace Road

Wood
Tick
Island

Louse
Point

East
Harbor

Landing
Road

The
Meadows

Springs Path Road

N

0   1/2   1
miles

The shorter plants—just eight inches high—endow the entire marsh with a more diminutive feel compared with the feeling generated by more typical salt marsh grasses several feet in height.

With the low grasses, even at midtide you can see out over the marsh for a great distance. At high tide, you're literally looking down on it. We could see great egrets a mile away, their slender white bodies prominent against the greens and browns of the marsh. Along with dozens of great egrets, we saw great blue herons, snowy egrets, several flocks of herring gulls madly picking at some sort of prey in the marsh, osprey, northern harrier, and various sandpipers, including lesser yellowlegs feeding on the mud banks. Several of the half-dozen osprey nesting platforms scattered around the marsh appear to have been used in recent years.

Look for sea lavender here. In some areas, this plant seems even more dense than the ever-present *Spartina patens*. One of the most beautiful plants of the salt marsh, sea lavender has a delicate bouquet shape and blooms in July with small lavender blossoms. It has often been collected for dried flower arrangements, but this practice should be discouraged. Vast areas of salt marsh in New England have been denuded of this wonderful plant—enjoy sea lavender in its natural environment.

You will also see glasswort, an odd plant with no obvious leaves and thick, succulent, jointed stems. In the autumn, glasswort turns a deep red, making it noticeable from quite a distance. Though not as common as sea lavender, you should still be able to find it.

Farther from shore the higher ground is forested principally with oak—mostly white oak but scarlet, black, and post oak as well. Pignut

Acabonack Harbor at high tide, with water flooding the Spartina patens.

hickory, sassafras, and sumac mix with the oak, and in places all are covered with a tangle of grape, greenbrier, and poison ivy vines. You will also see aromatic red cedar, *Juniperus virginiana*. This tree has the deepest green of any tree around, making it readily noticeable among the oaks and other deciduous trees. Red cedar is an evergreen with small whitish or bluish berrylike cones, ruddy-brown bark, and reddish, aromatic wood.

At the southern end of Acabonack Harbor, an area known as "The Meadows" forms the wildest and most attractive part of the marsh. From the boat access on Landing Road, paddle between Wood Tick Island and The Meadows as you snake toward East Harbor. At high tide you might want to paddle down some of the mosquito-control ditches. These long straight channels of water extend into the marsh here and there. Built in the 1930s and 1940s to drain interior portions of the salt marsh in an effort to control mosquitoes, most of these ditches remain after more than 50 years, showing us how permanent our effects on the salt marsh can be. People still debate whether this practice was ever a good idea.

Significant amounts of development intrude on the eastern side of East Harbor, as well as on much of the northern end of the main harbor. For a change of pace from paddling, beach your canoe at the north end of East Harbor and walk across the dunes to the ocean side and explore along here. To the south the quite dramatic Acabonack Cliffs rise from the sea. You might also want to explore a trail maintained by The Nature Conservancy between Springs Fireplace Road and Acabonack Harbor.

Getting There

Take Route 27 east to East Hampton, and bear left onto North Main Street (Route 40) in the center of town (if you get to the big windmill, you have gone just a bit too far). North Main Street becomes Harbor Road. After 0.6 mile, bear right onto Route 41, Springs Fireplace Road. Follow Springs Fireplace Road for 3.7 miles, then turn right onto Springs Path Road. Follow Springs Path Road for 0.7 mile, and turn left onto Landing Road. You will reach the boat access at the end of the road in 0.2 mile. You need to get a permit from the town of East Hampton to park here .

Long Beach Bay
Southold, Long Island

MAPS
New York Atlas: Map 28
USGS Quadrangle: Orient

INFORMATION
Area: Tidal, about 680 acres; maximum depth: about 6 feet
Shellfish and fish species: Scallop, whelk, razor clam, striped bass
Parking permit: Southold Town Clerk's Office; 516-765-1800
Canoe rentals: Narrow River Marina; 516-323-2660

Located just minutes from the terminus of the New London–Orient Point Ferry, Long Beach Bay offers excellent paddling. Little development intrudes on this area, currents remain modest (except at the mouth of the harbor), and on a calm day you can see the bottom on virtually the entire bay. Paddling here in the autumn is particularly rewarding, with the deep reds of oaks, bright orange reds of sumac, and spots of red glasswort in the high salt marsh. If you're as lucky as we were, you may also see and hear migrating snow geese in the fall. We watched three skeins pass over during a day's paddle in mid-October.

Long Beach Bay offers lots of opportunity for exploring the salt marsh environment. From the access on Narrow River, you can paddle "upriver" (to the north), passing through thick stands of salt marsh cordgrass (*Spartina alterniflora*). The tides submerge this dominant plant of the salt marsh twice daily. The grass has developed mechanisms to survive the high salt concentration, and it plays a critically important role in the salt marsh ecosystem, including providing habitat for young striped bass and other commercially important species.

If the tide is not all the way in when you paddle here, note the thick clusters of ribbed mussel at the base of the *Spartina*. This species of mussel is not commercially harvested—perhaps why they are found in such profusion. Some patches of *Phragmites*—a very tall grass that is displacing *Spartina* in some areas of the Northeast—grow on higher ground. Farther from shore you will see black locust, sumac, wild cherry, white and scarlet oak, and eastern red cedar.

Paddling east along the northern shore you can explore inlets into the salt marsh, particularly toward the eastern end. There is one place up here where, even at midtide, you can paddle a loop. We found the branch-

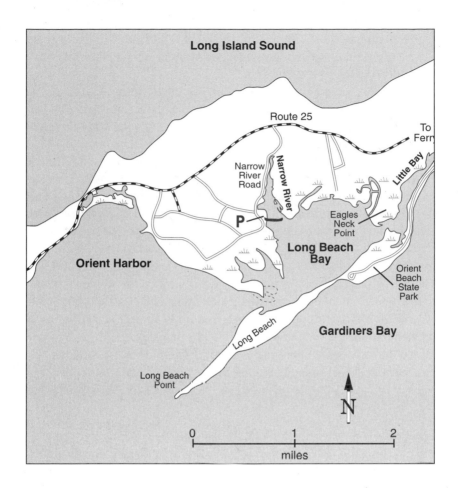

Long Island Sound

Route 25

To Ferry

Narrow River Road

Narrow River

Little Bay

Eagles Neck Point

P

Long Beach Bay

Orient Harbor

Orient Beach State Park

Long Beach

Gardiners Bay

Long Beach Point

N

0   1   2
miles

ing inlet just west of Eagles Neck Point to be especially interesting. At midtide with lots of exposed peat banks we saw thousands of skittering crabs. As you approach an exposed mud bank, a frenzy of activity breaks out as hundreds of the critters—appropriately called ghost crabs because of their disappearing act—scurry down their three-quarter-inch-diameter holes. We got our best look at them through binoculars, sneaking up as quietly as possible to within about a dozen feet.

At the far eastern end of the bay is Little Bay, which extends about a mile to the north-northeast. We saw several northern harriers along the wild shore here, along with osprey (there were more than a dozen osprey nesting platforms around the bay, and many had clearly been used), Canada geese, great egrets, snowy egrets, greater yellowlegs, cormorants, and common loons. If you do paddle here in the fall, notice near the north end of Little Bay the bushes that, from a distance, appear to be covered with bushy white blooms. This is groundsel bush, *Bac-*

charis halimifolia, an interesting member of the thistle family, and what you see are not blooms but cottony tufts (technically, each is a pappus) that aid in seed dispersal.

We were struck by the exceptionally clear water in the bay. We could see the bottom virtually the entire day (granted, it was very calm). For the first time, we got a good look at whelks crawling along the sand bottom, and we saw dozens of blue crabs dancing along sideways—one that we challenged with a paddle had a claw span of nearly a foot. In the section just south of the Narrow River mouth we saw quite a few striped bass, though all were below minimum keeping size.

The entire southeastern shore of Long Beach Bay is part of Orient Beach State Park, which definitely merits a visit. Unfortunately, some difficulty awaits those wishing to combine a paddling and hiking trip, because you may not beach a canoe at the park, but it's worth the drive around. This land has remained in public hands since 1774, when the residents entered into a written agreement providing that Long Beach should forever be reserved for common use, protection, and improvement according to the judgment of the majority of property owners. In October 1929, the owners turned the land over to the state to become Orient Beach State Park. The park covers 357 acres and offers hiking, picnicking, and swimming.

Getting There

Long Beach Bay is roughly 115 miles from New York City. From the west, take the Long Island Expressway (I-495) to the end, then Route 25 east toward Orient Point. Note your mileage where Routes 25 and 48 split after passing through Greenport. Continue another 5.5 miles on Route 25, then turn right onto Narrow River Road. Follow Narrow River Road for 0.9 mile, and you will reach the boat access on the left. Parking here is by permit only; stop by the Southold Town Clerk's Office on Route 25 in Southold to get a parking permit. If you want to rent a canoe, drive about 100 yards past the boat access to the Narrow River Marina.

If visiting from New England, another option is to take the New London–Orient Point Ferry. From the ferry terminus in Orient Point, drive west on Route 25 for 2.3 miles, and turn left onto Narrow River Road, then follow directions as above.

Sebonac Creek
Southampton, Long Island

MAPS
> **New York Atlas:** Map 28
> **USGS Quadrangle:** Southampton

INFORMATION
> **Area:** Tidal, 530 acres; maximum depth: 16 feet (Scallop Pond)
> **Prominent shellfish and fish species:** Scallop, whelk, razor clam, striped bass
> **Ramp use permit:** (West Neck Road access) Town of Southampton; 516-287-5740
> **Canoe rentals:** Peconic Paddler, 89 Peconic Ave., Riverhead, NY 11901; 516-727-9895. Canoe and kayak rentals and new equipment.

The contiguous waters of Sebonac Creek, Bullhead Bay, Little Sebonac Creek, West Neck Creek, Island Creek, and Scallop Pond offer, in our estimation, the finest canoeing on Long Island. The waters are manageable in size, yet extensive enough to provide for lots of exercise—we paddled more than 10 miles and didn't explore every last creek, let alone the dozens of mosquito-control ditches—many of which are accessible by boat at high tide. One could easily spend an entire day exploring all the nooks and crannies of this saltwater estuary.

Salt marsh cordgrass, *Spartina alterniflora,* dominates the entire shoreline of this estuary. One of the few plants able to survive regular flooding by salt water, much of the plant becomes submerged at high tide. At low tide the roots reemerge. *Spartina alterniflora* has evolved to fill a very important ecological niche in the salt marsh, and as you will note here, it indeed thrives.

On the higher salt marsh—land not flooded by the diurnal tides— you will see a much shorter cousin: *Spartina patens,* along with such plants as sea lavender and glasswort. If you paddle here in the autumn, the bright red glasswort stands out markedly amid the browns and yellows of other plants. Beneath the raised plain of the salt marsh grow thick clusters of ribbed mussel and masses of reddish brown seaweed.

A thick oak woods stands back from the shore, where white oak dominates, but you will also see lots of scarlet oak and may come across black oak, post oak, and scrub oak. Pignut hickory, beech, black gum (which turns crimson early in the fall), sassafras, and black cherry add variety to the tree-species mix.

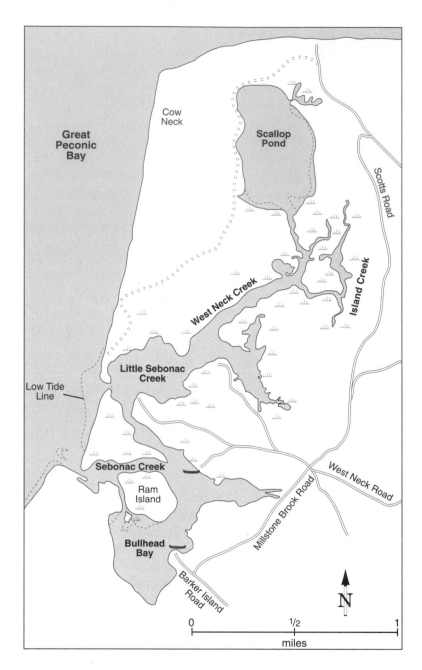

Bird life fills the estuary. We saw great blue herons, great egrets, snowy egrets, green-backed herons, hundreds of black ducks, a pied-billed grebe, several greater yellowlegs, kingfishers, osprey, northern harriers, and the ever-present herring gulls—to mention a few. Note that hunters also know about the many ducks here. We saw dozens of duck hunting blinds and would definitely choose to avoid this area during the duck-hunting season. Keep your eye out for deer, fox, mink, and otter as well, all of which dwell here.

Little development intrudes on the estuary. Most houses here are located on Little Sebonac Creek and Bullhead Bay. Many of these houses represent architectural statements, and we really enjoyed examining them as we paddled along. The northern sections of the estuary remain more remote and wilder, though Scallop Pond sports a few houses.

The eastern extension of Little Sebonac Creek and the extensive winding channels of Island Creek (both to the north and south) provide a wonderful paddling experience. In most of this area you feel truly alone, and even on a windy day you can find protected areas to escape the rougher water. Along Island Creek, you get a real feel for the marsh—the wide flat plain of grass seems almost like a sea, surrounded by oak forests where the ground is higher. If paddling at high tide, look out over this plain and note its flatness.

On the northern extension of Island Creek, you pass one mansion on the right, a colonial-style house set well back from the water. If you paddle within a few hours of high tide, continue paddling north, past the house. The channel looks as if it will peter out as you pass a gazebo, but it winds around, passes under a footbridge, and continues at least another quarter mile. The farther north you go, the more the channel narrows, with *Spartina* and other vegetation closing in, until your passage is finally blocked.

Scallop Pond, at the northern end of this estuary, is a large oval

Early morning light highlights the salt marsh cordgrass on Sebonac Creek.

pond, two-thirds of a mile long. *Spartina alterniflora* surrounds it too, but the band of grass is narrow. Trees extend much closer to the shore than elsewhere. One very prominent mansion and its associated buildings sit on Scallop Pond on the eastern side near the north end, lending a dramatic feel to this area. From a distance a large boathouse seems to appear on the water side of the mansion, but this turns out to be a curving concrete wall with windows that backs up to the water—creating what must be a very unusual space inside.

Just past the mansion a passageway cuts through to another, much smaller salt marsh. It looks as if one might be able to paddle (carefully) through this little man-made channel—almost a tunnel of wooden posts—but the wind blew a gale when we got to this end, and we weren't sure we could get into this channel without being bashed against the sides by the rough waves.

If you feel inclined to go for a walk on a fairly wild section of Peconic Bay shoreline when you paddle back into Little Sebonac Creek, pull your canoe up near the cut at the western end of the creek and cross over the the narrow band of dunes. Walking north toward Cow Neck you will find lots of shells and colorful stones.

You can easily paddle around Ram Island, passing under a road bridge that the island's owners use for access. There are some marshy islands just south of Ram Island worth exploring, but we found Bullhead Bay in general to be less interesting than the marsh north of Ram Island. The bay backs up on a huge golf course and has a road right along the western shore.

Getting There

Take Route 27 toward Southampton and turn north onto Route 52 toward North Sea. Drive 0.9 mile on Route 52, then turn left at the traffic light onto Route 38. Take an almost immediate left onto West Neck Road. Follow West Neck Road 1.8 miles, being sure to stay on the main road, and you will reach the boat access. A sign at the boat access says a ramp permit is required and that if you want to park a boat trailer you must display a ramp permit from the town of Southampton on your car. While these regulations are not altogether clear as regards canoes and kayaks, the safest thing would be to contact the town and ask for a permit to use this access (see above).

You can also launch your boat on Bullhead Bay. Follow West Neck Road 1.2 miles from Route 38, then turn left onto Millstone Brook Road. Follow Millstone Brook Road for 0.8 mile, and where the road curves sharply to the left, turn right onto Barkers Island Road. The access is 0.1 mile down this road.

Flanders Bay Tributaries and the Peconic River

Southampton and Riverhead, Long Island

MAPS

New York Atlas: Maps 27 and 28
USGS Quadrangles: Riverhead and Mattituck

INFORMATION

Flow: Tidal below the dam near the Peconic Avenue crossing in Riverhead. Flatwater above dam with several portages.

Canoe rentals and transportation: Peconic Paddler, 89 Peconic Ave., Riverhead, NY 11901; 516-727-9895. Canoe and kayak rentals and new equipment.

Nearby camping: Indian Island County Park near Riverhead; 516-727-5933

Hiking: The Suffolk County Parks Department maintains several trails in the Hubbard Creek area; 516-854-4949.

Flanders Bay is large and potentially dangerous on a windy day, but the southern shore and several of its tributaries offer superb paddling in the right conditions. Three creeks flow into the bay here that you should explore: Hubbard, Mill, and Birch. Of these, Hubbard Creek's islands, deep twisting coves, and winding channels through the salt marsh provide the most interesting paddling. Even when breezes blow on the bay, sheltered Hubbard Creek provides a quiet retreat from the world—though you have to paddle on the bay to get to it.

Two fairly nearby access points can get you into Hubbard, Mill, and Birch Creeks. Birch Creek provides the closest access, but this launch area and road can flood at very high tide. A better site, though somewhat farther away, is found on Red Creek Pond, located on the western end of Great Peconic Bay, across Red Cedar Point from Flanders Bay. We had some difficulty getting around Red Cedar Point on a breezy day and suggest you don't attempt it under windy conditions. On a calm day, you can put in at Riverhead and paddle west across Reeves Bay and along the southern shore of Flanders Bay to reach these undeveloped and more natural areas. Sea kayaks are most appropriate for the waters of Flanders and Peconic Bays.

Salt marsh cordgrass, *Spartina alterniflora,* dominates the salt marshes and tidal inlets on the south side of Flanders Bay. This grass

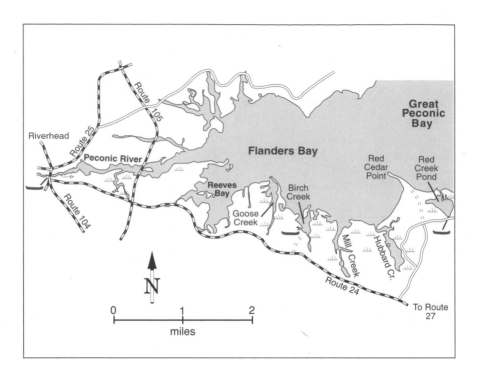

can survive—and indeed requires—regular flooding by salt water. In centuries past, Long Island settlers harvested this grass as winter feed for livestock.

Paddling here in the autumn we saw lots of black ducks, a half-dozen mute swans, an osprey hovering in search of a fish meal, and an assortment of songbirds preparing for fall migration. In the creeks, the shallow, mucky bottom could leave you high and, unfortunately, not very dry at low tide—it would not be fun to wade through the mud dragging a canoe if you became stranded.

On higher ground, away from the *Spartina* marsh, you will see thick oak-pitch pine woods. We recognize pitch pine as the only common pine with clusters of three needles in each bunch. Early settlers used pitch pine for making charcoal and fence posts, and they tapped the trees for sap, which they made into turpentine and resin. The most common oaks here are white oak and scarlet oak. Among the shrubs you will see are groundsel bush and bayberry with its highly scented leaves.

If you launch your boat in Riverhead, you can explore quite a way east in the river before actually getting into the bay. A little tributary on the south side of the river just west of the Route 105 bridge offers very pleasant salt marsh exploration, though it is a lot closer to heavily traveled roads than the tributaries farther east. The north side of Flanders Bay, including Sawmill Creek and Terrys Creek, suffers from quite a bit of development, and we do not recommend paddling there.

Paddlers can also enjoy a one-way trip along the Peconic River farther west. An outfitter in Riverhead, the Peconic Paddler, offers boat rentals and a shuttle service for the eight-mile stretch of river from Connecticut Avenue in Manorville to the center of Riverhead. This section of river offers fine paddling, although several landowner disputes and changing state regulations have recently made access and carries less certain in a few places. If you are considering paddling the river, be sure to check with the canoe outfitter to find out about the latest usage recommendations.

The Peconic River—the longest river on Long Island and one of the most popular canoeing locations—flows filled entirely with freshwater west of the dam at the center of Riverhead. The river winds through woodlands, farmland, old cranberry bog impoundments, and the backyards of various industries. Some narrow sections of the river flow with moderate current but no rapids; other sections flow through broad marshes. You must carry over several dams and roads. The Peconic Paddler has reasonable canoe and kayak rates, and even if you aren't renting a boat, the outfitter can ferry you and your boat to the access in Manorville for a modest fee.

Getting There

To reach the boat access at Red Creek Pond on Peconic Bay, take the Long Island Expressway (I-495) to Route 24 east. Note your mileage when you get to the traffic circle at Route 104, and continue on Route 24 east for 5.3 miles. Turn left onto Red Creek Road, stay on the main road where it curves sharply to the right, and you will reach the boat access in 1.7 miles.

To reach the Birch Creek access, take Route 24 east from the Route 104 circle in Riverhead 4.0 miles, and turn left onto Birch Creek Road. The access is 0.3 mile out this unimproved dirt road. This is not a maintained boat access. Be careful about leaving your vehicle here; flooding during very high tides is possible.

The Peconic Paddler is located on Peconic Avenue at the circle where Routes 24 and 104 meet in Riverhead.

Carmans River
Brookhaven, Long Island

MAPS:
  New York Atlas: Map 27
  USGS Quadrangle: Bellport
INFORMATION
  Length: Lower section 3.6 miles, tidal
  Prominent fish species: striped bass, flounder, brown trout, rainbow trout
  Canoe rentals and transportation: Carman's River Canoe & Kayak, 2979 Montauk Hwy., Brookhaven, NY 11719; 516-286-1966
  Wertheim National Wildlife Refuge: P.O. Box 21, Shirley, NY 11967; 516-286-0485

Carmans River and its surrounding marsh represent one of the last undeveloped estuaries on Long Island. One of the wildest and most pristine of the four major rivers on the island—the others are Nissequogue, Connetquot, and Peconic—it offers fantastic canoeing and wildlife observing. Though access is limited, we include here the lower section, a meandering 3.6-mile tidal flow from Route 27 to Bellport Bay through the 2,400-acre Wertheim National Wildlife Refuge.

Paddling here in the autumn is magical. *Phragmites,* the dominant plant, line the banks, and its tall, plumed stalks sway in the breeze, along with two species of cordgrass: *Spartina alterniflora* and *S. cynosuroides.* Though not far from major highways and concentrated development, you feel alone here and can immerse yourself in wildness.

The tributary streams Little Neck Run, Yapahank Creek, and Big Fish Creek particularly invite exploration—at high tide, that is, when they are most accessible. On these creeks, you gradually leave the marshland dominated by *Phragmites* to find much more variety: Atlantic white cedar, black gum, and pitch pine, for example. We saw lots of wood ducks here, along with herons, osprey, and a snapping turtle. A large, active osprey nest—one of three or four in the refuge—perches on an old pitch pine to the right as you paddle up Yapahank Creek.

On Carmans River and the various inlets, watch closely as you paddle along. In the shallow water we watched crabs skittering along sideways and caught a few glimpses of huge carp. We had the good fortune to spot two Virginia rails foraging in the mud for insects and crus-

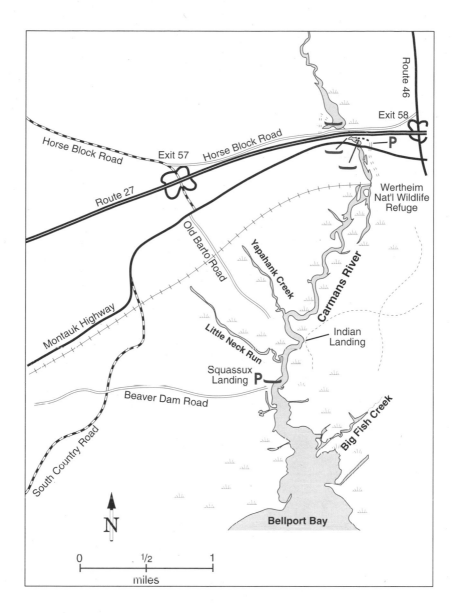

Route 46

Exit 58

Horse Block Road

Exit 57 Horse Block Road

P

Route 27

Wertheim
Nat'l Wildlife
Refuge

Old Barto Road

Yapahank Creek

Carmans River

Little Neck Run

Montauk Highway

Indian
Landing

Squassux
Landing P

Beaver Dam Road

Big Fish Creek

South Country Road

N

Bellport Bay

0   1/2   1

miles

taceans amid the *Phragmites* stems. This elusive and well camouflaged bird, about the size of a robin, has a fairly long, down-curved bill and very long toes to support the bird on soft mud. We also saw goldeneye, cormorant, mallard, and a loon—perhaps having just returned to the coast from the Adirondacks. Though loons spend most of their life in salt water, they breed only on freshwater lakes and ponds.

In late summer, you may also see the dramatic swamp rose mallow, *Hibiscus palustris,* a relative of the hollyhock, blooming here. We saw several plants—more of a bush really—with beautiful, five-petaled, pink, roselike flowers four or five inches across.

About a quarter mile north from the Squassux Landing boat access is Indian Landing, on the eastern shore. A trail leaves from here, providing opportunity to explore some of the wildlife refuge's higher ground on foot. If you pull your boat up here and leave for a walk, be sure to tie your boat—remember the river is tidal.

There are three primary access points for canoeing here: the canoe outfitter on the west side of the river between Montauk Highway and Route 27; a fishing access on the east side of the river, accessible off Montauk Highway; and Squassux Landing farther south, at the end of Beaver Dam Road. The Carman's River Canoe & Kayak shop and rental store charges two dollars to launch your own boat. The Squassux Landing access has very limited parking but provides closer access to Bellport Bay if you wish to explore to the south. From Squassux Landing, we suggest an upstream paddle, as the river gets a lot wider, windi-

Maples and other deciduous trees replace the salt marsh vegetation near the north end of the tidal portion of Carmans River.

er, and congested with powerboats toward the bay. The state fishing access off Montauk Highway is free, but you have to carry your boat about 250 yards to the river.

Carman's River Canoe & Kayak also operates river trips on the upper Carmans River. The upper river, above the dam at Route 27, has a very different character from the tidal river below Route 27. This 4.5-mile stretch of paddlable freshwater river meanders through woodland as well as marshy areas. The upper river has current, but it is all flat-water. For seven dollars (in 1995) the outfitter will shuttle you and your canoe to the upper end, and you paddle down to South Haven Park just north of Route 27, where you will have dropped off your car. Unfortunately, South Haven Park, where you will leave your car, will not permit you to launch your canoe there and paddle upstream; you can only take out at that point, after being dropped off at the north end by the canoe outfitter. Canoe and kayak rentals are available for paddling either the upper Carmans River or the lower stretch.

Getting There

To reach the state fishing access, take the Long Island Expressway (I-495) to Exit 68, and follow the William Floyd Parkway (Route 46) south. Cross over Route 27, then continue south for another 0.2 mile to the Montauk Highway (Route 80). Turn right here (west), and drive 0.9 mile to the traffic light, and turn right into the fishing access parking lot. The trail to the boat access is at the far end of the gravel parking lot. To reach Carman's River Canoe & Kayak outfitter, continue west on Montauk Highway across the river, and the store will be on the right, almost immediately.

To reach the Squassux Landing access, take Route 27 to Exit 57. Follow signs for Route 80/Montauk Highway, and turn right (heading west on Montauk Highway). Drive 0.3 mile, and turn left onto Old Stump Road. Follow Old Stump Road south for 1.4 miles, then turn left onto Beaver Dam Road. You will reach Squassux Landing at the end of this road in 0.2 mile. Parking is very limited here.

To paddle the upper river you have to use the services of Carman's River Canoe & Kayak. Staff will direct you to the southern terminus for this trip.

Stony Brook Harbor
Smithtown, Long Island

MAPS
New York Atlas: Map 26
USGS Quadrangle: Saint James
INFORMATION
Area: Tidal, 940 acres (high tide)
Prominent fish species: Striped bass, flounder

Located along the northern shore of Long Island, just across Long Beach from Smithtown Bay, Stony Brook Harbor provides a superb example of tidal estuary. Salt marsh cordgrass, *Spartina alterniflora,* dominates the harbor, including the entire shoreline and numerous islands. This species of grass varies in height from a foot to more than six feet; most of the grass here grows very tall. Throughout the Atlantic seaboard, thousands and thousands of tidal acres contain *S. alterniflora* as almost the only plant present.

Because Stony Brook Harbor is tidal, the place changes dramatically depending on when you visit. At low tide, vast mussel shoals and high peat banks become exposed, greatly restricting your paddling—in fact, the open water gets reduced by about half. At high tide only the upper portions of the cordgrass wave back and forth with the current and the wakes of passing boats.

You should see lots of herons and egrets as you paddle around the harbor, including great blue heron, green-backed heron, great egret, and snowy egret. Both the great egret and snowy egret boast a full coat of snow-white feathers, but the much larger great egret has a yellow bill and all-black legs. The smaller snowy egret has black legs but yellow feet. Both species nearly became extinct in this country near the turn of the century, when hunters harvested them for their gorgeous breeding-season plumes, then used in women's high fashion.

The double-crested cormorant, an ungainly bird that often stands with outstretched, bent wings drying in the sun, exists here in great numbers—you may see hundreds together in places. Cormorants' rear-set, webbed feet help them swim through the water hunting for fish. Because they spend so much time underwater, their wings get water-logged and need to be dried before the heavy birds can take to the air—quite a laborious process even with dry wings.

Expect to see gulls and terns as well. Watch for the endangered

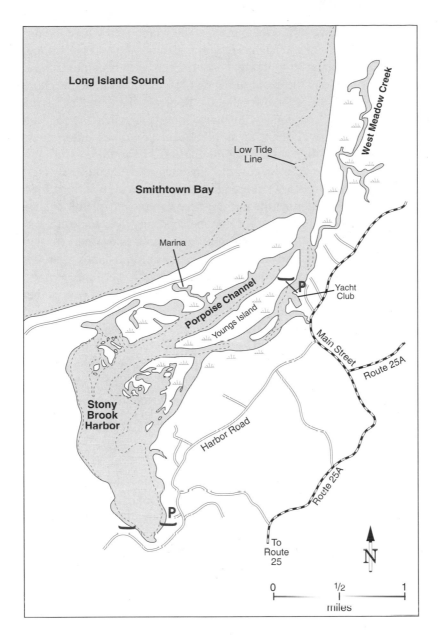

Long Island Sound

Smithtown Bay

Low Tide Line

West Meadow Creek

Marina

Porpoise Channel

Youngs Island

P

Yacht Club

Main Street

Route 25A

Stony Brook Harbor

Harbor Road

Route 25A

P

To Route 25

N

0   1/2   1

miles

least tern at Stony Brook Harbor, particularly along the northeastern end of Youngs Island. The island is posted off-limits to protect the least tern colony that nests here, so don't disembark on the island; bring a pair of binoculars to watch from a distance this smallest and most graceful member of the tern family. When we visited, we saw no evidence of recent osprey nesting at the several platforms erected on their behalf.

Our favorite section of the harbor is the island area where the harbor bends to the south. At high tide you can weave in and out through the cordgrass islands. At low tide, however, this area becomes impassable. Looking beyond the expanses of salt marsh cordgrass at the shore, you will see thick deciduous woodlands. In places there are huge white oaks and black birch, along with black locust, sassafras, beech, and black walnut. The well-kept lawns of expensive homes interrupt the woodlands on the hills overlooking the harbor. The southern section of the harbor has several almost castlelike estates overlooking the water.

If you put in at the town landing near the yacht club at the eastern end of the harbor, note that the current here can move right along. The current at the mouth of the harbor may be so strong that you can't paddle against it. The best time to put in here is as the tide comes in, with your trip timed so that you can explore the cordgrass islands at around high tide, then ride the outgoing tide back through the more southern channel to the access—avoiding the main Porpoise Channel altogether. If you paddle around Youngs Island, the only way to avoid dealing with strong current on one side or the other is to round the northeastern tip of the island as the tide turns. We really had to work to make our way southwest along this channel back to the boat access with the tide going out. If you want to explore West Meadow Creek without a whole lot of work, paddle north on the incoming or high tide and back south at high tide or after the tide has turned.

Getting There

Take the Long Island Expressway to Exit 53N. Follow the Sunken Meadow Parkway north to Route 25 (the Jericho Turnpike). Follow Route 25 east to Smithtown, where Route 25A joins from the west. Where Routes 25 and 25A split again, follow Route 25A east toward Stony Brook. From the point at which Route 25A turns to the right and Main Street continues straight, go straight on Main Street for 0.5 mile, then bear left onto Shore Road. The town landing by the yacht club is straight ahead in 0.2 mile. This boat launch is owned by the town of Brookhaven and the "ramp use" fees are quite high for nonresidents. We paddled here off-season (recommended) and did not run into any problems, but you may want to ask whether you can launch a canoe or kayak.

There were no signs restricting use at the two hand-launch sites near the south end of the harbor, but parking is very limited at those locations. These are reachable off Harbor Road, which winds among the estates on the eastern side of the harbor.

Nissequogue River
Smithtown, Long Island

MAPS
   New York Atlas: Map 26
   USGS Quadrangles: Saint James and Central Islip
INFORMATION
   Area: Tidal; about 5 miles one-way
   Prominent fish species: Striped bass, flounder; stocked brook, brown, and rainbow trout above Route 25 bridge
   Canoe rentals and transportation: Sunken Meadow Canoe & Kayak Rentals; 516-269-2929 or 516-269-2844. Nissequogue River Canoe Rentals; 516-979-8244. Bob's Canoe Rentals; 516-269-2761.

New York State designated the Nissequogue River a Scenic and Recreational River in 1982, and it remains almost totally undeveloped. It is one of Long Island's most popular canoeing locations. Three different canoe outfitters rent boats and provide shuttle service, making it possible to paddle both downstream and upstream—south to north on the outgoing tide, or north to south on the incoming tide. Except near the mouth of the river, the modest current would not prevent an up-and-back trip, but it's great to have the option of a one-way trip—especially if you have to deal with *both* current and wind.

Like nearby Stony Brook Harbor (see page 20), Nissequogue bristles with salt marsh cordgrass, *Spartina alterniflora*. This grass and its cousin, *Spartina patens,* have a remarkable adaptation to the harsh salt marsh environment, which alternates between salt water, brackish water, and freshwater. Among the few plants able to live in tidal salt marshes, *Spartina* thrives. It survives the salt marsh environment through several important adaptations. First, its cells maintain high salt concentrations to counteract salt water's osmotic forces, which would otherwise draw water out, dehydrating and wilting the plant. Second, *Spartina* secretes excess salt from its leaves through special pores. As the water evaporates from this concentrated salt solution, crystals usually form, which gives *Spartina* a whitish sheen until the next tide washes the crystals away—notice a whitish line partway up the grass.

Early settlers on Long Island and along much of the New England coast cut and dried *Spartina alterniflora* as winter feed for their livestock. The *Spartina* marshes provided spawning habitat for the fish that

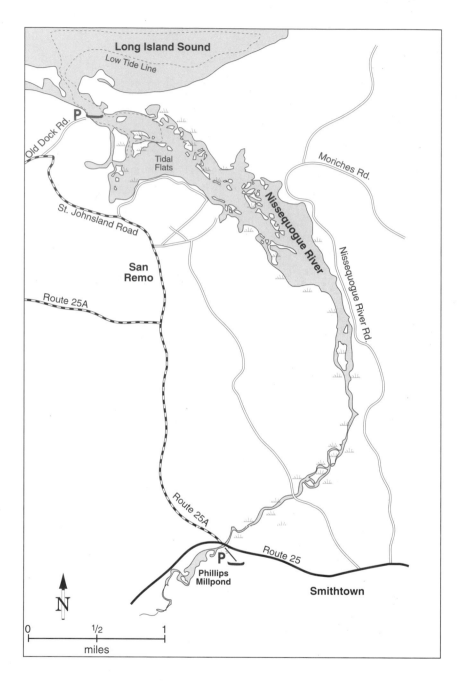

Long Island Sound

Low Tide Line

Old Dock Rd. **P**

Tidal Flats

St. Johnsland Road

Moriches Rd.

Nissequogue River

Nissequogue River Rd.

San Remo

Route 25A

Route 25A

P

Route 25

Phillips Millpond

Route 25

Smithtown

N

0   1/2   1
miles

supported generations of coastal fishermen. But this environment suffered from ecological havoc caused by intense use of DDT from the 1940s until the 1970s for mosquito control. The ecosystem is only now recovering—the ospreys you may see here provide evidence.

The *Spartina* islands and shoreline along the Nissequogue River offer hours of explorations at high tide—much less at low tide. As you explore along here, you never know whether a passageway you enter extends around an island or reaches a dead end. In places, the channels have gradually closed in, leaving just narrow sinewy creeks that wind among the islands like a maze. Particularly along the northeastern shore, you can almost get lost in these islands.

You will see many egrets and herons along the Nissequogue River. In one spot we saw a group of trees seemingly dripping with close to 100 egrets in the late afternoon. Even more cormorants covered another tree farther up the river. Kingfishers flew from snag to snag singing their rattlelike call. Both common and least terns—the latter an endangered species—nest near the mouth of the river. The least tern colony here is supposedly the largest on Long Island.

The farther south you paddle, the less saline the water. *Phragmites* mixes with, then replaces *Spartina alterniflora.* You may see another *Spartina* here: *S. cynosuroides,* or big cordgrass, with its much more distinctive, spreading seed heads. As you near the Route 25 bridge at the south end of the paddlable river, the water is fresh to brackish. South of the Route 25 bridge, you can paddle only a very short distance until your way is blocked.

Because water levels drop way down at low tide, outfitters recommend starting south-to-north trips shortly after high tide or north-

Herring gulls in flight over a Spartina patens *salt marsh.*

to-south trips a couple of hours after low tide. Those seeking solitude should note that novice paddlers in noisy aluminum canoes frequent this river; on a nice weekend day you might have a hard time finding peace and quiet.

Getting There

To reach the mouth of the Nissequogue River, where the canoe outfitters are located, and where a one-way river trip will start if the tide is coming in, take the Long Island Expressway to Route 111 north. At the intersection with Middle Country Road (Route 25), turn left. Continue on 25 for 1.3 miles, then bear right in Smithtown where 25A west (St. Johnsland Road) splits off from Route 25. In 1.9 miles, 25A west turns left at a traffic light; continue straight here, staying on St. Johnsland Road. In another 1.7 miles, turn right onto Old Dock Road. You will reach the river access in 0.6 mile. Parking at the boat access is limited if you are not a Smithtown resident—you must park on the right side of the road across from the diagonal parking for cars with boat trailers.

You can put in at the north end, just north of Route 25 by turning left onto 25 from St. Johnsland Road (25A), then taking an almost immediate right. There was construction here when we visited, so this access might change.

The canoe outfitters we spoke with were glad to ferry people who use their own canoes—though they will not carry your canoe. If you are paddling south, for example, at the end of the paddle you'll have to leave your canoe at the southern termination point and get a ride back to the north end where you can get your car and drive back to get your canoe. If the tide is going out and you want to paddle south, you will need first to drop off your canoe at the southern access, then drive north to the parking area and get a ride with an outfitter back to your canoe. Of course, if you are with a group with two vehicles, you can do the same without needing help from the canoe outfitters.

Harriman State Park Lakes
Tuxedo, Haverstraw, and Woodbury

MAPS

New York Atlas: Map 32

USGS Quadrangles: Thiells, Sloatsburg, and Popolopen Lake

Park Map: A very good map of the park is available for $3.00
from the Palisades Interstate Park Commission, Bear Mountain,
NY 10911-0427; 914-786-2701

INFORMATION

General: Nine canoeable lakes ranging in size from 36 to 297
acres; gasoline-powered boats prohibited from all lakes

Fishing: Fish species vary—see separate write-ups on each pond

Boat permits: Boating permit required for all paddling: Palisades
Interstate Park Commission; 914-786-2701

Canoe rentals: Available on Lake Sebago only—from the private
Baker Camp; 914-351-4609

Camping: Tent camping only at Beaver Pond Campground on
Lake Welch; 914-947-2792. Cabin camping at several locations
in Harriman State Park.

Situated just north of the New Jersey border and only about 45 minutes
from New York City, the lakes of Harriman State Park provided a real
surprise—and a wonderful treat. It is remarkable that such fine paddling can be found so close to the city. In two days of exploration we
visited eight different bodies of water here, paddling more than 20
miles, most of it at a very slow pace to maximize wildlife viewing.

Harriman State Park is the largest parcel of land managed by the
Palisades Interstate Park Commission, which owns 81,000 acres in New
York and New Jersey. In the late 1800s, when quarrying began to leave
serious scars on the Hudson's scenic west-bank cliffs, many people in
the region became upset. The cliffs and rubble beneath them provided
ideal stone for constructing New York's brownstone buildings and for
producing concrete aggregate. The New Jersey Federation of Women's
Clubs fought for legislation to protect the cliffs, and their efforts were
rewarded in 1900 with the establishment of the Palisades Interstate Park
Commission. Andrew H. Green, founder of the American Scenic and
Historic Preservation Society, sponsored a similar effort in New York
State. Harriman State Park had its actual beginnings in 1910 with the
donation of 10,000 acres of land to the state of New York from Mrs.

Mary Harriman—with the stipulation that the state abandon its plans to build Sing Sing Prison on what is now Bear Mountain State Park.

Harriman State Park prohibits gasoline-powered motorboats on all bodies of water here—a wonderful situation—but that doesn't mean you'll necessarily find peace and quiet. Because 10 million people live within an hour's drive of the park, it sometimes suffers from extremely heavy recreational use. During a typical summer weekend, the park has thousands of visitors, and hundreds of canoes and rowboats vie for space on some lakes. Annually, the Palisades Interstate Park Commission sells about 3,000 boating permits.

If you can, paddle here prior to mid-June or after Labor Day when the park has relatively few visitors. In fact, three of the bodies of water described below are open to boating only during these times. Also try to visit on a weekday: on a gorgeous Monday in mid-October—with trees in their full autumn splendor—we had the place to ourselves!

We cover each of the lakes and ponds we visited separately below, along with a map. To paddle here, you need to purchase a boating permit from the Palisades Interstate Park Commission. Permits run from April 1 through November 30. In 1995, permits cost $15. In addition, to get onto some of the lakes and ponds, you need to obtain a key from one of the park offices; these places are so noted in the detailed descriptions. For a better understanding of how to get on these bodies of water and how to get from one to another, we recommend that you purchase a map of the park from the commission.

Lake Sebago

INFORMATION

Area: 297 acres; maximum depth: 37 feet

Open for paddling April 1 through November 30. Boating permit required. Before issuance, boat and life vests will be inspected.

Prominent fish species: Largemouth bass, smallmouth bass, and chain pickerel

Canoe rentals: Baker Camp; 914-351-4609 (for use on Lake Sebago only). Sebago cabin camping; 914-351-2360.

Sebago, the largest lake in the park, has six miles of shoreline that offer splendid paddling. The widest portion of the lake extends in a northeast-southwest orientation, and a long arm extends to the north from its midpoint.

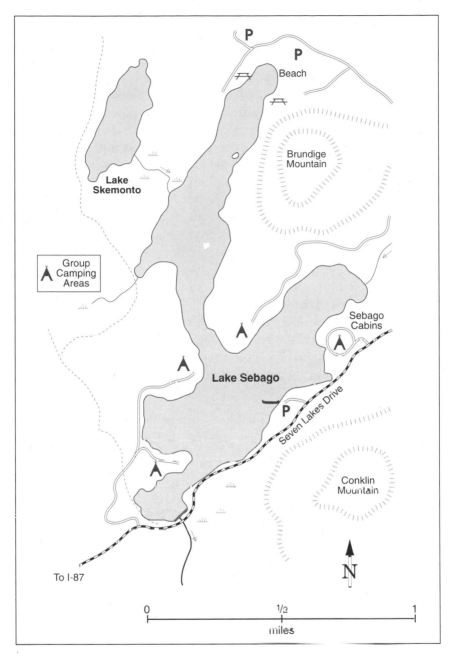

P

P

Beach

Brundige
Mountain

Lake
Skemonto

Group
Camping
Areas

Sebago
Cabins

Lake Sebago

P

Seven Lakes Drive

Conklin
Mountain

To I-87

N

| 0 | 1/2 | 1 |

miles

Sebago's shoreline is rocky. Massive slabs of granite and gneiss, a metamorphic rock, extend down into the water in places, some carpeted with mosses and polypody fern. Along the banks grow thick stands of mountain laurel, which should be spectacular when in bloom in June. Highbush blueberry also grows in profusion here, so if you're paddling in August, you may want to bring along a container and pick some for your pancakes or cereal.

Sebago's surrounding woodlands, comprised almost entirely of deciduous trees, include oaks (white, chestnut, scarlet, and red), beech, hickory, black birch, white ash, sugar maple, black locust, witch hazel, and American chestnut. Once one of the most abundant and economically important trees in the Northeast, the chestnut succumbed to the chestnut blight in the early 1900s. Saplings still sprout from rootstock, but these typically die after reaching 20 or 30 feet. We saw clumps of struggling saplings and hope someday a resistant strain will reclaim its place of importance in our eastern forests.

The open woodlands around Lake Sebago invite exploration. Take the time to explore the woods from shore, or hike some of the 200 miles of trails—including the Appalachian Trail—that extend throughout the park. From our canoe, we saw lots of deer browsing along shore, a beaver, mallard ducks, and a loon during a late-afternoon paddle around the lake in mid-October.

Recreational facilities include an extensive swimming beach at the northern tip of Lake Sebago, along with two picnic areas, playgrounds, ball fields, and rowboat rentals. Several group camping and cabin locations are scattered around the southern section of the lake.

Lake Tiorati

INFORMATION

Area: 292 acres; maximum depth: 43 feet

Open for paddling April 1 through November 30. Boating permit required. Before issuance, boat and life vests will be inspected. Key required for gate to boat launch.

Prominent fish species: Largemouth bass and chain pickerel

Located near the center of Harriman State Park, Lake Tiorati is the second-largest body of water in the park and the highest in elevation of any that are canoeable. It is also one of the most beautiful, with numerous wooded islands just south of the center of the lake. Tiorati—which means "skylike"—was created in 1914 by damming the existing 40-acre Cedar Pond and 15-acre Little Clear Pond, raising the water level by 17 feet and flooding 200 acres of swampland.

The southern shore stands out as our favorite part of Lake Tiorati. You escape the pavement here and will find many coves, inlets, and islands to explore. We saw a couple of beaver lodges at this end of the

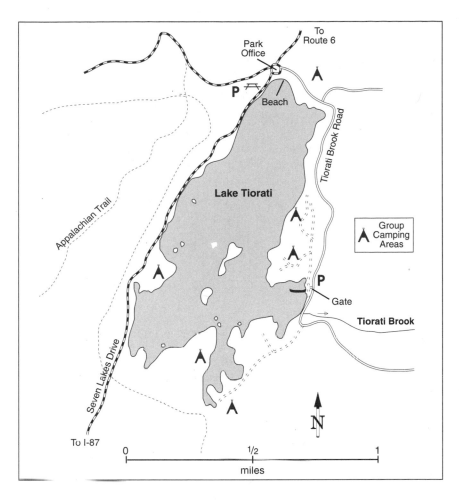

lake, one of which appeared active. Look for beaver early in the morning or at dusk. At dusk we have sometimes paddled right up to this largest of our rodents, though a loud slap of the tail as it plunges into the water's depths is the more common response.

In the shallow water south of the large islands, notice the extensive beds of underwater vegetation. By midsummer, long bushy tassels of coontail and various species of milfoil found here reach up toward the surface from the bottom. In the right light, these plants are really quite extraordinary—their feathery stems seem to capture the light and sparkle, standing out brightly against the much darker lake bottom. One can easily confuse these native species with the invasive Eurasian milfoil, which has taken over some lakes in New York and the nearby Hudson River—but which we did not see in these lakes, probably because of the gasoline-powered-boat prohibition (boat trailers transport it easily from one body of water to the next). Fanwort and several species of bladderwort also grow here, providing important underwater habitat for bass and pickerel.

Oak dominates in forests around Lake Tiorati, though you will see more pine and hemlock here than on most other bodies of water in the park. In many places, massive rock outcroppings reach down into the water.

Unfortunately, roads surround Lake Tiorati—Seven Lakes Drive passes along the entire western shore, and the less-traveled Tiorati Brook Road passes along two-thirds of the eastern shore. Considerable recreational development also encroaches on the lake, including group camping areas, picnic areas, the park office at the north end, and a swimming beach.

Lake Kanawauke, Little Long Pond, and Lake Skannatati

INFORMATION

Area: Konawauke, 170 acres; Little Long, 56 acres; Skannatati, 50 acres

Open for paddling April 1 through November 30, except the section of Lake Kanawauke that extends to the south. This southern

A lone white pine towers over the predominantly oak woods around Lake Tiorati in Harriman State Park.

part of the lake is closed to boating from the third Saturday in June through Labor Day. Boating permit required. Before issuance, boat and life vests will be inspected.

Prominent fish species: Largemouth bass and chain pickerel

Before 1915, only Little Long Pond existed here. Lake Kanawauke — "place of much water"—was created by damming Stony Brook at the southern tip of the present lake. Lake Skannatati, meaning "the other side," was not formed until 1947.

Route 106 bisects Lake Kanawauke. You can gain access on the south side of Route 106, about a half mile from the circle at the junction of Route 106 and Seven Lakes Drive. To reach the northern section of the lake and Little Long Pond (the only portions you may paddle during most of the summer), you have to paddle under the arched stone bridge where Route 106 crosses. The northern section of Lake Kanawauke has less development around it than the southern section.

Despite the group camping areas south of Little Long Pond and the road along the northern shore, we found this to be the most interesting of these three connected bodies of water. A very attractive cluster of islands greets you as you paddle into the pond, and across the pond exposed rock faces provide a delightful vista. Just east of the island, a shallow, stumpy area contains lots of floating vegetation and wildlife. Look for the small purple flowers of aquatic bladderwort here, along with fragrant water lilies, yellow pond lilies, and water shield. Near the island we saw a great blue heron, mallards, a ring-necked duck, several pied-billed grebes, a red-tailed hawk, and the remains of an old beaver lodge. As we paddled farther west along the southern shore of the pond into a small marshy area, we spooked about a dozen wood ducks getting ready for fall migration.

On the northern section of Lake Kanawauke you will see a large stand of red pine near the eastern end, along with the oak-dominated woodland found throughout the park. At the inlet stream at the northeastern tip, you might want to tie your canoe up and walk up along the creek through a gorgeous section of woods to Lake Skannatati. Gnarled tree trunks rising from massive rock outcroppings make this woodland here almost magical.

If you paddle here off-season, you can explore the southern section of Kanawauke. About halfway down the lake, just below a cove extending back to the north, you will find an attractive group of islands. Enjoy these from your boat, but refrain from getting out on them—

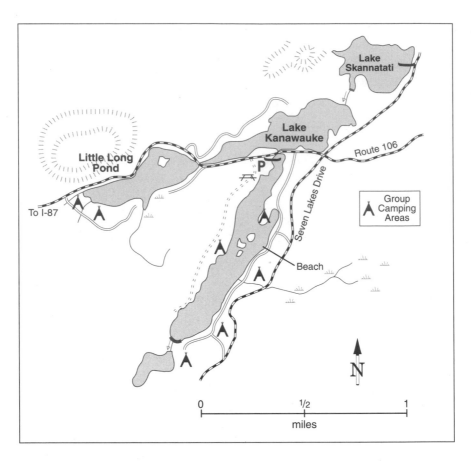

doing so might harm the vegetation and wildlife. The southern section of the lake extends a mile to a long dam at the outlet.

To paddle on Lake Skannatati, use the access off Seven Lakes Drive. Despite its small size (just 36 acres), Skannatati provides a real treat. Because no group camping areas exist on the lake, you will find it quieter than many of the other lakes in Harriman State Park. The shallow western end remains our favorite, where the coves and outlet arm get you out of view of the road. Some of the spectacular rock outcroppings here drip with ferns, while others sport moss-filled cracks in the rock faces, making them look a bit like massive road maps.

Most of the exposed bedrock in the park is igneous granite or metamorphic gneisses and schists. Bear Mountain to the east is composed of Storm King granite, a medium- to coarse-grained gray rock highly resistant to weathering. Information on the area's geology is available at the Bear Mountain Trailside Museum, located at the terminus of the Palisades Interstate Parkway.

Exploring the western end of Skannatati and the cove to the north, we found carnivorous sundew plants on moss-covered logs by the water's edge and on grassy hummocks. You will also find leatherleaf, a plant frequently associated with bogs and northern fens—it has small, leathery leaves and nondescript, white, bell-like flowers early in the season.

Lake Stahahe

INFORMATION

Area: 90 acres; maximum depth: 20 feet

Lake Stahahe is closed to boating from December 1 through March 30 and from the third Saturday in June through Labor Day. Boating permit required. Before issuance, boat and life vests will be inspected. Key required for gate to boat launch.

Prominent fish species: Largemouth bass and smallmouth bass

Located just a mile from the New York Thruway at the north end of Harriman State Park, Lake Stahahe extends one mile in a generally north-south orientation. The narrow northern end has lots of cabins and group camping areas, but these should not be actively used during periods when you can paddle on Stahahe. Even so, the southern end offers more interesting paddling. Here you'll find lots of islands to explore, along with shallow marshy areas rich in fauna and flora.

Near dusk on an October day, we watched a river otter for about a half hour as it fished—or perhaps just frolicked—in the shallow water. We also saw a small flock of Canada geese near the south end. Along shore at the south end, deer browsed all over the place—obviously fairly tame and too used to people. We also saw a beautiful red fox just south of the lake on Route 106.

Silvermine Lake

INFORMATION

Area: 84 acres; maximum depth: 20 feet

Open for paddling April 1 through November 30. Boating permit required. Before issuance, boat and life vests will be inspected.

Prominent fish species: Largemouth bass and smallmouth bass

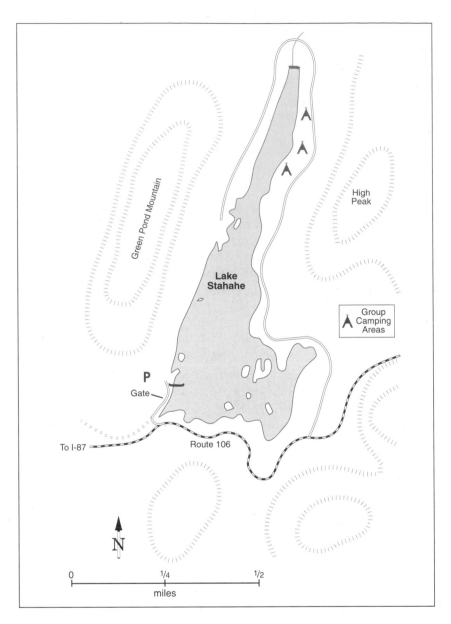

Green Pond Mountain

High
Peak

**Lake
Stahahe**

A Group
Camping
Areas

P

Gate

To I-87

Route 106

N

| 0 | 1/4 | 1/2 |

miles

When we paddled Silvermine Lake, located near the eastern end of
Harriman State Park, we got the sense that it sees somewhat fewer visitors than most of the other lakes in the park. Silvermine, created in
1934 by a dam on Bockey Swamp Brook, flooded a beaver swamp (this
may explain its earlier name, Menomini, meaning "wild rice"). The
lake still has a marshy feel and quite different vegetation from that
found in and around other lakes in the park.

A monarch butterfly sucks nectar from late-season asters in preparation for its long migration to Mexico.

A large stand of tamarack grows near the northeastern end of Silvermine, and thick clumps of alder, willow, red maple, red osier dogwood, sweet pepperbush, gray birch, and common reed (*Phragmites*)—all common marsh plants—line the northern shore. A dense oak-beech-maple forest—more typical of the region—rises from the water's southern edge. Submerged aquatic vegetation fills the relatively shallow lake, and various water lilies cover the arm to the northwest.

We saw lots of mallards and Canada geese near the boat access, while turkey vultures and red-tailed hawks soared overhead. Near the boat access is a ski area. Though we didn't climb up the steep slope, it looked as if one would get a great view to the north from here.

Lake Welch

INFORMATION

Area: 182 acres; maximum depth: 33 feet

Open for paddling April 1 through November 30. Boating permit required. Before issuance, boat and life vests will be inspected. Key required for gate.

Prominent fish species: Largemouth bass and smallmouth bass

Camping: Tent camping available at Beaver Pond Campground at the northern end of the lake; 914-947-2792

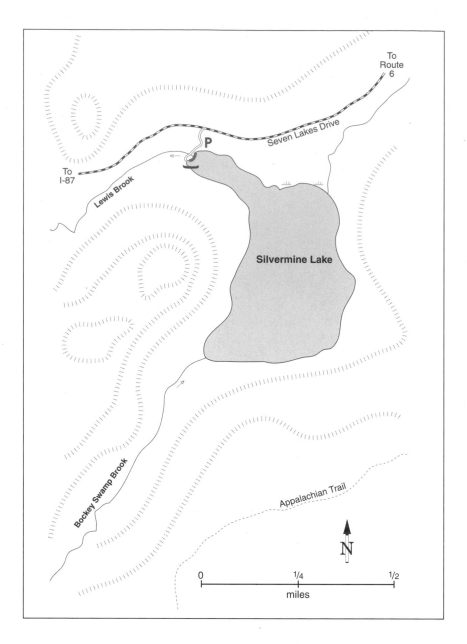

Of all the lakes and ponds we've paddled in Harriman State Park, Lake Welch remains our favorite. It's not the lake itself we find so appealing—though we did see a small flock of ruddy ducks and several Canada geese during our mid-October paddle. Lake Welch is fairly large, oval, and dominated by a gigantic swimming beach at the northeast end—we mean a *really* big beach, with perhaps a dozen lifeguard stands. Rather, it is the southwestern portion of the lake, reached by paddling under Route 106, and Beaver Pond Brook flowing into it, that we like.

Passage into this section of Lake Welch requires paddling southeast from the boat access and around the would-be island that is now connected by Route 106. After crossing under the road, paddle southwest, away from the cacophony of the beach and cars. As the lake narrows, it becomes quite rocky—expect a scratch or two. Ease your way past this area and into the marshy Beaver Pond Brook inlet. You will leave the rocks behind and enter a wild, magical area.

True to its name, we quickly came upon a beaver lodge in the broad outlet of the brook. Though hard to gauge distance here, we think we paddled at least a half mile along this highly twisted, slow-flowing brook as it meandered through *Phragmites* marsh and red maple swamp. In places the channel became so narrow and the curves so tight that we didn't know if our canoe would make it, but we always seemed to squeak through.

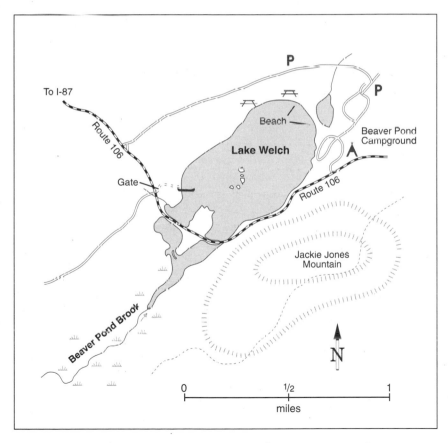

The farther we went, the shallower the water became. Eventually, sand replaced the mucky bottom; not long thereafter, we found our way blocked by a downed log. Fortunately, at that location we found a place where—with some difficulty—we could turn around. If you paddle a kayak back here, bring a break-down paddle or a single canoe paddle; using a two-bladed paddle would be out of the question along this creek.

Beaver Pond Brook teems with wildlife. We saw songbirds galore in the thick shrubs and grasses. Paddling back toward the main lake, after the brook widened out, we noticed movement by the shore and spotted a young otter making its way along the bank. It was obviously hunting as it alternately crawled over, slithered around, or swam under the tree roots and grass hummocks hanging out over the water. Until we watched this otter, we had not realized that these banks truly do overhang the water and that an animal can actually swim under a tree trunk or clump of grass. Sitting there in the canoe watching this otter—with no sign of people anywhere—we reveled in the fact that New York City was only an hour away.

Paddling back to the north toward the Route 106 bridge, look for a narrow channel heading to the left (northwest). This takes you into another part of the lake. Though within view of Route 106, this area felt quite wild. Immediately upon entering this cove, we spotted an osprey, which took off with a half-eaten fish in its talons.

Getting There

You can reach Harriman State Park from the New York Thruway (I-87) or the Palisades Interstate Parkway. From the Palisades Parkway, get off at Exit 18, and follow Seven Lakes Drive west for 9.6 miles to the access road on the right. Coming from the south on I-87, get off at Exit 15A, and turn left at the light onto Route 17 north. Follow Route 17 for 2.5 miles, then turn right onto Seven Lakes Drive. The access to Lake Sebago is on the left in 4.2 miles.

To reach the Lake Kanawauke access, continue another 2.9 miles past the Lake Sebago boat access to the circle at the intersection with Route 106. Go almost all the way around the circle and get onto Route 106 west. Follow Route 106 for 0.3 mile, and the boat access will appear on the left, just after crossing over the water. You can unload your canoe here but then should drive into the picnic and parking area just past the access, also on the left. There is a parking fee here. To launch your boat on Lake Skannatati, follow Seven Lakes Drive 0.8 mile from the Route 106 circle, and the access is on the left.

To reach Lake Tiorati, follow Seven Lakes Drive north 3.2 miles from the Route 106 circle to the Tiorati circle (the park office is located here). Bear to the right at the circle onto Tiorati Brook Road, and follow that around the lake to the south. The access is on the right in 1.1 miles. You need a key to open the gate. If there is inadequate parking space near the access, there is an additional small parking area across the road and slightly back toward Tiorati circle.

To reach Silvermine Lake, drive east on Seven Lakes Drive from Tiorati Circle for 2.1 miles, then turn right into the Silvermine Picnic Area. Drive past the parking area and across the small bridge, and you can hand launch your canoe to the left. After unloading your boat, park your vehicle in the parking lot.

To reach Lake Stahahe, take Route 106 west from the circle where Seven Lakes Drive and Route 106 intersect. Follow Route 106 for 3.9 miles, then take a sharp right onto the Lake Stahahe access road. You will reach the gate in another 0.2 mile (key required) and the boat launch and small parking area just beyond.

To reach Lake Welch, drive east on Route 106 from the circle where Seven Lakes Drive and Route 106 intersect. Drive 1.7 miles on Route 106, and the Lake Welch access road will be on the left just before getting to the lake—it is easy to miss. A key is required to unlock the gate. After passing through the gate (relocking it behind you), bear right and you will reach the access in 0.1 mile. There is limited parking here.

Snapping Turtle
Hidden Dweller of the Pond

Snapping turtles are the most common species of turtle in New York—even more common than painted turtles. In fact, they inhabit almost every beaver pond, millpond, lake, marsh, and slow-moving stream in New York. Hundreds may live in some bodies of water! But you wouldn't know it. Even if you spend quite a bit of time paddling ponds, lakes, and slow-moving rivers, you rarely see these large turtles. Unlike their sun-loving cousin, the painted turtle, snappers prefer pond-bottom depths and rarely bask in the sun. (The photo above shows an obvious exception to this generality.)

Snapping turtles, *Chelydra serpentina,* are easy to recognize if you come across them, especially out of water. They have long, spiny-ridged tails and very large heads relative to body size. The young have distinct ridges on the top shell (carapace), though on larger adults the shell may have worn smooth. On the underside, the small bottom shell (plastron) has a crosslike shape. If you pick up a snapping turtle, be very careful. Turtle handlers pick them up by the tail, holding them well away from their bodies (we recommend against messing with any large snappers).

Mature snapping turtles grow quite large—though usually not as big as the wide-eyed estimates of enthusiastic observers. The carapace can reach a length of 20 inches (which means an overall length, nose to tail, of more than three feet). A large turtle can weigh more than 60 pounds. No other turtle in the Northeast approaches this size.

When paddling relatively clear, shallow water, we occasionally see snappers underwater. On a few occasions we've seen them on the bank above a pond or slow-moving river—probably en route to a nearby body of water or, perhaps, a female out of water to lay a clutch of eggs. Snappers may travel great distances in search of suitable nesting sites—one marked individual traveled 16 kilometers round-trip! Our usual glimpse of snappers, though, is just the triangular nose sticking out of the water ahead of us as we paddle along. At first glance, we assume a water lily leaf has flipped over, but our binoculars tell us otherwise—if we get a chance to look before the nose submerges.

Many people fear snapping turtles—and we'll admit a bit of concern when two large snappers chased one another just inches beneath our canoe in a shallow pond—but they really pose no harm *as long as they remain in the water*. Even in the unlikely event that a snapper bites a swimmer's toe underwater, it quickly lets go, realizing that the quarry is more than it can handle. In the water, the shy snapper avoids any human contact. Watch out for snappers on land, though. They lash out with lightning speed if they feel threatened. A large snapper, with its massive jaw muscles and razor-sharp beak, exerts more than 400 pounds per square inch of force with its bite—enough to sever a finger easily.

If you look beyond their somewhat grotesque appearance and (at times) nasty disposition, snapping turtles are fascinating animals. They have existed for at least 80 million years, and scientists believe them to be the oldest reptiles in North America. Like all turtles, their rib cage and vertebrae have evolved into a bony carapace and plastron. With most turtles, this shell provides armored protection, but the snapper's small plastron offers almost no protection to its underside. So for defense out of water, the snapper does just that: it snaps. The small plastron also makes snapping turtles vulnerable to leeches, and they sometimes leave the water to rid themselves of this parasite.

Most turtles hibernate for long periods during winter, but snapping turtles are relatively resistant to cold. We sometimes see them swimming beneath the ice in the middle of winter, though in northern New York they typically hibernate in the bottom mud for at least a while during the dead of winter. When idle underwater, snappers do not need to surface for air. Special surfaces in their rear cloacal cavity extract oxygen from water, much like gills. When active, though, they need more oxygen and must surface for air—providing the quiet paddler an opportunity to catch a glimpse of one.

Omnivores and opportunists, snapping turtles dine on a wide range of animal and plant material, including fish, frogs, salamanders, occasional ducklings, dead animals, and aquatic plants. Snappers can kill anything their size or smaller, but they seem to prefer the easy meal. They have a superb sense of smell, which they use to scavenge for dead animals. Interestingly, this trait on occasion has been used to find human drowning victims. The snapping turtle literature recounts one story of a Native American who assisted officials in finding and retrieving drowning victims using a snapping turtle on a long leash. When released into the water, the turtle would unerringly head right for the decomposing corpse, latch onto it with its strong jaws, and its handler would slowly reel it in—corpse and all.

A mature female leaves the water in late spring or early summer to lay her eggs. She digs a hole and typically deposits from 20 to 30 (rarely, up to 80) eggs the size and shape of Ping-Pong balls, then covers the hole. Some females lay eggs in two or more holes; they often will dig several false holes to mislead predators, which take a heavy toll on snapping turtle clutches. The eggs usually hatch in the fall, some 70 to 100 days after laying (depending on temperature), and the inch-long hatchlings make a beeline for the water—often as raccoons, birds, and other predators gobble them up.

As with many turtles, temperature of the nest may determine the sex of young snappers. Several studies found that at very cool or very warm temperatures, the embryos all developed into females, while intermediate temperatures produced males. In most nests, the temperature regime varies with location, so both males and females develop.

Snapper populations remain quite secure in New York—unlike those of most other turtles. They seem to tolerate current levels of environmental pollution and live in even highly polluted marshy areas in cities. Some regard snapper meat highly, resulting in heavy trapping in certain areas. Roads result in fewer crushed snappers than the toll taken on more terrestrial turtles. If you come across a snapping turtle out of water, avoid the temptation to deliver it to the nearest body of water—chances are pretty good that she knows where to head to lay her eggs and does not need our assistance in this endeavor.

Mohansic Lake and Crom Pond
Yorktown

MAPS
New York Atlas: Map 33
USGS Quadrangle: Mohegan Lake

INFORMATION
Mohansic Lake area: 108 acres; maximum depth: 27 feet
Prominent fish species: Largemouth bass and chain pickerel
Franklin D. Roosevelt State Park; 914-245-4434. A onetime
yearly $15 fee provides access to the following lakes and ponds:
Taghkanic, Rudd, Canopus, John Allen, Mohansic, and Stillwa-
ter. FDR Park rents rowboats only.

Franklin D. Roosevelt State Park, one of several parks along the scenic
Taconic Parkway, contains both Mohansic Lake and the connected
Crom Pond. We paddled here during a Monday afternoon and evening
rush hour, and the road noise from the Taconic—which you can just
barely see off through the trees was a bit disconcerting at first.

FDR Park has few boaters. Most people come here for other types of
recreation: swimming in one of the U.S.'s largest pools, hiking on an
extensive network of trails, biking in the summer, and cross-country skiing and ice-skating in the winter. Dubious at first about the paddling,
given the road noise, we became converted after we paddled over into

*A female ruddy duck—one of the smallest North American ducks—paddles
about the surface of Crom Pond during fall migration.*

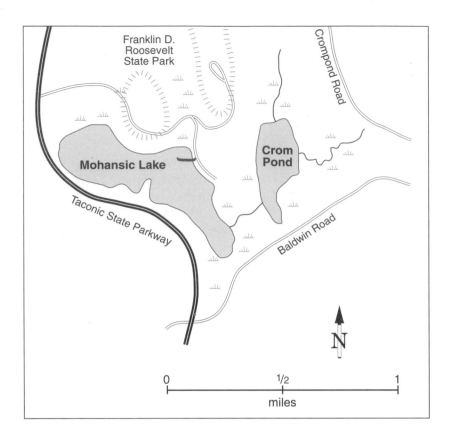

Crom Pond, a wilderness retreat, where you can just barely hear the road noise. It also helped that we visited in October, when few others were here.

A huge flock of tame Canada geese begged for food at the boat access, ignoring the sign that says Do Not Feed Wildlife. They also ignored the No Swimming in the Lake sign. Tame cottontails munched on the grass, and pied-billed grebes swam about in thick aquatic vegetation. A flock of coots over on the north end also tried to keep the abundant aquatic plants in check, seemingly to no avail, while a lone cormorant surveyed the scene from an exposed rock out in the middle of the lake.

We left behind the boat access, with its large beech, weeping willow, sugar maple, big-toothed aspen, and unfed geese, and headed for Crom Pond. As we paddled south to the connector, the sheer volume of white and yellow water lilies impressed us greatly. The entire southern cove was covered with their flat leaves floating on the water's surface. The large trees near the boat access gave way to a shrubby shoreline that included dwarfed red maples and black gum.

As we paddled the connector, ducks scurried into the tiny channels back under the shrubbery. A pied-billed grebe dove for cover; though we watched carefully, we did not see where it resurfaced. Shrubs and dwarf red maples dominate the connector. We found buttonbush, dwarf willows, and purple loosestrife growing in profusion, along with winterberry and lesser amounts of several other shrubs.

Two fishermen in a rowboat tried their luck along the northern shore, casting for bass, while eight ruddy ducks paddled about. As we drew near, we could see that the males were in winter plumage already. These unusual small ducks—also called stiff-tails—have short, stiff tails that often point straight up, revealing a bright white rump. Males in breeding plumage have ruddy necks, backs, and sides; a black head with large white face patch; and a bright blue bill—quite a sight to behold! In keeping with their strange visage, in the spring males putt-putt around in little circles and figure eights, using their stiff tails as rudders, trying to attract female attention; this perhaps does not look comical to female ruddy ducks.

Because they usually nest on small ponds, we rarely see these ducks, except in migration. Eventually this group decided that we had approached too close and dove for cover. They typically dive rather than fly when danger approaches.

As we sat out in the middle of Crom Pond surveying the countryside, we had to listen carefully to hear the Taconic Parkway road noise. We had forgotten all about it when we investigated the ruddy ducks. We noticed that tall trees grow only on one patch of the north shore, while a shrubby marsh with dwarf trees dominates the rest of the pond.

Having done all the surveying we could, reluctantly we paddled back to Mohansic Lake where we found the geese panhandling, again without much success. Obviously, given their robust size, they usually find a more responsive crowd. As we left the park near dusk and drove northward on the Taconic, rush hour had stopped, and the deer that like to dodge cars had emerged. We had not even merged onto the parkway when several deer appeared to browse on the roadside shrubs. As we drove back to Vermont in the gathering darkness, our headlights frequently caught the eyeshine of roadside deer. We had to stop abruptly more than a few times to avoid hitting them, though we did not see any dead along the road. The drivers who travel this road regularly must maintain quite a bit of caution. Frankly, nowhere else in our travels throughout New York can we remember seeing such a large population of deer. What is it about this road and deer?

Getting There

Take the Taconic Parkway to the north end of Westchester County, and get off at the exit for Franklin D. Roosevelt State Park, about 19 miles north of I-287. To get to the boat access, stay to the right at each junction.

Constitution Marsh

Philipstown

MAPS
   New York Atlas: Map 32
   USGS Quadrangle: West Point
INFORMATION
   Area: Tidal
   Prominent fish species: Saltwater species
   Constitution Marsh National Audubon Society Sanctuary; 914-
      265-2601

Constitution Marsh, owned by the National Audubon Society, provides a wonderful location to take children to learn about nature, including forests, streams, and tidal marshes. Three nature trails weave through the 270-acre sanctuary: one trail teaches tree identification, one leads to an ancient Native American rock shelter, and the third allows close inspection of the marsh by boardwalk. An archaeological dig at refuge headquarters has demonstrated Native American occupation dating back at least 5,000 years. Audubon naturalists also run guided canoe trips into the marsh for groups of up to 15 adults; programs for school-children accommodate up to 25 students, along with adult assistants. The Audubon Society Visitor Center is open from 9:00 A.M. to 5:00 P.M., May 1 to October 31 (closed Mondays).

   Unfortunately, you really cannot paddle your own boat out from the visitor center, because to get there you have to hike your boat about a half mile down a fairly steep gravel road; worse, you have to hike your boat back up. An alternate entrance to the marsh exists, however. You can launch from the Amtrak station parking lot in nearby Cold Spring and paddle for about a half mile through Foundry Cove into the northern reaches of the marsh. Because you can paddle the marsh only for about two hours either side of high tide, you should call the visitor center before venturing forth and ask about tides. Note that the time of high tide will differ significantly from what it is at the George Washington Bridge.

   We paddled in from Cold Spring, having parked our car down at the end of the Amtrak station parking lot (no, we didn't bring our canoe on the train!). Getting the boat through the overgrown bank, down over the jumble of rocks, and into the water took about 10 minutes; commuter cars partially blocked the obvious access ports. Paddle downstream for a

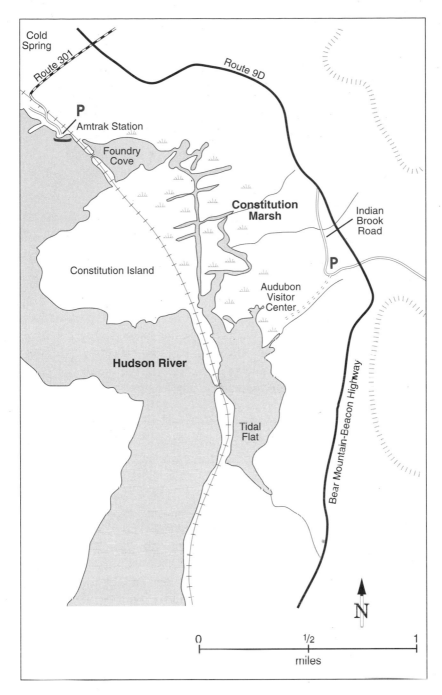

few hundred feet, and pass under the railroad bridge to the left. From there, head due east for the very back of Foundry Cove, where a wide passageway drains Constitution Marsh with the outgoing tide.

Cormorants

As we entered Foundry Cove, flocks of mallards and black ducks and five mute swans greeted us. Three of the swans spilled out of the EPA Superfund restoration site at the back of Foundry Cove on the outgoing tide. We eyeballed them pretty carefully but could discern no extra appendages or other mutations. The ducks and the other two swans had the good sense to stay out of this area.

Up close, the dramatic size difference between the swans and ducks stood out. The swans—five feet from beak tip to tail end—dwarfed the two-foot-long ducks, especially in bulk. An Old World import, wild populations of the generally tame mute swan have expanded along the East Coast from Cape Cod to Cape Hatteras.

We paddled back through acres of narrow-leaved cattails. Large deciduous trees line the eastern edge of the marsh and populate Constitution Island, which juts out into the Hudson. As we gazed out over the marsh and up the surrounding bluffs and hillsides, we found large, isolated homes overlooking this beautiful area through a glorious fall foliage.

According to the Audubon Society, the 154-mile tidal stretch of the Hudson from New York City to Troy represents the only major American river still functioning as a complete ecosystem. In spite of pollution and development, the Hudson has not lost a single fish species. It produces huge populations of striped bass, shad, blue crabs, and other species, all of which depend on tidal marshes for food. Tidal marshes rank at the top of biologically productive areas, producing three times as much biomass as the best farmland, up to 30,000 pounds per acre per year.

After we paddled many of the marsh's channels, we headed back to Cold Spring and drove around to the visitor center on Indian Brook Road. We walked the trails and, using their excellent guidebook, studied the 39 species of trees and shrubs described. We found interesting information about several tree species. For example, the last Ice Age nearly exterminated the black locust. Early settlers, however, transplanted it from its last holdout in Appalachian valleys to all over the East and Midwest. Settlers used it for many products; today, we still use it to make split-rail fences because of its tremendous durability. Locust also can substitute for pressure-treated wood, which we make rot resistant by impregnating with environmental toxins such as arsenic, copper, and chromium. Indeed, the boardwalk out into the Audubon marsh is made of black locust. We urge you to visit here, to paddle, to walk the trails, to talk to the staff. We especially urge you to bring children to this wonderful place.

Getting There

From the south, take Route 9 north through Peekskill. Just after leaving the city, turn left onto Routes 6 and 202, the Bear Mountain Highway. Do not cross the Bear Mountain Bridge on Routes 6 and 202; instead, go to the right onto Route 9D toward Cold Spring.

From I-87, get off at Route 6, the Bear Mountain Highway. Cross the Bear Mountain Bridge, and turn left onto Route 9D toward Cold Spring.

At the stoplight at the junctions of Route 9D and 301 in Cold Spring, turn left and drive down through town to the end of the street. Turn left onto Lunn Terrace, then take an immediate right across a bridge. At the T at the end of the bridge, turn left and drive down through the Amtrak station parking lot to the end. Park here and lower your boat down over the rocks into the Hudson River.

Paddle to the left under the railroad bridge into Foundry Cove, an EPA Superfund restoration site. At the back of the cove on the right is the entrance to Constitution Marsh.

To get to the Audubon Society headquarters for Constitution Marsh, leave the parking area, retracing your path back up through Cold Spring to the stoplight at the junction of Routes 9D and 301. Turn right onto Route 9D. Go 1.4 miles to Indian Brook Road, an easy-to-miss, narrow, gravel road that goes diagonally off to the right. Stay on Indian Brook Road for 0.4 mile to the Audubon Society parking lot. There is room here for precisely eight cars. When the lot is full, you must not park along the road—you will be towed. Instead, return later when there is room. Hike down the half mile to the visitor center.

Canopus Lake and Stillwater Pond

Kent

MAPS
   New York Atlas: Map 33
   USGS Quadrangle: Oscawana Lake
INFORMATION
   Area: Canopus, 120 acres; Stillwater, 64 acres
   Prominent fish species: Smallmouth bass
   Camping: Clarence Fahnestock State Park; 914-225-7207
   Fees: A onetime yearly $15 fee provides access to the following
   lakes and ponds: Canopus, John Allen, Mohansic, Rudd,
   Taghkanic, and Stillwater. The park rents rowboats only.

Canopus Lake

Canopus Lake, within the Clarence Fahnestock State Park, offers a wonderful paddling opportunity, especially in the off-season. Although the park prohibits gasoline motors on the lake, believe it or not, it can get overrun with rowboats and canoes, especially on sunny summer weekends. Three reasons account for this: the Appalachian Trail skirts the entire western edge of the lake, making the whole area a popular recreation destination; a popular campground lies within the park; and the Taconic Parkway has an exit within the park, making the area easily accessible to literally millions of recreation-starved, downstate city dwellers.

Even though we had to share the lake with other boaters, we loved paddling here, given its small, protected nature and incredible beauty. Beautiful tall hemlocks dominate the rocky hillside across from the boat access, and their lacy leaves droop out over the shores, especially on the upper lake, but the real attraction remains the tree-sized mountain laurel growing in the understory. A showy, evergreen member of the heath family—which includes leatherleaf, bog rosemary, sheep laurel, and blueberry—mountain laurel, like most heaths, prefers acid soil. Blooming in late May, the gorgeous clusters of pink-to-white flowers present a perfect pollen trap for honeybees. The 10 stamens of each flower press tightly against the petals. When a bee lands on the flower seeking nectar, the stamens spring out, dusting the bee with pollen to be carried on to the next flower for cross-pollination.

The twisted tops of oak, beech, and yellow birch dominate the hillsides, giving cover to the Appalachian Trail. After leaving the park, the

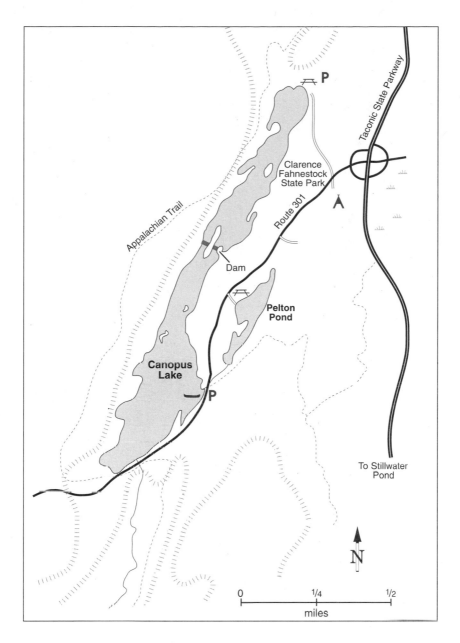

Clarence
Fahnestock
State Park

Appalachian Trail

Route 301

Taconic State Parkway

P

Dam

Pelton
Pond

Canopus
Lake

P

To Stillwater
Pond

N

| 0 | 1/4 | 1/2 |
miles

trail heads northeast, eventually entering Connecticut in northern Fairfield
County, on its way to its northern terminus in Maine's Baxter State Park.

Many smooth granite boulders dot the surface of the lake; unfortunately, the park does not allow swimming on the lower part of the
lake. To take a dip you have to carry over the dam that separates the two

Early-season fishermen try their luck for smallmouth bass on Canopus Lake.

halves of the lake and paddle up to the sandy swimming beach. Stay to the right for the carry.

When we paddled here in April, a pair of Canada geese nested on the south end of a tiny island near the east shore, just where the lower lake starts to narrow down. The bird sitting on the nest hunkered down, trying to look invisible, as we quietly paddled by. We hope that those who followed gave the nest a wide berth. Signs tell visitors not to feed the geese, which probably have gotten quite tame over the years. In addition, we saw several other species of birds, all of them newly arrived migrants thinking about nesting: eastern phoebe, robin, turkey vulture, flicker, and barn swallow.

Stillwater Pond

If you find yourself paddling with the crowds on Canopus Lake, try nearby Stillwater Pond. Though smaller than Canopus, it also receives far less traffic. When we paddled here on the Saturday afternoon of Labor Day weekend, we and the frogs had the pond to ourselves, probably because swimming is not allowed.

As you hike your boat the tenth of a mile down to the landing, take note of the huge, three-feet-in-diameter tulip tree along the path. This member of the magnolia family—with its large waxy yellow treetop flowers—is at the northern extension of its range here. Also note the

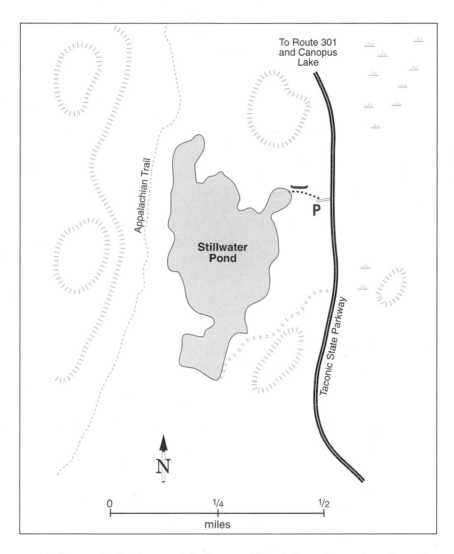

To Route 301
and Canopus
Lake

Appalachian Trail

P

**Stillwater
Pond**

Taconic State Parkway

N

| 0 | 1/4 | 1/2 |

miles

smooth gray-barked sweet birch trees (*Betula lenta*) growing along the path. Scratch off some bark from a branch, and note the sweet odor of wintergreen. You can use this characteristic odor to distinguish sweet birch from the similar river birch (*Betula nigra*), which lacks this odor.

Gorgeous rounded light gray granite boulders greet you in the access cove, many of them completely submerged in the clear water but others jutting way up out of the water. These beautiful rocks, though lending a scenic quality to the pond, also provide a hazard to navigation. Go slowly near shore.

As we paddled down the far shore, we spied many large mountain laurel, similar to the ones on nearby Canopus Lake. They had flowered long ago and set fruit, which have five-part symmetry and a prominent stalk (the leftover pistil) jutting from the end. The fruit do not spill their tiny brown seeds until fall, possibly to reduce seed predation by birds and mice.

Also along the shore in several places we spotted the heavily serrated nine-inch-long leaves of the American chestnut. This magnificent tree once was a codominant species in the Appalachians and its nuts an important food source for wildlife, but the inadvertent introduction of the chestnut blight, a fungus that gets under the bark, killed every mature tree. Stump sprouts such as these rarely live long enough to flower before they get felled by the disease. The stumps still sprout because the soft, resinous wood resists decay. It was used for railroad ties and split-rail fences. Many chestnut split-rail fences still survive after many decades.

We enjoyed paddling alone on this wonderful little pond, with its huge patches of water shield, studying its diverse plants. As we gazed at a red-tailed hawk circling overhead, we noted the lack of noise from the busy Taconic Parkway and were thankful that we had found this little jewel off in the woods.

Getting There

To get to Canopus Lake and the Clarence Fahnestock State Park, take the Route 301 Cold Spring exit from the Taconic Parkway, and drive south on Route 301 for 0.9 mile to the boat access on the right. There is limited parking across the road on the left.

The Pelton Pond Picnic Area and Nature Trail is on the left, 0.5 mile from the Taconic Parkway. The campground and swimming area entrances are 0.1 mile from the Taconic Parkway exit road junction with Route 301. The campground is on the left, and the swimming area is on the right.

To get to Stillwater Pond, head back to the parkway. Get on going south, and go about 1.5 miles, watching for a sign for Stillwater Lake. Turn right into the parking lot—avoiding the deep potholes. Park here and hike your boat about 0.1 mile down to the pond.

Chodikee Lake

Lloyd

MAPS
    New York Atlas: Map 36
    USGS Quadrangle: Hyde Park

INFORMATION
    Area: 61 acres; maximum depth: 20 feet
    Prominent fish species: Largemouth bass and chain pickerel

We paddled Chodikee Lake in the spring before the mosquitoes hatched out of the extensive marshes surrounding the lake and before more than an occasional fisherman plied the waters. What we found was a lake in an idyllic state, an extraordinary wildlife paradise free from the insects and people that would later appear in large numbers.

The plaintive calls of spring peepers, the chatter of chipmunks, and the mournful cry of doves greeted us at the boat access, and as we looked out over the lake from the end of the dock, two mute swans drifted slowly over the surface. These Eurasian imports, larger than our native swans at five feet from bill to tip of tail, continue to spread along the eastern seaboard from Cape Cod to Chesapeake Bay. They often swim with their necks carried in a graceful S-shaped curve and can be distinguished from our native swans by their orange yellow bills with a black knob at the top.

The most striking element of Chodikee Lake has to be its wildlife habitat, with acres of dead and dying trees, meandering streams on both the north and south ends, extensive wooded swamps, and stands of cattails and other marsh vegetation. The lake itself does not provide much habitat, so take the time to paddle both of the streams. At times of high water, you can paddle the south creek upstream to the road and the north creek downstream to a series of small waterfalls. You will be amazed, as we were, by the prodigious amount of wildlife.

Red-bellied woodpeckers and flickers have carved out holes in hundreds of dead trees, providing nests not only for themselves but also for other cavity nesters, including wood ducks, kestrels, bluebirds, and tree swallows. We saw hundreds of tree swallows cruising over the water, scooping up early emerging insects, as well as several kestrels and many bluebirds. The red-bellied woodpecker reaches the northern extension of its range in southern New York. It can be distinguished from flickers by

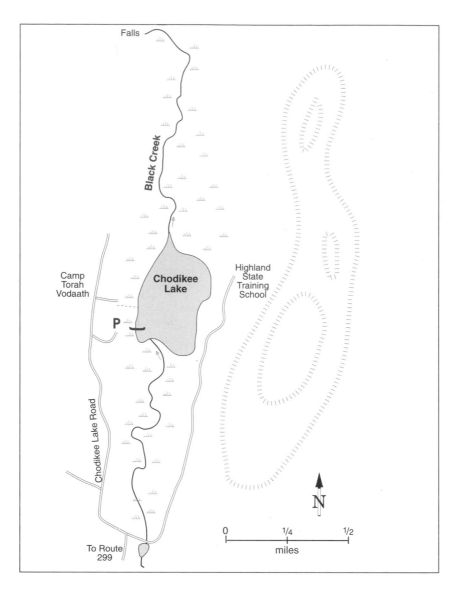

the large red patch on the back and top of the head and the alternating black and white stripes on the back—a so-called ladder back.

But the ducks provided the real attraction. Not only did we see many gorgeously colored wood ducks, especially in the wooded swamp along the northern stream, but we also saw hundreds of green-winged teal, quite a few mallards and black ducks, and many Canada geese. Several pairs of geese, which nest quite early compared with other waterfowl, hunkered down over their nests on rotting stumps, incubating their eggs just a foot or two above the water.

Dead trees, many with woodpecker excavations, line the banks of the inlet and outlet creeks.

At the northern end of the outflow stream, a hemlock canopy draped over beautiful rock formations. In the shade of the hemlocks, a pair of phoebes nested in a natural cavity in a vertical rock face. As the stream narrowed down and began to tumble gently over the rockfalls, the land was posted against further travel.

Getting There

From Poughkeepsie, cross the Hudson River on Route 44. At the junction with Route 9W, take 9W north. Turn left onto Route 299, and go 1.3 miles to Chodikee Lake Road. Turn right onto Chodikee Lake Road, and go 1.0 mile to a T. On the right is a yardful of interesting welded-steel sculpture. Turn left, and go 0.9 mile to the boat access road on the right. The boat access is 0.1 mile down this road.

Do not be fooled by the New York Atlas. It shows a boat access on the east side of the lake. That is a youth camp with a locked gate. The actual access is on the west side of the lake.

An alternative approach to the lake is to take the New York State Thruway to Exit 18 at New Paltz. Take Route 299 east for a few miles to Chodikee Lake Road, and proceed as above.

Lake Taghkanic and Rudd Pond
Gallatin and Northeast

MAPS
New York Atlas: Maps 37 and 52
USGS Quadrangles: Ancram and Millerton, NY & CT

INFORMATION
Lake Taghkanic area: 162 acres; maximum depth: 40 feet
Rudd Pond area: 64 acres; maximum depth: 10 feet
Prominent fish species: smallmouth bass and chain pickerel
Camping: Lake Taghkanic State Park; 518-851-3631
Fees: A onetime yearly $15 fee provides access to the following
lakes and ponds: Taghkanic, Rudd, Canopus, John Allen,
Mohansic, and Stillwater. Taghkanic Park rents rowboats only.

Lake Taghkanic

This small but popular park, located just off the Taconic Parkway in southern Columbia County, draws many recreation-starved down-staters to its shores. A popular picnic and day-use area for swimming, hiking, biking, and boating, it also includes a campground. The park permits boats without motors for a yearly fee of $15 that also allows access to other state-owned park waters in the Taconic region.

When we paddled here just before Labor Day as prefall colors just started to creep into the hillsides, people crowded the park, trying to get that last bit of warm, sunny recreation in before winter's onslaught. Still, boats did not crowd the water, and we felt as though we were paddling alone most of the time. The lake's small size means that even a leisurely paddle will end in about an hour, so this park remains mainly recreation and family oriented. You can teach your children about plants and wildlife here and, in these protected waters, how to paddle a canoe or kayak.

We especially enjoyed studying the oaks and found 5 of the 12 species that grow in downstate New York, including red oak, white oak, scarlet oak, pin oak, and chestnut oak. We did not find the other 7—bur oak, post oak, swamp white oak, chinkapin oak, bear oak, southern red oak, or black oak—but for tree lovers it would be interesting to try to find all of the oaks that grow in southeast New York.

Biologists theorize that oaks evolved millions of years ago in Mexico, where there are 150 species, and radiated southward and northward from there. The U.S. has about 50 species, with fewer and fewer species occurring as you approach the Northeast. Oaks fall into

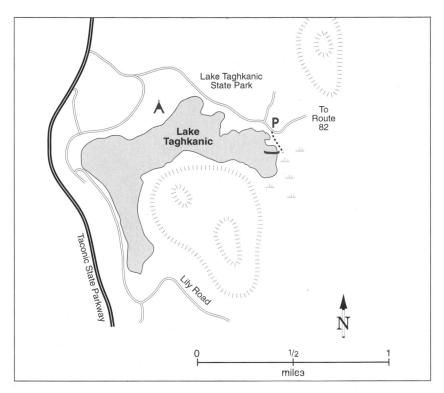

two major groups: red oaks and white oaks. The main differences between the two groups include bristles on the tips of red oak leaves, while white oak leaves are rounded, and white oak acorns mature in one year, while red oak acorns hang on for two years. Trees usually bear heavy crops of acorns on a two- to four-year rotation, and these seeds serve as an important food source for squirrels, wild turkey, grouse, black bear, deer, wood ducks, and small mammals.

We noticed that shoreside black gum trees had started to turn their brilliant scarlet color, which they do before other hardwoods begin to turn. We also found hickory, northern white cedar, red and sugar maple, though not nearly as frequently as oaks.

On the marshy east end of the lake, we found large patches of water shield, yellow pond lily, fragrant water lily, pickerelweed, purple loosestrife, buttonbush, fanwort, and pondweed.

Rudd Pond

If Lake Taghkanic is too crowded, you can also camp at Rudd Pond, a much smaller and more out-of-the-way member of the Taconic State Park group, almost to the Connecticut border. Because Route 62 trav-

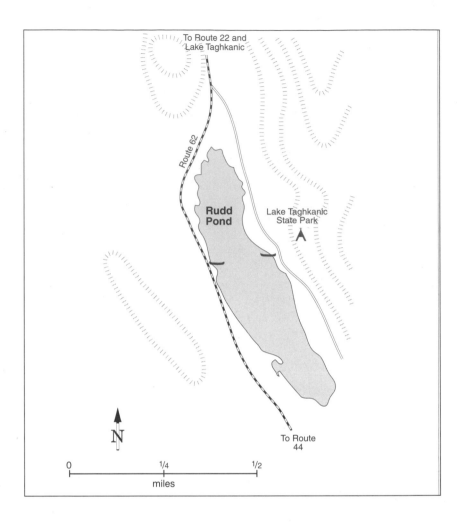

To Route 22 and
Lake Taghkanic

Route 62

Rudd
Pond

Lake Taghkanic
State Park

N

To Route
44

0   1/4   1/2
miles

els down the pond's western shore, paddling here will not be a wilderness experience. But it offers a nice place for camping, picnicking, and relaxing among towering white pines, spreading weeping willows, and tall black locusts. Oaks, paper birch, hickory, tall tamaracks, Norway spruce, and red pine round out the tree species. More so than most areas in the vicinity, this area boasts truly huge trees of all the abovementioned species. The forested hillsides of deciduous tree species glowed brightly with fall colors when we returned to this area in mid-October—a month and a half after our first visit.

The marshy north and south ends of Rudd Pond sport a blanket of aquatic vegetation, including pickerelweed, fragrant water lily, yellow pond lily, pondweed, cattails, *Phragmites,* purple loosestrife, and more.

Canoes and rowboats share the boat access on Lake Taghkanic.

You do not have to pay the park entrance fee if you put in from the pull-off on Route 62 as it travels down the west side of the pond. You do, however, need to have the same $15 yearly boat sticker that gets you onto Lake Taghkanic.

Getting There

To get to Lake Taghkanic, take the Taconic Parkway north or south to the well-marked Lake Taghkanic Road exit—roughly 40 miles north of I-84—and follow the signs into the park.

To get to Rudd Pond from Lake Taghkanic, head north out of the park to Route 82. Turn right onto Route 82, and take it to Ancramdale. There, turn left onto Route 3; in a little over a mile when Route 3 goes left, continue straight up over the mountain on Over Mountain Road. When Over Mountain Road forks, take the left fork downhill to Route 22. Turn right onto Route 22. After crossing the Dutchess County line, continue another 0.9 mile on Route 22, then turn left onto Route 62. Follow signs to Rudd Pond. You can enter the park and pay to use the boat access, or you could continue south on Route 22 and put in at the pull-off.

Basher Kill
Mamakating

MAPS
  New York Atlas: Map 35
  USGS Quadrangle: Yankee Lake
INFORMATION
  Area: 1,333 acres (entire wetland)
  Prominent fish species: Largemouth bass and chain pickerel
  Bashakill Wildlife Management Area: 914-255-5453

For observing wildlife near New York City, nothing beats the Bashakill (we do not know why the spelling differs) Wildlife Management Area of far southeastern Sullivan County. The largest freshwater wetland in southeastern New York, the Bashakill's 2,175 acres protect the habitat of deer, grouse, wild turkey, fox, beaver, muskrat, raccoon, rabbit, skunk, mink, opossum, and waterfowl, particularly wood ducks.

The middle section of the Shawangunk Mountains—the northern "Gunks" is famous with rock climbers and hikers—runs down the eastern shore of the Basher Kill, providing a scenic backdrop for paddlers and hikers alike. The western shore has beautiful hillsides as well,

Rising early-morning mists reveal clumps of purple loosestrife—an alien species—as it invades the marsh.

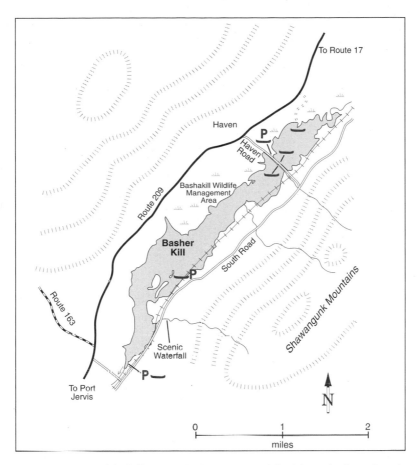

which dripped with fall colors when we paddled here in late October. We recommend, if you are so inclined, that you hike the perimeter trails: one along the west shore follows the historic D & H Canal, while one along the east proceeds over a long-abandoned railroad grade.

Because the state does not allow motors, you can paddle here for hours in peace, in and among the islands and drowned timber. The Department of Environmental Conservation tries to enhance nesting success of three species in particular within this refuge by erecting appropriate nesting structures: nesting platforms for osprey and nesting boxes for wood ducks and bluebirds.

We saw many wood ducks when we paddled here, as they gobbled acorns and aquatic plants to fatten up for migration. Flocks of Canada geese honked from the marsh, as they stopped off on their migration from the far north. Our visit also coincided with the tail end of songbird migration. In one mixed foraging flock, we saw chipping sparrow, white-throated sparrow, song sparrow, fox sparrow, junco, yellow-rumped warbler, a tail-bobbing palm warbler, and ruby-crowned kinglet. We spotted many hermit thrushes, tufted titmouse, and eastern phoebe.

Red and white oaks dominate the surrounding high ground. Their leaves had turned a burnished red in the fall air when we paddled here. Occasional sugar and red maples added accents of orange and red, and aspen and birch lent a vibrant yellow against a backdrop of dark green conifers. Beside providing food for wood ducks, oaks and beeches provide food for wild turkey and the abundant gray squirrels. Water lilies and other aquatic plants cover the surface of this shallow reservoir, while the alien invader purple loosestrife vies with buttonbush and arrowhead to dominate the shallows. In many spots, muskrats have built small brush piles that serve as their homes out in the marsh. Along stream banks, they usually burrow under roots in soft banks to find a home; here in an area with abundant food but no banks, they have to use an alternate strategy.

If recent rains have fallen, as well as in the spring, a beautiful waterfall tumbles down out of the Shawangunks, cascading over ledges in three drops, through an overhanging canopy of lacy hemlock boughs, to flow into the south end of the reservoir. You can easily see it from South Road as you approach the lake's south end.

Getting There

To get to the Bashakill Wildlife Management Area from I-87 or I-84, take the Route 17 west exit, heading toward Binghamton. Get off Route 17 at Exit 113, the Wurtsboro exit, and head south on Route 209. The first access point is on the left, 1.1 miles from Route 17, then down a short gravel road. We prefer to paddle out from either the bisecting bridge or the south end, as described below.

To get to the bridge from Route 17, go down Route 209 south for 1.8 miles, and turn left onto Haven Road. Just before the bridge, a parking area appears on the left. You can park there and launch your boat on the other side of the road. Alternatively, you can continue onto the bridge (0.5 mile from Route 209) and park your car along the side; there is room for only one or two small cars here.

You can also put in at two spots down along the southeastern shore. Continue on over the bridge and up the hill to South Road. Turn right, and drive south for 1.8 miles to the marked access road on the right. This is, perhaps, the best place from which to launch.

A final launch site exists at the outflow, where Pine Kill flows in. From the previous launch site, it is another 1.4 miles down South Road. Along the way, you pass the waterfall on the left at 0.5 mile.

Rio Reservoir

Forestburg, Highland, Deerpark, and Lumberland

MAPS

New York Atlas: Maps 35 and 31
USGS Quadrangles: Highland Lake and Pond Eddy

INFORMATION

Area: 460 acres; maximum depth: 85 feet
Prominent fish species: Smallmouth bass, largemouth bass, chain pickerel, and native brown trout

Rio Reservoir (rhymes with "bio") is the southernmost of three paddlable reservoirs on the Mongaup River near Monticello, New York. (See also the section on Mongaup Falls Reservoir—the third, Swinging Bridge Reservoir, is not included in this guide because of heavy motorboat use.) These bodies of water reside largely within the Mongaup Valley Wildlife Management Area, which was purchased or otherwise protected by the state of New York in 1986 to protect wintering bald eagles. As currently managed, the area remains off-limits to recreational uses from December 1 until April 1—cutting into the paddling season of only the most die-hard boaters.

Rio Reservoir extends roughly 3.6 miles in a north-south orientation, with several sweeping S-curves in the southern half. Maximum width reaches about a third of a mile. The primary access is at the north end and consists of a boat ramp and parking for about 20 cars. Fortunately for paddlers, the state prohibits gasoline-powered motorboats here, so this fairly large reservoir does not suffer from wakes and excess noise. When we went out for a morning paddle here on a sunny Labor Day weekend, only about a half dozen boats plied the water—mostly boats with electric trolling motors.

Rio's fairly uniform shoreline rises steeply from the water, so there are very few marshy areas. Hemlock dominates the banks, but you will see a large amount of diversity, including white pine, beech, black birch, red maple, sugar maple, ironwood, sassafras, shagbark hickory, and at least four oaks (red, white, chestnut, and scarlet). Of particular interest, particularly for paddlers in late June or early July, are the rhododendrons along the shoreline. While not as dense as you will find on nearby Lake Superior, this tall member of the heath family grows in profusion here and should be gorgeous during the flowering season in late June or early July. A few weeks earlier in the season,

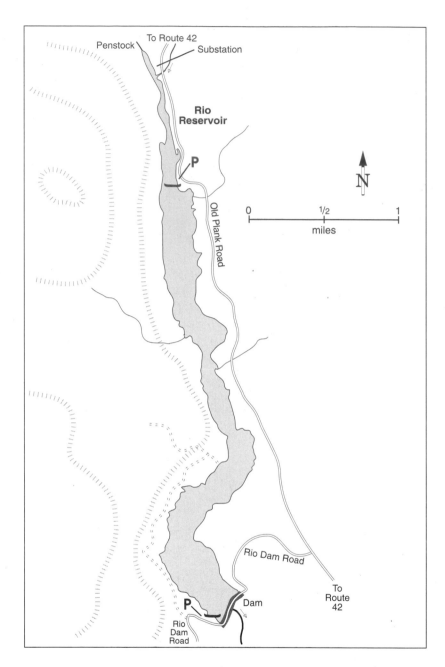

Penstock

To Route 42

Substation

Rio
Reservoir

P

Old Plank Road

N

0   1/2   1
miles

Rio Dam Road

To
Route
42

P   Dam

Rio
Dam
Road

paddlers will be treated to blooming mountain laurel—a shorter and smaller-leaved member of the same family.

The shoreline is quite rocky, with exposed outcroppings in some areas. As you paddle along, examine submerged branches or trees (called "structure" in the angler's lingo). You will likely see roundish blobs growing on the pieces of wood—these are bryozoa, a phylum of animals that live in associated colonies (like coral). Most bryozoa live in salt water, but a few freshwater species—such as the *Pectinatella magnifica* growing here—occur in New York. Each one of the knobs on the globular mass represents an individual animal. Hairlike appendages filter food particles out of the water.

Among the birds we saw here were common merganser, Canada goose, and great blue heron. We saw some evidence of beavers but not the critters themselves.

From the boat access at the north end, you can paddle a little ways north. Right away you will pass the remains of an old wooded structure for a gas pipeline that used to cross the reservoir here. Beyond that the reservoir narrows, and you quickly reach a rocky section of the river with quickwater. An old sign indicates that boaters should go no farther.

You can also use a second boat access at the south end, but it requires a short carry down to the water from the parking area. If it's a windy day, you might want to get dropped off at the upwind side, then get picked up at the other end—we didn't have that luxury and had to force our way back through a fairly stiff wind coming out of the north, funneling down the gorge.

Getting There

From I-84, get off at Exit 1 (Port Jervis), and follow signs for Route 97. Stay on Route 97 for a few miles, then turn onto Route 42 north. Drive 6.0 miles on Route 42, then turn left onto Old Plank Road. If you want to put in at the southern access, turn left onto Rio Dam Road in 0.8 mile—you will cross over the dam and reach a parking area in another 1.3 miles (there is room for 8 to 10 cars here). To put in at the northern access, drive north on Old Plank Road 2.6 miles from Route 42, and turn left at the sign for the Rio Access Site.

If you are driving here from the north, take route 17 to Exit 105A, Route 42 south. Stay on Route 42 through Monticello, following signs for Route 42 south at several places where the road turns. After driving 9.9 miles on 42, you will cross Route 43. Drive across Route 43, but take an almost-immediate right onto Mill Road. Follow Mill Road downhill for 0.6 mile. Just after crossing a small bridge, turn left onto Old Plank Road. You will reach the boat access in another 1.9 miles. It is on the right and well marked by a sign. There is space for 15 to 20 cars here.

Mongaup Falls Reservoir
Forestburg

MAPS
   New York Atlas: Map 35
   USGS Quadrangle: Highland Lake
INFORMATION
   Area: 120 acres; maximum depth: 20 feet
   Prominent fish species: Smallmouth bass, largemouth bass, stocked brown trout, and chain pickerel

Mongaup Falls Reservoir—a two-mile-long, dammed-up section of the Mongaup River, upstream from Rio Reservoir (see previous section)—has a much different feel from that of its southern neighbor. Smaller and shallower than Rio, this is a much better place to paddle on a windy day, as the surrounding hills seem to do a pretty good job shielding it from wind. Like Rio, Mongaup Falls Reservoir remains off-limits to gasoline-powered motorboats and Jet-skis. It is closed to all uses from December 1 until April 1 to protect an increasing population of wintering bald eagles.

From the boat access at the north end of the main reservoir, you can paddle upstream on a (usually) quiet section of the Mongaup River for another half mile or so. If you do paddle under the Route 43 bridge and up the river, be aware that the river can rise suddenly, carrying vastly more water—which can turn a relaxing paddle into a more exciting quickwater adventure. When both turbines upstream generate power, the flow can increase from about 100 cubic feet per second (cfs) to 1,600 cfs. We paddled up to the inlet brook from Lebanon Lake; above there, exposed rocks and rapids blocked our way.

Mongaup Falls Reservoir offers quite a bit of variety. Marshy areas contain all sorts of wetland plants (pickerelweed, bulrush, and sedges, for example). In one section of marsh just below the Route 43 bridge, we happened on a green-backed heron and got a chance to study this well-camouflaged bird before it flew. A few small patches of cattail marsh occur north of the bridge.

The eastern side of the reservoir—heavily wooded, except for a few stretches of marsh—has white pine as the dominant species, with deciduous trees comprising most of the rest of the woodland: oaks, maples, beech, and birch. A few small, well-hidden cabins do not intrude too much on the wild feeling here.

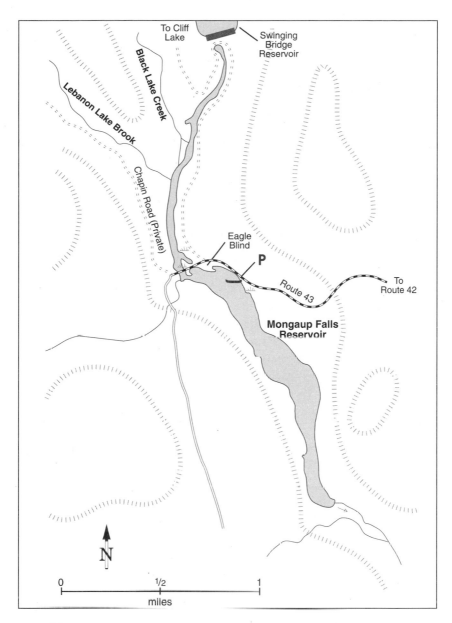

To Cliff Lake

Swinging Bridge Reservoir

Black Lake Creek

Lebanon Lake Brook

Chapin Road (Private)

Eagle Blind

P

Route 43

To Route 42

Mongaup Falls Reservoir

N

0   1/2   1
miles

The western shore is quite different. Here, trees have been cleared along a power line right-of-way, and open fields extend down to the water. In some areas, the fields consist mostly of hay-scented fern, which, by early September, had already begun to turn a golden brown. Where their feet can remain moist, closed gentian, cardinal flower, turtlehead, and false dragonhead grow along here. Cardinal flower was especially in evidence. When a dropping water level exposes new ground during the course of the summer, cardinal flower often springs up—and the level of Mongaup Falls Reservoir does drop.

We saw bryozoa colonies on most submerged branches in the reservoir, indicating fairly pure water. If you reach down into the water and touch a globular bryozoa colony, it will feel gelatinous.

Mongaup Falls Reservoir is best known for its wintering bald eagles, drawing eagles from all over the Northeast and Canada. As many as 100 eagles winter here, where the dam keeps water from freezing and the turbines kill some fish. An eagle-watching blind at the north end of the reservoir allows visitors to watch these majestic creatures without disturbing them. While eagles had historically wintered here, by the 1960s the population had fallen drastically because of DDT poisoning. New York eagles have made a dramatic comeback, largely the result of a bald eagle reintroduction program in the Adirondacks begun in 1976.

While eagle concentrations reach a peak during the winter, you might also see eagles here during the rest of the year. In the past few years, several pairs of eagles have nested in the Mongaup Valley and along the Upper Delaware River. We saw pairs on both Cliff Lake and Toronto Reservoir (see sections on those bodies of water). Even if eagle nesting becomes more common here, we do not anticipate addi-

Deep deciduous woods surround Mongaup Pond, along with state park campsites.

tional restrictions on summer recreational use of this area, though areas immediately around any nests will be kept off-limits.

Getting There

From the south, take I-84 to Route 97. Turn off onto Route 42 north, and follow Route 42 for 10.9 miles. Turn left onto Route 43, and follow it for 2.0 miles to the Mongaup Falls access sign. If you are coming from the north, take Route 17 to Route 42 south in Monticello. Follow Route 42 south for 9.9 miles (pay attention, because Route 42 makes several turns in Monticello), and turn right onto Route 43. Follow directions as above.

There is room for 10 to 12 cars at the boat access. You can drive down to the water to unload your boat, but then you have to park above in the designated parking lot. There is no camping here, but there is a nice spot for a picnic close to the parking area. If you continue on Route 43 for 0.3 mile past the boat access site, you will reach the eagle-watching area, with space for several cars and a blind so that you can watch the birds during the winter months without scaring them.

Cliff Lake

Forestburg

MAPS
> **New York Atlas:** Map 35
> **USGS Quadrangle:** Highland Lake

INFORMATION
> **Area:** 200 acres
> **Prominent fish species:** Smallmouth bass, largemouth bass, and
> chain pickerel

Cliff Lake and the surrounding upland belong to Orange and Rockland Utilities, but the company makes the area available for public use from May 1
through the end of November. As with nearby Rio and Mongaup Falls
Reservoirs, the utility prohibits gasoline motors on Cliff Lake; the difference here is that you have to carry boats in the last half mile. This makes
Cliff Lake all the nicer—the moderately strenuous carry discourages many
would-be users, making it more likely that you will paddle alone here.

The lake extends roughly two miles in a north-south orientation,
with a maximum width of about a quarter mile. In early September
when we visited, the markedly low water level detracted significantly
from the feel of the place. The level was down 6 to 8 feet in the drought

*A large beaver lodge along the shore of Cliff Lake. The residents of this
lodge had to keep extending it downward as the lake's water level dropped.*

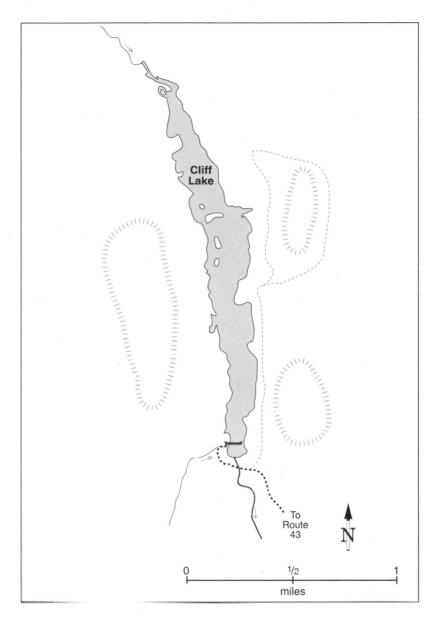

Cliff
Lake

To
Route
43

N

| 0 | 1/2 | 1 |

miles

year of 1995, which exposed quite a bit of shoreline. The utility company usually keeps the water level higher—within 5 feet of 1,070 feet in elevation. Interestingly, Cliff Lake connects hydraulically with Swinging Bridge Reservoir through an underground aqueduct, so the two water levels remain the same. We would recommend visiting before mid-July to improve your chances of finding the reservoir full. The sandy or pebbly shore suffers from erosion in some places.

We saw a curious beaver lodge where the ever-industrious animals worked hard to keep "growing" the beaver lodge downward, trying to keep it underwater as the lake's level dropped. Given the age of some of the material in the lodge, it appeared that the lodge, built into a fallen tree, holds firm through the seasonal water level fluctuation—they must have weighted the sticks down with stones to keep the lodge from floating away.

When we hiked up to Cliff Lake and around the reservoir, the open meadows—some carpeted with ferns, some filled with shade-loving grasses or sedges—struck us as particularly gorgeous. They give the woods a very open, inviting feel. If you choose to do any walking, though, pay attention to signs; only certain areas are open to public use. Sugar maple and white pine seem to be the dominant trees here, though beech is also common. We noted a few groves of red pine.

Several islands appear just above the midpoint of the lake. At the north end, we watched a number of sandpipers scurry over exposed mudflats, hunting for insects and crustaceans. Wilson's plover was most common here—it looks somewhat like a killdeer but shorter and with only one band around its neck.

Also at the north end we saw three bald eagles: two adults and a three- or four-year-old juvenile. Several pairs of eagles now nest in the Mongaup Valley. If you see a nest, or ground-feeding eagles, keep your distance so as not to disturb them. For more on bald eagles in this area, see the section on Mongaup Falls Reservoir.

Getting There

Follow the directions to Mongaup Falls Reservoir and continue 0.3 mile past the boat access. Just across Route 43 from the bald eagle observation area, you will see a sign indicating the Cliff Lake fishing access. Turn right here, passing through the gate, and follow the gravel road. After 0.9 mile, the road crosses the Mongaup River. Take a sharp left just after the river, following signs to the fishing access. At 1.5 miles, you bear left (again following signs) and pass below a portion of the Swinging Bridge dam. The parking area is 2.0 miles from Route 43.

From the parking area, you need to carry your canoe the rest of the way (a portage cart works very well, since you can stay on the gravel road the whole way). At one point, you will come to a T; turn left here, following signs to the public access. The road crosses the river just below the Cliff Lake dam, then follows a long switchback to get above the dam (there is a shorter, steeper trail up to the left of the dam, which we do not recommend if you are carrying or pulling a canoe). Follow the trail to the boat launch area, which is a bit north of the dam.

Toronto Reservoir
Bethel

MAPS
   New York Atlas: Map 35
   USGS Quadrangles: White Lake and Highland Lake
INFORMATION
   Area: 860 acres; maximum depth: 80 feet
   Prominent fish species: Smallmouth bass, largemouth bass, chain pickerel, and limited private stocking of walleye

Visit Toronto Reservoir *early* in the season. By mid-July, the reservoir typically gets drawn down considerably—and by late summer in a hot, dry year, it can be down as much as 15 or 20 feet, exposing hundreds of feet of ugly muddy shoreline around most of the reservoir's perimeter. We are told, however, that under provisions of recent federal relicensing of the dams owned by Orange and Rockland Utilities, changes will occur in the water management of Toronto Reservoir. The summer drawdown could become less extreme. While the utility and state permit powerboats here, the poor access means you shouldn't find too many pleasure boaters. People use the reservoir primarily for fishing. The state-record chain pickerel was caught on Toronto Reservoir in 1965 and remains as one of the longest-standing records.

The Iroquois Hunting & Fishing Club owns roughly half of Toronto Reservoir's fairly large surface area, posting it off-limits to the public. Large signs on the shoreline and several floating buoys mark this division. The club controls surface water access under an agreement with the utility company (then Rockland Light & Power) that built the dam creating Toronto Reservoir in the late 1920s. Because the reservoir inundated land owned by the club, the utility granted them exclusive hunting and fishing rights on that portion of the reservoir thus created.

Toronto's rocky shoreline has exposed outcroppings of a sedimentary, shalelike rock. Grasses and small shrubs prevail along most of the immediate shoreline, with woodland extending away from the shore. Scattered tall white pines extend above the canopy of beech-maple forest. Dense groves of hemlock occur here and there, and rhododendrons are scattered in the understory.

Half a dozen deer fed on grasses along the higher banks when we visited early in the morning, as mist still swirled above the reservoir. In

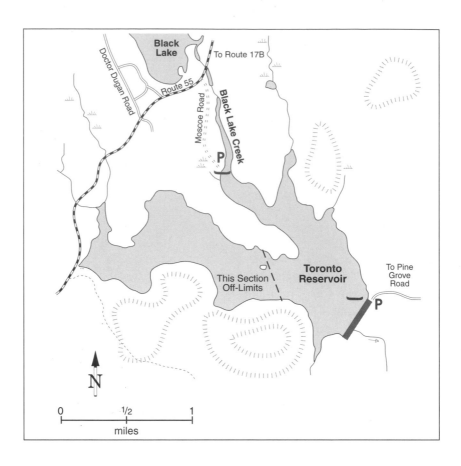

the water, a small flock of Canada geese and several families of common mergansers hunted for food.

Near the midpoint of the reservoir we heard a distinctive raptor
call and spotted a pair of bald eagles sitting side by side on an oak
branch. A little further scanning with binoculars turned up a juvenile in
a tree nearby. We watched these dramatic birds for some time and witnessed a rare treat. After awhile the immature eagle took off and began
flying above the water in search of fish. Shortly, one of the adults
joined it for what was almost certainly a fishing lesson. As we watched,
the two birds made dozens of passes over the same section of water,
each time dropping down and dipping feet into the water. Several times
they landed on the nearby shore. Eventually, the adult caught a small
fish, and the two flew off to tell stories about the big one that got away.

Bald eagles, which have long wintered near the dams along the
Mongaup River, have recently resumed nesting as well. To protect bald
eagle wintering grounds, the state of New York in 1986 purchased

A common merganser casts a wary eye in our direction.

6,000 acres along the Mongaup River and its reservoirs from Orange and Rockland Utilities and protected another 6,000 acres through easements. For more on bald eagles, see the section on Mongaup Falls Reservoir (page 70) and the nature essay on page 193.

Getting There

From Route 17 in Monticello, take 17B west for 7.7 miles. Then turn left (south) onto Route 55 west. Drive 1.9 miles on Route 55, then turn left onto Moscoe Road. Moscoe Road turns to gravel after a half mile and reaches the parking area and boat access in 0.7 mile. If the water level is down, however, you have to walk or drive (only if the ground is not too soft) as much as another third of a mile to get to the water. If driving in, use care, as the track is not maintained. The parking area has room for about 15 cars. Along the western side of the road driving into Toronto Reservoir is a dense stand of rhododendron, which should be beautiful when blooming in late June or early July.

Alternately, you can launch a boat at the Toronto Reservoir dam. This is reached via Pine Grove Road from the hamlet of Smallwood. There is room for about 15 cars here. At times of low water, this is a better access.

Lake Superior
Bethel

MAPS
  New York Atlas: Map 34
  USGS Quadrangles: White Lake and Lake Huntington
INFORMATION
  Area: 90 acres; maximum depth: 27 feet
  Prominent fish species: Largemouth bass and chain pickerel
  Lake Superior State Park, Sullivan County Government Center;
    914-794-3000

The bucolic, rolling countryside of Bethel rocked to a different tune for a week in the summer of 1969. The Woodstock Music Festival, held just a mile from Lake Superior on Max Yasgur's farm, drew several hundred thousand participants. The only hint of this historic event we could find at Lake Superior State Park—which no doubt bore a heavy impact from the overflow crowd just across Route 17B—was reference to the festival on the wrappers of the locally made ice-cream bars available at the park concession.

Lake Superior—really too small for the designation "lake"—offers a very pleasant spot for a morning or afternoon of paddling, mainly because of the prohibition on gasoline motors. Biologically, Lake Superior is highly productive. Thick mats of aquatic plants populate the extensive marshy areas at both the north and south ends. At the south end, a long outlet channel extends almost a half mile toward Black Lake. In the spring, you should be able to paddle this without difficulty, but by late summer we found it so choked with pickerelweed, bulrush, water lilies, and sedges we could not force our way through.

The north end is also marshy but very different ecologically. Here you will find typical swamp vegetation: red maple, buttonbush, leatherleaf, blueberry, royal fern, swamp rose, and swamp loosestrife. We had hoped to paddle up into Chestnut Ridge Pond, about a half mile north, but try as we might, we could not get through the dense growth. It might be possible—though unlikely—to wend your way through this swamp in the spring with the water level a bit higher—we'll leave the exploring to you.

Even in late summer, however, we would explore a little way into the swamp. We managed to squeeze in 50 or 100 yards after a number

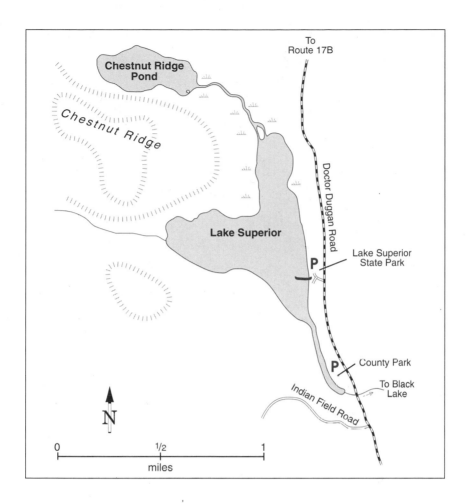

of false starts and were rewarded by the unusual sighting of a sora rail. This elusive marsh bird, a little smaller than a killdeer, is sometimes heard but rarely seen. We sat still for about a half hour as it darted in and out of view a mere 10 feet away. We recognize this brownish bird by its short bill; its short, triangular cocked tail; and its greenish legs with striations above and very long toes below. There was also evidence of beaver up here.

At the northeastern tip of the pond you will see a large stand of tamarack, with delicate, feathery needles that turn yellow then drop in the autumn. More common in northern New York, this species typifies the northern fen or bog, because it can become established in saturated soils—even on floating peat mats.

Buttonbush, with its spherical flower clusters and seed heads, is common in the marsh at the north end of Lake Superior.

Everywhere around Lake Superior are water lilies: fragrant water lily, yellow pond lily, and water shield. Typically, you will see emergent plants right along the shore, including bur reed and pickerelweed, then a fringe of floating water lilies slightly farther out in the water—in fact, you can pretty well judge the water depth by the plants—most water lilies cannot grow in water more than four feet deep. While the marshy areas have a mucky bottom, much of the rest of the lake has a sandy bottom, providing good habitat for freshwater mussels, which you will see in abundance. We also noticed a good-sized crayfish at one spot.

The fairly open woods around the lake abound with ferns, club-mosses, and wildflowers beneath a canopy of sugar maple, yellow birch, cherry, beech, red oak, hemlock, and white pine. You will also see rhododendron in abundance here. The groves of this largest member of the heath family grow thicker here than we have seen on any other lakes and ponds in the state. Visit in late June or early July, and you should be treated to rhododendrons in bloom. They are thickest along the eastern shore, just north of the boat access, and directly across from the boat access along the southwestern shore of the lake. At one spot on the eastern shore where we beached our canoe, a network of tunnels through the tall rhododendron groves extended away from the lake.

Near the boat access is a picnic area, concession stand, and roped-off swimming beach with lifeguard. The beach and concession stand open on Memorial Day and close after Labor Day.

Getting There

From Route 17 in Monticello, take Route 17B west for 9.3 miles, and turn left onto Doctor Duggan Road. The entrance to Lake Superior State Park is on the right in 1.5 miles. Between Memorial Day and Labor Day there is a two-dollar day-use charge for county residents and a three-dollar day-use charge for noncounty residents. Season passes are also available. Before Memorial Day and after Labor Day, you can use the boat launch without a charge. After passing through the gate, bear right and drive right down to the water; after unloading your boat, park above in the designated lot. Gasoline motors are prohibited on the lake.

Morningside Lake
Fallsburg

MAPS
>**New York Atlas:** Map 35
>**USGS Quadrangles:** Liberty East and Monticello

INFORMATION
>**Area:** 130 acres; maximum depth: 12 feet
>**Prominent fish species:** Largemouth bass and chain pickerel, but noted for its panfish
>**Camping:** Morningside Park, town of Fallsburg, P.O. Box 830, South Fallsburg, NY 12779; 914-434-5877

Morningside Lake really surprised us. While surrounded by relatively developed areas and dominated by the town of Fallsburg's Morningside Park, the lake is really very pleasant. On a gorgeous Sunday afternoon of Labor Day weekend, in spite of the seemingly incessant squeals of children and clanking of rental rowboats at the south end, we explored much of this small lake in peace.

Morningside Lake extends less than three-quarters of a mile in the longest dimension, but an extensive island area breaks up the center.

Feathery tamaracks on the boggy islands of Morningside Lake.

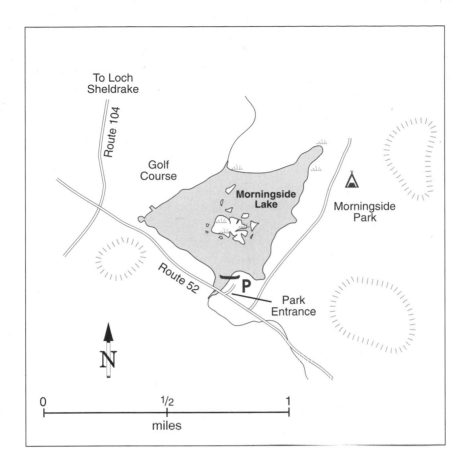

To Loch
Sheldrake

Route 104

Golf
Course

Morningside
Lake

Morningside
Park

Route 52

P

Park
Entrance

N

0   1/2   1
miles

Numerous small islands, some with tamarack stands, provide opportunity to explore for hours and, even on a sunny weekend afternoon, to feel a bit of solitude. On a weekday, you probably would paddle alone here, particularly before Memorial Day or after Labor Day. With their delicate tamaracks, these islands remind one of the many bogs and fens in the Adirondacks and northern New England.

Morningside is very shallow, only two to four feet deep in most places. This shallow water provides great wildlife habitat. In the extensive marshy areas at the northeast tip and around the islands, we saw dozens of wood ducks along with great blue herons, a few cormorants, and lots of painted turtles. In one section, masses of water lily tubers had somehow uprooted and floated on the surface. From a distance, these looked like huge dead carp, the leaf scars reminding us of scales. Paddling closer we watched turtles skitter from their floating platforms into the mucky water.

The water was quite eutrophic, its pea green color evidence of overfertilization—probably from the many Canada geese that call this home and from fertilizer applied to the golf course that adjoins the northwestern side of the lake. Golf courses can be significant sources of chemical runoff, and this one directly abuts the lake. Let's hope the golf course managers use chemicals wisely.

Stands of bur reed, cattail, arrowhead, pickerelweed, sedges, grasses, blueberry, winterberry, and leatherleaf dominate along much of the shoreline. Fragrant water lily, yellow pond lily, and water shield float in the water. Buttonbush, tamarack, and swamp loosestrife—a native cousin of the introduced purple loosestrife that continues to take over many wetlands—dominate the islands. Be careful paddling around these islands: when swamp loosestrife dies back, the woody stems rot away at about the water's surface, leaving sharp spikes. These could puncture a delicate fiberglass canoe.

Much more activity takes place at the southern end of Morningside Lake, particularly on a pleasant summer weekend. The park concession does a good business renting aluminum rowboats. A fairly thin row of trees and shrubs along the eastern shore buffers 144 campsites; expect to hear some activity from campers and from the ball fields, tennis courts, playground, swimming pools, and camp store that figure prominently in this park. But, somewhat surprisingly, we found that this campground does not dominate the shoreline as much as many others do.

Getting There

From Route 17 in Grassinger (Exit 100), drive east on Route 52 for 4.5 miles. Turn right onto Route 104 south. After 1.2 miles, turn left onto Sullivan County Route 52, and the park entrance will be on the left in 0.5 mile. There is no charge to enter the town park and launch a canoe, but fees are charged for camping and pool use. Although a sign states that canoes and kayaks are prohibited, we were assured that that is an old sign; canoes and kayaks are permitted as long as personal flotation devices are in the boats as per state regulations.

Carnivorous Plants
The Tables Get Turned

Carnivorous plants are fascinating—and a common sight as you paddle through bogs and marshy sections of New York's lakes and ponds. Their specialized adaptations make them one of nature's true wonders and make us wonder how their meat-eating habit evolved.

For many people, evolution brings Darwin's finches of the Galapagos Islands to mind. Supposedly, a few ancestral birds landed on the Galapagos Archipelago. Their offspring then radiated out among the widely scattered islands and encountered different types of seeds. In order to be successful seed predators, the birds on one island developed larger beaks and bodies to accommodate larger seeds, while another set of birds on a different island developed smaller beaks and bodies to feed on smaller seeds. Careful observations in this decade have lent credence to this theory, as one well-studied species of Darwin's finches evolved a different beak size as a direct result of changing seed resources. This is an example of divergent evolution, where an ancestral species evolved into several separate species, each with specialized adaptations.

Having published in 1875 a volume entitled *Insectivorous Plants*—a book that catalogued the known information on carnivorous plants—Darwin also figures prominently in this field. In contrast to the divergent evolution of Darwin's finches, however, carnivory in plants apparently resulted from convergent evolution: the taking on of similar traits among unrelated species. Carnivory in plants exists in many different, completely unrelated plant families on nearly every continent. These plants have two characteristics in common: almost all live in mineral-poor soils and so supplement the meager available soil nutrients with those from animals, and they use modified leaves to trap food.

Two main capture strategies have evolved: active and passive. Most people would recognize the active capture strategy of the Venus flytrap, a plant that grows in sandy soils in a narrow band along the coastal border between North Carolina and South Carolina. The plant's modified leaves form a bi-lobed trap. When an insect lands in the trap and touches the protruding hairs, the sides slam shut, sandwiching the hapless insect. The plant then secretes enzymes to aid digestion, a strategy common to most, but not all, carnivorous plants.

Unfortunately, collection and habitat destruction threaten this fascinating plant with extinction in the wild.

Few other carnivorous plants have adopted active capture strategies, but one that has grows abundantly—sometimes forming dense mats—in the quiet, shallow marshes and bogs of New York: bladderworts of the genus *Utricularia*. Bladderwort leaves, described more fully below, consist of minute bladders that, upon stimulation, inflate and ingest insect larvae and other organisms, to be digested by the plants' enzymes.

Passive capture strategies have taken two main paths among the remaining carnivorous plants of New York. Pitcher plants—*Sarracenia purpurea*—collect rainwater in their funnel-shaped modified leaves. Insects, attracted to nectar secreted around the top of the pitcher, fall in. Stiff, downward-pointing hairs in the plant keep most insects from climbing back out. Eventually the insects drown, and a combination of plant and bacterial enzymes reduces the insects to absorbable nutrients.

Another passive-capture plant uses sticky surfaces to ensnare insects. Sundews (genus *Drosera*) form tiny rosettes that protrude from a central root. Stalked glands of two types cover the surface of the modified leaves. One type secretes a sticky substance that glistens like dew in the sun, giving the plant its name. Entrapped insects, drawn initially by the nectarlike secretions, get digested by enzymes secreted by the second set of glands.

Each of the plants described above—bladderworts, pitcher plants, and sundews—captures its intended victims in a different way, but they all do so because, in the nutrient-poor marshes and bogs of New York, absorbing nitrogen and other minerals from insects and other prey gives them a selective advantage over other plants.

Do not be fooled by the black, fertile-looking soils of marshes and swamps. Black dirt like this in Iowa means fertile soil, but in bogs it means black carbon from undecomposed plants. The tea-colored water, laden with organic acids from decaying vegetation and supplemented by acid rain, effectively washes out the minerals necessary for plant growth. Although two primary nutrients supporting plant growth—carbon dioxide and water—remain plentiful, nitrogen, phosphorus, potassium, and other important elements get leached out or get bound up in the underlying layers of sphagnum and peat. Carnivorous plants, with their diet of insects and other organisms,

supplement the lost nutrients, making them effective competitors in the bog ecosystem.

Bladderworts: Bladderworts grow in quiet, shallow waters or in shoreline muck. Keep an eye out for small yellow or purple snapdragon-like flowers, leading on short stalks to their carnivorous underwater bladders. The vast majority of the plant lives underwater in dense feathery mats, bearing hundreds of tiny (0.02 to 0.1 inch long), bulbous traps that are the plant's leaves. The bladders have two concave sides and a trapdoor. When an insect larva or other small organism bumps into the door's guard hairs, the bladder's sides pop out, creating suction, the door swings open, and water along with the hapless critter get sucked in. All of this occurs in about 1/500 of a second, followed by slow digestion by plant enzymes.

In most ponds, mosquito larvae form the bulk of the diet, but the plant also ingests other insect larvae, rotifers, protozoans, small crustaceans, and even tiny tadpoles. As the animal is digested, its remains get absorbed by plant tissues, causing the trap's sides to go concave again, readying for its next meal. If the prey is small, chances are new prey will be captured before the first is fully digested. If it is large, such as a tiny tadpole, the door will close around the organism, and part of it will get digested. The next time the hairs get triggered, the plant ingests more of the organism, eventually sucking it all in.

Several species of bladderwort grow in New York, including 2 with purple flowers, one aquatic and one terrestrial, and possibly as many as 10 species with yellow flowers, mostly aquatic but including at least 2 terrestrials. We usually notice the presence of these plants when we see their snapdragon-like flowers protruding a few inches above the water's surface. Their dense underwater mats attest to their successful adaptation to nutrient-poor waters. If you lift a mat out of the water and listen carefully, you may hear crackling as the bladders suck in air instead of their intended prey.

Pitcher Plants: Although several other species of *Sarracenia* pitcher plant exist in North America, the northern pitcher plant, *Sarracenia purpurea,* has the widest distribution, growing from British Columbia to Nova Scotia, southward through the Great Lakes region and down the eastern coastal plain, crossing the Florida panhandle to the Mississippi River. Initially green in the spring, the pitcher plant's funnel-shaped leaves turn progressively more purple, becoming deep maroon in the

fall, and return to green again in the spring. During midseason, the red veins of the hood stand in stark contrast to the mostly green pitchers. Flowering occurs in June and July in New York, and single reddish flowers, borne on stout stalks, tower a foot or more above the cluster of pitchers.

In contrast to most other species, the northern pitcher plant does not have a hood to keep rain out. The curved pitchers recline, allowing rain to fall freely into the open hood. Because of this dilution of the pitcher's contents, insects drown well before digestion occurs. The stiff, downward-pointing hairs in the plant's throat keep insects from climbing back out, and the relatively narrow funnel leaves little room for airborne escape. The upper pitcher walls sport a waxy coating, making for slippery footing. A combination of plant and bacterial enzymes degrade the unlucky insects, and their nutrients pass easily through the unwaxed surface of the lower pitcher.

Amazingly, several different types of organisms can live in the pitchers, unharmed by the digestive juices. One harmless genus of mosquito, *Wyeomyia,* lives its aquatic life cycle in the pitcher, and other insects can escape by walking up the waxy cuticle and out over the downward-pointing hairs.

Pitcher plants usually grow near water, often with their roots submerged. Inexorably, plant material accumulates and marshes start to fill in. As shrubs and small trees begin to grow on the elevated ground, the pitcher plants get crowded out. Fortunately, with all the remaining water in bogs and marshes in New York, pitcher plants will remain for us to enjoy for quite some time.

Sundews: The best way to find sundews is to look for the glistening drops at the ends of their traps. Because they are so small—the smallest plants may measure only an inch across—sundews are easily overlooked. Four species occur in New York, and we describe the most common species here: roundleaf sundew (*Drosera rotundifolia*).

This remarkable plant grows mainly in sphagnum bogs, from Alaska to northern California, across the Canadian Rockies and plains, through the Great Lakes, north throughout Labrador, south to Chesapeake Bay, and down through the Appalachians. The same plant grows in Europe as well, where Darwin studied it in detail, devoting much of his book *Insectivorous Plants* to this one species. The entire plant averages about three inches across and about an inch high, and all of its leaves are modified into sticky traps. A short leaf stalk ends in a flattened oval pad, covered with red, stalked glands. The longer glands secrete a sticky fluid, while the shorter glands secrete digestive enzymes. Insects, attracted to the nectarlike secretions, become trapped. Slowly, imperceptibly, the pad edges roll over slightly, placing the insect in contact with digestive juices.

The usually white but sometimes pink flowers hover well above the plant's leaves, borne on a slender stalk. Although they are easy to miss, a little careful looking on sphagnum mats will show up many of these reddish rosettes. You should also see several small insects in various stages of digestion. And you, too, can wonder about how these plants developed the incredible ability to supplement the meager amount of available nutrients with those from insect prey.

Susquehanna River

Milford

MAPS
  New York Atlas: Map 64
  USGS Quadrangle: Milford

INFORMATION
  Prominent fish species: Largemouth bass, smallmouth bass, northern pike, and walleye
  Books: If you plan to run downstream sections of the Susquehanna River, purchase one or both of the following guidebooks: William P. Ehling, *Canoeing Central New York* (Backcountry Publications); Mark Freeman, *Canoe Guide to Western and Central New York State* (Adirondack Mountain Club).

From its modest beginnings in Otsego Lake—the famed "Glimmerglass" of James Fenimore Cooper—the Susquehanna River meanders quietly southward, gathering hundreds of feeder streams and rivers along the way. Because it drains so much of south-central New York, by the time it exits the state about 30 miles west of Binghamton, it has metamorphosed into a major river, one that eventually forms the Chesapeake Bay estuary. The Susquehanna, more than 400 miles in length, remains second only to the St. Lawrence among East Coast rivers in the size of its drainage.

The popular General Clinton Canoe Regatta over Memorial Day weekend includes a race on the Susquehanna that begins on Otsego Lake, ending 70 miles later at Bainbridge. In August 1779, General James Clinton and his forces floated a handmade fleet of 220 boats down the Susquehanna for more than 170 miles to join forces with General John Sullivan at Tiogo Point in Pennsylvania in a campaign to subdue the Finger Lakes Iroquois tribes loyal to the British. Because the upper Susquehanna had little water, Clinton had his men build a three-foot-high dam across the outlet of Otsego Lake. With his newly constructed fleet loaded and ready, he ordered the dam breached, and he and his men floated on a man-made crest down into Pennsylvania.

We have chosen for inclusion a section of the Susquehanna near its beginnings—just below Cooperstown—where it meanders slowly through farmlands, meadows, and woodlots, where at times of low water you can hardly tell which way the river flows. The section begins at the Route 166 bridge in Milford and continues south to Goodyear

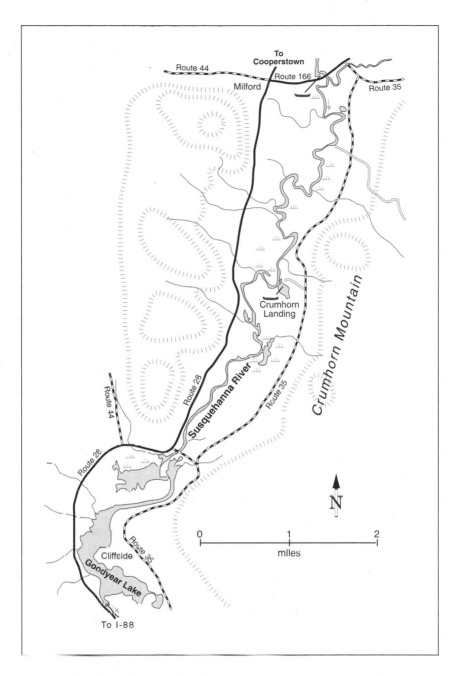

Lake, a distance of about 10 miles. After checking out the muddy banks at the access on Route 166, we decided to put in at Crumhorn Landing, paddle upstream to the Route 166 bridge, paddle downstream to Goodyear Lake, and then return upstream to Crumhorn Landing.

A northern harrier—fomerly known as marsh hawk—searches for rodents by hovering low over a field.

A rather tame osprey greeted us with its piercing cries as we put in at Crumhorn Landing, foreshadowing our close look at many more birds along the way. With the river's tight meanders and relatively high banks in some sections, if you paddle quietly close to the inside of the curve, you arrive on a new section of water with hardly any commotion, making for good wildlife viewing. We managed to sneak right up on a bittern—a reclusive, brown-streaked marsh heron that would rather hide than fly—causing it to bolt into the sky with a great thrashing of wings.

We came upon mallards dabbling for underwater plants, rear ends pointing skyward; spotted sandpipers bobbing along the shoreline, aiming for a better look at insects clinging to rocks; a northern harrier swooping over the fields with an uptilted dihedral, searching for rodents without the good sense to stay under cover during the day; chickadees foraging in small, loosely knit flocks, "chipping" to maintain contact; yellow-rumped warblers, the first warbler to appear in the spring, darting out over the water, feeding on spring's first insect hatches; a ruffed grouse drumming, trying to attract females to his territory to begin the rites of spring; and flickers tapping out holes in dead streamside trees, providing nest cavities for themselves, as well as for wood duck, hooded merganser, kestrel, tree swallow, and bluebird. We also saw or heard mourning dove, song sparrow, robin, crow, flicker, killdeer, red-winged blackbird, white-throated sparrow, and grackle.

Beaver have cut down many of the streamside willows that reach out over the water, and we managed to paddle right up to one before it dove for cover. We rescued a meadow vole that thrashed in the water before us, returning it to dry ground. Paddling here in the spring, we marveled at the numbers and variety of our furred and feathered friends. A warm southern breeze reminded us that a meandering river provides a great place to paddle when early- and late-season winds have turned large bodies of water to a foamy froth.

Occasional road noise intruded on our solitude as a meander in the river neared a road, but most of the time we had a peaceful paddle with great views of forested hillsides, a few with layered fields retreating off into the distance. We paddled by farms with fields edging on the water and occasional cottages, but most of the time we enjoyed in solitude the sounds, sights, and smells of spring.

Getting There

From Cooperstown (home of the Baseball Hall of Fame and the Corvette Museum), take Route 28 south to Milford. From the stoplight in Cooperstown on Routes 28 and 80, it's about 8.5 miles to the junction with Route 166 in Milford. At the junction of Routes 28 and 166, turn left. Reach the Route 166 bridge in 0.6 mile; this is the first of two access points. If you choose to put in here, park on the northwest side at the large pullout.

A better access exists at Crumhorn Landing. To get to the Crumhorn Landing access, continue east on Route 166 for 0.6 mile to the junction of Route 35, and turn right. After 0.2 mile the road forks; take the right fork to the south. From this fork, the boat access road is 2.7 miles south on Route 35 on the right; the landing is 0.3 mile down this gravel road.

Ninemile Swamp (Sangerfield River)
Brookfield, Hamilton, and Sangerfield

MAPS
>   **New York Atlas:** Maps 62 and 63
>   **USGS Quadrangle:** Hubbardsville

INFORMATION
>   **Length:** Approximately 8 miles round-trip, Wickwire Road bridge
>   to Swamp Road bridge
>   **Prominent fish species:** Largemouth bass and northern pike
>   **Books:** We owe finding out about this wonderful creek to William
>   Ehling in his outstanding guidebook, *Canoeing Central New
>   York* (Backcountry Publications). Descriptions of the Loomis
>   Gang are taken from there, rather than from *The Loomis Gang*
>   by George Walter.

The rich history of this creek includes the escapades of the notorious Loomis Gang, which operated in the swamp from the time of patriarch George Washington Loomis's arrival in 1802 until nearly 1900. Supposedly, shortly before his arrival, he had run stolen horses in Vermont and fled before a posse, ending up in Sangerfield where he married and raised a gang of outlaw children. This family of horse thieves, arsonists, highway robbers, and murderers lived on nearby Loomis Hill, overlooking the swamp from the west. Loomis Road crosses the swamp in the section above the one included here, and the gang used the swamp to hide themselves and their ill-gotten horses from local vigilantes.

When we paddled here, we made the mistake of trying to put in at the bridge in Hubbardsville, just to see how much of it we could canoe. Amazingly, the upper stretch has much more water than this section. We spent as much time out of the boat as in the boat because of shallows and logjams. The water did not really deepen appreciably until we reached the boat access on Wickwire Road, about a mile upstream. We do not regret pushing, poling, pulling, and carrying our boat up the stream, even though we believe that no one in his or her right mind should attempt this.

From the upstream launch at Wickwire Road, you begin an easy paddle up to Swamp Road. Even though we paddled here in the drought year of 1995, plenty of water carried us over the shallows and through the abundant aquatic vegetation. The snowmelt and winter rains funnel down off the surrounding hillsides, percolate through the

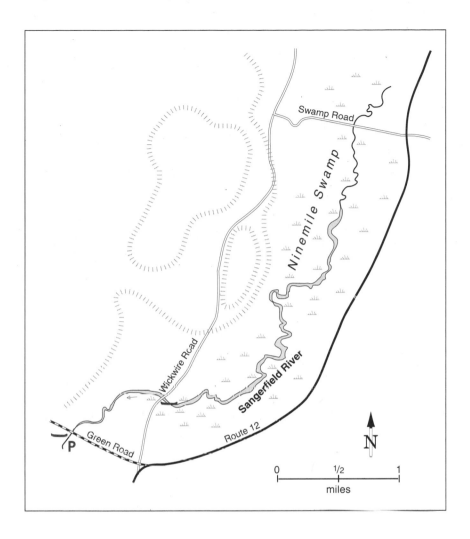

ground around the swamp, and slowly release into the creek. When other area water levels drop in midsummer, the Sangerfield usually still has plenty of water. Local fishermen, who fish for largemouth bass and 30-inch northern pike, told us that during high water, if you did not mind getting out of your boat on occasion, you could paddle past Swamp Road, all the way to Loomis Road and beyond.

When we checked out the bridge over the creek at Loomis Road in September (before launching farther downstream), the water—what there was of it—did not look at all inviting. At the Swamp Road bridge, however, even though willow, alder, and other branches draped over the meandering waterway, we could see that this section would be paddlable.

Ninemile Swamp alternately narrows down and broadens out on its mean-dering southward flow.

Paddling up this beautiful valley, with layered fields on the lower hills followed by timbered mountaintops, one can easily forget time. We never tired of paddling through this wildlife paradise, with deer crossing the stream in front of us in the morning mists; a crow-sized pileated woodpecker in undulating flight, looking for a dead tree full of carpenter ants; and several red-tailed hawks circling lazily above, wary eyes cast for rodents on the ground.

Alders and huge overhanging willows dominate this wooded swamp, along with occasional box elder, sugar and red maple, oaks, ash, cherry, big-toothed and quaking aspen, tall white pines, northern white cedar, and other conifers. In late September, the red maples of the swamp had started to turn their brilliant scarlet.

Red maples have red on them at all times of the year: buds in winter, flowers in spring, leaf stems in summer, and leaves in fall. Tree leaves remain green because the dominant pigment, chlorophyll, reflects mainly green light, absorbing other colors of the visual spectrum to do photosynthetic work. When cold temperatures destroy chlorophyll and its ability to absorb other colors, the brilliant reds, yellows, and oranges of fall emerge from the leaf's surface, reflected back by other selectively absorbing plant pigments. Against the brilliant blue sky of an arctic high-pressure cell, the river's fall foliage burned brightly when we paddled here.

With such fall beauty, we had difficulty focusing on paddling. Earlier in the year, we would have seen turtles and frogs out sunning, to go along with the swirling lily pads caused by bass and northerns as they chased bait fish in these productive waters. The mating calls of spring birds no longer sounded through the swamp, as we concentrated on the fall warbler migration. Prior to migration, warblers adopt a drabber fall plumage, making identification more difficult. Still, we identified six or seven species.

As fallen leaves began to clog the waterway, we recognized the approaching end of another paddling season, a season that would soon disappear along with the warblers. Wood ducks fattening up on acorns and aquatic vegetation jumped to the air at our approach, some blasting out from streamside branches. Soon they would join the warblers in migration. But we realized what a pleasure it is to paddle amidst the glorious foliage of fall, a season free from swamp-bred biting insects, when we have to share the wilds with few other humans. We would be back in the spring, fighting the bugs, just glad to be out there again.

Getting There

From Utica, take Route 12 south. Start measuring mileage at the junction of Routes 12 and 20, continuing south on Route 12. Turn right onto Green Road at 8.5 miles. Turn left after about 50 feet. Cross the railroad track, and take an immediate right (0.1 mile from Route 12) onto Wickwire Road. If you had veered left, you would end up at the downstream access point. The Wickwire Road bridge is 0.6 mile down this road with the boat access on the right. Do not block the drive down to the water, as fishermen launch small trailered boats here frequently.

Old Erie Canal
De Witt and Manlius

MAPS
> **New York Atlas:** Map 75
> **USGS Quadrangles:** Manlius and Syracuse East

INFORMATION
> **Length:** Approximately 2.5 miles from De Witt to Manlius Center
> and 5.5 miles to Kirkville Road
> **Prominent fish species:** Largemouth bass and northern pike
> **Erie Canal:** Old Erie State Park; 315-687-7821
> **Camping:** Green Lakes State Park; 315-637-6111

Perched on the edge of giant Syracuse, the Old Erie Canal State Park draws hundreds and hundreds of visitors on warm summer days. People hike, run, and bike along the towpath and historic canal, while paddlers ply the shallow, still waters. Because of disuse, the canal suffers from siltation and deadfalls; eventually it will fill in.

Work began on the 363-mile-long Erie Canal in 1817. When completed a short eight years later, it stood as an engineering marvel and a tribute to human genius. Think about trying to dig a wide, deep, 363-mile-long ditch with parallel road today... *with* bulldozers, draglines, and dump trucks.

In 1817, little was known about canal construction. Fortuitously, a surveyor named Canvass White (1796–1834) working near Chittenango in 1818, recognized and then perfected a waterproof hydraulic cement made from limestone that hardened underwater. Without motorized machines, workers felled and removed trees and pulled stumps; hand-dug the ditch through soil, rock, and swamp; and built towpaths, culverts, aqueducts, locks, gates, and bridges. At the ending, they had accomplished the foremost engineering feat of their time. Western New York flourished as goods moved cheaply from the port city of New York, up to Albany, and west over the newly dug canal out to the hinterlands and Lake Erie, hastening development of the Midwest.

A modern system of canals—taming major rivers such as the Mohawk and Seneca with dams and locks and using diesel-powered boats to cross major lakes such as Oneida, Ontario, and Erie—replaced the old Erie Canal in 1918. The modern system consists of the new Erie, Cayuga-Seneca, Champlain, and Oswego barge canals. In many

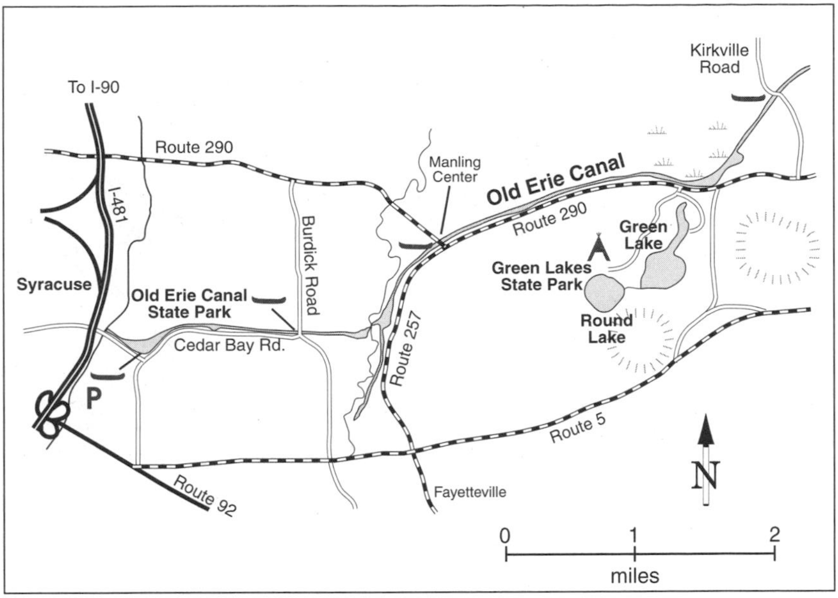

places—now crisscrossed with roads, farms, and development—no trace of the original canal can be found. Thankfully, we have preserved some parts of it in state parks. We wonder if the joggers, bikers, and paddlers appreciate the significance of Old Erie Canal State Park in, appropriately, De Witt, named for De Witt Clinton, the former 10-term New York mayor (1803–1815) and two-time governor (1817 1821; 1825–1828), who sponsored the building of the canal.

As we paddled out from the boat access in De Witt at the canal's beginning, we found a tree-covered south bank and a path-covered north bank. In between, the murky water of the canal hid much of civilization's detritus—except for occasional tires that popped into view. Tree species lining the south bank include black locust, lots of ash, black walnut, cottonwood, and box elder and the other maples, including one large silver maple whose grapevine-covered branches draped out over the water. Paddling under tree branches, grapevines, and Virginia creeper lends a closed-in, intimate feeling to the paddling.

Smaller trees and shrubs cover the banks on the north shore, at least down to the first automobile bridge at Burdick Road. The wide, rounded crown of sumac had turned brilliant red in the crisp, early morning October air. Clumps of clematis clung to streamside shrubs as the first joggers made their way down the towpath. By midmorning, vultures had started to ride the thermals, painted turtles had climbed

Paddlers cause the only ripples on leaf-strewn water in the fall.

out onto sun-facing logs, and more people on foot and on bikes came out onto the path. A few canoeists appeared as well.

An osprey fished a wide spot in the canal—how it could spot fish in the cloudy water remains a mystery. Gray squirrels appeared frequently along the ground, harvesting seeds for their winter stores. A flock of nine wood ducks fattening up for fall migration bolted skyward as we approached. We also saw a cormorant fishing for its morning meal and many black ducks and mallards dabbling along the canal's edge. Several muskrats pruned the canal-side grass, as more turtles climbed out into the midday sun.

We saw many more species of birds, which surprised us, given the level of recreational use here. Do not expect a wilderness experience in this recreation-focused environment. Expect to say "Hi!" constantly to cheerful passersby. If you continue on past tiny Manlius Center, the crowds thin out, trees crowd in, and wildlife abounds.

Several other potential launch points occur farther down Cedar Bay Road, but cars usually jam the small lots on weekends, and high banks make launching problematic. You can put in or take out at the bridges at Burdick Road, Manlius Center, and Kirkville Road. We prefer to paddle down and back; obviously, because the canal no longer has anywhere to go, current is nonexistent. Though the old Erie Canal no longer serves as a vital transportation corridor, it still holds immense historical significance—and provides a relaxing place to paddle to boot.

Getting There

To get to the canal from Syracuse, take Erie Boulevard (Route 5) or East Genesee Street (Route 92) east out of the city, crossing under the I-481 bridge. About a mile after crossing under the bridge, at the point where Routes 5 and 92 split, take a sharp left onto Lyndon Street. Go 0.9 mile to the three-way stop sign at a T. Turn left and then immediately right into the small parking area. This marks the beginning of the old Erie Canal in De Witt.

To get to Green Lakes State Park and to other potential access points, from the junction of Lyndon Street and Cedar Bay Road, drive east on Cedar Bay Road, past Burdick Road on the left (potential access point). Here, where Cedar Bay Road curves right, it turns into Burdick Road. Continue on to the stoplight on Genesee Street (Route 5) in Fayetteville. Turn left onto Genesee Street, and drive uphill through Fayetteville for 0.6 mile to the sign for Green Lakes State Park. Turn left here onto Route 257. At the stop sign in 1.8 miles, Route 257 ends at the junction with Route 290. Just across the canal to the left is Manlius Center, another potential access point. To get to the park, continue right at the stop sign for 1.6 miles to the entrance to Green Lakes State Park on the right.

Western
New York

Dryden Lake
Dryden

MAPS
  New York Atlas: Map 47
  USGS Quadrangle: Dryden
INFORMATION
  Area: 120 acres
  Prominent fish species: Warm-water species

Recreational opportunities abound in the Ithaca region. One can enjoy spectacular Taughannock and Buttermilk Falls, the Rim and Gorge Trails at Taughannock Point, bike trails—including one on the abandoned railroad grade near Dryden Park—several vineyards, state parks and forests, beaches, cruises on Cayuga Lake, and many more. With regional focus on Cayuga Lake—along with Seneca Lake one of the two largest Finger Lakes—quiet-water paddling opportunities are limited. Thus, the importance of Dryden Lake to the east of Ithaca becomes readily apparent.

The state and the town of Dryden, through farsighted efforts, have set aside Dryden Lake as a town park and a State Wildlife Management Area. A picnic area hugs the western shore, and a golf course covers a hillside on the east. Because of the lake's small size, the state does not allow motors, which would be nearly useless anyway, as vegetation mats the lake.

Scenic farms layer the hillsides, and fields march down to the lake's shore on the east. The cows in these fields, along with the abundant Canada geese—real feces factories—fertilize these waters ensuring abundant plant life. Neither cows nor geese move quickly, and that should serve as a metaphor for our approach to these waters. They should be enjoyed slowly; study the plants and watch the wildlife.

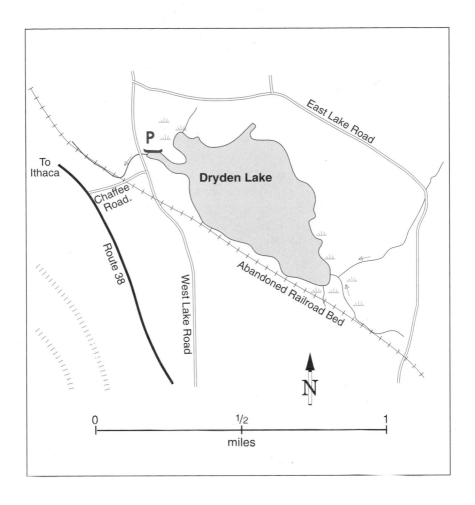

Usually on heavily vegetated bodies of water, one expects to see frogs using the fronds as furniture. In this lake, the vegetation in some spots supports turtles. A great blue heron even stood on it, trying with some difficulty to spot passing fish. Besides the usual water lilies, we found an aquatic member of the buttercup family in bloom, along with waterweed, a type of *Elodea*, with unusual underwater leaves one-quarter-inch long by one-sixteenth-inch wide, whorled in threes on slender stalks. It also bears the tiniest, barely visible purple flowers borne on tendrils; some flowers occur underwater, while others float in the surface film.

Narrow-leaved cattails cover much of the shore of this shallow lake. We paddled down the eastern shore, entering a marsh at the south end. Along with the usual turtles basking on logs, we spotted a young red-winged blackbird sitting on an exposed branch just a few inches above the water's surface. The male parent resented our proximity and flitted about the cattails, scolding us constantly. We hurried away, so as not to disturb the nest.

The inlet creek at the southeast corner meanders back through a cattail swamp, past a large beaver lodge with massive amounts of cuttings in the water. After a short distance, a beaver dam blocks the entrance to a broad meadow. As we paddled up, a green-backed heron family bolted skyward, accompanied by more loud squawking.

After things quieted, we listened to the metallic chip note of swamp sparrows among the streamside vegetation of *Rumex,* jewelweed, bur reed, and much more. Eventually one appeared in the brush, with its bright rufous cap and wings, pumping its tail as it flitted about. The melodious song of the marsh wren wafted by as tree swallows and cedar waxwings snatched insects on the wing.

Paddling back out onto the main lake and around to the southwestern shore, we surprised a few families of wood ducks that scurried into the surrounding marsh as we approached. You can paddle the entire circumference of this small lake and explore the inlet thoroughly in about two hours. We highly recommend a paddle here for those not in a hurry who want to study plants and animals.

Getting There

From Ithaca, take either Route 13 east or Route 366 east to the junction with Route 13 east. Continue on Route 13 east to the stoplight in Dryden. When Route 13 goes north, turn south (right) onto Route 38 south. Stay on Route 38 south for 2.1 miles, then turn left onto Chaffee Road. Chaffee Road dead-ends on West Lake Road in 0.3 mile. Turn left onto West Lake Road, cross the bridge over the outlet stream, and the boat access is on the right, just 0.1 mile from Chaffee Road.

Along the way, Chaffee Road crosses an abandoned railroad grade that has been turned into a bike path.

Howland Island (Seneca River)

Conquest

MAPS
  New York Atlas: Map 74
  USGS Quadrangle: Montezuma

INFORMATION
  Prominent fish species: Largemouth bass, smallmouth bass, and
    northern pike
  Montezuma National Wildlife Refuge: North end of Cayuga
    Lake; 315-568-5987

The Erie Canal takes a shortcut across a deep bend in the Seneca River,
neatly enclosing the Howland Island Wildlife Management Area and providing a wonderful loop trip of about 9 miles—10 miles if you paddle the
long way around Haiti Island. While you may encounter a few motorboats
on the canal portion of the trip, most motorboats stay off the Seneca River.
Portions of the river, particularly the long stretch that heads southwest to
northeast, suffer from siltation. When we paddled here in May, we ran
aground several times and hit bottom with every paddle stroke for a few
miles. Admittedly, this occurred in the drought year of 1995, and in wetter years the water level could be much higher. However, with most of the
water carried in the channelized canal and with little current in the river,
the low flow does not purge the river of the built-up silt.

Still, because the surrounding marshland provides an extensive
home for many nesting ducks, geese, and other wildlife, we found the
Howland Island loop well worth the paddling effort. When you start out
you have a choice of direction. Under calm conditions, toss a coin to
choose your direction of travel, but if the wind blows from the west or
northwest as it often does, we would paddle counterclockwise. The
western half of the loop, in contrast with the heavily wooded eastern
half, has low banks and few trees to block the wind. We tried to paddle
into a stiff northwest wind in a clockwise direction and wished we had
chosen to go the other way.

While we thought that the day would bring mostly a study of
plants, given our late morning start—when most birds and mammals
rest—instead it brought us great looks at two monarchs: the great blue
heron, monarch of the marsh, and the bald eagle, monarch of the skies.

Ducks and geese abound in this marshy paradise, but rarely have we
seen as many great blue heron standing stately knee-deep in water, patient-

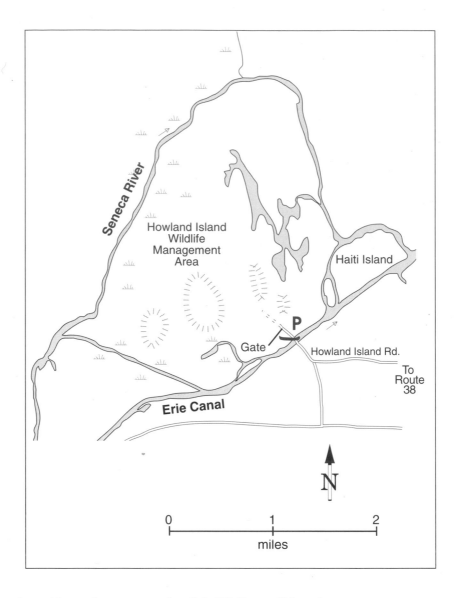

ly waiting to harpoon passing fish. While we did not keep count, we must have seen more than a dozen. If this were not sufficient inducement to paddle here, we also spotted two bald eagles. The first one we saw—a mature adult with white head and tail—soared effortlessly on huge broad wings. On some large individuals, wingspan can reach seven and a half feet. Females generally exceed the males in weight by a few pounds.

The second bird, judging from the white flecking on the underside, must have been a second- or third-year bird. First-year birds remain nearly totally brown, while older birds turn progressively whiter on the head and tail, reaching full adult plumage in four to five years. This bird, soaring ever higher, seemed totally oblivious to the raucous harassment engendered by several crows that tried to drive the eagle from their territory. The attacking crows seemed sparrow size compared to the massive eagle.

Twenty years ago, such a sight almost never occurred. DDT, introduced in the 1940s to control mosquitoes and other pests, accumulated in the environment. One of its breakdown products, DDE, caused disastrous eggshell thinning in birds at the top of the food chain, including eagles, osprey, and peregrine falcon. Coupled with habitat loss and illegal shooting, all eagle reproduction in the state had ceased. Sadly, one lone pair doggedly tried to reproduce year after year without success. Aided by the federal Endangered Species Act and banning of DDT in the U.S., the Department of Environmental Conservation began the New York eagle recovery program in 1976.

The eagle has traveled a long road to recovery in New York, from no successful hatchings for many years prior to 1976, to producing only three young in 1987, and to fledging an amazing 30 birds from 19 successful nests in 1995. Because of the success in New York and other states, the U.S. Fish and Wildlife Service, charged with overseeing the act, has removed the nation's symbol from the endangered species list and placed it on the threatened list.

Canada geese abound at Howland Island Wildlife Management Area.

This hard-won battle is far from over, however, because shortsighted economic interests continue to press for weakening of the Endangered Species Act. It seems that the vast majority of people would much rather see an eagle doing aerial battle with crows, a peregrine falcon stooping on a pigeon, and a California condor floating with the clouds than see some favored business get the green light to trash the preferred habitat of an endangered species for short-term economic gain for a few individuals. We all pay for such largesse by living in an altered environment very much less beautiful, interesting, and wild. Those who enjoy the out-of-doors—be they quiet-water paddlers, hikers, or sportsmen—should make their voices heard whenever the act is threatened: we must have a strong Endangered Species Act if we are to preserve any significant part of the environment for future generations to enjoy.

Lots more awaits you on your paddle around Howland Island. In addition to beaver activity, we saw a groundhog in a tree eating leaves! Admittedly, the tree trunk had bent down to a low angle, but this raises questions about the name "groundhog."

We never tired of paddling through the huge patches of fragrant water lily on the north side, nor of the chattering call of kingfishers as they fled before the approaching boat. Great crested flycatchers darted off their perches to snatch insects that fluttered on the breezes, and dozens of wood ducks provided dramatic sparkles of color. If you hear what appears to be a robin calling from the higher streamside foliage, take another look. It easily could be a beautiful rose-breasted grosbeak; we saw several along the way.

We are fortunate that we can paddle such a wonderful wildlife area, though we might think twice about paddling here during duck-hunting season! The nearby Montezuma National Wildlife Refuge—well worth a visit—provides similar habitat but no canoeing. It has self-guided auto trails, foot trails, and observation towers. One can often spot bald eagles at Montezuma, as well.

Getting There

Take I-90 to Exit 40 (Weedsport), and follow Route 34 south to Route 31 west. Take Route 31 into Port Byron, and turn right onto Route 38 north. Go 1.8 miles, and turn left onto Howland Island Road. Cross the bridge over the Erie Canal onto Howland Island after 1.9 miles. Turn right into the parking lot at the boat access.

Clyde River
Galen

MAPS
  New York Atlas: Map 73
  USGS Quadrangle: Lyons

INFORMATION
  Prominent fish species: Largemouth bass, smallmouth bass, and
  northern pike

Forgotten by time, the Clyde River gave up much of its water and its
character to the Erie Canal. Portions of it still run today along with the
waters of the canal. We do not cover those sections here, because they
include channelized water and too much boat traffic. Instead, we
include the headwaters of the Clyde, if they can be called such. With
almost no flow, the river collects snags and mountains of aquatic vegetation as summer wears on. Still, something primeval beckons one to
paddle the Clyde.

River Road parallels one shore, while the other shore marks the
beginning of deep, dark, brushy forests with towering trees and hanging
vines. Fields and occasional cottages line the eastern shore, making the

A tiger swallowtail perches on the leaves and flowers of a hawthorn.

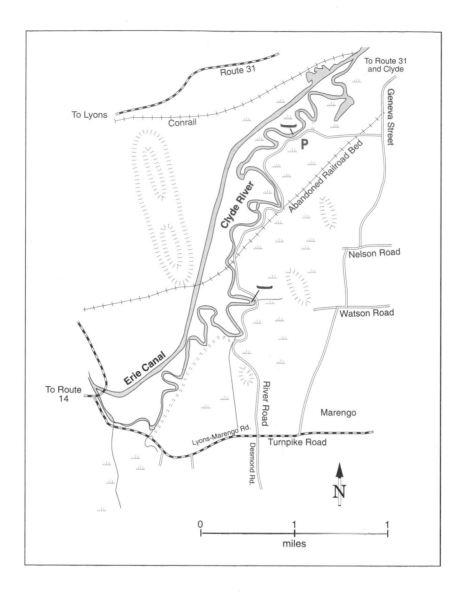

western shore vastly more interesting. Even though we paddled the Clyde up and back, we found ourselves clinging to the western shore the whole time, except where drowned logs made us detour to the other side.

While vultures circled lazily overhead, great blue herons fished the productive waters. From the more northern boat access, we paddled about five miles upstream and then back down, without seeing any other fishers besides birds and turtles, which were taking a break, basking on logs. While tree swallows skimmed the surface to drink, bullfrogs called from the lily pads. We stopped to photograph colorful orioles hanging from branches as they stooped to suck nectar from flowers with their narrow, pointed bills. Kingbirds patrolled the water, fluttering about to catch moths and other insects on the wing.

The dark swamp water harbored many fish that darted away as we approached, seeking cover under acres of floating vegetation. Along the far bank, ferns and swamp roses fought for light under the canopy of tall silver maple, ash, shagbark hickory, white oak, basswood, and many other tree species. Hawthorns with showy clusters of white flowers bloomed along the banks. Back in the woods, eastern wood pewees whistled "pea-o-whee," and veeries whistled their cascading, flutelike notes. Many more bird species announced their territories, including gray catbird, northern cardinal, yellow warbler, common yellowthroat, eastern phoebe, mourning dove, red-winged blackbird, rose-breasted grosbeak, great crested flycatcher, and American goldfinch.

It took quite a while to reconcile the two banks of the river, one with development, the other impenetrable jungle. We can only wonder what this wonderful swamp must have contained in precolonial times. Because people have forgotten this waterway, you probably will paddle here alone, perhaps joined by an occasional fisherman. Often the fishermen are just great blue herons.

Getting There

From I-90, get off at the Route 14 exit and go north. Just after crossing over into Wayne County, watch for Zohn Alloway Road going off to the right. Turn right, and start marking mileage. The road takes a sharp left after 0.8 mile. Continue on, and turn right onto Schwartz Road at 1.1 miles. At 2.1 miles cross a railroad track immediately after a steep downhill. At 2.2 miles, turn right onto Lyons-Marengo Road at the stop sign. At the crossroads at 4.2 miles, where Desmond Road goes right, turn left onto the gravel River Road. The first of several boat accesses is 1.2 miles down this road; we found the best boat access to be the last, after an additional 3.1 miles.

Sterling Valley Creek/The Pond
Sterling

MAPS
   New York Atlas: Map 74
   USGS Quadrangle: Fair Haven

INFORMATION
   Prominent fish species: Largemouth bass and northern pike
   Camping: Fair Haven Beach State Park; 315-947-5205

Sterling Valley Creek drains the hills immediately to the east and south of Fair Haven Beach State Park. As the tributaries flow together into the Sterling Valley, nearing the end of their journey to Lake Ontario, they spill out over an extensive marsh. This marsh—and many like it along Lake Ontario's broad plains—provides wonderful habitat for fish and waterfowl. While the waterfowl back in the tules, particularly the beautiful wood duck and ring-necked duck, try to escape human notice, those inhabiting the pond—called "The Pond," appropriately enough— have grown quite used to human presence, going so far as to beg for food. Signs suggest that feeding the abundant Canada geese and mallards will cost you more than the price of the food (illegal=fine).

This delicate, iridescent green damselfly folds its wings vertically over its back, in contrast with dragonflies that hold their wings out to the side.

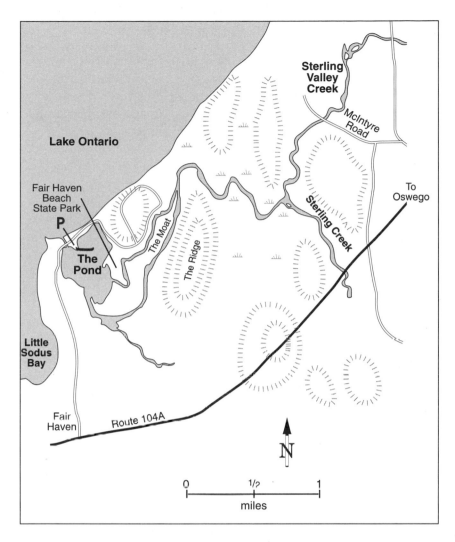

We saw several broods of mallards and Canada geese munching away on the abundant vegetation in The Pond by the boat access. Out in the middle, a common moorhen (formerly called common gallinule) grazed on the fanwort floating in the surface film. The moorhen resembles its relative the American coot, except that it has a red bill while the coot has a white one. Members of the rail family, they both swim and graze on aquatic plants just like ducks.

Two different species of yellow pond lily occurred in great mats, and duckweed—one of the smallest flowering plants—had started to fill in any available open water when we visited. By summer's end, paddling here can be a challenge.

The Moat, an impenetrable swamp filled with downed trees and duckweed, provides abundant habitat for numerous wood ducks. As you paddle out of The Pond and up the creek, an island ringed with cattails separates The Moat from the creek. We suggest that you paddle back through one of the several cuts through the island—particularly on the northern end—to The Moat. We watched numerous wood ducks feeding on aquatic vegetation and turtles basking on logs.

In addition to the wood ducks, Canada geese, and mallards, we saw many ring-necked ducks and common mergansers. Barn swallows swooped over the water's surface, alternately catching insects on the wing and dipping for a drink. Red-winged blackbirds sang from the cattails, bending the slender stalks with their weight, and eastern kingbirds darted out from their streamside perches to catch some of the all-too-abundant insect life.

Along Sterling Valley Creek, above The Pond, ramshackle cabins with boat docks askew line the banks for a short way on the right. After clearing these, you paddle up through an idyllic swamp to the fork, where Sterling Creek veers right, away from Sterling Valley Creek. The right fork turns into farm country after a short distance and becomes impassable as it nears Route 104A. Sterling Valley Creek continues to meander through the valley for several miles.

As we studied a beaver lodge with fresh cuttings and watched muskrat feeding on grasses, two Jet-skis roared up this narrow creek. Two-strokers create awful noise and smell as directly injected oil gets burned. They leave a huge wake and drive wildlife to cover. We should ban them from streams and ponds, as has happened in other states. If they want to roar around Lake Ontario, fine, but they have no business disrupting wildlife on small creeks such as Sterling Valley.

Paddling back in the setting sun to the boat launch, past huge willows, red oak, paper birch, and hemlock, we wondered about the fate of this wildlife paradise. Protection from development by the state is not enough; recreation disruptive to wildlife should be banned.

Getting There

From Oswego, take Route 104 west. When the road divides, take Route 104A to the right. Just as you start to enter Fair Haven, watch for signs to Fair Haven Beach State Park. Turn right, and follow the road for 1.8 miles to the boat launch area. As you near Lake Ontario, the park office and post office appear on the left. Immediately after these, the road curves to the right and crosses a wooden-rail bridge. Just after the bridge, the boat access and its large parking lot appear on the right.

East Bay

Huron

MAPS
   New York Atlas: Map 73
   USGS Quadrangle: East Bay
INFORMATION
   Area: 290 acres
   Prominent fish species: No information available

Great blue herons, marsh wrens, wood ducks, kingfishers, Canada geese, beaver, muskrat, painted turtles... these are some of the many animals you will see in the long winding inlet channels of East Bay. For a birder, botanist, or photographer, the marshland of East Bay provides tremendous opportunity for exploration.

Though we paddled around the northern section of East Bay—and through the breachway into Lake Ontario for kicks—most paddlers will prefer to stay in the more southern reaches. Several slow-flowing inlet creeks meander through extensive cattail marshes. From the westernmost boat access, paddle toward the main bay, then take the arm to the left (west). Paddling here in late June, we spotted a group of delicate rose pogonia orchids hidden among some ferns on sphagnum hummocks. This orchid has a single flower on a slender stem and a single oval leaf about halfway up the stem. While rarely abundant, this is one of the orchids you are most likely to see along New York's marshy lakes and ponds.

Cattails dominate the shoreline here, and water lilies dominate the water's surface. Both yellow pond lily and tuberous water lily grow here, but the white-flowered tuberous water lilies are more common. You can easily distinguish tuberous from fragrant water lilies (which are more common in eastern New York): tuberous water lily pads have green undersides, while fragrant water lily pads usually have purple undersides. If you can smell the flowers—leaning over to smell water lily flowers is a risky move from a canoe—the fragrant water lily is, as one might suspect, fragrant. Also, tuberous water lily leaves are much larger. East Bay had some of the biggest specimens of this plant we've ever seen: leaves up to 17 inches across and stems a half inch in diameter!

Interestingly, after they have finished blooming, the flowers of both species of white water lily get pulled underwater by a coiling action of the stems. This protects the seed head and permits the seeds

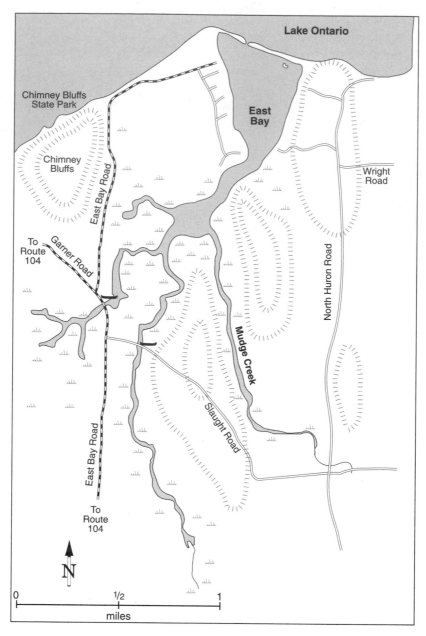

to ripen over a period of three or four weeks. After the seeds ripen, the seed head, or aril, breaks free and floats to the surface of the water. Here it gradually decomposes and deposits its seeds—which sink—into the pond bottom.

You will also see arrowhead, pickerelweed, nettles, alder, blue flag, wild morning glory, swamp loosestrife—a native cousin of the pesky purple loosestrife, which has taken over wetlands throughout the eastern United States—duckweed, fanwort, and bladderwort. Where the land rises from the water, deciduous trees dominate: red oak, basswood, beech, sassafras, red maple, and yellow birch, to mention a few.

In Mudge Creek we saw the most bird life. About a mile up this inlet creek (south from East Bay) we saw several dozen wood ducks. Most of the time you see these birds flying away far ahead of you, as they spook very easily, but if you paddle very quietly without talking, you can sometimes get quite close. Wood ducks now abound in our marshes, after nearly suffering extermination at the turn of the century. They were saved by passage of the Migratory Waterfowl Act, which protected migrating birds except during carefully timed waterfowl hunting seasons. Wood ducks got a further boost beginning around 1940 with the construction of wood duck nesting boxes in many areas—a practice that began in Massachusetts after most of the dead trees that the birds used for nesting got knocked down by the 1938 hurricane.

As we paddled up Mudge Creek, we were surprised to hear some commotion ahead. We watched an armada of about 75 Canada geese round the bend heading toward us. The flock included both adults and young at various stages of maturity. When they spotted us, they all began bobbing their heads in concern. This comical spectacle had the desired effect: after watching the geese for about 10 minutes, we turned around to leave them in peace.

We also got a great look at some huge carp here—feeding at the surface amid the water lilies, their humped backs extended out of the water an inch or more. We drifted over until we were almost on top of one particularly large individual and got a great look—when it finally noticed us and took off, the wake imparted a noticeable rock to our canoe.

The inlet creek extending farthest to the south—under the bridge from the more eastern boat access—was also very pleasant. It was here that we saw the most beaver activity. Paddling late in the day, we saw four different beavers and several lodges.

Merganser with chicks

The north end of East Bay has a fair amount of development on it, and you're likely to see water-skiers. When we visited it was possible to paddle through the breachway onto Lake Ontario, but the two excavators—one an antique quietly rusting in the shade of a willow tree—provide evidence that the access may not always remain open. Gravel deposits from the lake have to be cleared away regularly to keep the channel open. On a calm day, paddling out onto Ontario and around the point to the west offers a real treat.

Chimney Bluffs, about a mile down the shoreline from the breachway, is a remarkable geologic feature and definitely worth a visit—either by water in very calm conditions or by driving up East Bay Road. Dramatic, 150-feet-tall reddish spires of eroding sandstone and compacted soil look more like they belong in Utah or Arizona, not New York. Some of the knife-edge ridges and spires run so thin you wonder why they're still standing. You can walk or paddle along the shore beneath Chimney Bluffs, or explore above them on trails. Be very careful about venturing out onto Lake Ontario, however. It is more like ocean paddling than lake paddling.

Getting There

From Route 104, take Lake Bluff Road north at the point where Route 414 goes off to the south (this is 4.1 miles east of the intersection of Routes 104 and 14). Note your mileage here, and follow Lake Bluffs Road north. In 3.5 miles, where Lake Bluffs Road curves to the left, continue straight on Garner Road. Garner Road takes several sharp turns to the right. At 6.2 miles, where East Bay Road turns off sharply to the left, continue straight (you are on East Bay Road at this point). You will reach a small roadside park and boat access on the left at 6.3 miles (just before crossing over the creek).

To reach the second access, continue on East Bay Road for 0.2 mile past the first access, and turn left on Slaught Road. The boat access is 0.2 mile down this road.

To drive to Chimney Bluffs State Park, go back up East Bay Road past the first boat access and bear right (staying on East Bay Road) where Garner Road continues straight. The parking area for Chimney Bluffs Park is 1.0 mile up East Bay Road from here, and trails head down to the beach below the cliffs or up the ridge above them.

West River

Italy

MAPS
   New York Atlas: Map 58
   USGS Quadrangle: Middlesex
INFORMATION
   Prominent fish species: Largemouth bass and smallmouth bass

New York's Department of Environmental Conservation protects the West River, which flows—pretty much imperceptibly—into the south end of Canandaigua Lake. Part of the 6,100-acre High Tor Wildlife Management Area, the stream contains two portions, both worth exploring. When the wind has turned the big lakes to a foaming froth, paddle here instead. Canoeists can gain access to the river from three points: one from the southwest shore of Canandaigua Lake, the second from Route 245 five or so miles east of Naples, and the third from Sunnyside Road off Route 245. The last is the only hand-carry access, and the river's generally shallow and weedy character here make encounters with motorboats unlikely.

Putting in at the hand-carry access on Sunnyside Road, stay to the right (east) and head upstream under both bridges. This will take you back into the heart of the High Tor Wildlife Management Area and, more importantly, away from the motorboats. The sinewy West River reaches back upstream about two weed-choked miles before you reach the first beaver dam. We did not explore beyond it, although it looked as though you could go quite a bit farther. This beaver dam provided the first inkling that we were paddling upstream, given the seemingly nonexistent current. A sea of aquatic vegetation covers the entire river, from bank to bank, even where the river is 100 feet across.

Duckweed, a minuscule stemless flowering plant, covers the underwater vegetation in great floating mats. Tuberous water lilies and yellow pond lilies occur in profusion out in the water, with arrowhead lining the shore. Extensive stands of cattails course through the shallows, broken occasionally by clumps of dwarf silver maples, alders, large willows hanging out over the water, and lower-growing vegetation. We found large clusters of beautiful pink swamp roses, yellow irises, swamp milkweed, and many other flowering plants.

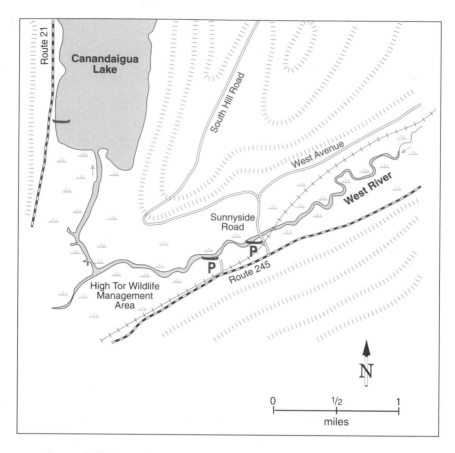

But wildlife provides the real attraction. Evidence of beaver activity appeared everywhere, and we saw muskrats both swimming and harvesting grasses. Turtles poked their heads up through the vegetation seemingly every few feet; we surprised several huge snapping turtles, which dove for cover under the boat. We saw several great blue herons, a green-backed heron, kingfishers, great crested flycatchers, eastern phoebes, red-winged blackbirds, and many other bird species. We saw more than 100 ducks, including mostly wood ducks. If you are lucky, you may catch sight of small, brightly colored hooded mergansers; they compete with wood ducks for cavity nesting sites. A family of Canada geese grazed the shoreline as well. Two young great horned owls sat on a log hanging out over the water.

Because this represents a very wild, truly productive environment, we strongly recommend against paddling upstream—downstream is okay at any time—from the hand-carry access during nesting season (before July 1). We paddled here in mid-July.

The slow-moving, marshy West River flows into the south end of Canandaigua Lake.

Downstream from the hand-carry access, motorboats maintain an open channel. We would avoid this area on weekends during the summer. When we paddled it down to Canandaigua Lake on a Wednesday in July we saw only a few boats. While the vegetation along the lower river remains pretty much the same as above the access, wildlife appears with less frequency, no doubt driven away by the boat traffic. You can also see layered farms on the hillsides off in the distance, whereas above the bridges we saw no development.

At the hand-carry access a plaque reads: Nundawao. Legendary site of the first Seneca Indian Village just across the river. This was the birthplace of the Seneca, members of the Iroquois nation.

Getting There

From Naples, at the junction of Routes 21 and 245, take Route 245 east. After 1.7 miles reach the Yates/Ontario Counties border. At 3.5 miles is the West River trailered-boat access. For the hand-carry access, turn left at 4.0 miles onto Sunnyside Road (marked by a green street sign on the left); go 0.1 mile to the access on the left.

Hemlock Lake and Canadice Lake

Canadice, Conesus, and Livonia

MAPS
  New York Atlas: Map 58
  USGS Quadrangles: Honeoye and Springwater
INFORMATION
  Hemlock Lake Area: 2,800 acres
  Canadice Lake Area: 850 acres
  Prominent fish species: Hemlock Lake—largemouth bass, small-
  mouth bass, landlocked salmon, lake trout, and rainbow trout;
  Canadice Lake—largemouth bass, smallmouth bass, lake trout,
  and lunker brown trout

Hemlock Lake and nearby Canadice Lake stand out as rare jewels
because of their positions as the only Finger Lakes not ringed by roads
or dominated by development and Jet-skis. Alas, their preservation did
not result from farsighted conservation efforts but because they serve
as water-supply reservoirs for the city of Rochester, which limits access
and controls uses.

Hemlock Lake

Only a couple of structures mar the view of the hillsides surrounding
Hemlock Lake, and while the city allows motors, it limits boats to 16
feet (except canoes) and to 10 horsepower. There is a picnic area on the
north end of this eight-mile-long, north-south-oriented lake, but boats
may not go north of the northern boat access (about one mile from the
north end).

You need a free permit, renewed annually, to paddle here and on
Canadice Lake. Obtain your permit at a self-service station near the
water-filtration plant off Rix Hill Road at the north end of the lake. This
same location provides the only access to the northern boat launch.
However, after you get your permit, you may want to travel down to the
southern access for two reasons: first, the southern section, including
Springwater Creek and marsh, provides more interesting paddling; second, the prevailing summer winds usually blow from the south, protecting those waters from the winds. When winds blow strongly up or
down the lake, we suggest that you paddle the nearby West River,
which flows into the south end of Canandaigua Lake.

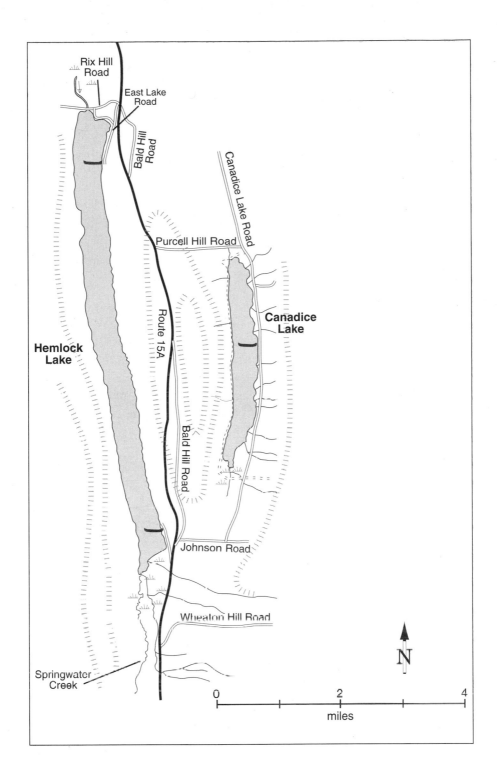

Rochester imposes several more restrictions, which we will not recount here, except for one. In order to halt the spread of zebra mussels—Eurasian import to the Great Lakes region in the ballasts of ships—you are not supposed to launch your boat in Hemlock Lake within three days of having it in other waters. These very destructive bivalves have reproduced prolifically in the Great Lakes, attaching themselves in many-deep clusters to water intakes and other marine structures, eventually clogging the water passages.

While giving out warnings we should mention that, although this is an unspoiled lake, its level does get drawn down in the summer by thirsty Rochester, revealing ugly barren shores, especially in dry years. In wet years, the level may remain quite high even in the middle of July. If you know people in Rochester, ask them to help preserve the lake by installing low-flow toilets and showerheads and sink aerators, and by using water judiciously.

Hardwoods, such as aspen, willow, red and white oaks, walnut, and sycamore, dominate the shoreline of Hemlock Lake. Occasional pines, mostly red, appear here and there, and a well-developed understory fights for light along the shore. Surprisingly, the quite clear water harbors a relatively large amount of submerged aquatic vegetation, even out in the open lake. The Springwater Creek marsh at the south end consists of a wide expanse of cattails, grasses, and water lilies. If the water is high, you can paddle down into it quite a way. It starts way over on the western shore and continues south.

When we paddled here, we saw many ring-billed gulls, a nesting pair of red-tailed hawks, spotted sandpipers bobbing on the rocks, belted kingfishers, eastern phoebes, great crested flycatchers, and tons of tree and barn swallows skimming the water's surface snatching up airborne insects. Unfortunately, we missed the main attraction, a nesting pair of bald eagles.

Canadice Lake

The same general rules about permits, boat length, motors, and zebra mussel precautions described above also apply to Canadice Lake. Much of what we said previously about Hemlock Lake remains true for Canadice. According to local fishermen, even a modest breeze can kick up rollers on Canadice Lake. Because it has a north-south orientation with steep hillsides all around, winds get funneled up and down the lake, even when they blow from off-axis directions. We would avoid

Canadice and Hemlock Lakes when the wind blows more than a modest breeze.

Canadice, slightly more than three miles long and less than a half mile wide, nestles in a deep valley, ringed with forested hillsides rising more than 1,000 feet above the lake's surface. A lone house appears near the northern shore, the only development visible from the water. Drawdown reveals a rock-filled shore, instead of exposed muddy banks, making the view a lot less ugly. Although a road travels down the eastern lakeshore, it contains very light local traffic only.

While crows, a red squirrel, and a gray squirrel harassed a perched red-tailed hawk, fish jumped out in the open water, rising for a late-May fly hatch. A few fishermen searched for the lunker trout that supposedly inhabit the depths. We were content to absorb the sights of dogwoods blooming on the hillsides and the songs of northern orioles and black-throated green warblers emanating from the treetops. Heart-shaped leaves of bankside cottonwoods rattled in the light breeze as we peered back into the undergrowth, trying to catch sight of a veery, yellowthroat, or other ground-dwelling songbird.

We enjoyed our early season paddle here, thankful that Rochester had not drawn the water down appreciably. Given the proximity to lakes infested with zebra mussels—Conesus, Canandaigua, Keuka, Seneca, and Ontario—we wondered how long it would take for Hem-

Flowering dogwood blooms in the spring on the hillsides surrounding Hemlock and Canadice Lakes.

lock and Canadice to become infested with the destructive bivalves. Will the warnings about zebra mussels at the boat access have any effect on their appearance here? Can the larvae hitchhike on the legs of long-legged waders such as the great blue heron? We all will have to wait to see how this plays out here and in our other favorite waters.

Getting There

Hemlock Lake: While the northern access is easily found, the southern one is not. From Rochester, go south on Route 15A. Where Route 20A goes off to the left, continue for another 0.7 mile, and turn right onto Rix Hill Road. Stop here for a free permit, following the signs to the self-service permit station. To reach the northern access, follow the gravel East Lake Road around to the right by the maintenance garages. The access is about a mile down this road.

To get to the southern access on Hemlock Lake, go back out to Route 15A, and drive 7.9 miles south until you come to signs for Livingston County and town of Springwater. A guardrail starts at these signs. When it ends in about 0.1 mile, turn right sharply back, almost a U-turn, onto the boat access road. At the turnoff, there is a big red sign with all the warnings about permits, etc.

Coming from the south, go 2.2 miles north of the junction of Routes 15 and 15A on 15A; watch ahead for the green sign on the right that says Hemlock Lake. The turnoff is on the left about 150 feet before the sign.

Canadice Lake: Go to the Rix Hill self-service free-permit station, as described above. After obtaining your free permit, go back out to Route 15A, and turn right. Go 2.5 miles south, and turn left onto Purcell Hill Road. After an initial, short uphill climb, the road drops steeply. At the bottom after 1.4 miles, the road curves right onto Canadice Lake Road. Follow this road to the boat launch on the right in another 1.4 miles.

Mendon Ponds

Mendon

MAPS
   New York Atlas: Map 72
   USGS Quadrangle: Pittsford

INFORMATION
   Area: Hundred Acre Pond: 120 acres; Deep Pond: 30 acres
   Prominent fish species: Warm-water species

Mendon Ponds County Park lies close by Rochester, just a mile or two south of the New York State Thruway. While it won't provide a wilderness experience, it is a great place for family recreation, a place to teach children about plants, wildlife, geology, and canoeing. The whole 1,000-acre wetland area has much to teach us about climate cycles and geology. The surrounding bog, underlaid with peat, provides an outstanding example of the rare bog community.

Kettle hole ponds are remnants of the last Ice Age. As the glacier retreated, it left behind huge chunks of ice buried in the glacial till. The melting ice formed kettle holes, which gradually fill in with sphagnum over thousands of years, forming peat lands. As the leading edges of glaciers retreated, they left behind low ridges of sediment called eskers, which we can see here and in many other areas of the north country. Eskers formed when under-ice rivers flowed through glacial cracks, depositing sediment along their borders.

Canoes may be rented at the Hundred Acre Pond access site off Route 65; other recreation and picnicking opportunities abound at the park, and while a beach exists, apparently swimming does not. Launch your boat at one of three access points: from the canoe rental facility off Route 65 on Hundred Acre Pond, from the opposite shore on Hundred Acre Pond, or from the southwest corner of Deep Pond, off Route 65 on Pond Road.

During our visit in mid-July, fishermen told us that in some summers the ponds get completely choked with aquatic vegetation. Clearly, with ever-increasing accumulations of dead plant material during each annual cycle, the ponds march inexorably to the filled-in bog condition, where a floating mat of sphagnum supports bog specialists, adapted to acidic conditions. Eventually, trees encroach as the bog fills in, squeezing out the water.

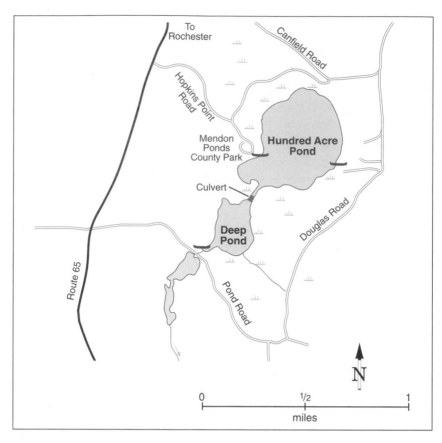

Trees such as Norway spruce, red pine, silver maple, ash, oak, and others grow well back from the water, with occasional willows on the shore. Cattails crowd the banks in shallow water, and arrowhead grows in huge patches where cattails have not yet crowded it out.

We saw ducks, great blue herons, red-winged blackbirds, and common yellowthroats. A hermit thrush called from the dense undergrowth, and several species of swallow skimmed the water's surface for a drink on a sweltering July day. Several eastern kingbirds patrolled the airways, performing the excellent service of snaring deerflies on the wing. Large flocks of Canada geese simultaneously mowed the grass and fertilized it, probably saving the county park a great deal of work.

As we approached the carry into Deep Pond at the south end of Hundred Acre Pond, a huge beaver lodge and lots of beaver activity greeted us. Traversing into the more secluded Deep Pond from Hundred Acre Pond should be a breeze; one could just paddle through the culvert that separates them. However, the beaver in the area must be

Acres of fragrant water lily dominate the southern end of Hundred Acre Pond, a kettle hole left by a melting glacier at the end of the last Ice Age.

really hard up, because they have chosen to dam up this culvert, thus requiring canoes to carry up and over the separating embankment.

We tried to paddle into the weed-choked southeastern cove on Deep Pond but couldn't penetrate more than 50 feet, because yellow pond lilies and fragrant white water lilies, along with arrowhead, some rushes, and a few cattails, choked the waterway. In this more secluded area we watched turtles bask and enjoyed the beauty of swamp rose and swamp milkweed. We found it hard to believe such tranquil surroundings exist on the very outskirts of Rochester.

Getting There

Take Route 65 south out of Rochester. A bike sign appears just before the green bridge over I-90, the New York State Thruway. From this bridge, continue 1.0 mile to the main park entrance, Hopkins Point Road, and canoe rental off Route 65. To get to the boat launch on the east side of Hundred Acre Pond, from the I-90 bridge, go south on Route 65 for 0.6 mile, and turn left onto Canfield Road. Go 1.1 miles, and turn right onto Douglas Road. Watch on the right for a green sign that says boat launch; it's about 0.8 mile down Douglas Road.

Genesee River Gorge

Rochester

MAPS
New York Atlas: Maps 71 and 72
USGS Quadrangles: Rochester East and Rochester West

The lower section of the Genesee River, from Genesee Dock at Turning Point Park to the spectacular falls four miles upstream (to the south), offers a wonderful morning or afternoon paddle within the city limits of Rochester. The river—wide and deep for most of this section—was a real surprise for us, given its urban setting. Large boats ply these waters—indeed, a cement tanker had docked just north of the park when we visited—but most boat traffic stays north of Turning Point Park and heads out onto Lake Ontario.

With the river's high banks, a paddler here feels remarkably separated from the surrounding city. You pass under a few bridges—including Route 104—and what appears to be a piped aqueduct, pass a large Kodak water treatment plant on the right, and catch a glimpse of a few large buildings and smokestacks. But mostly you paddle here separated from the urban congestion a quarter mile to the east or west. The walls of the canyon somehow muffle the noise as well; we really felt quite alone here—albeit during a paddle quite late in the day. The occasional rusting engine block, shopping cart, and partially floating tire reminded us that civilization is not far away, however.

From the park heading south, the shores are initially marshy, thick with cattails and sporting willow trees here and there. On higher terrain, farther from the banks, deciduous trees dominate: red oak, white oak, basswood, maple, walnut, sassafras. In some areas tall, red, sandstone cliffs probably serve the local kingfishers well. When we paddled here late in June, large carp spawned at the water's surface—sometimes you can paddle quite close and get a good view of these huge fish. We also saw a snapping turtle, several painted turtles, and a beaver during our exploration upstream.

Continuing south, the marsh gives way to a more abrupt shoreline, rising steeply from the river. About four miles south from the put-in, you pass an island on the left, the current picks up, and you have to dodge protruding rocks. Depending on the flow, you may be able to continue paddling upstream here, or you can beach your boat and walk

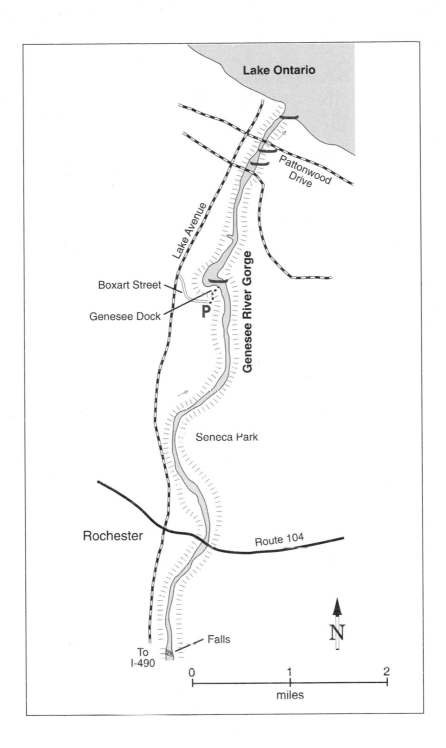

Lake Ontario

Pattonwood Drive

Lake Avenue

Boxart Street

Genesee Dock

P

Genesee River Gorge

Seneca Park

Rochester

Route 104

N

Falls

To
I-490

0   1   2

miles

on along the shoreline. A wide cirque of red cliffs appears ahead, and around the bend to the left the northernmost falls on the river roars off in the distance. Though not quite as dramatic as Upper Falls (just a little farther south on the Genesee), this one falls a greater distance, providing a spectacular sight. Water cascades over a broad brim, dropping approximately 150 feet into a widened section of the gorge.

We did not paddle north of Turning Point Park. Closer to Lake Ontario, the high banks of the river disappear, development encroaches to the water, and sections of the river are wall-to-wall powerboats—not our idea of a good time. Stick to the northern section, where you can watch a beaver foraging on cattails as dusk approaches, study basking painted turtles through your binoculars, and spot herons fishing in the marsh. You can almost forget that New York's third-largest city churns away above you.

Getting There

From the center of Rochester (Main Street), turn north on State Street. After 0.8 mile, State Street turns into Lake Avenue. Follow Lake Avenue north for 4.5 miles (5.3 miles from Main Street), and turn right at a traffic light onto Boxart Street—if you look carefully, you will see a small sign for Turning Point Park here. Follow Boxart Street to the right at the T almost immediately, and continue to the end of the road about 0.5 mile from Lake Avenue. There is a parking area inside the gate (check the closing time, and be sure to return before the gate is locked). From the parking area you have to portage your canoe about a quarter mile down to the river. The carry down to the water is paved, so a portage cart will work fine.

Salmon and West Creeks

Greece and Parma

MAPS
  New York Atlas: Map 71
  USGS Quadrangles: Braddock Heights and Hilton
INFORMATION
  Prominent fish species: Largemouth bass and northern pike

Braddock Bay, an inlet of Lake Ontario, lies just a few miles east of Rochester. The 30 or so creeks that flow into the lake from Braddock Bay to Round Pond, 4 miles away, drain at least 150 square miles of flat coastal plain. These bays should constitute wetlands of regional significance. Indeed, the state protects 2,125 acres as the Braddock Bay Fish and Wildlife Management Area, covering most of the marshes north of the Lake Ontario Parkway from Rose Marsh on the west to Buck Pond on the east.

Unfortunately, the protected area does not include most of Braddock Bay, which bristles with crowded marinas, development, large boats, and the dreaded Jet-ski. No paddler should venture out into Braddock Bay on a July or August weekend in a canoe for fear of getting run over or swamped. Fortunately, an alternative exists. One can paddle two relatively unspoiled tributaries—West Creek and Salmon Creek—or nearby Buck Pond (see the next description).

After paying five dollars to launch at Braddock Bait and Tackle at the Braddock Inn or at the Willow Inn, paddle south a short distance and cross under Route 261 at the Docksider Marina. That will put you on West Creek; the bridge over Salmon Creek lies a few hundred feet farther south. Try to time your passage so that no cars cross the bridge while you are underneath; the noise can be quite loud, especially under the Salmon Creek bridge. These low-clearance bridges exclude most boats other than canoes and kayaks. Further, weeds choke the two creeks so that props on motors would foul instantly.

Cattails dominate the marshes surrounding the creek, and pickerel-weed and acres of water lilies crowd the channel. We watched several red-winged blackbirds chase a red-tailed hawk from the cattails where it had stooped, looking for a meal. Hawks appear in abundance, especially during migration. In 1987, observers counted more than 100,000 raptors during spring migration, which peaks in late April.

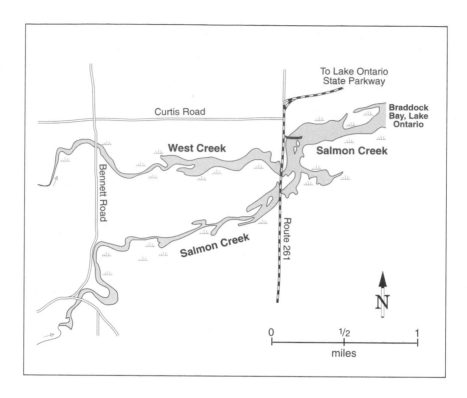

Tree species include towering Norway spruce, huge willows, and ash. Grapevines drape over the vegetation along the banks, and sumac appears here and there. Flocks of cedar waxwings and several species of swallow patrol the waterway, picking off insects born of these fertile waters, while great blue heron fish the shallows. Painted turtles dive for cover as you approach, and acres of tuberous and fragrant water lily flowers will greet you if you paddle in the morning.

Some botanists do not agree that tuberous and fragrant water lilies are separate species. Supposedly, they can be separated by the following: tuberous water lilies have rounded flower petals, no odor, and green leaf undersides; fragrant water lilies have pointed flower petals, abundant odor, and often purple leaf undersides. Tuberous water lilies do not occur in the Adirondacks or east of the mountains, while fragrant water lilies occur throughout New York. The leaves of tuberous water lily also get much larger—we measured one at 17 inches in diameter! Regardless of taxonomy, both produce beautiful white, morning-blooming flowers throughout the summer and into the fall.

You can paddle upstream through clear water and undisturbed habitat for about a mile and a half, all the way to the bridge on Bennett Road. After that, the creek gets too shallow for paddling. If you have time, paddle back downstream, cross back under the Route 261 bridge, turn south for a few hundred feet, recross back under Route 261, and paddle up Salmon Creek. While you are out in the south end of Braddock Bay, explore the extensive marsh, teeming with wildlife. If you get too close to the tiny islands where the black terns nest, they will dive-bomb your boat. After one warning, we steered clear of them and watched as they glided effortlessly over the water. A black bird with silvery wings, this tern has become increasingly rare over most of its breeding range, which stretches from coast to coast in the northern U.S. and Canada.

Salmon Creek has more water in it than West Creek, and consequently aquatic vegetation does not choke the main channel nearly as much. The Salmon also has more side channels to explore, it is longer, and there are fewer cattails, which can get boring after awhile. You can paddle upstream almost to the high school before riffles block your way. Common moorhens take time from grazing on aquatic plants to scurry back into the cattails as you approach. Kingfishers fly upstream from perch to perch, announcing your presence as they go. The unusual box elder, the only maple with a three-leaflet compound leaf, hangs out over the water in many places. Thick vines drape over the shoreline vegetation, and a rope swing dangles from a hemlock out over the water like a vine, inviting you to drop from it into a seven-foot-deep pool on hot, sultry summer days.

Getting There

Take the Lake Ontario State Parkway west from Rochester to Route 261, just after crossing the northwest arm of Braddock Bay. Follow Route 261 southwest, away from Manitou Beach. At the stop sign, where Park Beach Road goes to the right, continue on Route 261 to the left. Almost immediately, Curtis Road goes off to the right. From this junction, Braddock Bait and Tackle and the Braddock Inn are just a few hundred yards down on the left. Alternatively, you can launch at the Willow Inn, just a little farther down on the left. Both charged five dollars to launch.

Buck Pond

Greece

MAPS
  New York Atlas: Map 71
  USGS Quadrangle: Braddock Heights
INFORMATION
  Area: 550 acres
  Prominent fish species: No information available

Backed up against Lake Ontario and only a few miles from the city of Rochester, Buck Pond offers a pleasant escape from civilization. Though most of the marsh lies within earshot of automobiles and motorboats, you will feel alone here exploring the rich, bird-filled marsh. The few buildings on the northeastern shore and the vacation traffic along Edgemere Drive do not seem to spoil the wild character of the place. On a calm day, you can even paddle under the Edgemere Drive bridge and out onto Lake Ontario.

From the unimproved launch site near the eastern tip of the pond, Buck Pond itself is a little less than a mile across, but you can spend many hours exploring the long winding inlet channels and hidden coves of the pond. By early summer, marsh vegetation chokes the shal-

Thick vegetation dominates the winding channels of Buck Pond.

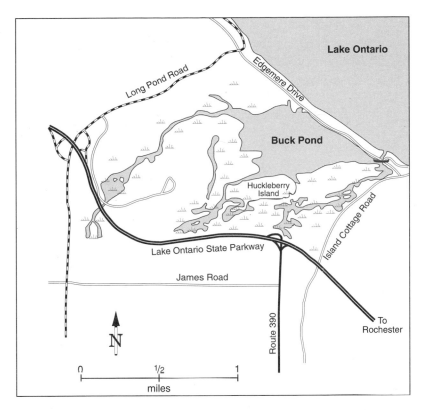

lower channels: cattails, bulrush, bur reed, swamp loosestrife, arrowhead, pickerelweed, fanwort, duckweed, and tuberous water lily. While cattails dominate the vegetation, there is quite a bit of diversity, which provides for the needs of the many animals of the marsh ecosystem. At the end of June, we could still paddle up the western inlet   where the current seemed nonexistent—and under the Lake Ontario State Parkway, but it was hard going through the thick vegetation in a few places.

Paddling around Huckleberry Island to the west was harder but well worth the effort. Open water gradually disappears amid the thick stands of cattail as you pass the island and head southwest. Watch for a stately great blue heron or osprey perched on the dead tree overlooking the marsh from Huckleberry Island. We saw several dozen wood ducks back here; watched great blue herons fishing; happened on a secretive, rarely seen least bittern amid the cattails; and enjoyed the song of numerous marsh wrens—we even watched one slipping in and out of its hidden nest woven of, and perched among, the cattail leaves.

The least accessible section of the marsh extends east from the boat access, then around to the south and southwest along Island Cottage Road. We didn't get very far attempting to paddle through the thick water lilies here, but we watched about a dozen black terns swooping and diving for small fish in the shallows. While most terns have white on their heads and undersides, black terns are mostly black, with silvery wings. They nest on freshwater marshes but are fairly uncommon in most of their territory and always a treat to see. If they seem upset with your paddling, though, they probably have nests nearby; to protect their young, keep your distance.

In addition to bird life, we saw lots of painted turtles, particularly in the westernmost section, huge carp splashing at the water's surface, and fleeting glimpses of a few lunker largemouth bass. Indeed, the fishing looks excellent.

In the spring, Buck Pond would be a very different place. Without the tall cattails, you would see where you were heading as you explored the marshy inlets and coves. And without the floating and submerged vegetation, you could explore a much larger area. It might even be possible to make your way around Huckleberry Island.

When we visited here in the early morning, wind barely rippled the surface, and we used the opportunity to paddle out on Lake Ontario. Paddle under the bridge from the boat access (you have to duck). Depending on recent storms and water levels, you may have to carry your boat over a narrow sandbar (as we did), but then you are out on the wide-open expanse of the lake. Ontario, smallest of the Great Lakes, is still plenty big—fourteenth largest in the world and nearly as big as New Jersey. Paddling on it, you feel you are out on the ocean, not on a freshwater lake. We recommend paddling on Lake Ontario only during the calmest of conditions and only near shore. Along the shore, note the quantity of zebra mussel shells washed up from the lake. This recently introduced nuisance species continues to wreak havoc throughout the Great Lakes.

Getting There

Take the Long Pond Road exit off the Lake Ontario State Parkway (about 2.0 miles west of where Route 390 goes off to the south). Head north on Long Pond Road for 1.1 miles, then turn right onto Edgemere Drive. Stay on Edgemere for 1.3 miles, and just after crossing over the channel connecting Buck Pond to Lake Ontario, take a sharp right turn into the unimproved boat access. There is room here for about a dozen cars and room for a few others just past the access on a widened section of shoulder of Edgemere Drive.

Oak Orchard Creek
Alabama and Shelby

MAPS
    New York Atlas: Map 70
    USGS Quadrangles: Knowlesville, Medina, and Oakfield

INFORMATION
    Prominent fish species: Smallmouth bass and northern pike
    Section described: Six miles one way
    Iroquois National Wildlife Refuge: P.O. Box 517, Casey Road, Alabama, NY 14003; 716-948-5445. Visitor center is open from 8:00 A.M. to 4:00 P.M., Monday through Friday, and is open weekends during spring and fall waterfowl migrations.

If you want a truly wonderful experience in western New York, come to the Oak Orchard Creek area in the spring or fall when thousands of migrating geese, ducks, and swans descend on three wildlife refuges surrounding the creek. Nearly 90,000 Canada geese have descended here during spring migration. In the spring of 1994, bald eagles nested within sight of the visitor center and fledged three young. Only twice

Canada geese keep a lookout for danger as their downy goslings feed on tender springtime shoots.

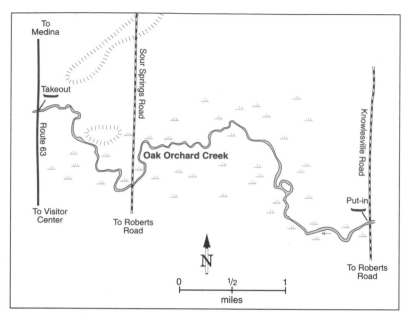

before have humans recorded the fledging of three eaglets from one nest. Prior to this extraordinary event, in 1993 the female laid only one egg, and that one did not hatch. For the several years prior to 1993, the eagle pair had fledged one young each year. Apparently, in 1994 there was a change of females. Because eagles mate for life, refuge personnel theorize that the original female probably died. In 1995, the pair returned to the nest quite early, perhaps because of the mild winter, and fledged two young.

The refuges include two state-owned Wildlife Management Areas, Oak Orchard on the east and Tonawanda on the west, with Iroquois National Wildlife Refuge sandwiched in between, comprising 20,000 acres of protected wetlands. Oak Orchard Creek meanders from east to west through the state's Oak Orchard Wildlife Management Area and through the Iroquois National Wildlife Refuge before turning north, heading for Lake Ontario. The section included here flows through Iroquois National Wildlife Refuge; no motors are allowed.

Paddle west from the boat access on Knowlesville Road, the dividing line between Oak Orchard Wildlife Management Area and Iroquois National Wildlife Refuge. One might be tempted to use two cars and make this a one-way trip. We advise against this except during higher water conditions or in the spring before aquatic plants choke the channel. Check stream conditions at the visitor center before embarking on such an adventure; sections may be impassable or extremely slow going. In mid-July, the lazy current allowed tons of duckweed—a minuscule, free-floating, flowering plant—to clog the waterway in several places, especially behind beaver dams and logjams, making paddling exceedingly difficult. Still, in spite of the duckweed and several downed trees, we loved paddling here among myriad plants, animals, and birds.

An alternative put-in spot exists upstream, in the Oak Orchard Wildlife Management Area at the bridge on Route 9 (the next road east of Knowlesville Road). We did not paddle this section of Oak Orchard Creek but did take notice of several downed trees blocking the waterway. Local fishermen confirmed that the waterway from Route 9 to Knowlesville Road abounds with downed timber and beaver dams, making passage difficult.

As you leave the boat access, look for the giant cottonwoods that send cotton balls carrying seeds on the wind drifting out over the water. The creek starts out about 30 feet wide but widens to 40 and 50 feet across as tree-lined banks of willow, ash, and silver maple give way to dense stands of cattails. Occasional beaver lodges and a few dams dot the waterway. As you pass, wood duck, coot, and other waterfowl scurry into the protective cattails, as common yellowthroats and hermit thrushes call from the dense undergrowth.

Beautiful stands of swamp rose and swamp milkweed grace the shores in places, and arrowhead and *Rumex* poke up from the shallows. During high water, side channels off the main creek flood the adjoining land, providing greater access to these very productive wetlands. Besides touring the area by boat, we recommend that you visit the waterfowl-viewing areas if you are here in the spring or fall.

Getting There

To get to the Iroquois National Wildlife Refuge Visitor Center take Route 77 north from I-90 (Exit 48A). At the junction with Route 63, continue straight on Route 63 north. Watch for the big green sign announcing the refuge and visitor center. Follow the sign, turning left onto Casey Road, continuing 0.8 mile to the center.

To get to Oak Orchard Creek, drive back out to Route 63. Turn left and jog north on Route 63, taking an immediate right onto Roberts Road. Pass Sour Spring Road on the left after 1.0 mile. Continue on for another 1.5 miles to the stop sign at Knowlesville Road. Turn left onto Knowlesville Road, and drive for 1.5 miles to the bridge over Oak Orchard Creek. There is room to park at most three or four cars.

Tonawanda Creek

Amherst, Clarence, Lockport, Newstead, Pendleton, and Royalton

MAPS
New York Atlas: Map 69
USGS Quadrangles: Clarence Center, Tonawanda East, and Wolcottsville

INFORMATION
Prominent fish species: Largemouth bass, smallmouth bass, northern pike, and walleye

Tonawanda Creek runs northward to Batavia from its source in Wyoming County south of Attica, then turns west, eventually emptying into the Niagara River just north of Buffalo. Before it reaches the river, however, it joins the Erie Canal in Pendleton (near the downstream end of this section). While some whitewater exists in the upper reaches of the creek, the 25-mile section included here drops well less than one foot per meandering mile, resulting in modest to no measurable current at most times of the year. Paddling upstream provided us with no great difficulty, but we did not paddle here during spring high water. We would suggest, however, that you use a two-car shuttle, or if you plan a round-trip, head upstream and let the current assist you on your return.

A study in contrasts, Tonawanda Creek alternates between ferns and fields, camps and woodlots, wooded shores and muddy banks, clear sailing and logjams. Beaver have contributed quite a bit to the logjams, some of which have been in place for awhile, as witnessed by the jewelweed growing out of some of the logs in the water. A series of jams just upstream from the Kelkenberg Road access were particularly annoying, given that we had to cross many slippery logs, both going upstream and back down. While houses do not crowd the banks in the upper reaches and few motorboats ply those waters, below Route 78 in Millersport development increases significantly.

Where tree density remains low, beautiful, aroma-laden honeysuckle alternates with dame's rockets—a widespread escape from cultivation—and irises along the banks. Willows lean out over the water, nearly closing the canopy. Wild grapevines drape over much of the shoreline vegetation. Three maples grow in profusion: mostly silver maple, along with lesser amounts of red maple and box elder. Other

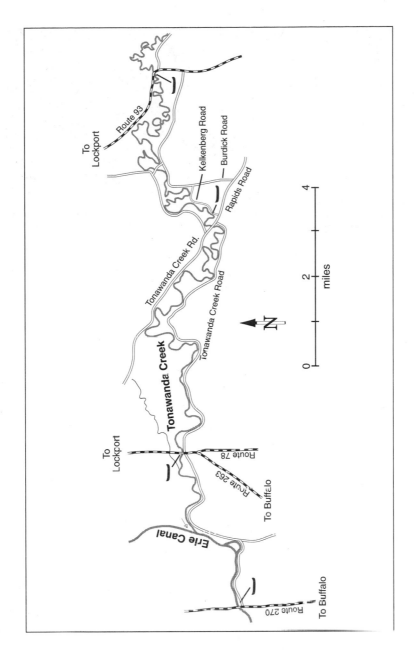

common trees include ash, basswood, white oak, black walnut, and cottonwood.

We never tired of the songs of the three dominant birds: northern oriole with its melodious, treetop song; red-winged blackbird singing "cong-ka-ree" from the tops of cattails and other low-growing vegetation; and the loud "witchety, witchety, witchety" sung from the under-

Western New York   145

Honeysuckle grows along the streambanks of Tonawanda Creek, along with many other flowering plants.

growth by the diminutive common yellowthroat, a small yellow warbler with a black mask across the forehead and through the eyes. Other birds included cardinal, grackle, song sparrow, mallard, robin, gray catbird, mourning dove, bobolink, American goldfinch, crow, eastern phoebe, black-capped chickadee, house wren, and blue jay.

Turtles basked on the many logs we passed, while groundhogs munched on the streamside grass. Raccoon tracks along the muddy banks told of nighttime foraging, and occasional discarded tires reminded us that many people do not recognize the nation's streams as recreation assets. As a light rain began, runoff from muddy banks and agricultural fields turned the clear water clay colored nearly instantly. One wonders where this huge silt burden eventually leads.

We never tired of the endless meanderings, although much of the shoreline looked the same. The stream straightened out in the lower reaches, and we made more progress. The last stretch between Millersport and Wendelville, particularly after the Erie Canal joins from the north, was not our favorite.

Still, this whole reach provides enjoyable paddling and a wonderful resource for the quiet-water enthusiast in an area with little else to offer. While glaciers carved out the Finger Lakes to the east and south and molded the Great Lakes, it left this area flat and without many ponds and small lakes. So we should all remain thankful for Tonawanda Creek and do our best to keep it untrammeled for future generations.

Getting There

There are several access points, starting from the upstream end: Route 93 bridge; from a bridge over a side creek on Kelkenberg Road (off Rapids Road); Route 78 in Millersport; and Route 270 in Wendelville. From Buffalo, to get to the Wendelville access, take Route 263 north (Buffalo-Millersport Road); turn left onto Route 270 (Campbell Boulevard); turn right onto Tonawanda Creek Road just before the bridge. The access is on the left just after the turn, right next to a bingo parlor.

To get to the Millersport access, start as before on Route 263, but instead of turning onto Route 270, continue on Route 263 to its junction with Route 78. Turn left onto Route 78, drive a few tenths of a mile, and cross the bridge over Tonawanda Creek. Immediately after crossing the bridge, turn left onto the widened shoulder; be careful here when entering and leaving the highway, as traffic is usually horrendous. Alternatively, you can reach this access by taking I-90 to the Route 78 exit (Exit 49) and traveling north.

To reach the other two access points, take Tonawanda Creek Road south (meaning it's on the south side of the creek as opposed to one on the north side). From Route 78, drive east for 3.9 miles, to the junction with Rapids Road, just after Goodrich Road enters from the right. Do not cross the bridge but stay right and continue for 3.2 miles more until you reach a T at Rapids Road. Turn right, then take an almost-immediate left onto Kelkenberg Road. From here, it is about a tenth of a mile to the Kelkenberg Road access on the left.

To get to the Route 93 access, continue on Kelkenberg Road another 1.2 miles to the junction with Burdick Road. Turn left onto Burdick Road and continue on for 3.5 miles to Route 93 (when Block Church Road enters from the left along the way, Burdick Road changes back to Tonawanda Creek Road). At Route 93, turn left and go 0.6 mile to the bridge, where you can launch from either side.

Allegheny Reservoir
Cold Spring, Elko, and South Valley

MAPS
  New York Atlas: Map 41
  USGS Quadrangles: Little Valley, Red House, and Steamburg
INFORMATION
  Area: N/A
  Prominent fish species: Smallmouth bass, muskellunge, northern
    pike, walleye
  Camping: Allegany State Park; 716-354-2545
  Seneca-Iroquois National Museum: On Allegany Indian Reserva-
    tion in Salamanca; 716-945-1738

Located almost entirely within the Allegany Indian Reservation,
Allegheny Reservoir represents one of the few quiet-water paddling
resources in southwestern New York. A dam just over the border in
Pennsylvania caused inundation of a many-mile stretch of the scenic
Allegheny River. The river begins in Pennsylvania, swings northward
into New York, flows west through New York for about 50 miles, exits
into Pennsylvania through the reservoir, and eventually joins the
Monongahela to form the Ohio River at Pittsburgh.

Portions of the reservoir's eastern shore, including the boat-launch
area, belong to Allegany State Park. This huge state park includes a
nice camping area, which fills up nearly every day of the summer, and
two popular swimming areas: Quaker Beach on Quaker Lake, just a
mile from the boat access, and Red House Beach on Red House Lake,
next to the Allegany State Park campground.

Leaving behind the Norway spruce, with their drooping branches,
and large white pine at the boat access, paddle to the left over to the
Quaker Lake outfall to look at the water cascading over the dam. Along
the way, note the groves of pine on the hillsides. Scrub vegetation,
including lots of willow, grows down to the waterline along the left
shoreline, while tall silver maple, white pine, hickory, oak, and hemlock climb the hillsides along the right shoreline.

Back by the boat access, two coves appear on the right just before
you get to the main reservoir. Willow dominates the shoreline here as
well, with silver maple farther back and basswood and aspen on higher ground. The first cove to the right contains many camps and boats.

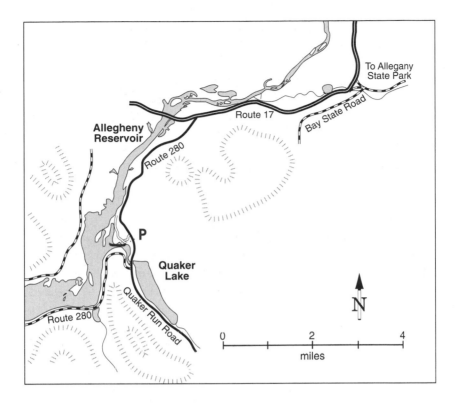

A peninsula forms the far shore, but during periods of high water, the peninsula gets cut off, forming an island. The camp on the high spot of the peninsula includes ducks, chickens, and mounds of trash. The second peninsula is a lot more scenic.

Moving out into the main reservoir, we noted that the shoreline in this area remains pretty much intact, punctuated only occasionally with camps. Wooded hillsides receding into the distance provide a scenic backdrop. Upon entering the reservoir, three choices immediately confront you: paddling upstream toward Salamanca, downstream toward Pennsylvania, or to the opposite shore. No matter which direction you choose, you should enjoy miles of scenery and plenty of wildlife.

When we paddled here during high water in early July, there was still barely any current out on the main reservoir. A breeze, just suffi cient to ripple the water's surface, blew us gently upstream, while a northern cardinal called from the dense undergrowth. American red starts, acting more like flycatchers than warblers, darted out to snare insects on the wing. Barn swallows and tree swallows skimmed the water's surface, doing their best to reduce the hordes of insects produced by these productive waters. While it was a treat to paddle here under these calm conditions, don't be deceived—any substantial wind will whip the surface of this large body of water to a foamy froth.

Some warnings: the state requires all people in boats less than 16 feet and in all canoes to wear PFDs; the state would like all of us to take precautions against importing exotic species such as Eurasian milfoil, water chestnut, and zebra mussels into Allegheny Reservoir and other nearby bodies of water.

By all means, especially if you have children with you, visit the Seneca-Iroquois National Museum in Salamanca.

Getting There

Limited-access Route 17, the Southern Tier Expressway, follows the course of the Allegheny River for many miles in southern New York. Get off west of Salamanca at Exit 18. Follow Route 280 south. Just before reaching Quaker Lake, follow signs on the right for Friends Boat Launch, Allegany State Park. There is no charge for the plentiful parking available here.

To get to the campground at Allegany State Park, from Route 17 use either Exit 20 at Salamanca or Exit 19 to the west and follow the signs to the state park.

To get to the Seneca-Iroquois National Museum, use Exit 20 from Route 17 at Salamanca.

Northern
New York

Grafton Lakes and Dunham Reservoir
Grafton

MAPS
   New York Atlas: Map 67
   USGS Quadrangle: Grafton

INFORMATION
   Areas: Long Pond, 122 acres; Second Pond, 31 acres; Mill Pond, 19 acres; Shaver Pond, 44 acres; Dunham Reservoir, 91 acres
   Prominent fish species: Smallmouth bass, largemouth bass (Second and Mill Ponds), pickerel, rainbow trout (Long and Second Ponds), brown trout (Long and Second Ponds), brook trout (Shaver Pond)
   Information: Grafton Lakes State Park, P.O. Box 163, Grafton, NY 12082; 518-279-1155

Grafton Lakes State Park contains five paddlable bodies of water: Long Pond, Second Pond, Mill Pond, Shaver Pond, and Dunham Reservoir, of which we paddled all except the smallest. We enjoyed our paddling here very much, and area residents should take note that the park lies close enough to Albany and Troy that you could come here on a long lunch break from work.

The large beach area at the southwest end of Long Pond gets crowded on nice summer weekends, so you may want to schedule your visit midweek or outside of the main summer season. The park does not allow motors of any kind (including electric) on Long, Second, Mill, and Shaver Ponds; they permit electric motors only on Dunham Reservoir. Unfortunately, quite a bit of trash had accumulated along most of the shorelines of these ponds and in the water.

We found Shaver Pond and Dunham Reservoir the most enjoyable to paddle, in part because they are less accessible. You have to carry into Shaver Pond about a half mile along a very easy nature trail, which

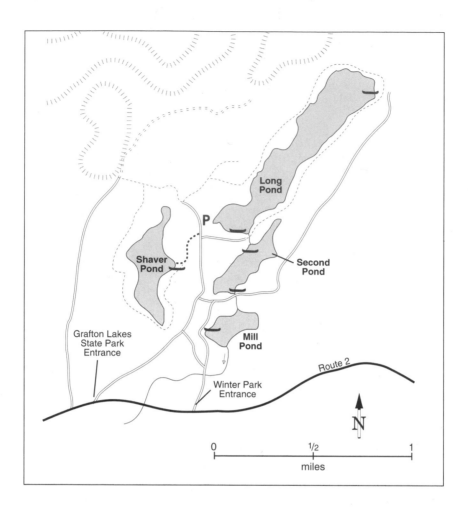

is suitable for a portage cart. Pick up a nature guide to the trees and other natural features of the Shaver Pond trail.

Dunham Reservoir has access at either end. Be sure to explore the eastern end of the reservoir and the winding inlet stream, which you can paddle for a quarter to a half mile before reaching quickwater and rocks. Paddling under the bridge, you initially enter a marshy area thick with grasses, sedges, and other marsh plants. When we paddled here in late April as dusk approached, spring peepers regaled us (and potential mates) with their high-pitched peeping. Mallards paddled about in the shallows. Several Canada geese eyed us warily from a likely nesting site. Several kingfishers announced their presence with their rattlelike call as they flew ahead of us. And beaver were out enjoying the just-beginning new growth of spring.

At the western end of Dunham Reservoir, you will see extensive berming and a dam. The reservoir was constructed as a water supply for the city of Troy. It supplied Troy's drinking water until the 1960s when the reservoir was transferred to the state to become a state park.

Beaver have overrun these ponds and appear to be eating themselves out of house and home. At the time of our visit, felled trees covered so much ground in some places that it looked like a logging operation. If you paddle here early in the morning or in the evening, you will likely get a good look at beaver at work.

Grafton Lakes State Park is a great spot to study clubmosses. Several different species of *Lycopodium* carpet extensive stretches of shoreline around most of the ponds. Clubmosses are among the most primitive vascular plants (vascular plants have xylem and phloem that conduct water and nutrients). Several species have the appearance of tiny trees, thus the common names "ground pine" and "ground cedar." Other species creep along the ground on long stems with short leaves extending from all sides. The soft branching stems of staghorn clubmoss resemble the velvet antlers of deer in spring. In the age of dinosaurs, relatives of these clubmosses grew as large as trees.

These ponds are all undeveloped and surrounded by primarily deciduous woods, including such species as red oak, beech, four dif-

Getting ready to head out on our first paddle of the season in late April.

ferent birches—paper, gray, black, and yellow—black cherry, red maple, and sugar maple. Along the shore, blueberry bushes grow alongside taller shadbush, both of which provide edible berries later in the summer. We watched an osprey ply the water for its next meal. Osprey often hover in the air—body tilted up slightly and wings flapping more quickly to maintain a stationary position—peering into the water for fish. Osprey are superb fishers, far better than their larger cousin, the bald eagle.

This is great place for families that enjoy both hiking and paddling. Easy trails extend around Long Pond and Shaver Pond, and several trails head off in various directions throughout the park. Be sure to pick up a trail map as you enter the park. There are also frequent guided nature walks and other events. Camping is not permitted.

Getting There

From the Albany/Troy area, take Route 2 east toward Clums Corner and Grafton. At the traffic light where Route 278 comes in from the left, note your mileage. To reach Dunham Reservoir, turn right onto Reservoir Road (gravel) after 5.1 miles, and continue for 0.6 mile to a pull-over area and gate. You can park here and carry your canoe down to the western end of the reservoir. There is space for only a few cars off the road here, but there is additional room along the side of the road. To reach the put-in at the east end of the reservoir, get back on Route 2, and take all available right turns. You will see an access just off the road before the road crosses the inlet stream.

To reach Long, Second, and Shaver Ponds, stay on Route 2 until you get to the well-marked main park entrance on the left. Follow the park road past the gate (there is a four-dollar/vehicle entrance fee during the summer), and follow signs to the boat launch area onto Long and Second Ponds. For Shaver Pond, park in the main parking area, and take the trail from the southwest end of the parking lot to Shaver.

Mill Pond, Second Pond, and Long Pond can also be reached via a town road without going through the park gate. Follow Route 2 to the center of Grafton (0.6 mile from the main park entrance), and turn at the sign indicating winter/maintenance entrance. You will pass the access onto Mill Pond on your right, Second Pond on your left, and the northwest end of Long Pond on the left near the dead end of the road.

Fish Creek (Saratoga Lake)
Saratoga and Saratoga Springs

MAPS
> **New York Atlas:** Maps 80 and 81
> **USGS Quadrangles:** Quaker Springs and Schuylerville

INFORMATION
> **Prominent fish species:** Largemouth bass, smallmouth bass, northern pike, and walleye

A huge stand of large willows and a RV park greet you at the boat access at the northern outlet of Saratoga Lake as it forms Fish Creek. We had originally intended to turn south under the bridge and to paddle down into Saratoga Lake, but it receives too much water-ski and Jet-ski traffic for quiet-water paddlers. Instead, we recommend that you paddle Fish Creek in its meanderings toward the Hudson River. Because of dams and occasional shallow rapids in a few spots, you cannot paddle it the whole way, at least at midsummer water levels. We include two sections here, separated by a short section of rapids and falls next to one of the Route 29 bridges. If there seems to be a lot of traffic on the creek, we recommend that you put in near the Hudson, just off Route 32 in the town of Victory, instead of at Saratoga Lake.

We paddled here twice, once in the spring and once in the summer. When we paddled out from Saratoga Lake in midspring, a bass fishing tournament had just begun, so we had to contend with dozens of 150-horsepower bass boats roaring up and down the creek, rushing to the next hot spot, of course putting the fish down from all the commotion. Because these boats hydroplane at high speeds and displace little water, they also leave very little wake. In order to avoid getting run over, we stayed along the edges of the creek and, not unexpectedly, did not see much wildlife in the heavily traveled portions of Fish Creek.

With springtime high water, however, we could paddle back into narrow creeks and coves where we saw numerous basking turtles and surprised a male wood duck in full breeding plumage right beneath a wood duck nesting box. We also saw mallards and black ducks—which sure beat the drowned tires, plastic buckets, and broken-up docks that mar the first few miles of Fish Creek.

About three and a half miles from Saratoga Lake, a nice little creek goes off to the right. Vines hang out over the water, and you have

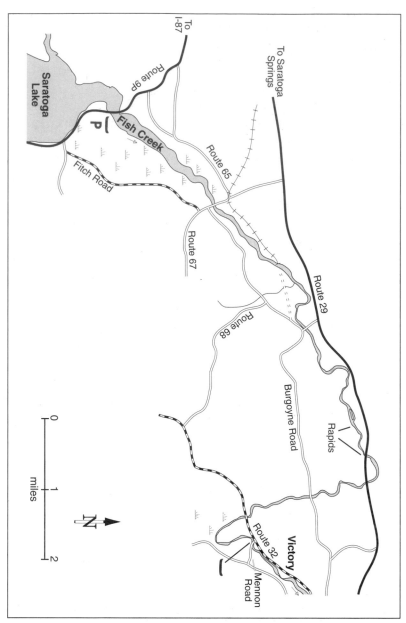

to thread your way through the narrow passageway. We found many ducks feeding and a pair of eastern phoebes nesting under a low bridge. Cardinals called "bir-dy, bir-dy, bir-dy" from the thickets, and red-winged blackbirds sang "cong-ka-ree" from the reeds. Once we got this far from Saratoga Lake, the number of boats dwindled to zero.

The lower portion of Fish Creek, closer to the Hudson, also receives much less boat traffic. We put in at Victory in midsummer and paddled upstream to the more western of two Route 29 bridges, where rapids block further passage upstream.

In contrast with Fish Creek's spilling over into broad marshes as it flows out of Saratoga Lake, low banks contain the lower section of Fish Creek. Dense grapevines drape over streamside willows and silver maples all along the creek, closing in much of the canopy. Great blue herons, as many as three at a time, stood poised over the water on downed trees, taking flight as we passed. We threaded our way upstream through this maze, listening to cardinal, eastern phoebe, gray catbird, brown thrasher, and mockingbird songs from the undergrowth. Barn and tree swallows dipped over the water for a drink, a spotted sandpiper bobbed along the shore, and a belted kingfisher paced us up the waterway.

We had no trouble negotiating the current of midsummer, until we reached the more western Route 29 bridge over the creek. Here, a small falls and rapids blocked our way upstream. We suppose that with two cars, you could paddle from Saratoga Lake to Victory, walking your boat through the shallows. As we drifted lazily back down to Victory, listening to the haunting song of the mourning dove and the high-pitched "pee-o-wee" of the eastern wood pewee off in the woods, we reveled in our solitude so close to crowded Saratoga Lake.

Serviceberry blooms in the early spring along the banks of Fish Creek.

Getting There

To reach the upstream section of Fish Creek as it flows out of Saratoga Lake, from Saratoga Springs or from I-87, take Route 9P east. From I-87, it is 2.0 miles to the iron bridge over the outlet of Saratoga Lake. After crossing the bridge, the boat access is immediately on the left.

To get to the downstream section, from Schuylerville, take Route 4 south. Turn right onto Route 32 near the south end of downtown. Take Route 32 1.3 miles to Victory. Turn left onto Mennon Road, cross the bridge in 0.1 mile, and park on the right (southwest corner).

The Playful River Otter

If you paddle the more remote lakes, ponds, marshes, and rivers of New York, and if you get out on the water early in the morning or remain out as dusk approaches, sooner or later a river otter—or perhaps a family of these adorable mammals—will bob into view. We have seen dozens of otters throughout the state: mostly in the Adirondacks but some much farther south and even in the highly visited waters of Harriman State Park, 45 minutes from New York City. Their playful antics, friendly facial expressions, and masterful swimming make them one of our favorite species.

The river otter, *Lutra canadensis,* once inhabited every watershed in New York and ranged virtually throughout North America. By the late 1800s, otter populations had declined significantly because of trapping for the mammal's valuable pelts. Because they eat at the top of the food chain, otters also suffer from pollution and toxic chemicals in the environment, such as heavy metals, DDT derivatives, dioxin, and PCBs. They do not thrive in polluted water.

In 1936, New York passed legislation to protect otters—totally prohibiting trapping for 9 years, then providing for an annual trapping season, to be determined each year by the Department of Environmental

Conservation. As a result, the otter has returned to New York's waterways and continues to expand its range. Their distribution has roughly doubled during the past 30 years, and in recent years, people have occasionally sighted otters on Long Island and in the western part of the state—areas that until recently had no otters.

River otters grow quite large. Adults can reach four feet in length and weigh up to 25 pounds. They have long thin bodies and a relatively thick, sharply tapered tail. Their dense fur, long prized by trappers, is dark brown above and gives way to lighter colors on the belly and throat. Their long, distinct facial whiskers probably aid in navigating or finding food underwater.

Otters have adapted well to their primarily aquatic environment. Their noses and ears close when underwater, and their webbed toes aid in swimming. Otters swim fast enough to catch trout in open water, though they usually opt for slower-moving suckers, minnows, crayfish, tadpoles, and salamanders. When hunting, otters come up for air every 30 seconds or so, though they can remain underwater for up to two minutes. When they come up to the surface, their heads generally pop up way above the surface and they look around—quite different from

beavers and muskrats, which barely rise above the water's surface.

Though primarily adapted for water, otters do pretty well on land as well, their undulating gait typical of members of the weasel family. Clocked at up to 18 miles per hour on land, they will travel as much as 100 miles overland in search of new territory. Otters generally place their dens at the water's edge, with an underwater entrance. Natural cavities under tree roots or an abandoned beaver lodge may be used.

Otters consume smaller fish and crayfish at the surface of the water, while they take larger prey to shore or to a protruding rock. In shallow water, you may see just an otter's tail sticking out of the water as it roots around in the mud for food. Ingenious hunters, otters sometimes herd fish into shallows where they easily catch their prey. They may even punch a hole in a beaver dam—allowing the water to escape—then wade in and feast on fish flopping in the shallow water. Because otters hunt so successfully, they have plenty of time to play—a justly famous otter trait.

The young of many mammal species play. Animal behaviorists believe such play provides practice for future hunting, territorial interactions, and courtship. But otters don't stop playing when they reach adulthood. They roll in the water chasing one another or climb repeatedly up on a mud or snowbank and slide down into the water (though otter slides are not quite as common as children's books seem to imply). Animal behaviorists have not yet found reasons for otters' play other than just to have fun.

Otters mate in the late winter or early spring, but often birth does not follow until almost a year later. As with many members of the weasel family, implantation of embryos is delayed in otters, and development stops until the following fall or winter. Otters give birth to two to four cubs in a well-protected den any time between November and April (usually February to April). The cubs emerge fully furred but with eyes closed and no teeth. They will not venture outside of their den for about three months, and they remain completely dependent on their mother for at least six months. Though the mother provides all care for the young cubs, the father may rejoin the family and help with care and teaching after they reach about six months of age. The young become sexually mature after two years.

Though otters are curious animals and relatively bold, keep your distance when observing them. Interference from humans may cause them to move away and search for more-remote streams or ponds. If you are interested in river otters or want to help recovery efforts, contact the New York River Otter Project, Inc., P.O. Box 39512, Rochester, NY 14604; 716-771-2113. Working with the New York DEC, the nonprofit New York River Otter Project hopes to reintroduce 180 to 270 otters in nine selected areas of the state between 1995 and 2005. Each release costs roughly $1,000; your tax-deductible contributions are gratefully accepted.

Northwest Bay of Lake George
Bolton

MAPS
New York Atlas: Map 89
USGS Quadrangles: Shelving Rock and Silver Bay

INFORMATION
Prominent fish species: Largemouth bass, smallmouth bass, northern pike, landlocked salmon, lake trout, and rainbow trout

Layered hills and forested islands—grand vistas of the north country—contribute to Lake George's very scenic setting and help attract multitudes of vacationers to its beautiful shores. The largest lake in the Adirondack Park, Lake George draws many large boats to its deep, clear waters. We recommend that you not paddle out onto the main lake to compete with the Jet-skiers, water-skiers, and speedboats. Because the long, relatively narrow lake also attracts wind, huge swells can build up over miles of lake, making treacherous paddling conditions for open boats.

The fishing access at the northern inlet into Northwest Bay allows cartop boats only. You can paddle to the left (north) up the creek for

Yellow pond lily grows in the shallow waters of Northwest Bay.

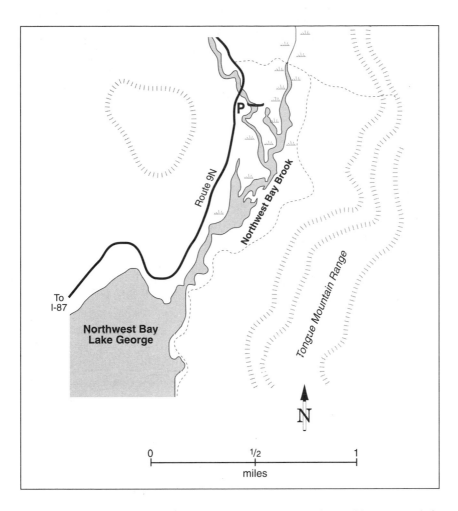

about a tenth of a mile where you will encounter lots of beaver activity, or you can paddle downstream into Northwest Bay Brook and out into Northwest Bay. However, before you paddle out into the bay, take time to explore the sinuous channel of the east fork of Northwest Bay Brook. You will have to elbow your way through pondweed, water celery, bur reed and other aquatic vegetation, but you should find a lot more solitude here than downstream.

Yellow pond lily covers the channel in places, and grasses and ferns cover the banks where alders haven't elbowed everything else out of the way. Tall trees, including lots of red and silver maples, hang over the alders and grassy banks. Farther down the lake, after the marshes disappear, tall white pines and hemlocks grace the shores.

In several places along the creek, you will see large beaver lodges, along with downed trees over the water, and many cuttings. Dragonflies mated on the wing along the protected, placid waters of the bay brook as we paddled here, and a large snapping turtle cruised by just under the water's surface. As we rounded a little island on the western shore just before the bay, we saw a sign on a dying white pine that said Caution, Rattlesnakes. Unlawful to Disturb or Take. The land belongs to The Nature Conservancy to protect a rare northern population of the timber rattlesnake that probably dens in the rockfall on this hillside.

Species become rare on the edges of their range. Because Lake George and Champlain Valley represent the northern extension of the timber rattlesnake's range, very few are found in isolated populations. Rattlesnakes probably arose in the southwestern U.S. and northern Mexico where they speciated and radiated outward, ranging as far as southern Argentina and southern Canada. About 30 species occur in a wide variety of habitats from sea level to over 10,000 feet. As you go north, their preferred habitats get closer and closer to sea level, probably in response to colder temperatures at higher elevations.

Two species occur in New York: the timber rattler (*Crotalus horridus*) occurs in isolated populations over much of the southern half of the state, while the massasauga (*Sistrurus catenatus*) occurs in two isolated populations near Lake Erie. As you move southwest, toward its evolutionary beginnings, more species appear. Three species occur in Missouri, 8 in Texas, and 11 in Arizona. A total of 15 species—half of all rattlesnakes species—occur in the U.S.

Forested hillsides surround Northwest Bay.

People fear rattlesnakes, probably because of their famed hypodermic venom injection system, the most highly developed poison delivery system among snakes. Indeed, some rattlesnakes stand their ground when aroused and vigorously defend themselves. People have eliminated them from much of their range through a combination of habitat destruction and direct killing. However, even with their sometimes lethal venom, rarely do rattlesnakes kill humans. Many more people die from lightning strikes or allergic reactions to bee stings.

As members of the pit viper family, rattlers have two small pits about midway between the nostrils and the eyes. (If you can actually see these pits, you have definitely gotten too close; look at them with binoculars.) These pits sense infrared energy and allow the snake to distinguish between warm organisms and the cooler environment. Rattlers dine mainly on rodents but will also take birds, frogs, and lizards.

Snakes grow throughout their lives, rapidly at first and slowing later. As the snake grows, it must shed its stretched skin, composed of dead cells. Each time it sheds, the rattlesnake adds a segment to its rattle. Young snakes may shed twice or more per year, while older snakes shed once, or not at all, each year. If the button is missing from the end of the rattle, it and possibly other segments have broken off. So the number of segments has little to do with the age of the snake.

Most people shun snakes of any stripe, and we understand if you choose to ignore this hillside. The Nature Conservancy does not want people traipsing all over this habitat, either. Unless the urge to look for them is irresistible, we recommend that you stay in your boat and explore the wonderful marshes of Northwest Bay Brook. Let us know if you find snakes here, but please do not molest them in any way.

Getting There

From I-87, get off at the Bolton Landing exit (Exit 24) for Lake George. Turn right and travel downhill for 4.7 miles to Route 9N. Turn left, and drive north on Route 9N for 4.3 miles to the Northwest Bay Brook fishing access on the right. The boat access appears abruptly: watch for a Driveway sign at 4.2 miles, with the access 0.1 mile farther.

Canada Lake and West Lake

Caroga

MAPS
  New York Atlas: Map 79
  USGS Quadrangles: Canada Lake and Caroga Lake

INFORMATION
  Area: N/A
  Prominent fish species: Stocked lake trout and brown trout
  Camping: Caroga Lake Campground; 518-835-4241

Canada Lake and West Lake mark the southwest corner of the Adirondack Park, and while the state owns huge tracts of forest all around the lake and its connected waterways, it does not own any significant fraction of the shoreline. Private inholdings abound, and with them wall-to-wall camps along the shoreline, bringing significant motorboat and Jet-ski traffic to the waterways. Consequently, we avoided the heavily developed eastern arm of Canada Lake and concentrated on West Lake, the southern shore of Canada Lake, and Lily Lake down to Stewart Landing. If you don't mind paddling by an occasional fishing camp or

Adirondack Peaks hover over the north end of Canada Lake on the southwest corner of the park.

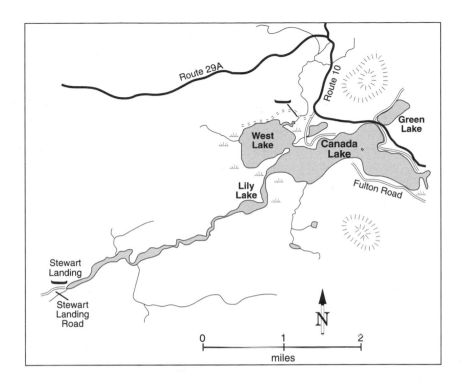

Route 29A

Route 10

Green
Lake

West
Lake

Canada
Lake

Lily
Lake

Fulton Road

Stewart
Landing

Stewart
Landing
Road

N

0   1   2

miles

summer home—particularly when you get near Stewart Landing—you can still have a wonderful paddling experience through scenic waterways chock-full of interesting plants and wildlife.

Paddling out from the boat access through the winding, twisting waterway leading to West Lake, with grasses and alders lining the banks, you wonder if any large bodies of water actually exist in this area. Muskrats break from harvesting the streamside grass, song sparrows sing from the undergrowth, and red-winged blackbirds flutter from the water's edge as you paddle by. Eventually you emerge in the northeast corner of West Lake. Although about a dozen houses appear on the northwestern shore, the picturesque southern shore remains unblighted. Paddle the shoreline counterclockwise, wind permitting, to get to the pine-covered peninsula that marks the entrance to Canada Lake.

Although hemlocks and white pines appear in good numbers along the shoreline, oaks, sugar maples, yellow birch, cherry, and other deciduous trees dominate the hillsides surrounding the lake. In places, a dense understory of balsam fir competes for light, stretching for the canopy. As you round the point into Canada Lake, notice the extensive marsh along the southern shore. We saw a deer here, taking a morning drink, as we headed for Lily Lake. Several loons plied the waters, but we arrived too early in the season to see them with young.

As we entered long, narrow Lily Lake, a chorus of songbirds serenaded us, announcing their breeding territories; white-throated sparrows with their "Old Sam Peabody, Peabody, Peabody" called from the undergrowth. Flickers drummed out holes for themselves and other cavity nesters, including wood ducks, hooded mergansers, and tree swallows, all of which we saw as we paddled down to Stewart Landing. Ducks appeared in profusion, some just migrating through, others looking to nest: hooded and common mergansers, wood duck, ring-necked duck, mallard, and black duck. We watched two osprey survey the water for fish near the surface; one swooped down and snatched up a fish, carrying it off to its aerie in a dead tree overhanging the water. Other prominent birds included blue jay, kingfisher, great blue heron, and killdeer.

The boat access at Stewart Landing surprised us—though it shouldn't have with the name "Landing"—as it is not on the map. After a few hours of paddling, mostly without other boats, we picked our way back to West Lake with care. Much of the passage along the way suffers from shallow water with many rocks. Stick to the center of these shallow waterways at times of low water, and you shouldn't have too much difficulty.

Getting There

From Gloversville, take Route 29A west to Caroga Lake. Start measuring mileage when Route 10 joins 29A in Caroga Lake. Pass through the small town of Canada Lake, with the waters of Green Lake on the right and Canada Lake on the left. At 4.3 miles, turn left onto Point Breeze Road. Immediately after turning off, take the right fork, West Lake Road, and you will reach the boat access in 0.3 mile. The access is on a small creek that leads to the northeast end of West Lake.

Alternatively, the blacktopped Stewart Landing Road leads to Stewart Landing from the west. Take Route 119 to Stewart Landing Road, and follow it to the end.

South Bay

Dresden, Fort Ann, and Whitehall

MAPS
   New York Atlas: Map 89
   USGS Quadrangle: Whitehall, NY/VT

INFORMATION
   Area: 1,100 acres
   Prominent fish species: Largemouth bass, smallmouth bass, northern pike, and walleye

South Bay lies along the western edge of the Champlain Canal at the southern terminus of Lake Champlain. Given that Route 22 crosses its northern reaches, we did not expect it would merit inclusion in this book. A pleasant surprise awaited us, however, as we gazed down to the southern end of the waterway. Gorgeous cliffs and hillsides receding into the distance beckoned us to paddle south.

Note the warnings about picking up "hitchhikers" at the boat access. This does not refer to the two-legged variety but instead

Steep cliffs and layered hillsides line the shores on the south end of the bay.

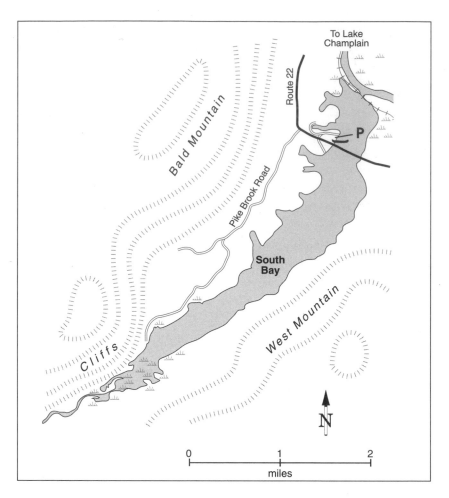

includes three serious aquatic pests: Eurasian milfoil, water chestnut, and zebra mussels. All three can easily hitch rides on boat trailers, in bilges, and even on canoe and kayak hulls, to be deposited later in the next waterway. South Bay and Lake Champlain already suffer infestation from these. Biologists worry that these three alien species, introduced from Europe and Asia to the East Coast by humans, will eventually infect most bodies of water in the East and Midwest. They arrived without their natural predators and now crowd out native species. As you paddle down South Bay, check out the first bay on the right (west). Along with a huge beaver lodge and a great blue heron patrolling the shallows, we found the large inlet choked with water chestnut, *Trapa natans*—yes, the plant that produces water chestnuts. Its rosettes eventually grow so thick that they push up over other aquatic vegetation, limiting access to light and smothering it. We tried to

Dense rosettes of water chestnut have clogged the northern coves of South Bay.

paddle through the sea of water chestnut—as we have done countless times before with stands water lilies or even pickerelweed—but to no avail. It was like trying to paddle over dew-covered grass.

As we paddled to the south end of South Bay at the end of July 1995, the first tentative rosettes of water chestnut had started to show up there, presaging the eventual onslaught. Eurasian milfoil already had made its way to the south end and, indeed, all the way up the inlet creeks. This underwater plant with its slender, lacy foliage also crowds out native vegetation by taking up root space. We do not believe that it poses anywhere near the threat posed by water chestnut, mainly because it has resided in these waters for several years, and where it grows we still usually find dense stands of water lilies, pickerelweed, bur reed, and many others.

We did not see zebra mussels when we paddled here, although they have likely made it to South Bay. They stick to underwater structures in many layers and threaten intake pipes and other human-made structures. Unless we can find an effective control mechanism that does not harm native species, zebra mussels will infest most waterways in the U.S. Ironically, this tiny mussel filters out microscopic plankton and other organisms, clarifying the water. Zebra mussels may filter out so many microscopic organisms that the whole food chain gets depleted, ultimately reducing fish populations significantly.

While our concern about alien pests continues unabated, they did not spoil our paddle here. We still enjoyed seeing stately great blue herons standing knee-deep in every bay. Near the Route 22 bridge, fields march down to the water's edge, but farther down the bay, fields give way to layered, forested hillsides and high cliffs. We wondered if peregrine falcons ever nested here; they would have had a spectacular view from their cliff-side aeries.

A great horned owl startled us as it flew off with powerful wing beats from a bankside willow. We explored all the deep inlets, choked with aquatic vegetation, that dot the western shore, paddling back in and among the cattails, bur reed, pickerelweed, yellow pond lily, and tuberous water lily. Rufous-sided towhees called from the under-growth, and barn swallows dipped low over the water.

We paddled up the creek on the south end, with its gorgeous cliffs, in among the water lilies, pondweed, water celery, and grasses. We paddled through thick stands of pickerelweed into a swamp with alders and cattails, cardinal flower, and purple loosestrife. Two new aquatic plants emerged in great mats: yellow-flowered bladderwort and one of the small yellow pond lilies—*Nuphar rubrodiscum.* Silver maple continued as the dominant tree species. We watched large schools of fish swim in the clear water of the creek, in sharp contrast with the milky water of the bay.

We paddled back to the boat access, again hugging the picturesque western shore, wondering what we will find here next year. Because of the huge expanse of water, South Bay often suffers from strong winds, the same winds that carry water chestnut and Eurasian milfoil to the far reaches of the waterway. But that same wind should keep water chest-nut piled up in protected areas. Would it be possible to harvest these masses with an aquatic harvester? We should pursue containment, because South Bay would become a far different—and disappointing—place if all the native aquatic plants were to disappear.

Getting There

From Whitehall next to the Vermont border, at the junction of Routes 4 and 22, travel north on Route 22, cross the bridge over South Bay, and take the second right, which leads to the boat access. The access is 2.8 miles from Whitehall.

Putnam Pond

Ticonderoga

MAPS
  New York Atlas: Map 89
  USGS Quadrangle: Graphite
INFORMATION
  Area: 330 acres
  Prominent fish species: No information available

Nestled in the Pharaoh Lake Wilderness—with high Adirondack peaks all around—Putnam Pond sports a scenic campground, lots of hiking trails—some accessible only by water—and no development. Because the hiking trails and the surrounding wilderness, including Pharaoh Mountain, attract hundreds of hikers all summer long and well into the fall, try to visit Putnam Pond in the spring or fall; if you must travel here in the summer, avoid weekends. When we paddled here in mid-September, we shared the water with three other canoes.

Putnam Pond contains many beautiful features. Smooth granite boulders rise from the pond's surface and protrude from the shore. About a dozen widely separated, water-accessible, scenic campsites spread along the shore, seemingly wherever it is flat—and finding a flat space along the edge of the Pharaoh Lake Wilderness is no mean feat. Most include fire grates, picnic tables, and outhouses. As you paddle out from the grassy boat-launch area, the point on the right harbors a wonderful picnic area. The cove around to the right, filled with pickerelweed and other aquatic vegetation, leads to the main campground.

On the drive in, towering hemlocks line the way in places; around the pond, the occasional dense stands of hemlock include considerably smaller trees. Red maple, northern white cedar, and paper birch line the shore, interrupted occasionally by dense stands of red pine. Large white pine stand farther back from shore. Marshy coves occur in several places, and way down on the southwest shore a nearly pure stand of tamarack covers a boggy island. Other, larger islands have more diverse tree species, along with groups of flat granite boulders, perfect for picnics. Be careful when paddling near shore, because the jagged surfaces of some barely submerged boulders are incompatible with smooth boat hulls.

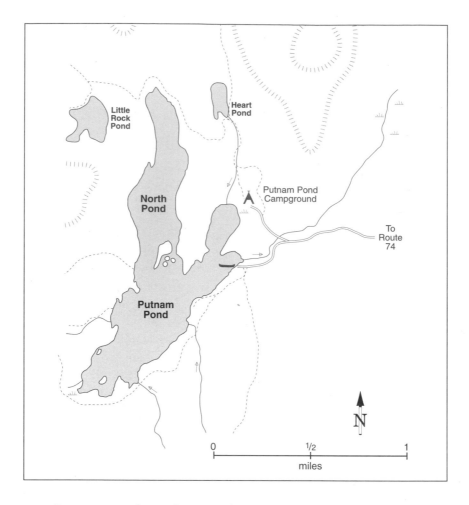

Large areas of aquatic vegetation accumulate later in the season—
mostly water shield, along with some fragrant water lily, yellow pond
lily, pickerelweed, and water celery.

In places, mussel shells litter the shore and pond bottom, probably
left there by foraging raccoons. The heavy visitation has not driven out
the healthy beaver population. Paddling along the western shore, we
were taken by the large numbers of downed trees, floating and submerged, felled by these industrious waterway engineers. In the early
evening, we saw two beaver swimming along. As we approached, they
slapped the water's surface with their broad, flat tails to show their
annoyance at our intrusion before diving for cover, only to surface a
short distance away and repeat the ritual. Besides the beaver's tail slap-
ping, several red squirrels and a kingfisher scolded us as we paddled by
their pond-side perches.

The boggy south end of Putnam Pond.

Two loons cruised around the center of the lower pond, and several flocks of ducks, including wood ducks, fed in the shallows. A family of red-breasted mergansers watched us warily from close range as we glided by, in stark contrast to the chaotic fluttering across the water's surface that occurs when the brood is much younger.

Putnam Pond provides an ideal getaway for a day or two. If possible, visit after Labor Day or in the spring to improve your chances of finding solitude.

Getting There

From Ticonderoga, take Route 74 west, and watch for a sign on the left that says Pharaoh Wilderness and Putnam Pond (this turn is about 5 miles west of 9N). Turn left, and follow the road 3.9 miles to Putnam Pond. The boat access is at the Putnam Pond Campground.

Ausable Marsh

Ausable and Peru

MAPS
  New York Atlas: Map 103
  USGS Quadrangle: Keeseville

INFORMATION
  Prominent fish species: Largemouth bass, smallmouth bass, northern pike, and walleye
  Camping: Ausable Point Campground; 518-561-7080
  Books: If you plan to run any section of the Ausable other than the one described here, purchase a copy of Paul Jamieson and Donald Morris's outstanding guidebook: *Adirondack Canoe Waters: North Flow,* published by the Adirondack Mountain Club.

Three separate paddling areas await you at Ausable Marsh: Dead Creek, Ausable River, and the marsh between the mouths of the river. We paddled all three in the several hours we spent on Ausable Point, a broad delta formed from silt carried by the Ausable as it tumbles down from the Adirondack High Peaks—including the state's tallest, Mt. Marcy—to the Champlain Valley.

To get to the river without paying a fee, you can put in at the hand-carry launch on the park road 0.4 mile from Route 9. If the wind has kicked up whitecaps on Lake Champlain, we would pay the park entrance fee and launch from the campground directly into the river. Given the choice, we would launch into the lake to take advantage of the panoramic views of Vermont from the water.

As you paddle south on Lake Champlain from the first access, you initially paddle through *Equisitum,* or horsetail, growing near shore. This plant has a segmented stalk and is related to ferns. Look for ducks feeding among the rushes in deeper water. We saw many, including a female mallard herding her brood before her. The sand bottom, easily visible in the clear water, harbors hordes of freshwater mussels. Looking to the shore, silver maples stand shoulder to shoulder along the bank all the way down to the campground.

Belted kingfishers paced us as we paddled upriver from the sand-bar at the Upper Mouth of the Ausable. A ground-dwelling warbler, the northern waterthrush, patrolled the shore bobbing its tail constantly. This five-inch bird, with its streaked breast and white eye stripe, has a

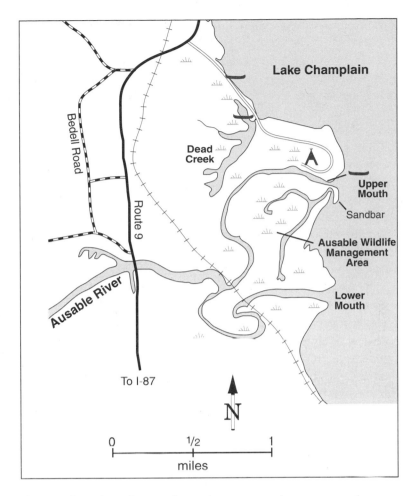

Lake Champlain

Dead
Creek

Upper
Mouth

Sandbar

Ausable Wildlife
Management
Area

Lower
Mouth

Bedell Road

Route 9

Ausable River

To I-87

N

0   1/2   1

miles

loud song, thought to be an adaptation to attracting mates and announcing its territory over the streamside roar of rushing water.

A sea of underwater vegetation undulated over rippled sand in
the clear current as we passed by gravel bars, eroded banks, and tree
trunks waiting to be washed out into the lake. Although the water
reached very low levels in the drought summer of 1995, we still had
to work paddling against the current, particularly after passing under
the railroad bridge. As we neared the Route 9 bridge, we were working harder than we wanted to and turned around to drift back downstream with the current, enjoying ostrich ferns towering over the
banks, beautiful iridescent green damselflies mating on the wing, and
a fat groundhog munching on the lush streamside grass. Paddling
downstream, before reaching the railroad bridge, a channel cuts back
to the right (south) leading to the Lower Mouth. Unfortunately,

because of low water we could not return to the lake in a loop trip via the Lower Mouth. At higher water this may be possible, but you would have to paddle through heavier current to get this far upstream.

As we emptied back into the lake at the Upper Mouth, we turned right to clear the quarter-mile-long sandbar and paddle back up into the sloughs of the Ausable Wildlife Management Area. In retrospect, it would have been a lot easier to carry over the 30-foot-wide sand barrier spit than to paddle around it, especially given that we continually ran aground trying to stay in an elusive channel.

However, we're glad we took the long way around, because we got a close-up sight of a very rare shorebird in full breeding plumage. It was a ruff, a Eurasian shorebird slightly larger than the killdeer with which it shared the sand spit. Ruffs appear only occasionally along the East Coast and rarely this far inland. The male's breeding plumage includes long tufts of feathers (ruffs) that stream for several inches from the head and neck down either side of the breast. The highly variable color of the ruff ranges from steel gray to red to white. This bird had a striking reddish orange head with snow-white ruffs and bright orange legs. We watched this bird run and fly over the sand for at least 10 minutes, so close we did not need binoculars. Other than seeing bald eagle nests with young or otters noisily chomping on fish, this provided perhaps the biggest treat of the paddling season.

The sloughs of the wildlife management area provided our most enjoyable paddling. Except for the occasional fisherman, you likely will find yourself paddling alone in this marshy wilderness, just a few tens of feet from the bustling lake. Immediately upon entering the marsh you have to choose a direction—west or south—and neither channel goes far.

We paddled the whole area because of the abundant wildlife and the opportunity to study the huge variety of marsh plants. According to some plant keys, there are nearly 50 different species of pondweed (genus *Potamogeton*), with more than 30 occurring in the Northeast. We saw several species here, but they all have two things in common: the floating leaves have parallel veins, all running the same direction as the midvein; and the small, knobby flowers look sort of like a pale raspberry, extending a few inches above the water's surface on a stout stalk. These serve as aerial landing pads for diminutive blue damselflies that leap to the air as the boat glides by.

We also studied bladderworts, with their yellow snapdragon-like flowers borne on short stalks above the water. The vast majority of the plant lives underwater in dense, feathery mats, bearing hundreds of tiny

Abundant deadfalls occur in the clear waters of the Ausable River.

(0.02 to 0.1 inch long), bulbous traps that are the plant's leaves. When an insect larva or small animal bumps into the trigger hairs, a small door opens and the concave sides of the trap inflate, sucking in water along with the hapless animal. The ingestion process occurs in about 1/500 of a second, followed by several days of digestion by plant enzymes. If you lift a mat out of the water and listen carefully, you may hear crackling as the bladders suck in air instead of their intended prey. In most ponds, mosquito larvae form the bulk of the diet, but the plants also ingest other insect larvae, rotifers, protozoans, small crustaceans, and even tiny tadpoles (for more on carnivorous plants see page 87).

We hated to leave the marsh with its abundant wood ducks, eastern kingbirds, flickers, and muskrats, but we wanted to paddle the third body of water, Dead Creek, before dark. You can get into Dead Creek in two ways: paddle in from Lake Champlain through a culvert (or portage over the top if there's too much water) or drive 0.3 mile farther down the park access road to the parking area by the culvert.

Surprisingly, when we paddled here, water flowed from the lake into Dead Creek. Does it flow the other direction in nondrought conditions? We enjoyed paddling this placid water while the setting sun drew pastel colors across the western sky. While we did not see anything new, we had to marvel at the sheer abundance of ducks, great blue heron, muskrat, and the insect-eating tree swallow, barn swallow, and purple martin, doing their best to keep down the ubiquitous deerflies.

We left this wildlife paradise knowing that we would return. Habitats such as these have become increasingly rare as urban sprawl, strip development, and consumptive land practices have gnawed away at these priceless habitats. We thank the farsighted individuals who set aside this marshland for us and for future generations to enjoy.

Getting There

From Plattsburgh, take Route 9 south. From the stoplight at the air force base, enter Adirondack Park at 3.9 miles, and turn left into Ausable Point Park at 7.2 miles. The first boat launch on Lake Champlain is 0.4 mile in on the left; the second launch point at the bridge at Dead Creek is another 0.3 mile. Campers may launch from their campsites, as well.

From I-87, get off at the Route 442 exit (Exit 35). Turn right, and drive 2.8 miles to the junction with Route 9. Turn left onto Route 9 and proceed north to the park entrance on the right in about 0.3 mile.

Davis Lake and Salmon River
Peru and Schuyler Falls

MAPS
   New York Atlas: Map 103
   USGS Quadrangle: Peru
INFORMATION
   Area: 60 acres
   Prominent fish species: Stocked brown trout
   Camping: Macomb Reservation State Park; 518-643-9952

We really enjoyed paddling this small lake and the Salmon River that flows into its west end. Surrounded by hills and wilderness, Macomb Reservation has a wild feel to it, even though it's so small. One of several Salmon Rivers in the north country, it should be renamed "Salmon Creek" in keeping with its size and to avoid some confusion.

Four other boats ambled about on this paddle-only lake. We traversed Davis Lake slowly to savor its beauty. Vegetation layers back from the water's edge, starting with ferns or cattails and various shrubs, giving way to paper birch and other small trees, ending with large red pine and a few scattered white pine. Near the stream entrance, narrow-leaved cattails give way to wooded shores. Where alders hadn't crowded everything else out, a fine grove of walnut grows. Look for feather-like leaves resembling ash and deeply furrowed bark on straight trunks in older trees.

We did not get out of the boat to check to see whether the grove contained butternut or black walnut trees. Butternut ranges over the entire state, while black walnut occurs primarily in the southeast and in isolated populations in the central region. But these could be black walnuts nonetheless, because horticulturists have planted them widely, mainly because of their very valuable dark wood. Butternut has lighter bark and 11 to 17 leaflets per leaf; black walnut's bark can get almost black in older trees and has 15 to 23 leaflets per leaf.

Black walnut (and butternut to a lesser extent) has adopted an interesting strategy to limit competition for light and space from other trees. Established trees exude into the surrounding soil a chemical called juglone that inhibits germination of other walnut seeds and many other plants. It also limits growth of other plants. So when we looked at the grove of even-aged walnuts on Davis Lake, we thought black

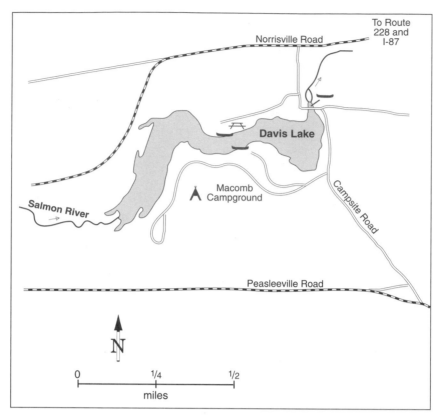

walnut. In retrospect, we should have checked them out more thoroughly to make sure they weren't butternut.

As we paddled upstream on the Salmon River, trout rose from their underwater haunts, deftly sucking in floating insects from the evening's hatch. Beaver own this stream. We turned around after carrying over three dams, one with a two-foot drop and jcwelweed sprouting from its bulwarks. In contrast to the muskrat that slipped quietly under the water's surface at our approach, three beaver on separate occasions slapped the water with their tails, splashing water bank to bank, showing annoyance at our intrusion.

We only wished the beaver had done a better job at pruning back the alders that converge on the channel, leaving only a few feet of passageway in spots. As we worked our way back down the meandering stream in the fading light, veeries called from the undergrowth. A mallard hen reenacted its broken wing trick, leading us away from its brood. Grapevines draped over the streamside vegetation, giving sanctuary to song sparrow, yellowthroat, yellow warbler, brown thrasher, cardinal, and catbird. The strains of the night—cicada, barred owl,

A well-kept beaver dam provides a momentary impediment to paddling up the Salmon River.

frog, veery, white-throated sparrow—flooded the summer air as we paddled back out onto Davis Lake and back to the campground in the semidark. We strongly recommend an evening paddle into this wilderness.

Getting There

From I 87, get off at Exit 35, Route 442. Travel west on Route 442 to the junction with Route 22. Take Route 22 north for 0.2 mile to Route 22B. Turn left onto Route 22B in Peru. Continue north, watching for the sign for Macomb State Park in 4.5 more miles. Turn left onto Norrisville Road at the Sunoco station just after the park sign. Turn left onto Campsite Road after another 2.6 miles at the sign for Macomb Park. In 0.1 mile, you can turn right to reach the beach and north shore boat-launch entrance. You can launch there (fee) or continue on to the bridge a short distance beyond and launch there free. Finally, you can launch from the lower campground loop if you're camped there.

Taylor Pond

Black Brook

MAPS
>   **New York Atlas:** Map 96
>   **USGS Quadrangle:** Wilmington

INFORMATION
>   **Area:** 803 acres; maximum depth: 95 feet
>   **Prominent fish species:** Lake trout and rainbow trout
>   **Camping:** Taylor Pond Campground; 518-647-5250

State forest lands surround Taylor Pond on all sides, giving it a wilderness feel. Because of its out-of-the-way northern Adirondack location, the pond does not draw large numbers of people to its shores. The small state-run campground, given its rustic character—outhouses, picnic tables, and simple fire grates—does not provide the amenities that would bring in crowds of campers. We appreciated the 25 well-separated, wooded campsites, but we preferred those accessible only by boat. Campsites I-1 and I-2 on the tip of the peninsula separating the eastern arm from the main lake appealed to us the most. Each nestles

A beaver lodge in the mouth of Bear Brook as it flows into Taylor Pond, with Catamount Mountain looming large over the pond.

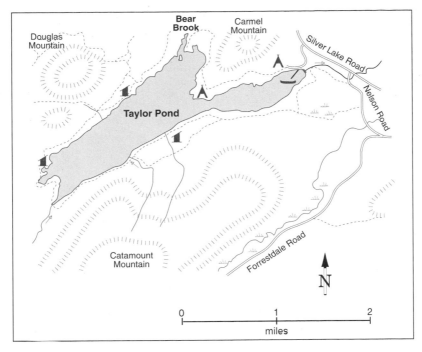

in a grove of hemlock, paper birch, and pine and has an outhouse, picnic table, and fire grate.

Most of the lake has a sandy bottom, at least where there are no exposed or barely submerged pink granite boulders. A very narrow-leaved water celery floats on the surface in shallower areas, but the deep pond does not support an abundance of aquatic vegetation. We found cranberries growing among the shoreside shrubbery, under a canopy of stunted birch and red maples. A wide array of deciduous trees dominates the hillsides, and conifers cling to the crest of Catamount Mountain.

Paddling up the mouth of Bear Brook, with large, lichen-covered, pink granite boulders lining the shore, we glided by a large beaver lodge mounted on a small island. The lodge had nearly obliterated the island, we looked but could not seem to find the underwater entrance to the lodge. It seemed pretty rocky for digging such an entrance.

Looking out over the water as we paddled back to the main lake, the wooded peaks and extensive shoulders of Catamount Mountain seemed to guard the entire southern shore, providing a picturesque backdrop for a leisurely cruise down the pond. While the mountain lion no longer patrols the shadows of the mountain named for it, we did see another species that has recently retreated from the endangered species list: a mature bald eagle. As we approached the peninsula, it took off from a tall pine and soared ever higher on Catamount's thermals, becoming barely visible among the billowing white clouds. Given the midfall season, we suspect that it had just started its migration to the coast or other body of water that does not freeze in the winter.

In addition to the bald eagle, we noted the presence of wood ducks and great blue herons in the quieter coves, along with the usual array of songbirds back in the woods. Hiking trails ring the pond and extend into the nearby hills, adding an extra dimension to this beautiful location.

Getting There

Take Route 3 north out of Saranac Lake. At the stop sign in Bloomingdale, turn right, staying on Route 3; start marking mileage from this point. In 0.2 mile, turn right onto Essex County 18, which turns into Franklin County 48. Pass the Moose Pond entrance at 1.8 miles, and cross the Saranac River at 7.5 miles. When County 48 turns right at 9.1 miles, go straight onto Plank Road (which turns into Forrestdale Road). At 17.4 miles at the stop sign, turn back sharply left onto Nelson Road. At the T at 18.3 miles, turn left onto Silver Lake Road. At 18.9 miles you will see a sign for Taylor Pond; turn left here onto a dirt road that ends at the Taylor Pond Campground and boat launch.

Alternatively, you can get to Taylor Pond from Wilmington or from Au Sable Forks. From Wilmington, take County Road 19 north to Silver Lake Road. Turn left onto Silver Lake Road, and proceed to the campground entrance.

From Au Sable Forks, take Turnpike Road northwest. When Silver Lake Road veers off to the left, take Silver Lake Road, and proceed to the campground entrance.

Moose Pond

St. Armand

MAPS
> **New York Atlas:** Map 96
> **USGS Quadrangles:** Bloomingdale and Saranac Lake

INFORMATION
> **Area:** 173 acres; maximum depth: 52 feet
> **Prominent fish species:** Brook trout, rainbow trout, lake trout, and smallmouth bass

With a depth of over 50 feet, Moose Pond differs from most of the shallow, boggy lakes and ponds in the area, and because of its depth, it supports a cold-water trout fishery. Trout seem to succumb readily to acidified water; apparently, these waters remain alkaline enough for them. Bogs, especially those with sphagnum—a plant that secretes hydrogen ions that acidify its environment—do not support trout very well. In addition, the decaying vegetation common in bogs gives off tannic and other acids during the oxidation process that add further acidity. While trout might survive, barely, under such conditions, they certainly cannot survive the added import of acid rain from the Midwest. The sulfur

High Adirondack peaks overlook the placid waters of Moose Pond.

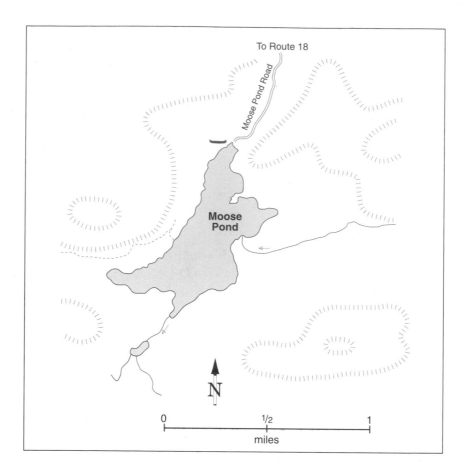

dioxide—eventually converted to sulfurous and sulfuric acids in the atmosphere—along with hydrochloric and nitric acids emanating from unscrubbed, coal-fired power plants toll a death knell for the high Adirondack lakes. Hundreds of them no longer support trout or other game fish. Thankfully, such environmental insults have not ruined this body of water...yet.

Precambrian rocks—mostly granite and gneiss (pronounced "nice")—poke up through sedimentary rocks to form the High Peaks regions of the Adirondacks. Although the upthrust is relatively new, and evidence suggests it's ongoing, the high peak rocks date to about a billion years ago. These rocks do not react with acids and, therefore, do not reduce acidity of acid rain or high-altitude bogs. Most low-elevation lakes in the Adirondacks lie over marble, a type of calcium carbonate, just like limestone. Acids readily react with calcium carbonate, liberating carbon dioxide and water, effectively neutralizing acid rain.

So fish have not disappeared from low-elevation lakes as they have from higher elevations.

Surrounded by scenic, forested Adirondack peaks, Moose Pond nestles in a deep, pristine valley. These same peaks also funnel and intensify any north-south winds, making the waters of this small pond treacherous during windy periods. Large, smooth granite boulders line the shore in places, adding to its scenic character. These vegetation-free boulders offer easy egress, allowing people to convert the areas around them into unofficial campsites. We spotted obvious camping spots at several locations. In the fall, deer hunters use them for base camps as they foray off into the huge, roadless McKenzie Mountain Wilderness—home of 2 of the 100 tallest Adirondack peaks—that surrounds Moose Pond.

A stand of hemlock grows near the boat access, and northern white cedar ring the pond. Thick stands of birch reflect off the clear water, standing in stark contrast to the evergreen conifers. Occasional yellow birch blend in with the hemlock and tall white pine. Although it does not take long to paddle the complete shoreline of Moose Pond, one could camp here for days, relaxing, reading, philosophizing, and, of course, paddling in relative isolation, surrounded by clear, trout-filled waters and scenic mountains.

Getting There

From the town of Saranac Lake, take Route 3 north. Route 3 takes a sharp right in Bloomingdale, where Route 55 enters from the left, and just after this, Route 3 crosses a bridge. Immediately after crossing the bridge (0.2 mile from the sharp turn), turn right onto Route 18, a paved road. Go 1.6 miles down Route 18, watching for an unmarked paved road going off to the right. Turn right onto this paved road, which turns to gravel after 0.6 mile. The boat access is 1.5 miles from the junction with Route 18.

Deer River Flow and Horseshoe Pond

Duane

MAPS
  New York Atlas: Map 101
  USGS Quadrangle: Lake Titus

INFORMATION
  Area: 500 acres
  Prominent fish species: Largemouth bass, smallmouth bass, and northern pike
  Camping: Deer River Campsite (private campground); 518-483-0060
  Books: If you plan to run downstream sections of Deer River, purchase a copy of Paul Jamieson and Donald Morris's outstanding guidebook *Adirondack Canoe Waters: North Flow,* published by the Adirondack Mountain Club.

Paddling out in the shallow, tea-colored water, we felt transported into the time of nineteenth-century Adirondack guides. Ringed with spire-like conifers—tall tamaracks, balsam fir, black and red spruce, northern white cedar, white pine—and gorgeous mountain views to the south and west, Deer River Flow retains a magical aura, even though Route 30 intrudes a little on its southern arm.

The magic increased dramatically when we spotted a bald eagle nest with two nearly grown fledglings perched on side branches. Seeing four eagles at once made our paddle here superbly enjoyable. Bald eagles nested widely in the Adirondacks until done in by DDT poisoning and habitat destruction. Beginning in the late 1980s, they resumed nesting—the result of a massive reintroduction program that began in 1976. Even though we saw several bald eagles in our two-year intensive exploration of the state's quiet waters, we still marvel at the grace and power of this remarkable bird. Awe inspiring is the only way to describe seeing one swoop over the water on powerful wing beats to snatch a dying fish from the surface with its talons. For more on the bald eagle, see page 193.

As we scanned the skies for more raptors, a northern harrier glided low over the marsh, on the watch for rodents. But the habitat along the shore of both Deer River Flow and Horseshoe Pond belongs to red-winged blackbirds. The territories must be worth defending against other red-wings, because the males sing from cattails every few feet along the marsh. The shrubby shoreline, lined with sweet gale, bog rosemary—with its long, narrow leaves, green on top, white underneath—sheep laurel, and more, provides excellent habitat for common yel-

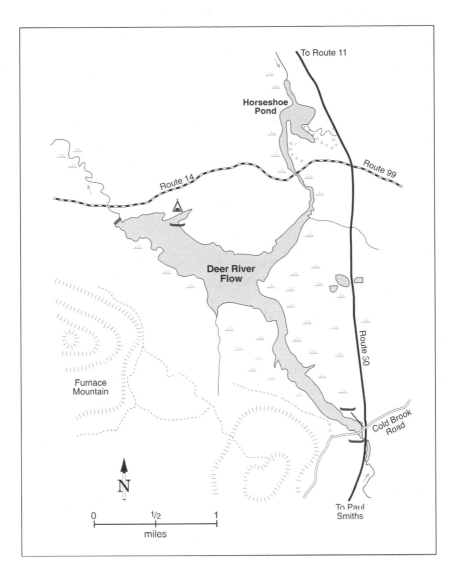

lowthroats, a diminutive yellow warbler with a black mask through its eyes, looking rather like a robber ready to pounce on unwary insects.

Out on the flow, mussel shells litter the bottom near shore, much of which consists of peat bogs. While tamaracks have started to invade the bogs, eventually filling them in, they still support tons of bog specialists, including such carnivorous plants as sundew and pitcher plant. Because pitcher plants and sundews live in nutrient-poor soils, they supplement the meager nitrogen available by capturing and digesting insects. Pitchers fill with rainwater, into which the plant secretes digestive enzymes. When unlucky insects fall in, downward-pointing hairs keep them from crawling back out. Eventually they drown and give up their precious nutrient stores to the plant.

Sundews operate in a similar manner. Glistening dewlike secretions on stalks emanating from the sundew pad attract insects, which become entrapped on the sticky secretion. The plant rolls the insect inward slightly to come in contact with shorter stalks that contain digestive enzymes. The degraded insect material provides needed nitrogen to the plant.

The shallow water harbors acres of yellow pond lily, fragrant water lily, and water celery, with its long narrow leaves floating on the surface, especially on the long connecting stream into Horseshoe Pond. As you enter Horseshoe Pond, an occasional house intrudes on the right-hand shore, while the left-hand shore is covered with sphagnum, black spruce, tamarack, and carnivorous plants.

We loved paddling here and found it hard to leave. We spent quite a bit of time trying to photograph iridescent green damselflies. Besides interruptions from our photographic pursuits by the eagles and harrier, we watched deer come down to the water's edge for a drink and numerous muskrats harvesting aquatic vegetation. We saw one beaver and evidence of many more.

We highly recommend paddling here, especially early in the morning or in the late afternoon. If you want to see wildlife and study myriad bog and aquatic plants, this is the place. But please keep your distance from wildlife, especially eagle nests.

Getting There

From Paul Smiths, travel north on Route 30. As you pass the turnoff to Meacham Lake Campground, start marking mileage. Continue north for 3.5 miles, and turn left onto Cold Brook Road. The boat launch is a few hundred feet down the road on the right. Alternatively, you can launch by the bridge on Route 30 just before Cold Brook Road.

From Malone, travel south on Route 30. When you reach the Red Tavern Road fork, with Route 14 going right and Route 99 going left, start measuring mileage. From this junction, Cold Brook Road is 2.2 miles south on the right.

Deer River Campsite is 1.5 miles down Red Tavern Road (Route 14).

Bald Eagle
Our National Bird Back from the Brink

Without a doubt, the bald eagle is our most dramatic and recognizable raptor. With its unmistakable white head and tail, contrasting with a dark brown body, an adult bald eagle flies over the nation's waterways on powerful wings. In flight, its large size stands out   it soars with wings straight out, spanning up to eight feet. From beak to tip of tail, eagles measure from 34 to 43 inches; males weigh 8 to 9 pounds, while the larger females weigh 10 to 14 pounds. Bringing new meaning to "light as a feather," up to 15 percent of the bird's body weight may be in the feathers!

Adults do not attain their distinctive plumage until reaching four or five years of age. Until that time they may be mistaken for golden eagles—a rare species in New York—as they are mostly dark brown with some white mottling on the underside and tail. As they mature, the head and tail become progressively whiter. At close range, the adult's large yellow beak and piercing yellow eyes convey a fierce strength. Our country's founders evidently felt this image symbolized what our young nation stood for, selecting *Haliaeetus leucocephalus* as our national symbol. Appropriately, this is the only eagle found exclusively in North America.

The bald eagle ranges throughout New York and can be seen either nesting or in migration in all but the most populated regions of the southeastern part of the state. Eagles generally locate their nests in trees at the water's edge. Pairs return to the same nest for years, adding to it annually. An old eagle nest may be 6 feet in diameter, more than 8 feet deep, and weigh more than a ton. The largest nest ever found was 9.5 feet in diameter and 20 feet deep. Because eagles often build nests in dead trees, the huge mass of the nest eventually topples the tree.

Bald eagles usually lay two eggs several days apart. Incubation lasts 30 to 36 days, during which time the male and female share in nest sitting. The young hatch several days apart; the earlier born, larger chick may outcompete its younger sibling for food. If food is scarce, the younger chick usually dies, a strategy that improves the chances of fledging at least one chick. Because eagles live long lives—as long as 30 years in captivity but usually less in the wild—they really only need to fledge a few chicks to replace themselves, thus maintaining a stable population.

They mate for life, although when an adult dies its mate will usually succeed in finding a new partner. This change undoubtedly occurred at Oak Orchard National Wildlife Refuge recently. In the spring of 1994, bald eagles nested within sight of the visitor center and fledged three young, an unprecedented occurrence in the Northeast and one that we were fortunate to witness. Only twice before have humans recorded the fledging of three eaglets from one nest. Prior to this extraordinary event, in 1993 the female laid only one egg, and that one did not hatch. For the several years prior to 1993, the eagle pair had fledged one young each year. Apparently, in 1994 there was a change of females. Because eagles mate for life, refuge personnel theorize that the original female probably died. In 1995, the pair returned to the nest quite early, probably because of the mild winter, and fledged two young.

After 10 to 12 weeks of a diet consisting mostly of fish, chicks reach the fledgling stage, when they begin to fly. For the next 7 or 8 weeks, they increasingly gain independence, eventually leaving the nest to migrate to coastal areas and to outfalls below dams where the water does not freeze. In past years, when eagles were plentiful, they congregated in great numbers off both coasts and in the Mississippi drainage each fall. Eagles still congregate by the thousands in mid-November along a 10-mile stretch of the Chilkat River in Alaska, to feed on hordes of dead and dying salmon.

While bald eagles occur more frequently in New York today—thanks to efforts by the Endangered Species Unit of the Department of Environmental Conservation—just a few years ago only a few remained. New York's population of eagles plummeted to just one nesting pair in the western part of the state. This pair doggedly nested in the same tree for more than 20 years. Only once during that time—in 1973—did they successfully hatch and raise a chick. But they served as successful foster parents for captive-born chicks over several years, starting in 1978, in the fledgling reintroduction program of the DEC.

In the late 1960s and 1970s, incubation success dropped to zero because toxins in the female eagles' bodies resulted in thin eggshells that broke during incubation. Long-lasting chlorinated hydrocarbons—such as DDT and its breakdown product DDE, left over from mosquito-control projects—reached high concentrations in eagles, peregrine falcons, and other species at the top of the food chain.

Eagle populations have rebounded to about 4,000 nesting pairs in the U.S. outside Alaska, 25 of them in New York (1995)—with the greatest concentration around remote lakes in the far western, far northern, and southeastern regions. In 1995, New York eagles fledged 30 young, up from 20 in 1994, 15 in 1990, and 3 in 1987. In addition to the increasing number of young produced in New York, another satisfying statistic has occurred: nest success rates are relatively high, from 1990 to 1995 averaging 1.2 chicks fledged per breeding pair. This stands in contrast with less than 1 chick fledged per breeding pair in Maine with 150 nests. Possibly, eagles in New York suffer from less contamination by DDT, DDE, dioxins, mercury, and PCBs.

Because eagle populations have risen gradually during the past 20 years since the banning of DDT, aided by reintroductions in many areas of the country, the U.S. Fish and Wildlife Service removed the bald eagle from the Endangered Species List in 1994. U.S. Fish and Wildlife still lists the bird as threatened, however, and it is still protected from hunting and trapping.

We feel privileged to paddle on lakes with resident bald eagles, keeping ever watchful for their glorious presence. Some people have accused them of being opportunists, and indeed we have watched a few chase smaller ospreys laboring with heavy fish, circling to gain altitude before flying off to their aeries. In one case, after the osprey dropped its hard-won catch, a bald eagle snatched it, flying off gracefully with its ill-gotten goods. In our view, this is not a case of good and evil; instead it represents the triumph of bald eagle adaptation, ensuring its survival.

Humans still shoot eagles and build high-tension lines that electrocute them—although designs and devices exist that reduce eagle mortality from these high lines—and many eagles die from flying into human-made structures (towers, smokestacks, power lines, and buildings). But the biggest threat to the eagle's continued survival comes from an expanding human population, one that spews forth toxic chemicals into the environment and develops the shoreline of every lake in sight. If we wish to continue to enjoy this majestic creature as it patrols the waterways of America—and keep it from returning to the Endangered Species List—we must take steps to keep some of its habitat undeveloped and unadulterated by the toxic wastes of a consumer society. The eagle represents an enduring wildness that we must protect for future generations to enjoy.

Meacham Lake and Osgood River
Brighton and Duane

MAPS
  New York Atlas: Map 101
  USGS Quadrangle: Meacham Lake

INFORMATION
  Area: 1,023 acres; maximum depth: 63 feet
  Prominent fish species: Splake, smallmouth bass, and northern pike
  Camping: Meacham Lake Campground; 518-483-5116
  Books: If you plan to paddle from Meacham Lake more than a few miles up the Osgood River or down the East Branch of the St. Regis River, purchase a copy of Paul Jamieson and Donald Morris's outstanding guidebook *Adirondack Canoe Waters: North Flow,* published by the Adirondack Mountain Club.

Although the state owns the land surrounding Meacham Lake, it allows motorboats and Jet-skis out on it. In the summer, especially on weekends, the lake's surface crawls with noise and wakes. We vastly prefer paddling up the Osgood River on the south end. Although a free, hand-carry, public boat launch exists at the north end of the lake, we would put in at the dam on the outflow on Route 30 at the south end of the lake. From there it's an easy paddle over to the Osgood River. Even when the wind blows from the north, the abundant aquatic vegetation on the south end of the lake damps the wind-driven swells. On a very windy day, we had little difficulty traversing over to the river and back, even though we had to paddle in the wave troughs.

We paddled up the Osgood River, and the same scene unfolded before us that we had experienced earlier when we paddled the upper reaches flowing out of Osgood Pond. Few deciduous trees appear along the marshy shores; conifers abound. This northern conifer forest supports an unusual array of species rarely seen farther south in New York, including gray jays—the so-called whiskey jack or camp robber—that exhibit little fear of humans; boreal chickadees, with their gray brown cap and nasal call; spruce grouse, a quite tame, chunkier relative of the ruffed grouse; and crossbills, both red- and white-winged, with bills that cross instead of meet together when closed, an adaptation they use to good advantage in prying seeds loose from pinecones.

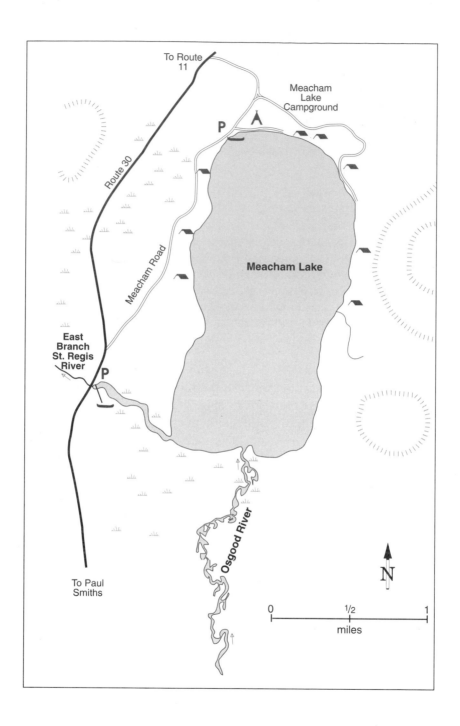

To Route 11

Meacham Lake Campground

P

Route 30

Meacham Road

Meacham Lake

East Branch St. Regis River

P

Osgood River

To Paul Smiths

N

0   1/2   1
miles

Tamarack and black spruce, both of which can withstand partially submerged roots, grow on the sphagnum substrate. Balsam fir and white pine grow on the banks and on islands, with red and white spruce on drier ground. Paddling here in the fall provides a rare but beautiful treat: the golden-needled tamarack against a backdrop of dark green conifers. Tamarack is the only conifer in our area that drops all its needles in the fall. The other conifers drop their needles as well but do so after two or three years, leaving a healthy crop of new green needles at the end of growing twigs.

Another interesting plant that grows in the Osgood River is the smallest of the four yellow pond lilies, *Nuphar microphyllum,* which as its name suggests has very small leaves—less than five inches long—compared to the larger water lilies. Its diminutive flowers measure less than an inch across when fully open.

You can paddle up the Osgood for many miles before it becomes impassable. Unbelievably, it disappears underground for some distance, according to Paul Jamieson and Don Morris in their *North Flow* book. To paddle from Osgood Pond to Meacham Pond would be an extraordinary undertaking; if you wish to attempt this, you must refer to their book first.

Reluctantly, after a few miles of making very slow progress on this endlessly meandering stream, having to carry over downed logs and

*The smallest yellow pond lily—*Nuphar microphyllum—*grows amid pondweed leaves on the Osgood River.*

halfhearted beaver dams, we had to contemplate paddling back to the boat launch.

The dams, beaver lodges, and abundant cuttings reminded us that beaver generally do not forage on the resinous bark of coniferous trees, thereby limiting the numbers in the Osgood River. As they hack down the streamside alders, they literally eat themselves out of house and home. As the fast-growing alders return, so do the beaver to hack them down once again. Amazingly, the beaver had been trapped out of existence in New York in the late 1800s. In 1904, conservation officials released 6 beaver near Old Forge, and in 1906, they released 25 beaver from Yellowstone Park. From this nucleus, the prolific rodents reached a population of nearly 20,000 by 1915. The New York population, scattered all over the state, now numbers about 100,000 individuals. You will see them on this lower section of the Osgood River in the early evening . . . unless they decimate the alders again.

Paddling back to the river's mouth on calm water, we had almost forgotten the north-wind-driven swells on Meacham Lake, but after a short sprint to the outlet channel, we again met calm waters.

The outlet channel leading to and from the dam differs significantly from the Osgood River. It has rounded boulders poking up above the water's surface, and the boggy areas contain sundews and pitcher plants in profusion. What sets it apart, however, are deciduous trees along the bank. And instead of the exotic bird species of the coniferous forest, here red-winged blackbirds, black-throated green warblers, and white-throated sparrows serenaded us from their streamside perches. Dwarf gray birch graced the shores along with alders, sheep laurel, and other shrubs, and *Equisetum,* floating heart, pickerelweed, and pondweed covered patches of water.

Getting There

From Paul Smiths, travel north on Route 30. From the junction of Routes 30 and 458, the dam is 0.2 mile farther north on the right; turn in just past the bridge.

To get to the campground and upper access, there are two ways. From the dam, drive 0.2 mile north on Route 30, then turn right on Meacham Road, which leads to the campground and the upper boat access. Alternatively, continue north on Route 30 for 2.5 miles from the dam, and turn right on the upper road into the campground.

Osgood Pond, Jones Pond, and Osgood River

Brighton

MAPS

New York Atlas: Map 95
USGS Quadrangles: Bloomingdale and St. Regis Mountain

INFORMATION

Area: Osgood Pond, 530 acres; Jones Pond, 170 acres

Prominent fish species: Stocked brown trout and brook trout

Books: If you have any notion of paddling down the Osgood River beyond what is covered in this guide, we strongly suggest that you purchase a copy of Paul Jamieson and Donald Morris's guidebook *Adirondack Canoe Waters: North Flow,* published by the Adirondack Mountain Club.

Tall white pines ring the cove that contains the boat access onto Osgood Pond. Occasional tamarack and red maple and a few paper birch appear as well. The shoreline surrounding the rest of the pond also contains large numbers of pine. Despite the forested shores, noise from Route 30 and summer cabins intrude on the solitude of Osgood Pond. Fortunately, solitude begins just about a mile from the boat access, as you paddle north down the Osgood River out of the pond.

Water lilies

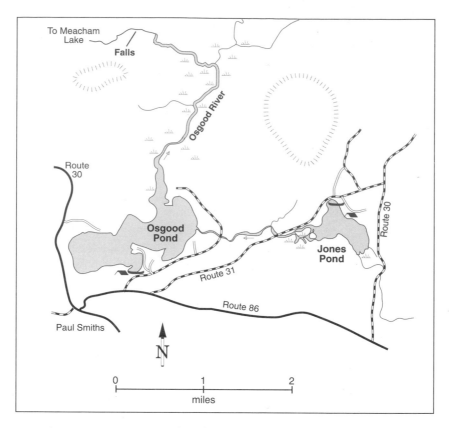

As you start out on the river, tamarack, spruce, northern white cedar, and balsam fir dominate the western bank, while pines cover the eastern side, with its higher ground. In and amongst these trees, many of which are actually red pines, lies White Pine Camp, the home of the 1926 summer White House where Calvin Coolidge stayed. With its 20 buildings and walkways surrounded by rhododendrons, it has been restored and opens to visitors from 10:00 A.M. to 5:00 P.M., mid-May through mid-October. One of the great rustic estates of the Adirondacks, the camp boasts 3,900 feet of shoreline and 35 acres.

As the camp gives way to state-owned land along the river, note the stunted, spirelike spruces of the sphagnum bog; these are black spruce, the only spruce species that tolerates partially submerged roots.

We paddled downriver about three miles, until we reached a series of waterfalls. You should not attempt to go past here; if you really want an adventure and intend to continue on, refer to Jamieson and Morris's *North Flow* book. The river actually disappears down a hole along a portion of the stretch leading to Meacham Lake.

On the river, we did not see more than a handful of deciduous trees. Conifers completely dominate the boggy northern boreal forest here. A wide variety of shrubs perch on the sphagnum hummocks, including sweet gale, leatherleaf, sheep laurel, bog laurel, and bog rosemary. Large clumps of pitcher plants line the shore in spots, and diminutive sundew rosettes glisten in the sun, awaiting insects drawn to the sticky "dew" of their traps. Yellow pond lily, fragrant water lily, pondweed, and water celery crowd the channel, while bur reed and pickerelweed compete for space along the shore.

As we rounded each bend, through the early morning autumn mists drifting slowly across the water, small flocks of black ducks would leap to the air, beating their wings furiously. Many groups of three to a dozen wood ducks, some all males in bright plumage, erupted from the water while sounding out their mournful, unducklike cries. They circled around behind us, only to be disturbed once again on our return trip. This beautiful duck, driven to the verge of extinction around the turn of the century by unregulated hunting and clearing of forests, has rebounded nicely. Prompted by the newly formed National Audubon Society, the government passed legislation in the early 1900s that protected the wood duck and other migratory species. Bird-watchers and wildlife management officials began erecting wood duck nest-

Tamaracks and balsam firs line the shores of the Osgood River as it flows out of Osgood Pond.

ing boxes in the 1940s, leading to greatly increased populations of this beautiful bird, one of our few cavity-nesting ducks.

As we neared the end of our travel on the river, road noise, which had receded from our consciousness, announced the proximity of Route 30 once again. A logjam followed by a series of falls indicated the end of the line. Lichens festooning some of the spruces provided a primeval look as the bog gave way to forest. Reluctantly, we turned around to retrace our way back to the lake.

When we reached the lake, we paddled southeast to find the outlet from Jones Pond. Even though the creek is small, we paddled all the way up into Jones Pond, having to carry over a few beaver dams and one road. Water had breached some abandoned dams, and we eased our way through the narrow channels. Most of the alders that formerly lined the banks had disappeared, leaving only stumps and conifers, which beaver rarely eat. Apparently, the beavers had eaten themselves out of house and home, leaving only grasses to feed the muskrats that we saw occasionally.

On Jones Pond, a pleasant, informal camping area surrounds the boat access. Ovenbirds call from the midstory level in an extensive red pine grove. We camped here and at the boat access on Osgood Pond a number of times in 1994 and 1995 and never tired of the nighttime sounds of whippoorwill, barred owl, and great horned owl.

Getting There

From the junction of Routes 30 and 86 at Paul Smiths, take Route 86 east. Go 0.6 mile to an unmarked paved road, and turn left. Continue for 0.2 mile, then turn left onto a dirt path that leads down to the water in 0.1 mile. You can camp here at the Debar Mountain Recreation Area, as well as launch your boat. However, of the five times we visited here, only once—in the fall—was there an available camping spot.

An alternate place to camp is at the boat access on Jones Pond, where there are two designated campsites, also part of the Debar Mountain Recreation Area. To get to Jones Pond by car, return to Route 86. Turn left, and go 0.3 mile to the next paved road to the left. Turn left here, onto Franklin County Route 31. Cross the bridge over Jones Pond outlet in 0.7 mile, and reach the Jones Pond access site on the right in another 0.9 mile.

Lake Kushaqua and Rainbow Lake

Franklin

MAPS
New York Atlas: Maps 95, 101, and 102
USGS Quadrangles: Loon Lake, Debar Mountain, Bloomingdale

INFORMATION
Area: 1,290 acres
Prominent fish species: Largemouth bass, northern pike, and stocked brown trout
Camping: Buck Pond Campground; 518-891-3449
Books: If you plan to paddle up from Jones Pond to Rainbow Lake or down the North Branch of the Saranac River beyond Lake Kushaqua, purchase a copy of Paul Jamieson and Donald Morris's outstanding guidebook *Adirondack Canoe Waters: North Flow,* published by the Adirondack Mountain Club.

The Kushaqua Lake area contains several different types of water; you could spend several days here exploring it all. To keep you oriented, we'll start our descriptions on the north and move south. If you intend to paddle the North Branch of the Saranac River downstream from the dam on Lake Kushaqua, we strongly recommend that you purchase a copy of Jamieson and Morris's *North Flow;* potentially dangerous rapids await those who have not scouted these waters carefully.

Lake Kushaqua

Lake Kushaqua offers picturesque scenery with forested hillsides and wonderful lakeside camping, but the lake itself is big and relatively round. The delicate branches of gray birches, suspended over the water, add to the scenic beauty. Fall foliage—crimson and orange from many sugar and red maples, coupled with vibrant yellows of striped maples and big-toothed aspens, viewed against a dark, green backdrop of white and red pine—makes fall camping here an invigorating experience.

Kushaqua Narrows

Kushaqua Narrows has interesting coves and islands to explore; it also has Buck Pond Campground and boat ramp, but neither intrudes on the narrows significantly. A rope swing dangles from a red pine bough, and

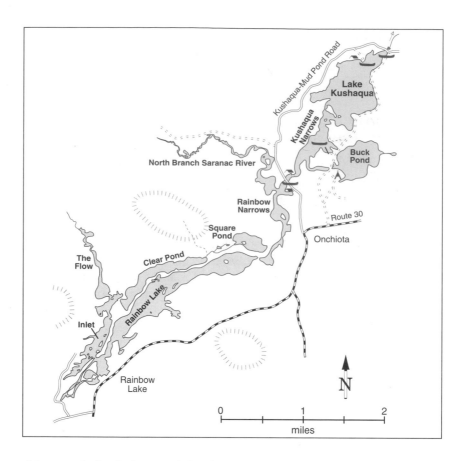

deer nonchalantly browsed the shoreside brush and drank from the cool waters as we cruised by. A great blue heron took flight at our approach. Sweet gale and sheep laurel draped the shores, while bracken fern stretched for filtered light from the pine canopy. Mussel shells littered the bottom in the clear water.

If you paddle back through the narrow cove that goes off to the south and then east down near the base of the narrows—a quiet, idyllic spot with ducks swimming and lacy green hemlock branches draping out over the water—you can get to Buck Pond . . . eventually. You have to carry up over a steep bank and road first.

North Branch of the Saranac River

The North Branch of the Saranac River coming into the narrows from the west, beginning with a primeval waterway maze of drowned timber, floating vegetation, and a large, thickly forested island, provides a haven for wildlife and quiet-water paddlers. We saw one other canoe at the mouth and nary a soul in the upper reaches. If you have limited time, make this your prime destination. It not only avoids the congestion and noise of the lakes, but it provides hours of solitude in pristine and varied wildlife habitat.

We felt transported back to a distant time as we paddled among the towering tamarack, spruce, white pine, and balsam fir at the river's mouth. The primeval forested swamp funneled down to a narrow, boulder-strewn passageway, then opened into a series of wide beaver meadows. We wondered how the aquatic plants divide the habitat as we paddled first through acres of pondweed, followed by acres of water shield, and then several acres of yellow pond lily. Water celery undulated in the light current, as alders began to appear along with rafts of beaver cuttings, beaver dams, and lodges. Large birds appeared: turkey vulture, northern raven, and great blue heron.

An alder flycatcher cried a buzzy "fee-bee-o" from, appropriately enough, the alder swamp. This uncommon, inconspicuous, and very drab warbler-sized bird has an olive brown back and pale yellow belly, with two white wing bars and a small white eye ring. Like the eight other similarly drab flycatcher species found throughout the U.S. and Canada, it sits upright on exposed branches, waiting to pounce on juicy insects that fly by. Listen for its song anytime you are near alder stands in the spring and early summer.

Conifers line the shore in many places on Lake Kushaqua, Rainbow Lake, and the North Branch of the Saranac River.

As we gazed into the distance, the tall, cathedral-like spires of bal-sam fir provided a mesmerizing effect—we didn't mind carrying up over beaver dams to penetrate farther back into the wilderness. The metallic chip of the swamp sparrow, followed by a musical trill, made us want to locate the furtive little bird. A painted turtle swam up to greet us in the clear water. Reluctantly, we paddled back down the river, not wanting to leave this wildlife paradise.

Rainbow Narrows

Rainbow Narrows, really just a continuation of Kushaqua Narrows, has much the same beauty of the latter but with slightly more boat traffic. A waterways crossroads of great beauty, with spirelike spruce, balsam fir, and other conifers, it transports boaters between Rainbow and Kushaqua Lakes and the mouth of the North Branch of the Saranac River. The exceedingly narrow concrete passageway keeps the bigger boats in Rainbow Lake from polluting Lake Kushaqua.

Rainbow Lake

Rainbow Lake's development started with an inn and a few rustic camps back in 1856; it now gets too much attention from Jet-skis, water skis, and motorboats. Cottages and houses line the banks in places. We had hoped to spend a short time on Rainbow Lake by car-rying up over the esker that separates it from Clear Pond, but we decid-ed that it was too brushy and steep. For a fascinating discussion of eskers, see the Rainbow Lake section of *North Flow*.

Clear Pond and The Flow

To reach Clear Pond and The Flow, paddle southwest on Rainbow Lake about two and a half miles to a fairly developed area known as Inlet. Paddle through the narrow break in the esker into The Flow. As you paddle north here, you will leave the traffic of Rainbow Lake behind and return to the peace and quiet you hope for in the northern Adiron-dacks. About two-thirds of a mile north from the opening into Rainbow Lake, a narrow channel to the right (east) leads into Clear Pond. The esker separates Clear Pond—a little more than a mile in length—from far busier Rainbow Lake.

As we paddled back to the boat access at the narrows—listening to the calls of white-throated sparrow, hermit thrush, ovenbird, white-

*Pine seeking light
over open water*

breasted nuthatch, red-eyed vireo, and several species of warbler—the nesting barn swallows under the bridge once again exploded into the air at our passage. We knew we would be back for further explorations.

Getting There

From Paul Smiths, take Route 86 east. Turn left onto Route 31. Go to the junction with Route 30, and turn left. Continue on to Onchiota, and where Route 30 turns right, go left onto Kushaqua–Mud Pond Road. The first boat access in 0.7 mile is at the bridge over Kushaqua Narrows.

If you continue north on Kushaqua–Mud Pond Road, take the right fork in 0.6 mile. The next boat access is on the right 1.8 miles from the fork; it's across from a field and easy to miss. If you miss it, it's 0.4 mile back from the bridge over the outlet. Several camping sites occur at this site.

You can also launch at the bridge over the Lake Kushaqua outlet.

You can launch at Buck Pond Campground. From the junction of Route 30 and Kushaqua–Mud Pond Road, it's 0.3 mile east on Route 30.

St. Regis Lakes and Spitfire Lake
Brighton and Harrietstown

MAPS
>**New York Atlas:** Map 95
>**USGS Quadrangles:** St. Regis Mountain and Bloomingdale

INFORMATION
>**Area:** St. Regis Lakes, 490 acres; Spitfire Lake, 310 acres; St. Regis Lakes, 790 acres
>**Prominent fish species:** Splake, landlocked salmon, smallmouth bass

The St. Regis Lakes and Spitfire Lake provide access into the St. Regis Canoe Wilderness Area, but they also offer enjoyable paddling in their own right—especially if you enjoy Adirondack-style architecture.

Lower St. Regis Lake

Lower St. Regis Lake (the northernmost of these lakes) is less developed than the other two and much more varied, with extensive marsh areas, wildlife habitat, and several lean-tos for camping. While the area immediately around Paul Smiths College is dominated by the college and a few houses, most of the shoreline remains undeveloped. Botanists will find the small inlet west of Paul Smiths College particularly interesting. Along its boggy perimeter you'll find a classic northern fen ecosystem, thick with leatherleaf, sheep laurel, bog rosemary, cranberry, sweet gale, sphagnum moss, pitcher plant, rose pogonia orchid, and tamarack. Cattail and pickerelweed provide evidence, however, that this area is biologically richer than a true fen, which has very little nutrient flow. There is a hand-launch access off Keese Mill Road.

Paul Smiths College on Lower St. Regis Lake gets its name from Paul Smith, who owned thousands of acres in this area. In 1859, Paul Smith opened the Saint Regis House on Lower St. Regis Lake, and it quickly became a playground for the rich and famous, including three U.S. presidents and P. T. Barnum. The original Saint Regis House—commonly known as Paul Smith's—had a modest 17 rooms, but the building mushroomed to a sprawling 225-unit complex by the early 1900s, with gardens, casino, bowling alley, and—for visiting financiers—even a direct line to the New York Stock Exchange! The hotel long gone, a college bearing Smith's name now sits on the lake.

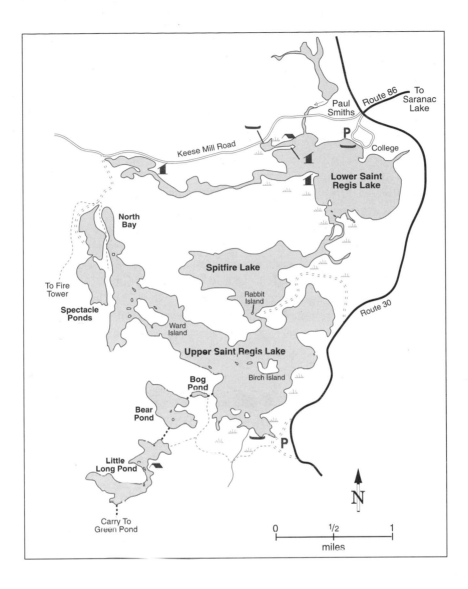

Much more important than the luxury accommodations found here in ages past was the role the area played in awakening interest in the environment. As well described in the wonderful book *An Adirondack Passage: The Cruise of the Canoe Sairy Gamp,* by Christine Jerome, the region played an important role in cementing a young Theodore Roosevelt's interest in natural history into a lifelong commitment that would help to usher in this nation's conservation movement. During several visits here as a boy and during a June 1877 visit as a Harvard student, Roosevelt published his observations of the area's bird life in what became his first natural history contribution: *The Summer Birds of the Adirondacks in Franklin County, N.Y.*

It was not too far from here 24 years later that Teddy Roosevelt, as vice president of the United States, climbed the state's highest peak, Mt. Marcy. On the hike back down, he learned that President McKinley had been shot and lay gravely wounded. By the time he made it to North Creek by horse, McKinley had died and Roosevelt was president. Appreciation of the out-of-doors gained in the Adirondacks no doubt played an important role in his determination to protect some of the nation's natural treasures—which he did with the creation of the National Park Service and the National Forest System.

There is a beautiful lean-to on Peters Rock, across from Paul Smiths College, and several others, all built by college students along the wide, two-mile-long outlet channel toward Keese Mill. The marshy south end of Lower St. Regis Lake and the channel into Spitfire Lake abound with thick floating vegetation by early summer. Depending on the water level, there may be several navigable channels and islands to explore in the marsh here, but when we visited, the water level had dropped somewhat, limiting our passage to one channel.

Spitfire and Upper St. Regis Lakes

Spitfire Lake is about a mile across and fairly developed around the entire perimeter. At the south end of this lake is tiny Rabbit Island, which played a role in important medical research. Here in 1886, Dr. Edward Livingston Trudeau studied how the environment influenced the spread of tuberculosis within a colony of rabbits. The island kept the rabbits—and presumably the disease—isolated, according to a plaque. (We are not told how the rabbits were contained in the winter when the lake froze over....)

Upper St. Regis Lake is much larger than Spitfire and also quite developed. But, as with Spitfire, most of the places you see here aren't tacky new vacation homes. Here you will find classic old Adirondack vacation homes, many dating from the late 1800s when this was the "wilderness" retreat for New York's wealthy aristocracy. Vacationers traveled by train from Albany and New York City. Architecturally spectacular vacation homes adorn the shoreline, many with large three- or four-bay boathouses that store classic wooden motorboats from the early 1900s. One could spend a day paddling the 11-mile shoreline of these two lakes gazing at the buildings, whose rustic architecture became known as the Adirondack style.

Looking across Upper St. Regis Lake from the carry into Bog Pond and the St. Regis Canoe Area.

Upper St. Regis Lake has long been a sailing lake. Summering New York Yacht Club members founded their own sailing club here in 1897 and designed their own sailboat—the Idem class. Their idea was to have all the boats be identical, so that the races would test the participants' skills, not differences in their boats.

The most grandiose of the estates on Upper St. Regis is Camp Topridge, on the western arm extending to the north. The scattered 60 or so buildings were built in the early 1900s by Marjorie Merriweather Post, heiress of the cereal company that later became General Foods. At one time, the "camp" employed eighty-five staff! When the mistress of Topridge died in 1973, the estate was given to the state of New York, which then sold it in 1985 for $1 million to New Jersey millionaire Roger Jakubowski, who went bankrupt in 1993.

From the end of the north arm of Upper St. Regis Lake (North Bay), a trail extends around Spectacle Ponds and up to the top of St. Regis Mountain at an elevation of 2,874 feet. It looks as if the fire lookout tower on the peak would provide tremendous views out over the St. Regis Canoe Wilderness Area.

Despite the level of development on the St. Regis Lakes and Spitfire Lake, loons nest successfully, as evidenced by the parent with two chicks we watched on our paddle through. To enjoy your time on these lakes, paddle early in the morning, midweek, or before or after the main vacation season. Or, be prepared for a lot of activity.

Gateway to the St. Regis Canoe Area

Near the south end of Upper St. Regis Lake, a carry into Bog Pond and many other ponds of the St. Regis Canoe Wilderness Area begins (see following section). Even if you are not planning an extended back-country trip, it's worth carrying into Bear Pond and Little Long Pond to get a sense of the wild, remote country in this spectacular region.

The carries to Bog Pond and Bear Pond—only 50 to 60 yards each—give you a taste of what a canoe carry is like, but not enough to wear you out. Tiny Bog Pond is aptly named, a great place to see pitcher plants and other bog vegetation. The bottom is mucky and the shores thick with sheep laurel and other shrubs.

By contrast, the deeper Bear Pond sparkles with clear water and sections of sandy shore. You will see some huge specimens of white pine here, along with hemlock, spruce, and balsam fir in the predominantly conifer woods. We saw a loon and several great blue herons.

Getting There

From Exit 30 on I-87, take Route 9 then Route 73 toward Lake Placid. Before getting into Lake Placid, take a left onto Military Road, which bypasses the town, following signs to Saranac Lake. In Saranac Lake, take Route 86 north, passing Route 186 to the left. Continue for another 7.2 miles, where Route 86 Ts into Route 30. Drive straight across into Paul Smiths College. Bear to the right, and you will reach the boat access on Lower St. Regis Lake in 0.2 mile. If you plan to leave your vehicle here overnight, check in with the campus security office to let them know your plans. A smaller, roadside boat access is found off Keese Mill Road, 1.0 mile west from Route 30.

The primary boat access on Upper St. Regis Lake is a few miles south, off Route 30. From the intersection of Routes 30 and 86, take Route 30 south for 3.4 miles, and turn right. Continue roughly straight to the boat access in about a quarter mile. Another boat access is shown on some maps at the north end of North Bay, but we did not investigate this access location.

St. Regis Canoe Area
Santa Clara

MAPS
New York Atlas: Map 95
USGS Quadrangles: St. Regis Mountain, Upper Saranac Lake

INFORMATION
General: Dozens of ponds in this 18,000-acre St. Regis Canoe Wilderness Area are covered in this section.

Outfitter: St. Regis Canoe Outfitter, P.O. Box 318, Lake Clear, NY 12945; 518-891-1838. Complete supplies, including canoe rentals. Located on Floodwood Pond.

Wild. Remote. Gorgeous. Pristine. The St. Regis Canoe Area offers some of the finest backcountry paddling in New York. Fifty-eight lakes and ponds—most of them accessible by water or short carries—dot the landscape throughout this 18,000-acre wilderness section of the Adirondacks. In the 1970s this part of Adirondack Park was set aside for nonmotorized use and temporary (rather than seasonal) camping. The state bans all motorboats, motorized vehicles, airplanes, and snow-mobiles from the canoe area.

For the paddler, several excellent canoe trips wend their way through the St. Regis Canoe Area. Some can be paddled in extended multiday loops or in-and-out trips, but the best way to see the area is a through-trip—putting in at one location and taking out at another. You can drop off one vehicle at the terminus of the trip, then drive with gear to the put-in. Or you can hire an outfitter to shuttle you and gear or to ferry your car from the put-in to your destination.

The most common loop trip takes you through Hoel, Turtle, Slang, and Long Ponds in the canoe area, then several ponds just to the south (Floodwood, Middle, and Polliwog). For a through-trip, you can put in or take out on Lower St. Regis Lake, Upper St. Regis Lake, Little Clear Pond, Hoel Pond, or Long Pond. For an even more extended trip, you can put in on Osgood Pond or Rainbow Lake to the northeast or on any one of a number of bodies of water to the south, such as Rollins Pond, Fish Creek Pond, or the Saranac Lakes. We describe several canoe routes through the canoe area.

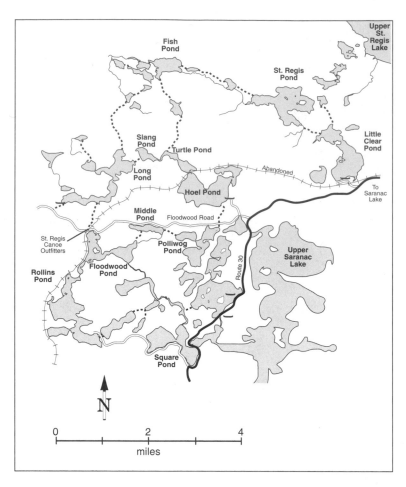

From Upper St. Regis Lake to St. Regis Pond

The trip from Upper St. Regis Lake into St. Regis Pond is fairly easy, though it does involve five relatively short carries. Near the south end of St. Regis Lake (see section on the St. Regis Lakes and Spitfire Lake, page 210), you will find a short carry into Bog Pond. This marks the eastern end of the Canoe Area. The very short carry (about 50 yards) makes it just as easy to carry canoes upright, leaving the lighter gear in them, and make a return trip for the rest.

Bog Pond is tiny, just a few hundred yards long. From the put-in—which may be quite muddy—you initially paddle along a winding channel amid leatherleaf, sheep laurel, pitcher plant, and other vegetation typical of bog ecosystems. The large number of frogs here—as on most of the ponds in the canoe area—surprised us. A quick paddle (longer if you take the time to study some of the plants) brings you to the western end of the pond, where you will see the rectangular white sign marking the carry into Bear Pond.

Almost as short as the carry into Bog Pond, the carry to Bear Pond brings you into a very different pond—one with deep, clear water and sandy sections of shoreline. Tall, ancient white pines rise from the shoreline of this picturesque pond. We watched loons dive for fish and great blue herons wade along the shallows. There are a few small islands in the pond worth exploring. Even if paddling the shoreline and around all the islands, you will quickly reach the next carry—into Little Long Pond.

Though a little longer than the first two—with a bit of up and down—the carry into Little Long Pond remains very manageable (warming up the through-paddler for some more strenuous carries to come). Little Long Pond, with an S-shaped configuration about a mile in length, has the highest elevation of any pond in this section of the canoe area. Little Long Pond, Bear Pond, and Bog Pond drain into the Middle Branch of the St. Regis River, while the other ponds covered in this section drain either into the West Branch of the St. Regis or into the Saranac River.

Conifers, including hemlock, spruce, fir, tamarack, and some towering, wind-sculpted white pines, dominate the shoreline of Little Long Pond. Most paddlers choose to push on into St. Regis Pond to camp, rather than take advantage of the several very nice campsites here. At the southernmost tip of Little Long Pond is the carry into Green Pond.

Note on the carry into Green Pond the abundant wildflowers—we saw pink lady's slipper, trillium, and Indian cucumber root, for example, nestled among the thick clubmosses and hobblebush viburnum. The trail winds through a deep yellow birch-sugar maple-beech woods. On tiny Green Pond—like quite a few others in the canoe area—you can see the portage sign on the far side of the pond before you get in your boat. This last carry, from Green Pond into St. Regis Pond, is short (100–150 yards).

St. Regis Pond is a gem—one of the finest camping ponds in the Adirondacks. On a map, the pond looks a bit like a flying duck, with the bill at the far west end by the dam. From the tip of the bill to the tail is about a mile and a half. Several island campsites were posted no-camping when we paddled here—we suspect either to allow the vegetation to recover from overuse or to reduce shoreline erosion. A well-kept shelter perches on the south shore where the pond narrows toward the west. Across the pond from the shelter is a superb campsite with a massive slab of granite extending down into the water from which

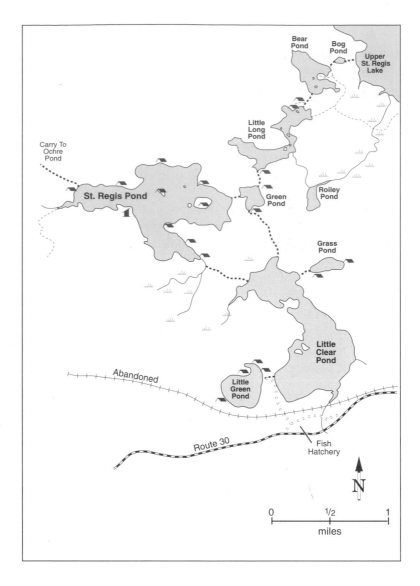

swimmers can enjoy the cool, refreshing water. To the north from St. Regis Pond you can see St. Regis Mountain, which rises to 2,874 feet and has a fire lookout tower on the top.

Visitors here should know that, even though this is a true wilderness pond, it's no secret. Lots of people know that St. Regis Pond provides a wonderful place to camp. Most of the dozen or so campsites on the pond are frequently in use, and you may not succeed in getting one of the nicest sites. If you want more solitude here, visit after Labor Day, when most of the summer vacationers (and mosquitoes) have gone.

Inlet creeks flow between many of the lakes in the St. Regis Canoe Areas.

In the southern arm of St. Regis Pond, you can paddle up the winding inlet creek for several hundred yards—probably much farther in the early spring. This creek is rich with aquatic vegetation, including pickerelweed, yellow bladderwort, sundew, pitcher plant, wild calla or water arum—with heart-shaped leaves somewhat rounder than those of pickerelweed—and yellow pond lily. Sweet gale lines the banks, and feathery spires of tamarack rise from the ground farther from the bank. If you paddle up this creek, you will get to a boardwalk extending across the boggy shore from the left—this is the carry to Little Clear Pond.

Exploring Little Clear Pond

Some canoeists reach St. Regis Pond from the boat access on Little Clear Pond (just west of the State Fish Hatchery). For others, Little Clear Pond makes a great day trip from St. Regis Pond. From the southern arm of St. Regis Pond, paddle up the meandering creek for a few hundred yards, and take out at the boardwalk on the left. The third-of-a-mile carry to Little Clear Pond starts out somewhat steeply, with lots of exposed tree roots, then levels out for most of the distance.

From the access onto Little Clear Pond, you can paddle to the right (southwest) into a shallow cattail marsh leading to a small inlet creek. By midsummer, water shield and other floating vegetation cover the surface of this cove in dense mats. We saw wood ducks here, watched great blue herons hunting methodically in the shallows, spooked a few painted turtles, and noticed a sizable beaver lodge. In the spring it might be possible to paddle up the inlet creek here, but by mid-July we could not even get over to it.

Because the State Fish Hatchery uses the waters of Little Clear Pond at the south end, the state maintains various restrictions to ensure water quality and to prevent the introduction of unwanted fish species. Fishing and camping are prohibited, which suits the resident ospreys just fine, assuring plenty of fish. Along with several ospreys, we saw as many as a half-dozen loons here, including one adult with two chicks near the small islands. We were troubled, though, to see one loon with a deformed bill—possible evidence of dioxin or PCB poisoning.

At the north end of Little Clear Pond, a short carry leads into Grass Pond, but the tiny pond did not seem terribly interesting. When we visited, the water level was way down, exposing a rather unappealing muddy shoreline. We did not check out the two campsites supposedly on the pond.

If you get a chance while in the area, visit the State Fish Hatchery at the south end of Little Clear Pond. You cannot paddle to it, as the small cove at the southeast end of the pond remains off-limits to boats. The easiest way to visit the hatchery is by car at the beginning or end of your paddling trip. You will see the mammoth breeding stock of landlocked salmon and brook trout they keep here, some about two feet long. They even had pails of fish food at some of the tanks for you to feed the fish. Open daily, the visitor center at the fish hatchery is a great place to take kids.

The Fish Pond Area

You really have to work to get into Fish Pond, which helps to make it such a wonderful spot. You can carry to Fish Pond from Hoel Pond, Long Pond, or St. Regis Pond. With most of the routes in, the trails are up and down and very uneven, though it is also possible to use a portage cart along much smoother abandoned logging roads all the way from the dam at St. Regis Pond to Fish Pond—a distance of about two

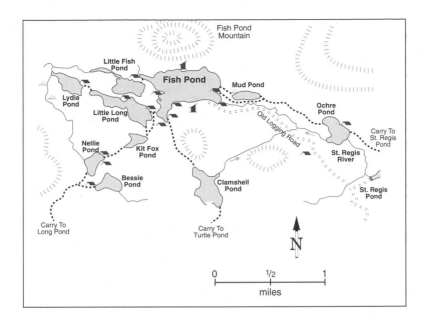

miles. (Portage carts are not effective on the carry trails because of steepness, roots, and rocks.) We describe the carry-trail route from St. Regis Pond here.

In the spring it may be possible to paddle or pole a canoe from the dam on St. Regis Pond down the West Branch of the St. Regis River to Ochre Pond, though when we visited during a dry summer this was not possible. The carry trail begins on St. Regis Pond near the western end, but northeast of the dam. We made the mistake of bringing a portage cart with us into the St. Regis Canoe Area and tried to use it here. Forget it. Not only did many roots and stones bar the way, but if you do use it you'll end up having a significant ecological impact on the trail by trampling wildflowers or churning up the trail with the tires. Unless you plan to come in to Fish Pond via the logging road, leave your portage cart at home.

The carry to Ochre Pond involves some up and down, and the well-used trail has lots of exposed rocks and roots. Ochre Pond is small—one of those where you can see the carry trail sign on the other side of the pond before you even get in your canoe from the last carry. The pond gets its name from the color ochre. Rust-colored deposits form in certain mountain lakes when just the right conditions provide a food source for bacteria that live on iron. Acidic groundwater from bogs can dissolve iron out of the rock and soils and put it in solution as ferrous ion (Fe^{++}). When iron-rich—but oxygen-poor—water wells up

Alex at the St. Regis Pond end of the carry between Little Clear Pond and St. Regis Pond. The boardwalk protects fragile vegetation.

through a spring into oxygen-rich water, just the right environment is created to support a type of aerobic "iron bacterium." This bacterium obtains its sustenance from ferrous ion, oxygen, and carbon dioxide—converting these chemicals into organic matter, just as plants convert carbon dioxide and water into organic matter through photosynthesis. The bacterium-catalyzed reaction precipitates ferric oxide in flocculate orange masses. Deposits of this precipitate build up in certain areas—including Ochre Pond—and the chemical state of the ferric oxide gradually changes into less hydrated forms, which have earthy colors ranging from yellow to red and brown.

Going from Ochre Pond to Fish Pond entails one of the longest carries of the trip, but it is a gorgeous trail, with part of it passing along a ridge studded with mammoth old-growth white pine and hemlock. You can either carry all the way to Fish Pond on this Ridge Trail, or turn off to the right after about two-thirds of a mile into Mud Pond (a sign clearly marks the trail split). Mud Pond's tiny size hardly justifies loading and unloading the canoes. We carried most of our gear on to Fish Pond but paddled Mud Pond anyway—and we were glad we did.

Surrounded by tall cathedral white pines, the shallow pond is rich with bog life. Most exciting were floating logs festooned with fascinating plants: delicate pink of rose pogonia orchids; upright nodding spikes and long, cuplike leaves of carnivorous pitcher plants; terrestrial horned bladderwort, with small yellow flowers that have long drooping spurs (most bladderworts are aquatic); and a low reddish carpet of sundew plants, which use sticky droplets to entrap tiny insects. This floating-log ecosystem provided a veritable classroom of plant adaptation to nutrient-poor conditions.

From the western end of Mud Pond, the short carry traverses a recently improved trail to Fish Pond. Nestled beneath Fish Pond Mountain to the north and less than a mile across, the pond is spectacular. Since you will work hard to get here, plan to spend a few days—if there is an available campsite. We counted two lean-tos on Fish Pond and another eight campsites. Enjoy the excellent brook trout and lake trout fishing, as well.

The northwestern cove of Fish Pond—by the outlet into Little Fish Pond—offers a great spot to watch beavers. Paddle up here in the evening, and you'll likely see (and hear) this industrious rodent hard at work. On some large boulders extending out of the water here, we watched two large snapping turtles soaking up the late afternoon sun.

Alex and family on Fish Pond.

Rarely have we seen snappers sunning—as painted turtles do all the time—yet the references we saw in the journal at the Blangden Lean-to lead us to believe that these particular turtles sun themselves frequently. Some reptile guides claim that male snapping turtles may never leave the water after entering it as hatchlings.

From Fish Pond you can take wonderful day trips into nearby ponds, including Little Fish, Little Long (a different Little Long Pond from the one described earlier), Lydia, Kit Fox, Nellie, Bessie, and Clamshell.

Reach Little Fish Pond—tranquil and pristine—from near the end of the outlet cove on the northwest end of Fish Pond. During an evening paddle on Little Fish Pond, the still air scarcely rippled the water's surface. The shoreline is shrubby—not easy to disembark on—with leatherleaf, sheep laurel, and bracken and royal ferns. Along the southern shore a few spots exist where you can pull over and walk up and over the steep esker ridge into Little Long Pond. (It would be difficult to carry a canoe over, however).

In the water along the southern shore we saw several freshwater sponge colonies. Though we find sponges (phylum Porifera) far more commonly in the ocean, a few freshwater species exist. The species we saw, probably *Spongilla lacustris,* looks more like a plant than animal. (Sponges are loosely aggregated colonies of primitive animals.) It is bright green and branching, living underwater attached to submerged sticks or rocks. The green color comes from the single-celled algae, *Zoochlorellae,* which live symbiotically with the sponge colony. We have seen branching colonies of these sponges more than a foot in height, though the sponges we saw on Little Fish Pond were smaller. They only inhabit very pure water.

From the southern arm of Fish Pond, you can carry over the ridge into Little Long Pond. Watch your footing on this short up-and-down carry! Little Long Pond is a deep oligotrophic pond that had an odd milky blue color when we visited—quite different from the color of other ponds in the area. We saw one campsite on the pond, roughly in the center on the northern shore. Much of the north shore is quite steep and sandy—the ridge between Little Long Pond and Little Fish Pond is an esker created as a retreating glacier left a deposit of sand and rock.

The sand suits nesting snapping turtles very well, as they use the steep exposed sand banks for building nests. When we visited in mid-July, we saw the remains of several nests and hundreds of curled pieces of leathery eggshell. These were likely remains of nests dug up by skunks, raccoons, otters, or some other predator—very few of a snapping turtle's offspring make it to the water, but the species does well because, once in the water, it may live for 30 or more years.

Lydia Pond, accessible by a portage from the western end of Little Long Pond, lies along the same esker as Little Long Pond. As on Little Long, we saw evidence of snapping turtle nests on the sandy northern shore. Although whitened drift logs blocked our way from further exploration of the marshy outlet at Lydia Pond's west end, we did see lots of rose pogonia orchids, pitcher plants, sundews, and a muskrat here. A lone loon swam and dove about the pond when we visited. There is one campsite on Lydia Pond—right at the end of the carry from Little Long Pond.

A hike into Clamshell Pond makes another pleasant day trip from Fish Pond—with or without canoe. The carry heads south from near the tip of the southern arm of Fish Pond (across from the carry into Little Long Pond). This half-mile hike has significant ups and downs, but it winds through a beautiful old-growth yellow birch and hemlock forest. Some of the largest yellow birch we've seen line the trail. Clamshell Pond has a generally sandy bottom. Occasional boulders dot the shoreline, and a mixed hardwood-conifer forest surrounds the pond with white pine, hemlock, northern white cedar, spruce, sugar maple, and yellow birch. Through-paddlers can carry from here down to Turtle and Hoel Ponds, though the carry from Clamshell to Turtle is quite long and steep.

The other route out of (or into) Fish Pond is via Kit Fox, Nellie, and Long Ponds. From the south arm of Fish Pond, take the carry to Little Long Pond, as described above, then paddle to the southern tip of Little Long Pond to find the carry to Kit Fox Pond. Coming from Fish Pond, you can alternately bypass Little Long Pond, carrying all the way to Kit Fox Pond and avoiding a steep trail down into Little Long Pond. This alternate trail to Kit Fox Pond branches off from the carry trail between Fish and Little Long Ponds. We found it fine for walking but not as well maintained for carrying a canoe when we visited (tree branches closed in on the narrow trail), so you will be better off sticking to the marked carry trail with a canoe.

Kit Fox Pond, an easy carry from Little Long Pond, is tiny but well worth exploring. Slowly skirting the perimeter, we happened on a bullfrog bedded down in a soft (sticky) mat of sundew beneath a healthy clump of pitcher plant atop a floating log. Many ancient logs extended out from shore or floated in the shallow water and muck. The carry to Nellie Pond is significantly longer. Expect this trail to be quite

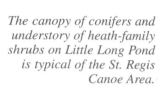
The canopy of conifers and understory of heath-family shrubs on Little Long Pond is typical of the St. Regis Canoe Area.

wet in the spring, but the walking was easy when we visited. A couple of campsites greet you right as you reach the pond.

The carry you've been building up for traverses from Nellie to Long Pond. Not only is it long—about a mile and a half—but parts of it were exceedingly wet when we visited. About a tenth of a mile from Nellie Pond, a trail bears off sharply to the left to Bessie Pond. There is a gorgeous campsite on Bessie Pond on a thick carpet of pine needles. A huge floating log extends 60 or 70 feet into the water from shore, providing a great swimming or fishing platform. If you make two trips at the Long Pond carry, Bessie Pond offers a great midpoint break. Along the first half of the carry trail, a few sections can be pretty wet in the spring, as evidenced by the carefully placed stepping-stones. One section of trail passes through a beautiful pitch pine forest, a very unusual sight in this part of New York, seeming most out of place.

The greatest excitement of the carry, however, was the section of trail that passed over (through) a beaver-flooded swamp near the south end. We had to use fancy footwork—especially when carrying a canoe—to negotiate the sections of floating bridge across the swamp. As we stepped on one end of a section of log bridge, it would sink three or four inches into the mucky water. Conveniently, there was an ample supply of sticks at both ends of this swamp to help one maintain balance on the acrobatic carry. With the water only slightly higher, one would have to paddle across this wetland. This should be only a temporary problem, but it made for quite an adventure during our visit. Indeed, we were glad to arrive finally at Long Pond.

Long Pond to Hoel Pond

Long Pond is a wonderful place to become acquainted with backcountry canoe camping. Reaching the two-mile-long pond from Floodwood Road requires just enough effort to give one a feeling of accomplishment getting there—it is a real feat getting here from Fish Pond! While more than a dozen campsites dot the shoreline, they spread out enough so that you can find some solitude here. Totally within the St. Regis Canoe Area, Long Pond remains free of motorboats.

From a campsite on Long Pond, you can take a pleasant evening or early morning paddle up to Pink Pond, where you are likely to see beavers and other wildlife. Near the western end of Long Pond, watch for a creek that comes in from the north, and paddle up the narrow channel. When we visited, we had to carry over a beaver dam almost immediately, then we quietly wended our way up into the small pond. The channel banks grow thick with leatherleaf, sheep laurel, sweet gale, royal fern, pickerelweed, wild calla, and grasses and sedges on the many sphagnum hummocks. In the late afternoon, sunlight filters through feathery branches of tamarack along the banks. In the water are yellow pond lily, fragrant water lily, water shield, and long floating leaves of bur reed.

We had the good fortune here to watch a family of beaver lazily munching on yellow pond lily stems. While the adult disappeared as our canoe drifted close, we got a great look at the young, who seemed oblivious to our presence. As evening settled in, we spotted a deer drinking from the shore and listened to the melodious song of the white-throated sparrow.

From the eastern end of Long Pond, you can make a short carry into Slang Pond, where you will find a few campsites. From Slang you can usually paddle through to Turtle Pond, but at low water it may be necessary to wade with your canoe through the shallow passage. There is one campsite on Turtle Pond, where the carry goes off to Clamshell Pond.

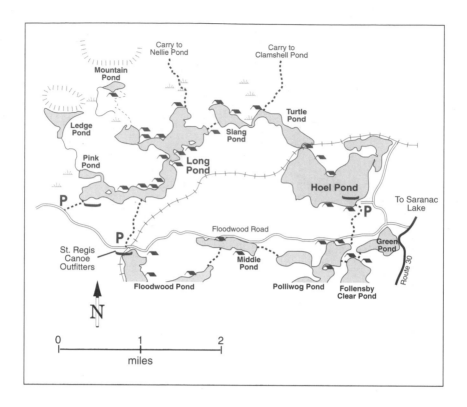

At the eastern end of Turtle Pond, you have to carry your canoe and gear up over the abandoned railroad tracks to get into Hoel Pond. Hoel Pond—about a mile long and half a mile across—offers an alternate put-in point for a trip into the St. Regis Canoe Area. There is some development on the eastern side of the pond, and you may see powerboats here. The canoe outfitter on Floodwood Pond told us that Hoel Pond is actually one of the most dangerous bodies of water in the area. Winds whip up waves very quickly across the broad expanse, and the shoreline affords little protection on most of the pond. A more protected cove exists on the northern end of Hoel Pond, but development at that end makes it less appealing.

Getting There

There are five primary access locations for the St. Regis Canoe Area: off Route 30 at the south end of Upper St. Regis Lake; at Paul Smiths College at the north end of Lower St. Regis Lake (see previous section on the St. Regis Lakes and Spitfire Pond); at the south end of Little

Clear Pond west of the State Fish Hatchery; on the southeastern end of Hoel Pond; and at the western end of Long Pond, off Floodwood Road. You can drive right to the put-in sites on all but the Long Pond access, which requires a carry of about a quarter mile. To get to these access sites, use the directions below:

Access on Upper St. Regis Lake: From the junction of Routes 186 and 30 at Lake Clear Junction, drive north on Route 30 for 2.9 miles, and bear left onto a gravel road. Follow this road for 0.4 mile to the public boat access (right next to a private access). Only a few cars can park here.

Access on Lower St. Regis Lake at Paul Smiths College: Drive north from the town of Saranac Lake on Route 86. After 11.8 miles, where Route 86 (also shown on some maps as Route 192) ends at Route 30, continue straight across, into Paul Smiths College. Follow the campus road around to the right to the boat access and parking area in 0.2 mile. If you plan to leave a car here overnight, check in with the campus security office, which is located back toward Route 30 (to the right as you are heading toward Route 30).

Access on Little Clear Pond: Take Route 30 west from Lake Clear Junction (where Route 186 intersects with Route 30) for about 2.5 miles, and turn right toward the fish hatchery. Follow signs to the boat access, where there is plenty of parking.

Access on Hoel Pond: Take Route 30 west from Lake Clear Junction for 5.3 miles, then bear right onto Floodwood Road. Bear right at the fork after 0.3 mile, and follow this road to the boat access.

Access at the western end of Long Pond: From Route 30, drive west on Floodwood Road, passing the St. Regis Canoe Outfitters on the left. After 5.0 miles from Route 30, turn right into the boat access, where you will find parking for about 20 cars. The carry trail from here to Long Pond is wide and suitable for a portage cart. (Most other carries in the St. Regis Canoe Area are not suitable for portage carts, and we suggest that you do not bring them along.)

Fish Creek Loops
Santa Clara

MAPS
> **New York Atlas:** Map 95
> **USGS Quadrangle:** Upper Saranac Lake

INFORMATION
> **Prominent fish species:** Brook trout
> **Canoe Outfitting:** St. Regis Canoe Outfitters, P.O. Box 318, Lake Clear, NY 12945; 518-891-1838. Complete supplies, including canoe rentals. Located on Floodwood Pond.
> **Camping:** Rollins Pond Campground; 518-891-3239. Fish Creek Pond Campground; 518-895-4560.

There is something wonderful about being able to paddle a string of lakes or ponds with minimal portaging and end up at the starting point. The Fish Creek Loops described in this section provide just such opportunities. The compact scale of these trips, with just a few short carries, makes them ideal as the first such trips for young paddlers. Our five- and eight-year-old girls did a half-dozen carries superbly and explored nine different ponds during three days and two nights here.

Floodwood Pond—Fish Creek—Whey Pond—Rollins Pond Loop

Several points provide access for this loop trip, as shown on the map. One approach is to camp at the Rollins Pond Campground, then paddle this loop as a day trip from your lakeside campsite. We visited this area in early May (before the campground was open—and before the bugs were out) and launched onto the northern tip of Floodwood Pond. We paddled to the large island and set up a base camp, from which we explored this loop as well as the loop described below.

We recommend traveling in a clockwise direction, which permits paddling downstream on Fish Creek—though the current is not too strong, the section between Floodwood and Little Square Ponds flows right along. If you start out on Rollins Pond, paddle north from the campground (or from one of the primitive campsites along the western shore). At the northern end of Rollins Pond, paddle to the east (right). The pond narrows to a small stream, which connects into Floodwood Pond. In May, the stream contained enough water to float our boat,

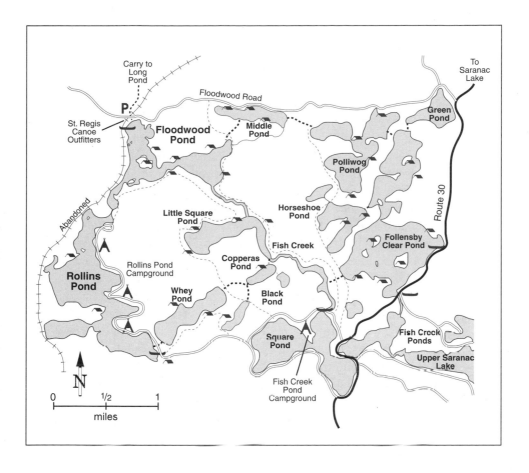

though we had to lie down at one point to maneuver under a fallen birch tree and had to drag our canoe over a small beaver dam. Later in the season you usually need to carry along a small portage trail on the left bank. Look for a path leading off to the left as the pond narrows to a stream. If you do paddle through, watch for rocks.

The western end of Floodwood Pond is narrow, with an abandoned railway bed on the northern shore. A few vacation houses crop up along the shore—the only ones you will encounter on this trip. Floodwood Pond, like most of the ponds here, has a fairly sandy bottom and not too many rocks. The thick understory along the shoreline makes landing a canoe just anywhere out of the question, but the woods rising from the water are much more open. Hemlock, white pine, yellow birch, white birch, beech, and sugar maple are the predominant trees. Because the area has not been logged for over 100 years, some hemlocks have grown to a huge size.

Red pine and hemlock—both of which provide an open, accessible forest floor—dominate the large island on Floodwood Pond. Three or four campsites and several outhouses are scattered at various points on the island. When we camped here in 1995, a pair of merlins nested in one of the tall red pines on the island. Their frequent peening cries alerted us to their presence many times during our two-night stay. This relatively rare falcon looks very much like a peregrine but is about half the size—just slightly larger than another, more common falcon, the kestrel. It is a delight to watch these agile-winged birds. We watched with binoculars as one devoured a small rodent 50 feet up on a dead snag. We have also seen them nesting on islands in northern Maine.

Floodwood Pond resembles a butterfly. Fish Creek flows out of the bottom tip of the eastern wing toward Little Square Pond, Copperas Pond, and the Fish Creek Ponds. The first section of Fish Creek—between Floodwood and Little Square Ponds—is the shallowest and quickest. While there are no rapids, some rocks and many logs provide an obstacle course of sorts. In periods of low water, passage here may be difficult. Shortly after leaving Floodwood Pond, pass under a wooden hiking-snowmobile trail bridge. In several places, kind souls have notched out large submerged logs to provide canoe passage. We had to squeeze over a couple of tiny beaver dams when we visited, so be forewarned: Fish Creek could be a lot different depending on how busy our furred friends have been before your visit.

Be sure not to rush through here too fast. Beautiful Fish Creek winds through quite varied vegetation. In some sections the streambed meanders through a shaded woodland, with trees overhanging the channel. In other places, it winds through a marsh thick with grasses, sedges, and cattails, where you can expect to startle a great blue heron from its patient fishing. Everywhere in the gently flowing stream you will see yellow pond lilies and various other floating and emergent aquatic plants. Leatherleaf dominates most of the shoreline. You can recognize this shrub by its small leathery leaves and drooping clusters of small white, inconspicuous bell-like flowers.

About a half mile below Floodwood Pond, Fish Creek flows into the eastern end of Little Square Pond. If the winds coming out of the west do not blow too strongly, you may want to explore this pond, but both times we paddled through here the waves coming off Little Square Pond discouraged us from more thorough exploration.

Below Little Square Pond, Fish Creek widens and the vegetation becomes more fenlike. You will see feathery tamarack, particularly along the western shore. On the sphagnum tussocks watch for carnivorous pitcher plants. As the channel begins to narrow again, keep an eye out for the narrow stream heading off to the right into Copperas Pond. You can easily miss this turn in the summer when thick pond vegetation covers the water's surface. Paddle southwest through Copperas Pond to the carry into Whey Pond. Conspicuous rectangular white signs and yellow trail markers point the way to and down all the carries. The trail to Whey Pond heads due west from the takeout point; another trail from the same point leads south into Black Pond.

Like most of the carries on state land in Adirondack Park, the Whey Pond Carry traverses the terrain gently, taking you through thick beds of wildflowers, ferns, and clubmosses. While paddling your boat is distinctly easier than carrying it, the carries provide a chance to stretch your legs, exercise your sore buns, enjoy the woods from a distinctly different perspective, and study the wildflowers—particularly when the bugs don't patrol the woods. During our early visit, when the huge velvety buds of hobblebush viburnum were just beginning to unfurl, the yellow bell-like flowers of trout lily were in full bloom.

A portage cart can make light work on a carry, as Lillian and Frances demonstrate.

Whey Pond, just under a mile long, runs in a northeast-southwest orientation. At the southwest end, look for the sign identifying the carry into Rollins Pond. There are two carries: the more southern one is shorter and ends up at a boat launch into Rollins, while the other brings you out onto the campground road.

Rollins Pond is much larger than the other ponds on this loop and can become quite choppy on a windy day, so use caution. The eastern shore is lined with 288 campsites—so don't expect to find solitude when the campground is open. Rollins Pond Campground offers an attractive setting with ample room between sites, and it seems well managed. For those seeking the convenience of car camping, this spot would be ideal. To get the most out of a paddle on Rollins Pond, though, stick to the western shore, where you can escape into several deep coves and keep your distance from the bustling campground activity—or paddle here early in the season, as we did.

Follensby Clear Pond—Polliwog Pond—Floodwood Pond—Fish Creek Loop

This trip covers six ponds connected by Fish Creek and four relatively short carries. The carries are somewhat longer and a bit steeper than those in the preceding section, but you can still manage the loop as a day trip. Camping opportunities abound on Follensby Clear Pond, and several campsites nestle along the shores of most of the other ponds on this loop. Or you can camp at the Fish Creek Pond Campground and paddle north into Follensby Clear Pond via the Spider Creek Passage.

If you start at Floodwood Pond, paddle southeast into Fish Creek. The state prohibits motors on Fish Creek, so it should be pretty quiet. Pass through the eastern end of Little Square Pond, pass the somewhat hidden channel into Copperas Pond on the right, and continue in a generally southeastern direction, keeping an eye out for the carry to Follensby Clear Pond on the left. A wooden boardwalk extends out into the water, but vegetation may hide it by early summer.

The carry trail into Follensby Clear Pond is less than a quarter mile in length, well marked, and lined with ferns, clubmosses, and wildflowers. Perhaps the prettiest pond in this immediate area, Follensby Clear Pond remains our favorite. The wide southern section—about a mile across—has two boat access locations along Route 30. Seven islands dot the surface of the two-mile-long pond, most with campsites on them. While we didn't camp here, several of the sites looked great, sandy beaches topping off the wilderness splendor. Hemlock dominates the forest around Follensby Clear Pond, its shade providing an open, inviting woodland and its needles leaving a soft carpet that quiets one's footsteps. We paddled alone here, sharing the water only with loons and mergansers.

After paddling north through the narrowest part of the pond, you can get into Horseshoe Pond by paddling into the cove on the left. A well-marked and very short carry over a slight rise brings you into Horseshoe Pond. True to its name, this pond is shaped like a horseshoe. From the trail you can look into both arms of the small pond. Several campsites cluster near the portage trail and one lies directly across.

Near the north end of Follensby Clear Pond on the west side is the somewhat hidden carry to Polliwog Pond. This beautiful trail passes through old-growth hemlock forest. While much of the Adirondacks was clear-cut in the mid-1800s, some 60,000 acres remain as virgin forest, some of those acres right here. Since 1892 there has been no logging on public lands in the park, so much more of the forest is returning to old-growth. The carry into Polliwog Pond will give you a sense of what virgin forest looks and feels like. Note the standing dead trees, the moss-covered logs slowly rotting into the ground, the tremendous variation in age of trees, and the high diversity of tree and plant species.

Polliwog Pond has a sandy bottom, and several of the campsites we saw offered beautiful sand beaches. Depending on the water level,

A northern water snake suns on a dense patch of aquatic vegetation. It swims underwater to catch small fish.

the point of land to the left after you enter the pond will either be a peninsula or an island. Another peninsula comes in from the west across the pond. To paddle through to Middle Pond, you have to pass through a narrow section of Polliwog into the western extension of the pond. At the western end of the pond, you will see the sign marking the carry to Middle Pond. The exception that proves the rule about gentle carries, this trail goes up and down somewhat steeply for a third of a mile—again, passing through gorgeous, deep woods.

Middle Pond is less than three-quarters of a mile long and just a few hundred yards wide. With its east-west orientation, a westerly breeze can generate surprisingly large waves. Several campsites dot the far side, along Floodwood Road, and one is on the south side. Tree swallows patrolled the air, swooping for flying insects, then returning to dead trees that no doubt provide nesting sites. A solitary loon, clearly oblivious to the cold wind and choppy waves, dove for fish near the center of the pond. Watch for the carry to Floodwood Pond along the south shore about three-quarters of the way up this pond. This final carry in the loop starts out steep but then becomes an easy walk.

Getting There

To reach this area from I-87, get off at Exit 30 and take Routes 73 and 86 to Lake Placid and Saranac Lake. In the town of Saranac Lake, Route 86 briefly joins Route 3 east. Bear left on Route 86 west where it splits off Route 3. Continue on Route 86 for another 4.6 miles from this point, then turn left onto Route 186, following the sign to Lake Clear. Stay on Route 186 for 3.8 miles to where it feeds into Route 30 south. If you want to launch your canoe onto Floodwood Pond, follow Route 30 for 5.3 miles, then turn right onto Floodwood Road (you will see a sign for the St. Regis Canoe Outfitters here). Drive west on Floodwood Road for 4.0 miles to the small public parking area across the road from the canoe outfitter's headquarters. There is a short carry down to the launching area on the left just before the outfitter.

If you plan to camp at the Rollins Pond Campground, continue south on Route 30 for 4.2 miles past Floodwood Road to the campground entrance on the right. You can also reach the campground by turning onto Route 3 west in Saranac Lake, then onto Route 30 north, following signs to Rollins Pond and Fish Creek Pond Campgrounds.

To launch on Follensby Clear Pond, continue south on Route 30 past Floodwood Road. There are two access sites on the right: the first 1.6 miles from Floodwood Road and the second 2.4 miles.

Middle Saranac Lake
Harrietstown and Santa Clara

MAPS

New York Atlas: Map 95
USGS Quadrangles: Saranac Lake, Tupper Lake, and Upper
Saranac Lake

INFORMATION

Area: 1,384 acres; maximum depth: 20 feet
Prominent fish species: Largemouth bass, smallmouth bass, and
northern pike
Camping: Permit required for the 25 campsites on Middle and 60
on Lower Saranac Lakes. Saranac Lake Islands Campground
(office at Second Pond fishing access); 518-891-3170.

The middle of the three Saranac Lakes remains the least heavily traveled, probably because of more difficult access. You can launch from
the South Creek hand-carry boat access on Route 3, or carry the half
mile through Bartlett Carry from Upper Saranac Lake, or pass through
the stream and lock that connect Middle and Lower Saranac Lakes.
Middle Saranac Lake lies along two popular long-distance canoe
routes. One comes down from the hamlet of Saranac Inn, traversing the
length of Upper Saranac Lake to Bartlett Carry, east to Middle Saranac
Lake, through the outlet stream and lock into Lower Saranac Lake, and
then either directly to the town of Saranac Lake or through Ossetah
Lake and then to the town site. The second route travels the length of
Long Lake to Axton Landing, up through Stony Creek Ponds, with a
three-quarter-mile carry to Upper Saranac Lake, a two-mile paddle to
Bartlett Carry, then finishing as above.

Both times that we paddled here, we launched from the South
Creek boat access on Route 3. We could not resist paddling up South
Creek, away from an expected boat-clogged lake, through a cedar-lined
beaver swamp. We carried over a few beaver dams, but we decided not
to clamber over the downed timber that clogs the waterway.

Resist the temptation to bolt out onto the lake. Take the time to
study the South Creek channel. We found many huge clumps of pitcher plants perched precariously on sphagnum hummocks, trying to
elbow the ubiquitous leatherleaf out of the way. Rarely does one have
the opportunity to see pitcher plants in such easily viewed locations; in

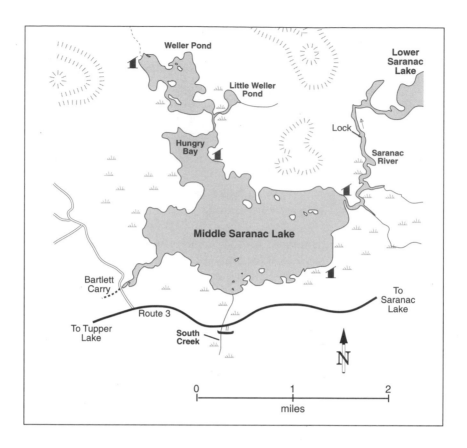

all of our travels through New York, this may be the easiest place to view them from a boat.

Tamarack, northern white cedar, and black spruce have invaded the sphagnum bog as it makes the gradual transition from wetland to upland. Eventually, trees crowd out the sheep laurel, leatherleaf, bog rosemary, sweet gale, winterberry, pitcher plant, and other shrubs, and the decaying vegetation builds up an overlying soil.

Surprisingly, we did not see boats at every turn when we paddled out onto the lake. Even though traversing the lock from Lower Saranac into Middle Saranac remains a popular pastime for motorboat enthusiasts, Middle Saranac retains a wilderness character, mostly because of lack of development along the shore. The state owns about three-quarters of the shoreline, starting at the southwest corner of Hungry Bay, moving clockwise up through Weller and Little Weller Ponds, down along the northern shore through the lock into Lower Saranac, down the eastern shore of Middle Saranac, and around the southern shore, stopping just short of the South Creek entrance.

As we paddled clockwise around the lake, we noted the many conifer species lining the shore, the few, small birches fast disappearing as beaver cut them down to drag to their lakeside lodges for winter food. We wonder whether the preponderance of white pine, northern white cedar, tamarack, hemlock, and spruce along the shore results from selective cutting by beaver. We also noted the conspicuous browse line on the cedars along the shore, where deer reached up from the winter ice to gnaw on the branches.

As you paddle the western end of the lake—most of its cedar-clad shore owned by the Bartlett Carry Company—look back to the east and savor the view of saw-toothed peaks in the McKenzie Mountain Wilderness. The protected coves contain patches of pickerelweed, pondweed, and water celery, as well as feeding ducks. We paddled here once in the fall, finding many loons in twos and threes and hundreds of ducks feeding furiously in the protected coves, trying to gain those last few ounces of fat to fuel their migratory flight.

One of the most interesting, secluded, and scenic portions of the lake is Weller and Little Weller Ponds. Among the side channels, coves, and islands, a sea of aquatic vegetation floods the marsh. Tamarack, a deciduous conifer with golden needles in the fall, has invaded the marsh; leatherleaf lines the waterways. The cedars and scrub birches

View of Adirondack High Peaks from the lock that separates Middle and Lower Saranac Lakes.

along shore give way to conifer-clad hillsides. And wildlife abounds—from frogs to great blue heron, from red-winged blackbird to beaver, from yellow-rumped warbler to belted kingfisher—and one can enjoy it in quiet seclusion. As you paddle back to Middle Saranac, Stony Creek and Ampersand Mountains dominate the skyline, but you can also see several other peaks, including a few off in the distant High Peaks Wilderness.

A similar marshy area exists along the narrow connecting river between Middle and Lower Saranac Lakes, but you will have to share it with motorboats. The channel rules include a five-mile-per-hour speed limit in the presence of other boats, so you should keep your speed down when passing the motorboats that you're sure to see. You can explore the beaver-dammed side channels during high water, where you will see lots of wildlife, including wood, black, mallard, teal, and ring-necked ducks. We listened to the strange call of bitterns (sounds sort of like "woooom'-pah-pah") as we paddled back in and up over beaver dams and saw yellowlegs and spotted sandpipers.

When you get to the lock, you have four choices: turn around, go through the lock, carry around the lock, or run the river to the right at medium to high water. Scout it first because of boulders and a sharp left turn at the bottom of the run. The lock intrigued us because of its counterweighted wood construction and its hand operation. It's worth a visit just to see it in operation. If you go in the off-season, you can operate it yourself, following the posted instructions; it's a lot faster to carry around unless your boat is loaded with gear.

Camping is permitted at several wilderness campsites and at four lean-tos scattered around Middle Saranac Lake.

Getting There

From the town of Saranac Lake, drive west on Route 3 to the South Creek boat access on the left. The access is 5.6 miles from the Second Pond boat access on Lower Saranac Lake on Route 3 and 9.7 miles from the stoplight on Route 3 in downtown Saranac Lake. From Tupper Lake, drive east on Routes 3 and 30; when the roads divide, take Route 3 for 5.4 miles to the South Creek boat access on the right.

Lower Saranac Lake

Harrietstown

MAPS
   New York Atlas: Map 95
   USGS Quadrangle: Saranac Lake

INFORMATION
   Area: 2,286 acres; maximum depth: 60 feet
   Prominent fish species: Largemouth bass, smallmouth bass, and
      northern pike
   Camping: Permit required for the 25 campsites on Middle and 60
      on Lower Saranac Lakes. Saranac Lake Islands Campground
      (office at Second Pond fishing access); 518-891-3170.

You will encounter more boat traffic here than on Middle Saranac
Lake. Trailers often jam the large parking lot at the fishing access on
Second Pond. You can also launch at the much-less-used access on
Middle Saranac Lake at South Creek, then paddle into the lower lake.
Despite the motorboat traffic, Lower Saranac Lake is a wonderful, his-
toric place to paddle, especially because the state owns the vast major-
ity of shoreline surrounding it and First and Second Ponds.

*Views of the Adirondack tall peaks lend scenic character to Lower
Saranac Lake.*

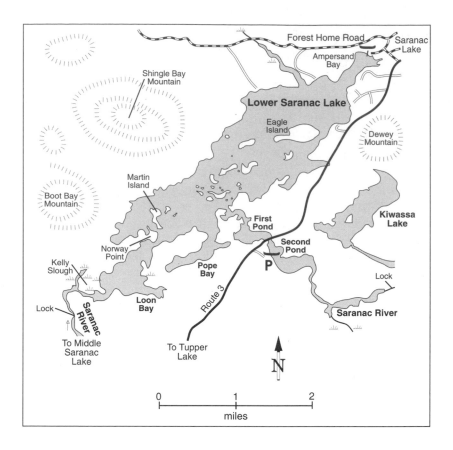

Much of the early guide lore and its literature took place on the Saranac Lakes, which served as a gateway to all northern Adirondacks drainages. This should not be surprising, given the area's central location, its linkages to other river and lake systems, and its beauty. The surrounding Adirondack peaks form a dramatic backdrop, providing many hiking trails for those seeking a wilderness experience.

The many islands dotting the surface of Lower Saranac Lake break up the view, making it seem much smaller than its large area would indicate. These same islands provide many beautiful campsites and block the wind—indeed, winds can pose more of a problem on the smaller, but less protected, Middle Saranac Lake.

Because development on Lower Saranac concentrates at the north end, we focused on the southern half and the winding coves and bays to the southwest. It takes quite a while to explore fully the lake's 17 miles of shoreline and many islands—making this a great location for a several-day vacation, especially off-season.

As you enter the boat access on Second Pond, note the many towering hemlocks; as you paddle out onto the pond, northern white cedar dominates the shoreline, joined by an occasional paper birch and a few very tall white pine. From here, we paddled northwest onto First Pond and worked our way out onto Lower Saranac Lake, continuing left, and worked our way around to the Saranac River lock leading to Middle Saranac Lake. As the lake narrows at the Saranac River inlet, quite a contrast unfolds: sheer, cedar-clad cliffs stand guard on the left, while flat, bird-filled marshes spread out on the right. When we paddled here, red-winged blackbirds, eastern kingbirds, and ducks filled the marshes with their spring calls and songs. Ring-billed ducks scattered into the emerging marsh vegetation in Kelly Slough.

We heard or saw eastern phoebe, chickadee, crow, winter wren, song sparrow, hermit thrush, spotted sandpiper, grackle, yellow-rumped warbler, black duck, ring-billed duck, robin, red-eyed vireo, black-throated green warbler, and white-throated sparrow.

When we paddled here, winds were negligible, and we meandered around the islands, enjoying the emerging spring plants and the gorgeous mountainside scenery.

Getting There

From the village of Saranac Lake at the downtown stoplight on Route 3, drive west on Route 3 for 5.0 miles. The Second Pond boat access is on the left. Paddle under the Route 3 bridge to the left.

From Tupper Lake, drive east on Routes 3 and 30 for about 5 miles. When Route 30 turns north, continue on Route 3. The Second Pond boat access is 11.0 miles from the divergence of Routes 3 and 30.

Adirondack Park

Little Long Pond, Adirondack Park.

Sweeping mountain vistas, sparkling waterfalls, the haunting cry of the loon and playful antics of river otters, clear mountain lakes in the steep glaciated terrain, broad expanses of untrammeled wilderness—all these identify Adirondack Park, one of the most remarkable parks in the United States. Located less than a half-day's drive for more than 30 million people and covering an area larger than either Massachusetts or New Hampshire, Adirondack Park has a fascinating history.

History

Before the Industrial Age and the resource consumption that fueled it, the region that became Adirondack Park was little known. Native Americans traversed the mountains, but mainly in the summer. They also traveled the region's rivers, linking with lands as far away as Maine (today the AMC and other organizations are developing a proposed canoe trail that traces the historic paddling routes from New York to Maine). High northerly elevations, where winter lingered long and cold, relegated humans to a transient existence here. Our early adventurers explored the Pacific Northwest and Rockies long before the Adirondacks were mapped.

During the 1800s, the area fell victim to greed and waste. Loggers penetrated nearly every corner of the park, mainly to remove the tall white pines—some towering 150 feet or more—standing well above the other forest trees. Logs were floated down the Hudson and every other river of consequence. Hemlocks were cut and stripped of their bark to extract tannic acid for the tanning industry. When the logging boom ended in the late 1800s, only 1 percent of the original six million acres remained untouched. Hunters killed the last moose in the 1860s; extirpated the cougar, wolf, lynx, and wolverine by 1900; and relentlessly trapped beavers until only a handful remained in 1904.

Ironically, though, it was the wealthy industrialists, whose mills and factories depleted the region's forests and despoiled its air and water, who finally saw the Adirondacks for what they were and led the charge to protect the area. The wealthy literally fled to the mountains for its clean air and water. Recreational visitation to the Adirondacks mushroomed in 1869, when Boston preacher William H. H. "Adirondack" Murray wrote the widely read book *Adventures in the Wilderness; or, Camp-Life in the Adirondacks*. He likened the "magnificent scenery" to that of Switzerland. In the 1880s, George Washington Sears, under the pen name Nessmuk, wrote in *Forest and Stream* exciting accounts of his adventures paddling the *Sairy Gamp*, a 10-pound canoe designed and built by J. Henry Rushton, through the Adirondack wildlands.

They came in droves for the pure mountain air that might cure tuberculosis or offer relief from the polluted air of New York City and Boston. Intellectuals, including Ralph Waldo Emerson, James Russell Lowell, and Louis Agassiz, came to "rough it" at the "Philosophers' Camp" on Follensby Pond. Waterways were the corridors as they explored the remote wilderness in famed Adirondack guide boats. Entrepreneurs catered to the wealthy with dozens of grand hotels—the hotel at Blue Mountain Lake was the first in the world to have electric lighting in every room—and luxurious fishing and hunting camps. The guiding industry flourished, and many of the carry trails we use today were in use long before the roads. While enjoying the out-of-doors, these industrialists also witnessed the destruction of the Adirondacks around them, including their own rampant overfishing and overhunting.

They were ready to hear the message from Vermont lawyer George Perkins Marsh in his 1864 book *Man and Nature*. Marsh convinced many powerful New Yorkers that denuded slopes would hold neither soil nor water, that floods and droughts would increase, that the prized artery of commerce, the Erie Canal, might go dry.

A young, well-to-do Albany lawyer, Verplant Colvin, reinforced Marsh's message. Colvin gave up lawyering to survey the Adirondacks for more than 20 years, climbing its peaks and mapping its valleys, taking every opportunity to write and to speak about the threats to this glorious land. Colvin and his powerful allies convinced the state legislature in 1872 to set up a commission to study the Adirondacks, eventually leading to the Forest Preserve Law of 1885: the Adirondacks and Catskills would be "forever kept as wild forest lands."

But because of continuing abuses, Governor David Hill asked the Forest Commission to draw a line around those lands most worthy of protection, resulting in 1892 in the first "blue line" around two million acres of the Adirondack Forest Preserve. A state constitutional convention in 1894 gave constitutional protection to these lands with the passage of Article 14:

> The lands of the State, now owned or hereafter acquired, constituting the forest preserve, as now fixed by law, shall be forever kept as wild forest lands. They shall not be leased, sold, or exchanged or taken by any corporation, public or private, nor shall the timber thereon be sold, removed, or destroyed.

The publicly owned lands within the Adirondack Park blue line are among the most fully protected lands in the nation. To open these lands for logging or development would require not just the passage of a new law, but amending the state constitution. Over the years, the blue line has expanded to its present boundaries, encompassing approximately six million acres.

Adirondack Park is unique, too, because it includes a mix of public and private land. When the Forest Preserve was first created, the hope was eventually to acquire all of the land within the blue line, but that will not occur. The state has managed to acquire roughly 42 percent of the land within Adirondack Park, and that fraction is expected to continue gradually creeping upward as the state purchases additional lands or tracts are deeded to the state.

Geology

The Adirondacks' unique character stems, in large part, from its geological history. The region is a section of the Canadian Shield that was inexplicably pushed up through the overlying sedimentary rock. This is one of the few locations where the ancient Precambrian metamorphic rock of the shield is now exposed. Viewed on a raised-relief map, one can see this distinct dome, which extends in a generally northeast-southwest orientation and covers an area of roughly 120 miles by 80 miles. Although much of the exposed rock of the Adirondacks is more than a billion years old, the mountains themselves are very young in geologic terms. They are believed to be only about 15 million years old—far younger than the weathered, 350-million-year-old Appalachian Mountains of neighboring Vermont. Some geologists believe that the Adirondacks continue to rise, but no one seems to know why. Because no active tectonic plates collide beneath the Adirondacks, the usual mechanism of mountain building does not explain the mountains' recent, and possibly continuing, uplift.

The Adirondacks' high mountain granite, quartz, and gneiss (pronounced "nice") do not react with acid. Thus, airborne acids from coal-fired power plants in the Ohio River Valley—deposited on the peaks as acid rain, dew, frost, and snow—acidify high-elevation waterways. Native brook trout and other game fish cannot reproduce under moderately acidic conditions, so many lakes and ponds in the Adirondacks have become depleted of fish. In contrast, at lower elevations the underlying marble, made up of calcium carbonate just like limestone, neutralizes the acidity. Consequently, lower-elevation lakes have not suffered the drastic declines in fish populations that have occurred at higher elevations.

Looking toward the Future

The Adirondacks, part of 26 million acres of the Northern Forest, which stretches from northern New York to northern Maine, should serve as a model for preserving these magnificent forests for future generations. But major conflicts have arisen over management—as one might expect when nearly 10 million visitors per year descend on an area that is the home of just 130,000 residents. Most residents depend on visitors for their livelihoods, but many resent regulatory controls from "downstate."

Ultimately, the goals of residents and visitors should be the same. Both want scenic vistas, deep forests, and pristine waterways that support hiking, canoeing, camping, hunting, and fishing where game and fish can be caught. But keeping the privately owned portions of the park attractive to the visitors, upon whom the residents depend, means some controls on development. Cheek-to-jowl vacation homes dotting the shorelines of the Fulton lakes is not a future most residents want to see in other parts of the park—yet this is a very real risk for much of the 58 percent of the park in private ownership. A recent ballot measure to appropriate funds for purchase of additional park lands failed, and property rights activists sidetracked a major effort to strengthen regional controls on development.

The challenge of finding workable solutions to the differing needs of residents and visitors is difficult. But the goal is a worthy one. Adirondack Park includes the largest wilderness area east of the Mississippi River and the vast majority of remaining virgin old-growth forest in the eastern U.S. The region offers a tremendous resource for learning about forest ecosystems and wildlife habitat, and it could serve as the site for reintroduction of species long extirpated from the Northeast. Many creative solutions—benefiting locals and visitors alike—are available to those willing to open their minds to new ideas. Among the highest priorities for Adirondack Park, in our estimation, are the following:

1. Control shoreline development. Current zoning requires that single-family homes sit on parcels of at least several acres, except along shorelines, where the minimum lot size is only 1.2 acres. The result is a carving up of private land around our waterways and introduction of pollutants from high population densities. A moratorium should be placed on shoreline development until we can agree on a master plan that adequately protects river and lake shores.

2. Establish the 400,000-acre Bob Marshall Great Wilderness in the core of Adirondack Park. Link the Oswegatchie wildlands into one wilderness corridor. When the New York legislature agreed to the original blue line that enclosed the most significant natural features on the Adirondacks, their intent was to purchase all the lands inside. Many of those lands still remain in private hands more than a hundred years later. We should move now to protect the most significant natural resources of the park before it's too late.

3. Use voluntary check-offs on tax returns, the sale of vanity license plates, funds from nonprofit organizations such as The Nature Conservancy, designated surcharges on recreational equipment (including binoculars, canoes, and fishing gear), and renewed emphasis on bond issues to fund land acquisition within the park's core. Pay year-round residents for conservation easements, which provide a way for residents to receive money for their land, yet keep the land intact—as most would choose to do.

4. Support sustainable, nonpolluting businesses that strengthen the local Adirondack economy. Look for products labeled as "Made in the Adirondacks," for example. If residents have a dependable source of year-round income, the pressure to develop or sell their land will decrease.

Those of us who share a love the Adirondacks—residents and visitors, loggers and birders, anglers and paddlers—must work together to guarantee its continued splendor for future generations to know and enjoy. Get to know this most remarkable of parks. Paddle its lakes and rivers, climb its mountains, hike its trails, explore its history, study its wildlife and geology.

Organizations

The Adirondack Conservancy Committee (regional chapter of The Nature Conservancy)

The Adirondack Council

Adirondack Mountain Club

Adirondack Park Agency

New York State Department of Environmental Conservation

Raquette River

Harrietstown

MAPS
New York Atlas: Map 95
USGS Quandrangle: Tupper Lake

INFORMATION
Prominent fish species: Smallmouth bass, walleye, and northern pike

Books: If you plan to paddle long distances on the Raquette River, purchase a copy of Paul Jamieson and Donald Morris's outstanding guidebook *Adirondack Canoe Waters: North Flow,* published by the Adirondack Mountain Club.

The Raquette River, second longest river in New York, features prominently in the early lore of the Adirondacks, from Emerson's poem "The Adirondacs" about his explorations in 1858, to Nessmuk's voyages in Rushton's 10-pound Sairy Gamp in the late nineteenth century, to the Old Forge-to-Saranac-Lake guide-boat race of this century. Still very popular with canoeists today, the Raquette accommodates many paddlers in July and August.

Black ducks, along with many other species, nest and feed in the marshes along the Raquette River.

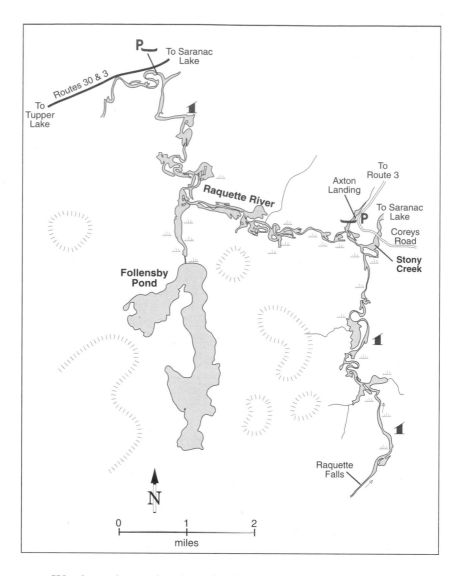

We chose the section described here—between Raquette Falls and the boat access on Route 3 east of Tupper Lake—because of its slowly meandering wilderness character, where sometimes one questions current direction. According to Jamieson and Morris in *North Flow,* the river is so flat in this area that a 10-foot-high dam constructed in Piercefield in 1870 flooded the valley for nearly 30 miles, all the way back to Raquette Falls near Long Lake. Fifteen years later, after many protests, they lowered the dam to where it stands today. In the spring and during other times of high water, much of the formerly flooded marshland becomes accessible by boat again for a short time.

The state owns both sides of the river between Route 3 and a mile or so upstream of the entrance to Follensby Pond. After that, up to Raquette Rapids, the state owns only the east shore. The High Peaks Wilderness Area borders the east shore of the river upstream from Axton Landing.

One could spend days here exploring the oxbows and inlets, the braided channels and side streams, watching the professorial great blue heron preside over the marsh, quietly, stealthily hunting for fish, frogs, and indeed anything that moves. The channel turns back on itself over and over, occasionally doubling or even tripling the water distance between two points. Ducks erupt from the water's surface as you round the bend, startling you as much as you startle them.

The flooding of a century and a quarter ago killed the large trees that lined the banks, although some tall white pine and some relatively large northern white cedar have grown back. Today, the streamside silver maple, even large ones, provide forage for the many beaver that make this home. Watch to the sides as you paddle. The number of beaver dams on inflows and side channels will surprise you. If you have time, carry up over one or more of these to explore in quiet seclusion, away from the motorboats that occasionally come roaring around the bend. We found the fishermen to be quite courteous toward paddlers . . . if they see you!

One particular side excursion we enjoyed, as did Ralph Waldo Emerson nearly 150 years ago in a guide boat, was a paddle up the expansive marshy connector to Follensby Pond, where he camped for a few weeks in August 1858, under some huge pines and maples.

Next morn, we swept with oars the Saranac,
With skies of benediction, to Round Lake [Middle Saranac],
Tahawus, Seward, MacIntyre, Baldhead,
And other titans without muse or name.
Pleased with these grand companions, we glide on,
Instead of flowers, crowned with a wreath of hills,
And made our distance wider, boat from boat,
As each would hear the oracle alone.
By the bright morn the gay flotilla slid
Through files of flags that gleamed like bayonets,
Through gold-moth-haunted beds of pickerel-flower,
Through scented banks of lilies white and gold,
Where the deer feeds at night, the teal by day,
On through Upper Saranac, and up

Pere Raquette stream, to a small tortuous pass
Winding through grassy shallows in and out,
Two creeping miles of rushes, pads, and sponge,
To Follansbee Water, and the Lake of Loons.

While Follensby Pond itself remains off-limits, one can explore the outflow creek. You will need a map and compass to find this inlet into the Raquette; if you succeed, you won't regret it. As you paddle upstream, look for a broad, marshy expanse off to the right as the river curves left. As you enter, paddle over the barely submerged posts of a long-abandoned bridge, back into a broad expanse of pickerelweed and other aquatic vegetation. Grasses line the banks, and many ducks raise their broods here, fattening them up for fall migration. When we paddled here in the fall, we saw many black ducks—the smaller wood ducks and teal having migrated earlier. The biggest flock numbered about 30 individuals.

Two shelters are located where indicated on the map. Several other obvious camping spots—flat grassy and needle-carpeted areas—exist under hemlocks and pines. We saw little other evidence of human activity, save two rope swings hanging from paper birches out over the water.

Getting There

There are several ways to gain access to the Raquette River. One access point is on Routes 3 and 30 east of Tupper Lake, 3.9 miles east from the downtown stoplight in Tupper Lake. A second point is at Axton Landing. To reach this, head east from the junction of Routes 3 and 30 for 2.6 miles to Coreys Road. Turn right onto paved Coreys Road, and take it to the short gravel connector to Axton Landing on the right. Finally, long-distance paddlers can paddle from Long Lake, carrying around Raquette Falls, and take out at either access point or continue on through Stony Ponds into Upper Saranac Lake.

Five Falls, Rainbow Falls, and Blake Falls Reservoirs

Colton and Parishville

MAPS
New York Atlas: Maps 94 and 100
USGS Quadrangles: Carry Falls Reservoir, Rainbow Falls, Stark, and Sylvan Falls

INFORMATION
Five Falls Reservoir area: 145 acres; max. depth: 40 feet
Rainbow Falls Reservoir area: 1,453 acres; max. depth: 45 feet
Blake Falls Reservoir area: 1,458 acres; max. depth: 45 feet
Prominent fish species: Smallmouth bass, northern pike, and walleye
Camping: Available at the McNeil's Point Campground, Blake Falls Reservoir; no reservations accepted. Niagara-Mohawk Power Corporation information: 800-NIAGARA (800-642-4272).
Books: If you plan to paddle long distances on the Raquette River, purchase a copy of Paul Jamieson and Donald Morris's outstanding guidebook *Adirondack Canoe Waters: North Flow,* published by the Adirondack Mountain Club.

On the northwestern edge of Adirondack Park, a series of seven reservoirs in succession drown out Raquette River rapids and falls to provide electric power. What was once a beautiful wilderness river—second longest in the state after the Hudson—succumbed to our continuing thirst for power. Thankfully, Niagara-Mohawk allows continued public use of the Raquette River by providing public fishing access, picnic areas, and campgrounds on the reservoirs. We have chosen for inclusion here three connected intermediate reservoirs. If you have limited time, we suggest that you paddle Blake Falls Reservoir, the nicest of the three.

Five Falls Reservoir

Five Falls is a small, quiet reservoir that receives little attention. If chaos reigns on the others, then we would paddle here. During drawdown, however, it gets quite shallow in its upper reaches, and passage up into the most interesting part may be difficult. Where the main body

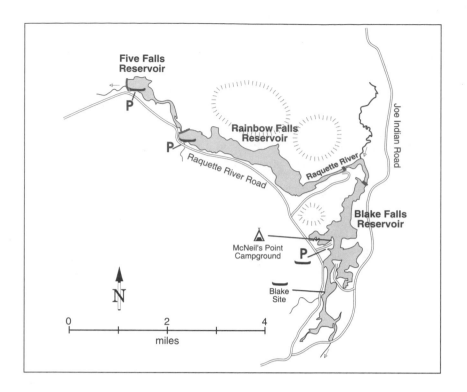

necks down as you paddle around to the right from the boat access, note the rock formations near shore. These extend out into the water, making passage difficult during times of low water.

The forested shoreline contains a wide variety of tree species, including both of our aspens—big-toothed and quaking—paper birch, red maple, yellow birch, red pine, white pine, northern white cedar, eastern hemlock, and several others. A relatively open understory contains a large population of ferns.

We recognize aspens, members of the willow family, by their smooth, light green or yellow bark. In a light breeze, their leaves quake. They grow in association with pines and other conifers, and when their leaves turn a golden yellow in the fall, they provide a beautiful contrast with the surrounding dark evergreens. The two species can be distinguished most easily by their leaves: quaking aspen (*Populus tremuloides*) has very fine teeth on its leaf margins, while big-toothed aspen (*Populus grandidentata*) has large serrations on the margins. Also, the trunks of big-toothed aspen lose their smoothness as they grow larger.

Both species regenerate quickly after fire or other disturbance, serving as soil anchors. Quaking aspen also propagates readily by sending out root suckers, forming dense clones, all with the same genetic makeup. In the East, they frequently get crowded out by taller species. In the West, crowding out is less frequent, and while individual trees may live for only 100 years, the clone may survive for thousands of years, placing aspens (or at least their roots) among the oldest species on Earth. Furthermore, some scientists claim that an aspen clone is actually a single organism, interconnected by the root system. That would make some large western clones the largest organisms in the world—far outweighing the largest redwoods, sequoias, and blue whales.

A few hundred species of wildlife—including moose, beaver, bear, elk, grouse, quail, and deer—rely on aspen for food from its bark, leaves, buds, flowers, and fruits. Coupled with its early successional soil-holding character, this food production makes aspens one of the most important tree species in the North Country environment.

We saw, bustling among the branches, yellow warbler, black-throated green warbler, American redstart, and black-capped chickadee, while song sparrow and wood thrush hunted insects along the ground. A deer snorted at us from the brush, and we searched in vain for the beaver that had been feeding on tender aspen branches. We enjoyed paddling here among forested shores with a rich mixture of conifers and deciduous trees, but it doesn't take more than a few hours to paddle the entire shoreline.

Rainbow Falls Reservoir

Rainbow Falls Reservoir, located between Five Falls and Blake Falls Reservoirs, takes much more time to explore. In spite of the 20 or more houses that crowd the southern shore of Rainbow Falls Reservoir, we feel that paddling here still provides a quiet-water experience, especially early and late in the season. The broad expanse of water near the dam on the west end gives way to an island that blocks the view of many of the houses. At the east end, the reservoir takes an abrupt left turn as it heads toward Blake Falls. The most beautiful area on the reservoir, this narrow arm sports forested shores and tall banks covered with lush vegetation, very similar in character to that found along Five Falls Reservoir.

Paper birches, very similar to aspens in ecological niche, grow in profusion, and beaver hack away at them just as they do to aspens on Five Falls. In some sections, deer have created a conspicuous browse line by munching heavily on lakeside branches.

Besides the birds mentioned above on Five Falls, we saw red-eyed vireo, belted kingfisher, common loon, two families of common mergansers, spotted sandpiper, black duck, and ring-billed gull.

Blake Falls Reservoir

Blake Falls Reservoir—by all odds the most scenic of the three reservoirs—provided us with the best looks at wildlife, even though we paddled here in the middle of the afternoon. Plant species also appear in greater abundance, and the aquatic habitat includes marshes, which are absent in the other reservoirs.

A wild turkey hen and her brood greeted us as we approached the water. These magnificent game birds, standing over three feet tall, once inhabited most of the forested parts of eastern North America, foraging on acorns, chestnuts, beechnuts, seeds, and insects. With the clearing of forests, loss of the American chestnut to chestnut blight, and unregulated hunting, the wild turkey disappeared over much of its range. Recently reintroduced in many areas, wild turkeys now range over large tracts of New York.

As we approached the southern end of the reservoir, we spotted two mature bald eagles. Though we searched for their large nest of sticks, we never found it. Eagle nests may reach six or more feet in diameter, and the adults, which mate for life, usually return year after year to the same nest, adding a new layer each year. Eventually, the nest may reach eight or more feet in depth and weigh up to a ton.

A majestic bald eagle clings to its perch in a hemlock on the south end of Blake Falls Reservoir.

Because they often nest in dead trees that stand on partially rotted trunks, eagle nests make trees top-heavy, eventually bringing them down in windstorms.

As we paddled north, back to the boat access on Blake Falls, we reflected on the differences among the three reservoirs. While the other two have relatively open understories filled with bracken and hay-scented ferns along the shore, this one has much more shrubbery. It also has a narrower channel, giving it a more closed-in, riverlike feeling. Its close-by shores make it seem smaller; indeed, because of peninsulas and meandering channels, from most locations it looks much smaller than the other two reservoirs.

Blake Falls Reservoir had much more water in it, as well, when we paddled here in mid-July. Perhaps Niagara-Mohawk's keeping this reservoir full has something to do with the campground and consequent increased recreational use. The higher water allowed us to penetrate back into marshy areas, where we found swamp rose and swamp milkweed growing among many other wetland species. More conifer species grow here as well, including some large tamaracks, spruce, balsam fir, and red and white pines. The lacy green foliage of eastern hemlocks hanging out over the water shades the shoreline in several areas.

Getting There

From Potsdam, take Route 56 south. When you reach South Colton, just after crossing the Raquette River bridge, turn left onto Snell Road. Then take an immediate left onto Raquette River Road. The Five Falls Reservoir boat access is on the left after 2.6 miles.

To get to Rainbow Falls Reservoir, continue east on Raquette River Road from the Five Falls boat access for an additional 1.4 miles.

To get to Blake Falls Reservoir, continue east on Raquette River Road past the Blake Falls Dam Road for 0.8 mile (3.8 miles from the Rainbow Falls Reservoir access) to the Blake Falls Reservoir McNeil Site, where camping and boat launching occur; also, there is an access 0.9 mile farther south called the Blake Site, where there is a lot less congestion.

From the south, take Route 56 north from Route 3 for about 12 miles to Stark Road. Turn right onto Stark Road, and go 1.0 mile to Raquette River Road. Turn left onto Raquette River Road. The Blake Site access is 1.6 miles north, and the McNeil Site is another 0.9 mile after that.

Massawepie Lake and Grass River Flow
Piercefield

MAPS
New York Atlas: Map 94
USGS Quadrangles: Childwold and Piercefield

INFORMATION
Area: Massawepie Lake, 490 acres
Prominent fish species: Lake trout, brown trout, and smallmouth
bass
Books: Our description of the South Fork of Grass River comes
from Paul Jamieson and Donald Morris's outstanding guidebook
Adirondack Canoe Waters: North Flow, published by the Adiron-
dack Mountain Club.

Massawepie Lake

The Otetiana Council of the Boy Scouts of America owns Massawepie
Lake and the immediately adjoining ponds: Catamount, Round, Long,
Horseshoe, Boottree, and Pine. The lake serves as a source of the Grass
River as well. The lake and ponds remain closed to the public from the
last week in June to the last week in August. But we include this area
anyway, because it offers early- and late-season paddling, with no gasoline motors allowed, in an extraordinarily scenic and secluded location.
Other access points on the Grass River remain open throughout the
summer. The ponds and streams are maintained to produce trout.

Just out from the small, unmarked boat access on Massawepie
Lake, hemlock, with its lacy, drooping branches, dominates the conifer
stands along the shore. Eastern hemlock, one of four hemlocks that
occur in North America, grows from Georgia up through the backbone
of the Appalachians to Nova Scotia, spreading west through the Great
Lakes region. The tree grows best in cool, moist locations, particularly
on protected northern and eastern slopes.

Every three or four years, each hemlock produces a huge crop of
cones with tiny winged seeds, an important food for pine siskins, crossbills, and other northern birds. Snowshoe hares and deer browse the flat
green needles, and porcupines eat the bark. Dense stands of hemlock
provide protection for birds and animals, including ruffed grouse, wild
turkey, and deer. We noticed a conspicuous browse line on the hemlocks growing along the water in the southern cove. Deer stand out on
the ice in winter, reaching up to browse the branches they can reach.

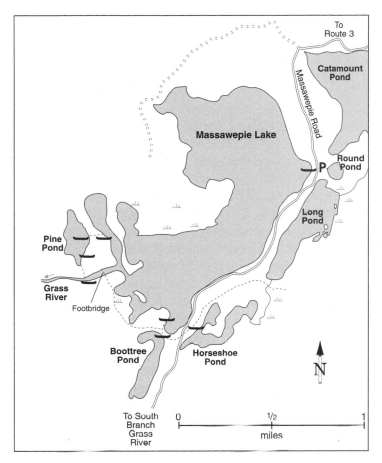

Besides paddling Massawepie Lake, one has several other options. We carried into Horseshoe, Boottree, and Pine Ponds and paddled down Grass River, which has one source in Massawepie Lake. We did not paddle Catamount Pond because it lies along the road and has some development along the shoreline. We did not paddle tiny Round Pond or Long Pond. We also paddled another section of the Grass River, but not from Massawepie (see below).

To get to Boottree Pond, head for the southern cove of Massawepie Lake and look for a small white marker with a blue center square in a tree on the right-hand shore. Hike up over a short hill about 100 feet to Boottree Pond where a stand of drowned spruce and pines greet you. Out in the water, a pine-, spruce-, and hemlock-covered peninsula juts out. This is truly a beautiful, quiet spot.

From here, a trail leads to Horseshoe Pond, following a woods road that goes gently uphill for several hundred yards. Along the way, you'll pass through a stand of tall pine, hemlock, and yellow birch, along with some huge big-toothed aspen that are getting crowded out by the conifers. The trail crosses the road, then heads steeply downhill to the pond. But the effort to get to quiet, secluded, gorgeous Horseshoe Pond is worth it.

After exploring the side ponds, we traveled down to the western outlet of Massawepie Lake, a source of the Grass River. A sphagnum bog surrounds the whole western side of the lake, with black spruce, tamarack, sheep laurel, and lots of pitcher plants—particularly on the left-hand (southern) shore. Pickerelweed, fragrant water lily, bur reed, and water celery crowd the outlet channel. After a short paddle, you'll come to a footbridge over the creek; carry over it to continue down Grass River and to reach the carry to Pine Pond on the right. Leatherleaf, bog rosemary, and various grasses compete for space on the hummocks. About a half mile down the river, the waterway is posted with No Trespassing signs. We stopped here, even though we believe that travel on this navigable waterway may not be restricted. Access restrictions on paddlable rivers and streams in the Adirondacks has become an ongoing issue of contention and the source of several lawsuits in recent years.

Paddling back toward the footbridge, we stopped and carried into Pine Pond boat access, guarded by huge hemlocks, the biggest we've seen this far north. Some huge white pine occur as well, but much closer to Grass River. Given that hemlocks surround Pine Pond, we're a bit stumped by its name.

On the way back to the Massawepie boat launch in the late afternoon, we managed to sight a few ever-busy beaver bustling about in the waterway and out on the lake. They seem particularly hard up in this environment, reduced to gnawing on tamarack bark.

Grass River

Early the next morning, we hiked back in to Grass River from Shurtleff, about nine miles by road west of Massawepie Lake, to see how far we could paddle back up toward Massawepie Lake. We had some difficulty finding the boat access, but that was nothing compared to paddling the river. This is not a place to take young children—intrepid explorers, who remain undaunted by carries over several serious logjams, would do best here.

We paddled the narrow river up to an impoundment with a road and a bridge across the breastworks. A logjam on the upstream side of the earthen dam—where the river sluices through—pressing up against the cribbing, threatens the bridge with a washout. Above the dam, the

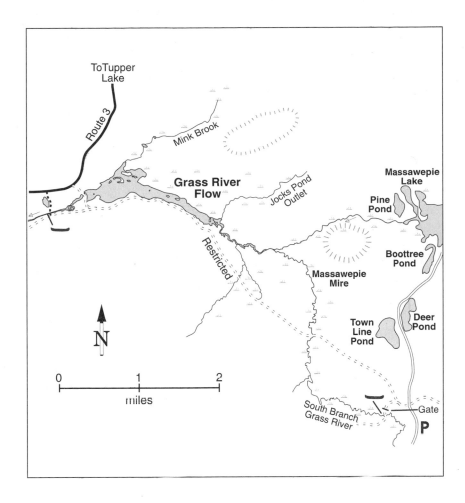

impoundment—called Grass River Flow—stretches away in all directions. Aquatic vegetation of every kind covers the wide expanse of shallow water, with many stumps breaking the surface. We studied the flow with binoculars but turned back without paddling it. Even though we had paddled only about a mile up to the flow and a mile back, going over the same five logjams each direction, it took us the entire morning. We decided to change the name of this watercourse from Grass River Flow to Dead Tree Blockage.

We also checked out the access to the South Branch of Grass River about two and a half miles south of Massawepie Lake. Access requires hiking your boat around a locked gate and putting in off the edge of a bridge. The paddling looked great, but we did not have time to explore this area. According to Jamieson and Morris in *North Flow,* this area has recently opened to the public through a conservation easement from the Yorkshire Timber Company. The area remains closed during deer season, however. Farther downstream, the Grasse River Club owns both shores and expects you to stay in your boat as much as possible—no camping, picnicking, or trespassing allowed, except to carry around obstructions.

As you paddle downstream on the South Branch, just before reaching Grass River Flow, you pass through Massawepie Mire—at 900 acres the largest peatland in the Adirondacks and proposed for national registry as a natural area. From here you have three choices: if you have two cars and had the foresight to place one down at Shurtleff, you could continue down through the flow, over the rickety impoundment, and take out on the section of Grass River described above. Or, because the river has little current, you could return to your car. Finally, you could take a right turn and head up to Massawepie Lake.

If you decide to paddle the Grass River, you should be prepared for obstructions and some slow going. Paddling here provides a wonderful opportunity to study plants and wildlife in quiet seclusion. Take time to enjoy this wild area. If moose inhabited New York in appreciable numbers, they would certainly thrive in the Grass River area.

Getting There

Drive west out of Tupper Lake on Route 3. Watch for a Massawepie Scout Camp sign on the left. At the sign, turn left onto a gravel road leading into the camp. Stop at the sign-in area next to the superintendent's residence after 0.3 mile. Just after the sign-in area, the road sweeps to the left and passes Catamount Pond. Pass the parking area on the left 0.7 mile after the sign-in. The boat launch on Massawepie Lake is on the right after another 0.1 mile.

To get to the South Branch of Grass River, drive south from Massawepie Lake for about 2.5 miles, passing the entrance to the Grasse River Club on the right. Take the next right at the crossroads, and proceed about 0.2 mile to the locked gate. Parking is on the right, just before the gate. The river flows under the bridge about 0.1 mile past the gate.

To get to the downstream end of Grass River below Grass River Flow in Shurtleff, drive west from the Scout camp entrance on Route 3 for 9.2 miles. The canoe launch sign on a tree on the south side of the road is next to impossible to see from the road as you drive by at 55 miles per hour, unless you know exactly where to look for it. Out on Route 3, there are jumping deer warning signs on both sides of the road. This is it! Follow the woods road back about a half mile to Grass River; ignore the small pond on the right.

Lows Lake (Bog River Flow)
Clifton, Colton, Long Lake, and Piercefield

MAPS
    New York Atlas: Map 94
    USGS Quadrangles: Little Tupper Lake and Wolf Mountain

INFORMATION
    Area: 2,838 acres; maximum depth: 55 feet; average depth: 5.2
    feet
    Prominent fish species: Brook trout
    Camping: Permits required for stays of more than three nights.
    Obtain permits from New York State Department of Environ-
    mental Conservation, P.O. Box 170, Piercefield, NY 12975.
    Books: If you plan to include a trip on the Bog River below the dam
    down to Tupper Lake, purchase a copy of Paul Jamieson and Don-
    ald Morris's outstanding guidebook *Adirondack Canoe Waters:*
    North Flow, published by the Adirondack Mountain Club.

Extraordinary is the only adjective needed to describe Bog River Flow
and its lakes and ponds, islands and shores, floating bogs and surrounding forests. Two dams built by A. A. Low in 1903 and 1907 provide sufficient water to allow us to paddle the 14.5 miles from the
access at the lower dam to the west end of the main lake. A trail, three-
plus miles, through the woods connects the far western end of Lows
Lake with the upper reaches of the East Branch of the Oswegatchie
River. But as of this writing, because of the violent windstorm that
swept through the Adirondacks in mid-July 1995, thousands of downed
trees now block the trail.

    Twenty-one numbered campsites and another 19 under construc-
tion, available on a first-come basis, provide wonderful camping
opportunities. Check the bulletin board at the parking area for campsite
locations. If required, you may camp at nondesignated sites, but make
sure that you are on state land and not on private land. The state
restricts parties to nine or fewer but encourages you to travel with six
or fewer to reduce impact on fragile bog habitat. This popular recreation destination can suffer from too many canoeists in the summer. We
recommend that you paddle here on weekdays during the summer or in
the spring or fall.

    Tall pines and spruce perch precariously on the huge granite boul-
ders that line the narrow passageway leading out from the boat access

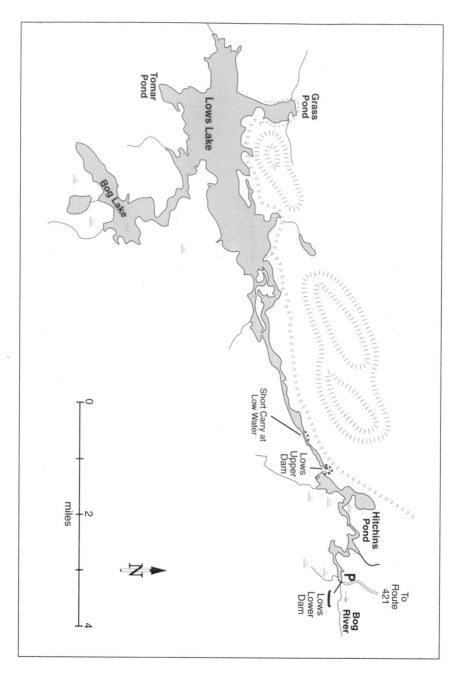

at Lows Lower Dam at the east end of the flow. Mosses, lichens, and ferns cling to the rock faces, and pine needles carpet the forest floor.

Bears patrol the shores and islands, looking for an invitation to destroy food bags and coolers left carelessly lying about. The careful observer who searches dense conifer stands might find spruce grouse, an increasingly rare northern cousin of the ruffed grouse. Spruce grouse usually stand out in plain view, allowing humans to approach closely, which probably explains something about their reduced numbers. Ravens appear in pairs, croaking out their hoarse calls. When we paddled here, we saw lots of deer as well. In the not-too-distant past, one might have seen a rare golden eagle soaring overhead, along with the much more common osprey. Today, with the return of nesting bald eagles to New York, we may soon see eagles again on Bog River Flow.

Perhaps most impressive, however, is the large concentration of loons that populate the far reaches of each lake and pond in the flowage. Loons suffer from human disturbance; boat wakes drown their nests, and repeated encounters with humans drive them away. Fortunately, the Department of Environmental Conservation excludes motors between Lows Lower and Upper Dams. The upper lake borders the Five Ponds Wilderness Area, and we hope the state will include it in the wilderness someday, which will eliminate all motors.

The Bog River roars down through a small canyon at the outlet of Lows Lower Dam, sending mists billowing into the crisp fall air.

We saw many other species of animals in our all-too-brief stay in this wildlife paradise. We noted a large number of beaver lodges, along with mounds of fresh cuttings set aside as winter food. One enterprising beaver had just downed a large paper birch. Given that beaver prefer deciduous trees, probably because of the resins in conifers, one wonders why they eat so much resinous paper birch. Anyone who uses paper birch for firewood will tell you that unsplit logs rot from the inside out in short order, because the resinous bark does not allow moisture to escape. Beaver also trim the leaves and twigs from ends of branches to lessen drag as they swim, sometimes for long distances, hauling branches back to their lodges.

After a short carry around the Lows Upper Dam, we ran into a floating bog after about a mile up the relatively narrow channel leading to Lows Lake. In high water you can possibly paddle over or around it, but we had to carry around it on the north side, taking care not to harm the fragile sphagnum mat with its few dwarf tamaracks, along with sundew, pitcher plant, leatherleaf, sweet gale, and other bog specialists.

Spirelike spruce and balsam fir ring the shore of much of the main lake, providing habitat for spruce grouse and many other species of wildlife. Appropriately enough, an extensive sphagnum

A tall beaver dam holds back the water on a tributary just upstream from the launch site.

bog guards the entrance to Bog Lake. Scattered tamaracks and a carpet of leatherleaf cover the bog, along with sweet gale and grasses around the edges. A great blue heron, watched warily as we paddled by, and an osprey wheeled overhead. This extraordinarily rich and varied habitat, filled with myriad plants and wildlife, offers one of the finest paddling experiences in the Adirondacks.

The St. Lawrence County Historical Association, in January 1974, chronicled the enterprises of A. A. Low. A bulletin board at the Upper Dam contains a copy of their quarterly. Built in 1903 and 1907 by A. A. Low, the dams generated electricity for the small enclave and for Low's residence on nearby Lake Marian and provided water for log drives. Low owned 40,000 acres, which he used to produce timber and maple syrup. He tapped more than 10,000 maple trees and produced 20,000 gallons of maple syrup in the peak year of 1907. Low was an innovator—he used tubs, pipes, and troughs to bring sap to railcars to transport to his huge evaporator. Among his more than 200 patents were several on sap-boiling devices. He also held a patent on a square bottle used to package virgin Adirondack forest springwater that he sent off to New York City. His company, the Horseshoe Forestry Company, met its demise in the devastating fire of 1908. Low died in 1912.

The historical association finishes its account of this amazingly accomplished man with these words: "In life his aim had been to develop, improve, and utilize the fruits of his mountain empire without despoiling it. His spirit roams the Bog River Valley. Today it must be pleased that two monuments to his enterprise still stand tall and proud after more than 60 [now 90] years. They are the two dams...."

Getting There

Going north out of the village of Long Lake or south out of Tupper Lake on Route 30, turn west off Route 30 onto Route 421. Pavement ends in 5.7 miles. About 0.1 mile farther, watch for a sign to Lows Lower Dam Canoe Access. Turn left onto the dirt access road, and you will reach the small parking area in 0.7 mile.

Cranberry Lake
Clifton, Colton, and Fine

MAPS

New York Atlas: Map 94

USGS Quadrangles: Cranberry Lake, Five Ponds, and Newton Falls

INFORMATION

Area: 7,040 acres (11 square miles); maximum depth: 38 feet

Prominent fish species: Brook trout and smallmouth bass

Camping: Cranberry Lake Public Campground is located about one mile east of the village of Cranberry Lake on the south side of Route 3. There is no boat launch facility at the campground; you could launch from a shoreside campsite; 315-848-2315.

Camping at one of the 46 water-access sites for more than three nights or in parties of 10 or more requires a free permit from the forest ranger at P.O. Box 104, Wanakena, NY 13695; 315-848-3370.

Books: If you plan to include Cranberry Lake in a longer paddle of the East Branch of the Oswegatchie River, purchase a copy of Paul Jamieson and Donald Morris's outstanding guidebook *Adirondack Canoe Waters: North Flow,* published by the Adirondack Mountain Club.

One might easily be intimidated by Cranberry Lake's size, the third largest in the Adirondacks, especially if one has familiarity with Lake George and Great Sacandaga Lake. The main body of Cranberry Lake can have wind-driven swells that might swamp an open canoe, but compared to the other two, this one is calm, especially in its many quiet coves. Cranberry Lake looks more like a Rorschach ink blot, with jagged fingers that contain 55 miles of shoreline running to the edges of the map in all directions, rather than the well-defined north-south channels of the other two that funnel even modest breezes into threatening swells. And while the two larger lakes attract hordes of large boats and Jet-skis, Cranberry attracts far fewer boaters and about equal numbers of canoes and motorboats.

Perhaps Cranberry's attraction lies in its protective islands that shelter quiet-water paddlers from the wind or the 46 water-accessible campsites scattered about the shore and islands. It could be the extensive marshes of Bear Mountain Swamp, the network of hiking trails of

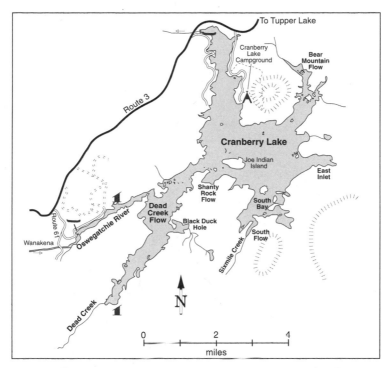

the surrounding Five Ponds Wilderness (96,000 acres) and Cranberry Lake Wild Forest (24,000 acres), the abundant wildlife, or the lake's relative seclusion. These combine to make Cranberry Lake one of the finest paddling destinations in the Adirondacks.

Instead of putting in at the state-run boat access off Route 3 just west of the village, we drove down to the quieter southwestern arm in Wanakena, where the East Branch of the Oswegatchie River enters the lake, thereby avoiding the congestion and development that characterize the village and surrounding shoreline at the north end. The Wanakena arm also provides access to the more sheltered coves and bays of the lake, allowing you to avoid the windier open water of the main lake.

As you paddle out from Wanakena, hemlocks line the banks in places, sporting a conspicuous browse line where deer munch the vegetation from the ice in winter, particularly right across from the ranger school. A rope swing dangles from a yellow birch; it looked enticing, but it was too early in the morning for a swim. The ranger school represents the last development on this arm of Cranberry Lake; indeed, the state owns and protects three-quarters of the lakeshore and most of the surrounding hillsides.

We saw numerous great blue herons patrolling the shallow coves, and we listened to hermit thrushes singing from the understory in the early morning hours. An osprey fished the quiet waters of Shanty Rock Flow, and two flocks of common mergansers tried to hide along the shore as we cruised by. Ring-billed gulls dive-bombed us if we got too close to their nests on bare granite boulders, and we watched a pair of loons with a half-grown black chick swimming between them.

We had a picnic lunch on the smooth ledges surrounding the falls where Sixmile Creek enters South Flow. We hiked back along the trail leading away from the falls, searching the marshes for beaver; none seemed to be out in the middle of the day.

Granite boulders, some really huge, crowd the shoreline. Glacial erratics form small islands, even out in the middle of the main lake. Spruce, hemlock, tamarack, red maple, yellow birch, aspen, and many other tree species cover the hills that recede off into the distance.

Marshy areas exist at the back of Black Duck Hole on the east side of Dead Creek Flow and much more extensively up in the northwest in Bear Mountain Flow. When we paddled back into Black Duck Hole, there were black ducks dabbling for the abundant succulent underwater vegetation. We also watched an otter cavorting, and a huge beaver lodge provided the final confirmation that this area has abundant wildlife. A fellow paddler we met who visits Cranberry frequently said that he often sees otters in the southern portions of the lake.

You can travel back for a couple of miles into Bear Mountain Flow to a very long line of black spruce that mark the end of the marsh, and you probably will paddle alone here. We turned around at the second beaver dam.

Extensive mats of small, red-tinged sundews cover the hummocks of Bear Mountain Flow, in as great a concentration as we have seen. As we looked carefully at these small, carnivorous plants, we could see the dewlike, sticky secretions on short stalks that crowd the outer margins of their rounded pads—their only leaves. Insects, attracted to these glistening secretions, become entrapped. A slight roll of the pad pushes the unlucky insects onto shorter stalks that contain digestive enzymes. The digested insects get incorporated into plant tissues, supplementing the meager nutrients available in swamps and bogs.

But large patches of a beautiful yellow-flowered bladderwort provided our biggest treat. When you push gently on the long spur protruding from the rear of the flower, it opens the front two petals, revealing the interior reproductive parts. We often see both yellow- and, more rarely, purple-flowered bladderworts, particularly in shallow, stagnant water, with only the small bloom stalk above the surface. However, the bladderworts found here, members of the genus *Utricularia,* shared the hummocks with sphagnum and the sundews. One of the few terrestrial bladderworts, these plants trap insects on dry land, with their bladders immersed in mud. They function much in the same way as their aquatic cousins, but this variety captures small, land-based insects.

We spent several hours back in Bear Mountain Flow and saw nary another paddler. Ducks, great blue herons, and kingfishers kept us company. This was the last part of Cranberry Lake that we paddled, and the memory of the wonderful sights and sounds of the marsh kept our minds off the long paddle back to the boat access at Wanakena.

Getting There

Head west on Route 3 out of Cranberry Lake village, keeping an eye out for a boat launch sign just outside of town. About 0.1 mile after the sign and just after crossing a bridge, turn left to get to the state-maintained boat access.

Alternatively, continue on for 6.7 miles from the state-maintained access road to the road to Wanakena, Route 61. Turn left onto the paved road. Go 0.9 mile to the sign for the ranger school. Turn left onto Ranger School Road, and go 0.4 mile to the boat access on the right.

The state-run campground is about 1.0 mile east out of Cranberry Lake village on Route 3. Turn right, and drive quite a way back in to the campground.

Oswegatchie River

Fine

MAPS
New York Atlas: Map 94
USGS Quadrangles: Five Ponds and Newton Falls

INFORMATION

Length: Approximately 13 miles from Inlet to High Falls

Prominent fish species: Brook trout

Camping: Limited camping available at the boat access at Inlet, as well as at 46 campsites along the river. Camping for more than three nights at one site or in parties of 10 or more requires a free permit from the forest ranger at P.O. Box 104, Wanakena, NY 13695; 315-848-3370.

Also, Cranberry Lake Public Campground is located about one mile east of the village of Cranberry Lake on the south side of Route 3; 315-848-2315.

Trails: For trail information, call the Canton office of the DEC; 315-386-4546.

Books: If you plan a longer paddle of the Oswegatchie River, other than the section described here, purchase a copy of Paul Jamieson and Donald Morris's outstanding guidebook *Adirondack Canoe Waters: North Flow,* published by the Adirondack Mountain Club.

The remarkable Oswegatchie River upstream from Inlet, an extraordinary canoe wilderness, drains the high country of the Five Ponds Wilderness Area. Because the river remains one of the few places in the Adirondacks without motors, it has become very popular among paddlers; do not expect to paddle alone here: we encountered eight other boats.

The trip described here travels upstream (south) to High Falls and returns. Although you can paddle a few miles beyond the falls, penetrating ever deeper into wilderness, that has become much more difficult. The Five Ponds Wilderness, once a large tract of virgin timber, suffered a devastating blow in mid-July 1995, when a violent windstorm ripped through this section of the Adirondacks.

We camped out near Inlet on the night of July 14 and had planned to paddle the Oswegatchie the next morning. As first light neared on the 15th, we awoke to great tent flapping. Desperately, we held onto the tent's fragile fabric. After a few minutes, the wind subsided, and we emerged to find the landscape littered with fallen trees. With all roads

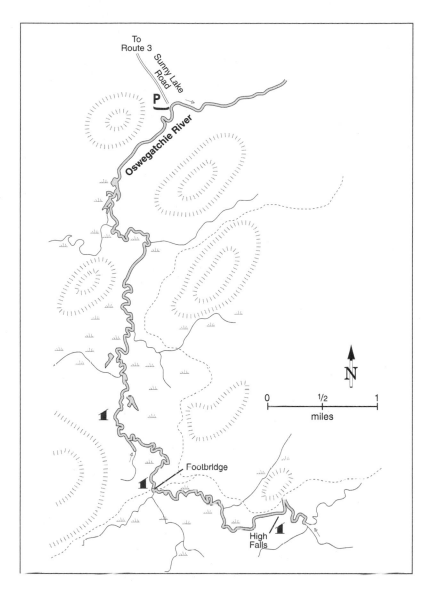

blocked by downed trees and power lines, we retreated outside the park to the north, the only direction with open roads.

But we returned to paddle the Oswegatchie three weeks later. What we witnessed was indescribable devastation. The Five Ponds Wilderness had been the epicenter of a storm that destroyed much of 1 million acres of timber. Just over 100,000 acres suffered greater than 60 percent tree loss, while the rest sustained about half that percentage loss.

Blown-over and snapped-off trees—all facing west to east—dominated much of the river's course. We skirted countless treetops, ducked under many leaners, and carried over several logjams. Many sections remained untouched, but then hundreds of acres of twisted wreckage would confront us as we rounded the next bend.

Hardly a tree remained standing on the right side of High Falls. One large cherry tree had crashed down on the lean-to on the right side of the falls; we heard that the lean-to had occupants—as it always does—at the time of the blowdown. Fortunately, the log structure held, protecting its occupants. Amazingly, none of the more than 30 paddlers and hikers in the wilderness died, though one camper was killed by a falling tree at Eighth Lake Campground and another at Lake Lila.

Shortly after this trip, three friends paddled to the end of Lows Lake and decided to try the three-plus-mile trail to High Falls. They turned back after 100 yards because downed trees had obliterated the trail. Most of the trails in the Five Ponds Wilderness suffered a similar fate. It will take years for this area to be cleared or for the downed timber to rot away. We hope timber companies will not try to harvest this timber, even if given permission to penetrate the wilderness.

Upon our return trip, signs at the launch area warning Caution, Wind Damage, Unsafe Conditions did not deter us or the several other paddlers we encountered. Paddling out in the early morning mists through spirelike balsam firs, our questions about what became of the wildlife during the storm were answered immediately as a beaver

Early-morning mists rise from the surface of the Oswegatchie River in the Five Ponds Wilderness Area.

Joe-pye weed

swam by, totally unconcerned by our presence. The many beaver have done a good job at pruning back the streamside alders.

As we penetrated farther into the wilderness, beaver meadows appeared on side channels. If you have time, carry up over the banks through joe-pye weed into these meadows, as they provide excellent wildlife habitat. A bittern that had stationed itself upright to blend in with the streamside grass bolted skyward as we got too close. A snow-shoe hare, wearing its summer browns, munched on grass, while flocks of cedar waxwings ate everything in sight, except the ripening winter-berries. Their bright red fruits persist well into winter because of their low nutritional value. Birds and mammals prefer more nutritious fruit and insects. However, after depletion of other food sources, the waxwings and other wildlife do eat these berries, eventually scattering the plant's seeds to new locations in their droppings.

As we neared the first of five obstructions across the stream, near campsite 33, a river otter that had sat feeding on a fish slid gracefully into the tea-colored water. Tannic and other organic acids liberated from decaying vegetation in the surrounding swamp turn the water into a rich yellow brown. Animal droppings on nearly every exposed rock tell us that this otter and the beaver we saw earlier have much company.

The surrounding boreal forest of tamarack, black spruce, white pine, and balsam fir provide habitat for rare northern species, including spruce grouse, gray jay, and boreal chickadee. The only one we encoun-tered was the boreal chickadee, with its gray cap and hoarse "chick-a-dee-dee" call. This habitat should include moose, as their wide cloven hooves and very long legs—the largest moose stand seven and a half feet at the shoulder—adapt them to life in swamps and beaver meadows. Instead, in a sorry chapter of mid-nineteenth-century history, hunters vied to kill the last moose in New York State. Recently, moose from northern New England have made their way to New York in what we hope will form the pioneer stock for widespread dispersal.

A little way upstream, you reach a footbridge at the top of a riffle. At high-water levels, you will have to carry over or pole through the riffle. Just after the footbridge, at campsite 22, a sign says Spring with an arrow pointing the way. Until the blowdowns get washed out or removed, it will take quite a bit of time to reach High Falls with a loaded canoe. Start early, and expect to take two days to reach the falls. The downstream trip with the current and with lighter food packs should take well less than a full day. If you want to explore the wilderness more fully, you will need more than three days.

As we drifted back lazily with the current, we remarked at the abundant wildlife. In addition to the species noted above, we saw crow, catbird, yellow warbler, common yellowthroat, northern harrier skimming over the surface of the marsh, yellow-rumped warbler, downy woodpecker, wood duck, American redstart, black-and-white warbler, and magnolia warbler. A garter snake swam in S-shaped arcs across the river before us, and a pair of ospreys and a pair of red-tailed hawks circled above. We wondered if their nest trees got blown down—at least the adults survived to build new nests next year. We would be back to check on their progress.

Getting There

From the village of Cranberry Lake, travel west on Route 3 to Sunny Lake Road (called Inlet Road on the New York Atlas) on the left. The turnoff is about 3.0 miles past the turnoff to Wanakena. If you get to Newton Falls Road (Route 60) going off north, you have gone 1.0 mile too far. Turn around, and measure 1.0 mile back to Sunny Lake Road. After turning onto Sunny Lake Road, take an immediate sharp left after 10 feet; do not go straight. The road ends at the boat access in Inlet. Paddle to the right, upstream, from the boat access.

Lake Lila

Long Lake

MAPS
New York Atlas: Maps 86 and 94
USGS Quadrangles: Beaver River, Forked Lake, Little Tupper Lake, and Wolf Mountain

INFORMATION
Area: 1,446 acres; maximum depth: 64 feet
Prominent fish species: Brook trout, lake trout, landlocked salmon, and smallmouth bass
Camping: Permit required for stays longer than three nights. Contact forest ranger at Long Lake at 518-624-6101.

Autumn-hued foliage of beech, sugar and red maple, paper and yellow birch reflected off the glasslike surface of Lake Lila. Wisps of mist rose gently into a cloudless sky, burned off the lake's surface by the rising sun, as we paddled out early one October morning. We paddled alone—not surprising this late in the season.

Lake Lila is a wonderful place to paddle. The state owns the entire shoreline and prohibits motors in the Lake Lila Primitive Area, which encompasses the entire lake. Great campsites exist all around the lake's perimeter and on some islands. Shingle Shanty Brook offers hours of pleasant diversion, and the Beaver River can be paddled down to the falls, about halfway to Nehasane Lake, which lies about two miles to the southwest. Intrepid explorers could paddle through Nehasane Lake all the way to Stillwater Reservoir, at least during high water. Clear water makes it possible to avoid the barely submerged boulders that rush up to greet your hull.

Rocks, shrubs, and tall white pine dominate the shoreline of Lake Lila, along with occasional stands of red pine, spruce, northern white cedar, red maple, and a few mountain maple. Pine and paper birch cover the islands. In contrast to the lakeshore, deciduous trees dominate the hillsides, along with some patches of dense conifers.

Yellow-rumped warblers searched for insects, still fattening up for their fall migration. Of the 52 species of warblers that nest in the U.S., 31 nest in New York, and 2 more pass through during migration. Of these, yellow-rumped warblers arrive first in the spring, leave last in the fall, and winter farther north than any other warblers—as far north as coastal Massachusetts. Given that warblers feed nearly exclusively on

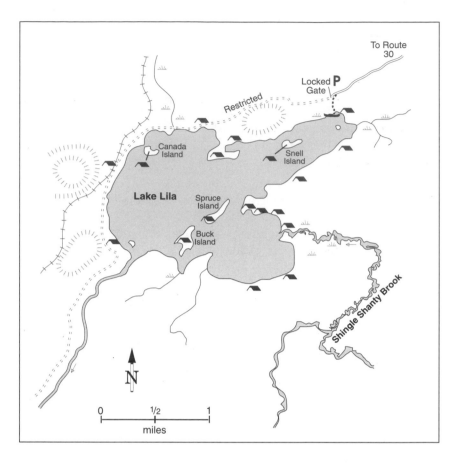

insects, the yellow-rumped—formerly called myrtle—warbler has had to adapt to insectless conditions in the fall and winter by eating berries. While insects remain their preferred food, they commonly eat poison ivy's white berries, bayberries, and others during cold weather. This adaptation has served the yellow-rumped well, as it remains one of our most abundant warblers.

Another late migrant, an osprey, hovered over the placid waters of Lake Lila, waiting to crash-dive onto unsuspecting fish. Occasionally, we have seen a bald eagle swoop over the water's surface, gracefully sweeping up a dead or dying fish in its crooked talons, in contrast with the noisy immersion and splashing of the osprey. We suspect that the eagle may be too heavy, at up to 12 pounds, to extricate itself from the water laden with a fish. We have also watched bald eagles attempt to steal fish from ospreys, which are better fishers. The eagle attacks in midair as the osprey labors to gain altitude, trying to force the osprey to release its prey.

Bald eagles winter as far north as Canada—and in increasing numbers in southern New York—wherever there is open water. Osprey, on the other hand, winter in Florida, southernmost Texas, southern California, Mexico, and points south.

Shingle Shanty Brook, Beaver River, and the lake itself all showed evidence of extensive beaver activity. We saw beaver out foraging in the middle of the day. Beaver naturally forage during daylight hours, but in the presence of human disturbance, they become crepuscular (out in twilight), if not completely nocturnal.

We very much enjoyed our three-hour paddle on Shingle Shanty Brook, one of the most meandering bodies of water we've ever paddled. Grasses, clematis, sweet gale, alder, swamp rose, and other shrubs line the banks, with the pointed spires of golden-needled tamarack, spruce, and balsam fir providing contrasting habitat. Bur reed and water celery, our constant companions, had little trouble in the light current. Eventually, a few miles back up the stream, we encountered a purposely downed log across the stream, accompanied by several Warning, No Trespassing signs. Because the stream remains clearly navigable, even during low water in the fall, we believe that access restriction violates the law.

The Beaver River that flows out of Lake Lila cuts a broad, shallow swath through the forest. A slow, scenic river bounded by coniferous

Mists lift from the waters of Lake Lila near the boat launch at sunrise.

forest, it connects Lake Lila with Nehasane Lake and eventually Still-water Reservoir. About halfway to Nehasane Lake, a short falls bars your way. A private bridge over the falls warns that proceeding farther would be trespassing. People who canoe this area frequently tell us that no one gets hassled who paddles down the Beaver River to Stillwater Reservoir, but that you should attempt it only during high water to avoid walking your boat through miles of shallows.

Our experience on Lake Lila points out the extraordinary advantages of fall paddling, from the gorgeous red leaves of sumacs lining the Adirondack Northway, to a total lack of biting insects and motors, to the glorious fall colors surrounding the lake, to the presence of beaver in the middle of the day, to the generally windless, cloudless skies, and to the lack of crowds. Try it out!

Getting There

Coming from the north, from the stoplight in downtown Tupper Lake, head south on Route 30 for 11.3 miles, and turn right onto paved Circle Road (this road is 2.6 miles past the junction with Route 421). Bear right at the fork after 3.0 miles, and drive another 4.5 miles on Sabattis Road. Turn left onto the access road; the boat access is 5.7 miles down this gravel road. This last section of road passes through private land; although the state owns a conservation easement, you may not park along this road at any point. If the parking lot at the end is full—and it can be on popular summer weekends—you must turn around and drive back out!

Coming from the south, from the green iron bridge over Long Lake, the Circle Road turnoff is 10.0 miles north on Route 30. Watch for the small sign for Sabattis. You can join Circle Road about 3.0 miles closer to Long Lake—if you can find it. It is at the top of the hill and lacked a marker before the recent major road reconstruction. Perhaps a new sign has been placed there.

The launch point is about a quarter of a mile down a trail that goes south out of the parking lot. Do not take the hiking trail that leaves from the end of the parking lot and goes along the northern lake shore.

Long Lake

Long Lake

MAPS

New York Atlas: Maps 87 and 95

USGS Quadrangles: Deerland and Kempshall Mountain

INFORMATION

Area: 4,077 acres; maximum depth: 50 feet

Prominent fish species: Smallmouth bass and northern pike

Camping: Permit required for stays of more than three nights or parties of 10 or more people. Contact Forest Ranger, Long Lake, at 518-624-6101.

Books: If you plan to do a long-distance paddle of the Raquette River, purchase a copy of Paul Jamieson and Donald Morris's outstanding guidebook *Adirondack Canoe Waters: North Flow,* published by the Adirondack Mountain Club.

The 4,000-foot mountains of the High Peaks Wilderness dominate the view to the northeast from Long Lake, which lies in a glaciated valley on the Raquette River. The view alone makes the northern stretch of Long Lake worth paddling. Long-distance paddlers travel up Long Lake on their way to Tupper Lake via the Raquette River or to the Saranac Lakes via the Raquette River to Stony Creek Ponds.

Long Lake's 14-mile length, traversing southwest to northeast, funnels winds that can make boating hazardous. We paddled here twice—both times on the northern section—once with two-foot waves occasionally crashing over the bow and a second time under dead calm conditions. Although well worth paddling, we advise that you paddle smaller, more protected bodies of water during strong winds, and if you do paddle Long Lake, pay attention to the weather forecast. Remember that paddling back to Long Lake from the northeast you will paddle into the current and—most often—into the wind.

Don't let the Jet-skis, floatplanes, and motorboats hovering about the village of Long Lake intimidate you. The lake stretches for many miles and includes several small paddlable streams where you can escape the noise and congestion. On the north end of the lake where it narrows down, and continuing on to the carry around Raquette Falls—a distance of about six miles—the Raquette has earned a scenic river designation, which keeps out the motorboats and Jet-skis.

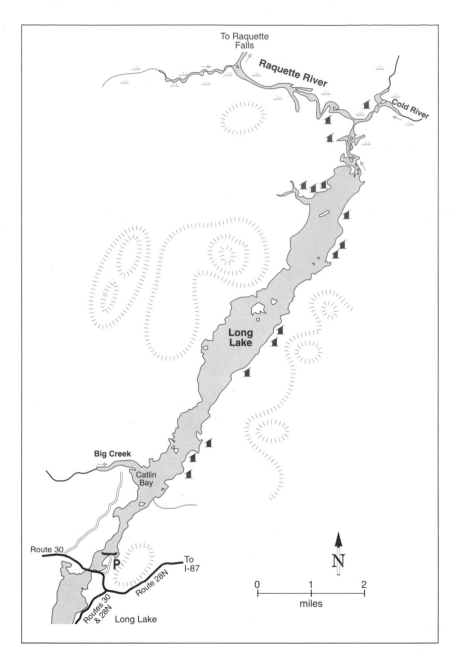

The lake's high elevation (1,627 feet) and considerable depth keep the water quite cool until midsummer, so early season swimming can be a brisk experience. Twenty shelters dot the shoreline, providing some wonderful camping spots, especially those with a view down the scenic valley with the High Peaks Wilderness hovering over the lake's north end. The state owns much of the eastern shore but not the western until you get far down the lake. A grove of large red pines helps conceal the first shelter on the eastern shore, announcing the beginning of state-owned land. Unfortunately, the view here over Catlin Bay includes cottages intruding on the opposite shore.

Because the 133-mile-long Northville-Placid Trail follows the right-hand shoreline, you may have to compete with hikers for use of the shelters. Near the northern end of the lake, several shelters occur on the opposite shore, away from the trail. We suggest taking a tent along in July and August, as the shelters are likely to be in use.

Northern white cedar, paper birch, and hemlock line the shore of Long Lake, along with a wide assortment of pine and deciduous trees. We saw few ducks when we paddled here, but loons appeared in good numbers. And we watched several crows chase a Cooper's hawk. Like the other accipiters—the larger goshawk and the smaller sharp-shinned hawk—this hawk preys on birds. The Cooper's hawk has become increasingly rare, and so we delighted in watching its agile flight on short, rounded wings as it used its long tail as a rudder. Although we have not witnessed a kill by a Cooper's hawk, we have witnessed several by the similar, but smaller, sharp-shinned hawk. Their agility allows them to take songbirds on the wing, leaving nothing but a puff of feathers drifting slowly to the ground.

Beautiful views await paddlers on Long Lake.

Take time to explore the two creeks that flow into Long Lake: Big Creek and Cold River. Big Creek flows into Catlin Bay on the left as you paddle north. Pickerelweed, bulrushes, and grasses greet you at the outlet, along with lots of beaver activity. We passed by more beaver lodges than human houses. We paddled through two breached beaver dams and carried up over a third. About a half-mile upstream, we passed under an unusual bridge with four laminated wooden support beams; they must have been eight inches wide and at least three feet deep.

About two-tenths of a mile after the bridge, a fall of rocks blocks the way—the decent-sized, rounded boulders form a sizable rapids, flanked by a very large stand of tall, pointed balsam firs. Yellow birch dominate the southern shore, with some alders along the bank. Occasional red maple and paper birch occur, as well, in this beautiful and peaceful setting. We noted lots of open mussel shells in the clear water and many species of aquatic plants, including fragrant water lily, yellow pond lily, and pondweed.

We did not paddle Cold River, which flows into the Raquette River about a mile downstream from the north end of the lake, because of low water, but we were told and have read that you can paddle back up its marshy wilderness for nearly two miles during high water. Other coves and inlets on Long Lake harbor marshes and their assorted plants and animals as well. And the myriad Raquette River channels at the north end down to Raquette Falls provide many more exploration opportunities. One has to paddle here for a few days to explore it all, the whole time under the magnificent backdrop of the High Peaks Wilderness.

Getting There

The boat access is in the village of Long Lake. From the junction of Routes 28N and 30 in Long Lake, go north on Route 30. After one block, as the road curves left at the post office, turn right at the flashing yellow light. The boat access is 0.4 mile down the paved road to the left.

Harris Lake and Rich Lake
Newcomb

MAPS
  New York Atlas: Map 87
  USGS Quadrangle: Newcomb
INFORMATION
  Harris Lake area: 310 acres
  Rich Lake area: 342 acres; maximum depth: 65 feet
  Prominent fish species: Harris Lake—smallmouth bass and north-
    ern pike; Rich Lake—lake trout, smallmouth bass, and northern
    pike
  Camping: Lake Harris Campground; 518-582-2503

Harris Lake

We decided to include Harris Lake for two main reasons: first, because
of the really gorgeous scenery as you paddle down to the Hudson, and
second, because three cavorting river otters thought it remote enough
for them. River otters, large members of the weasel family, with a body
length of 30 inches and weighing up to 25 pounds, range coast to coast,
from northern Alaska to Labrador, south to the tip of Florida, and
across to Yuma, Arizona. In spite of this huge range, people rarely
encounter this magnificent creature, mainly because it has grown
increasingly rare. Development and commotion drive river otters away,
so finding them playing—one of the few animals that seem to cavort
for fun—on the rocks in Harris Lake made our paddle a real treat.

Scattered development along the southern and western shores did
not seem to bother the resident loons, either. Crows searched the shoreline for washed-up food, and a kingfisher eyed the water, looking for
those last few fish to eat before migrating on to warmer climes. Northern white cedar grows along the shore, along with patches of tall, pointed firs, occasional white pines, and sugar and red maples. Note that on
the cedar white-tailed deer have browsed a conspicuous line up as high
as they can reach from the ice in winter.

Rushes inhabit the shallows, along with pondweed, pickerelweed,
water celery, yellow pond lily, and fragrant water lily. Bur reed also
occurs in the shallows in places, and royal fern graces the banks. Water
shield, a member of the water lily family, with stems entering the center of a floating oval leaf, occur in large patches. Notice the slimy,
gelatinous coating on the underside of its leaves.

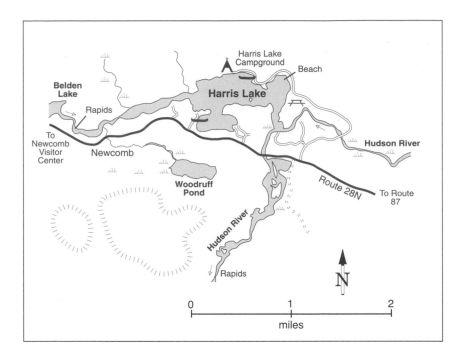

Paddling east from the boat access, you encounter the mighty Hudson River, longest river in the state, near the beginning of its almost 300-mile-long sojourn from Lake Tear of the Clouds on the slopes of Mt. Marcy down to the Verrazano Narrows Bridge and the Atlantic Ocean. Entering the river channel, you can paddle upstream a short distance before you meet quickwater. You can paddle farther to the right, passing under the Route 28N bridge. Take note of the warning signs, referring to the impending rapids—about three-quarters of a mile downstream—that eventually lead to the Hudson River Gorge. Use caution here, because you do not want to get swept into these Class III rapids, not usually run in open boats. Only really serious whitewater paddlers traverse the Class V water of the gorge farther downstream.

Along the lake's northern shore sits Harris Lake Campground, which provides pleasant family camping and easy canoe access to these waters and to nearby Rich Lake. On the western end of the lake, you will find most of the development, including a nice town park with swings and a beach along the southern shore. Rocks lining the banks and out in the water mark the inflow from Belden Lake, really just a wide spot connecting Rich and Harris Lakes.

On the way to Rich Lake, stop in at the Newcomb Visitor Center, one of two in the Adirondacks. Three nature trails originate here, and a guidebook can help you learn about the area's plants and animals.

Rich Lake

When we paddled out one early fall morning, mist swirled slowly down this shallow, sandy-bottomed lake. Mussel shells lay in piles near shore where the raccoons feasted on nightly forays. Looking out from the sand beach at the boat access, we could see a marsh across the way...and no development. This wild place offers hours of exploration where not even allowed electric motors will bother you.

Rich Lake allegedly got its name when early settlers discovered graphite flakes in the surrounding rocks and thought that the mineral was silver ore. Miners later extracted graphite, a form of carbon, from the deposits near Ticonderoga for the "lead" in lead pencils.

Paddling around to the right from the boat access, you reach the eastern tip of the lake, which narrows to a rocky stream with definite current. A footbridge on one of three nature trails crosses overhead;

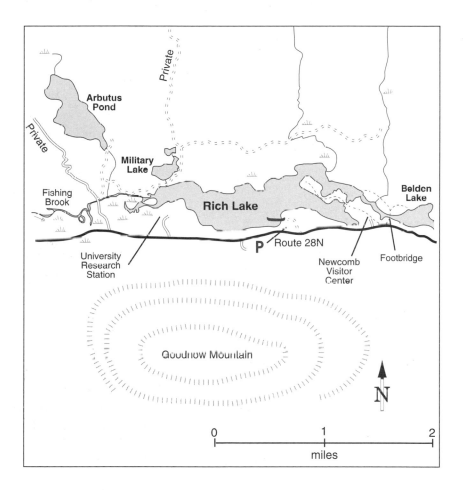

after this, a short rapids leads to Belden Lake and eventually Harris Lake. At low water, you would have to walk your boat down these rapids.

Back out on the main lake, we saw loons, kingfisher, and an osprey, all three fishing in different ways: the loon gliding underwater, snaring a fish with its bill; the kingfisher folding its wings at the last moment, diving headlong into the water, and catching a fish in its beak; and the osprey hovering overhead, swooping down, crashing into the water, and grabbing a fish with its talons.

Down on the western end of the lake, Fishing Brook enters on the north, but you can also paddle through an extensive beaver swamp on the south. The beaver swamp extends back quite a way through encroaching pickerelweed to a few-hundred-acre marsh. At various places along the way, if you carry up over a few well-kept beaver dams, some surprisingly high, you enter Fishing Brook. Many more dams occur on the myriad channels of the brook.

Grasses grow on the banks, along with thick shrubbery. Sweet gale, leatherleaf, swamp milkweed, sheep laurel, bur reed, and many

A handicapped-accessible boardwalk and observation platform make the beauty of Rich Lake accessible to all. The trail starts at the Adirondack Visitor Center.

more swamp specialists grow here. Northern white cedar, with a few towering white pines, occasional hemlocks and balsam fir, some paper and yellow birch, and lots of red, sugar, and silver maples, occur on higher ground.

We paddled back up the alder-lined brook, with occasional dogwood and viburnum interspersed, for about three-quarters of a mile, until we reached a large area flooded by a beaver dam. Having carried over many beaver dams already, we decided to turn around and paddle back to the lake.

On our travels through the marsh, several small flocks of wood ducks and ring-necked ducks sprang to air as we interrupted their attempts to fatten up for fall migration. But the real wildlife highlight came as we were leaving the lake. Right in front of us, a female black bear with two young cubs bounded across the road, with mom woofing copious instructions to her young. Black bear populations have increased significantly in Adirondack Park in recent years. In the dry summer of 1995, they seemed to move around often, undoubtedly because traditional food sources were not as plentiful. If you spend a significant amount of time in wild areas such as these, your chances of seeing them are quite good.

Getting There

Harris Lake: From the village of Long Lake, at the junction of Routes 28N and 30, take Route 28N east for 11.7 miles to the Newcomb Visitor Center. To get to Harris Lake, continue on past the visitor center for 2.0 miles, and turn left at the sign for Newcomb Town Beach and Boat Landing.

If coming from the south, take I-87 to Exit 29, then follow Route 28 north to North Creek, where Route 28N bears off to the right. Take Route 28N north toward Newcomb. After crossing the Hudson River, continue 0.8 mile to the access road on the right.

Rich Lake: From the visitor center, drive west on Route 28N for 0.6 mile and turn right onto an easy-to-miss gravel road. Turn left almost immediately to go down to the parking lot 0.1 mile from Route 28N; the paved road to the right leads to a research and training center. You can drop your boat off a few hundred feet closer to the access by driving past the parking lot and then returning your car to this lot.

Harris Lake Campground: From the visitor center, drive east on Route 28N for 3.2 miles. The turnoff to the left is 0.3 mile past the Hudson River bridge.

South Pond

Indian Lake and Long Lake

MAPS
> **New York Atlas:** Map 87
> **USGS Quadrangle:** Deerland

INFORMATION
> **Area:** 442 acres; maximum depth: 55 feet
> **Prominent fish species:** Splake, Kokanee salmon, and lake trout
> (unless the otters ate them all)

We loved paddling South Pond . . . after we finally found it. This large, scenic pond cannot be seen from the road, Route 28N. After you've found the unmarked parking area along the road, which looks just like any other roadside pullout, then you have to find the trail to the pond. Look for it back down the hill toward Long Lake a few hundred feet. You can drop your boat off there, but then you must remove your car to the pullout. The steep trail down to the shore passes through a grove of massive hemlocks, punctuated with a few large yellow birches and a needle-carpeted floor; the path waxes slippery when wet. Of course, once you get your gear and boat down to the lake level, somehow you have to get it back up.

Sunlight filters through the hemlocks at the boat launch on South Pond.

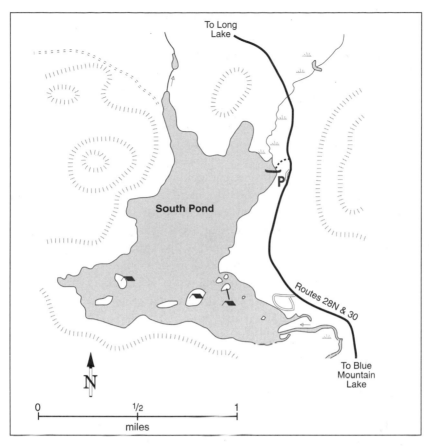

To Long
Lake

P

South Pond

Routes 28N & 30

To Blue
Mountain
Lake

N

0   1/2   1

miles

We found our efforts amply rewarded. Because of difficult access, the lake receives only modest attention and that primarily from fishermen. The state owns more than three-quarters of the shoreline and all of the beautifully forested islands; we found state campsites on three islands on the south end of the lake. The superb views from the pond—of 3,600-foot Blue Mountain, a member of the tallest 100 Adirondack High Peaks club, and sister peaks to the south, and of Inlet Mountain Ridge ending in 2,900-foot Mt. Sabbatis to the northeast—sometimes kept us from casting a wary eye on barely submerged granite boulders.

The sheer numbers of these boulders—lining the banks, submerged, and emerged, some standing taller than a person—greatly impressed us, and impressed *upon* us the need to go carefully. Generally, you can see submerged boulders in the clear water; most of those poking up through the surface, particularly on the pond's south end, had fish skeleton adornments. After viewing several of the many picked-clean carcasses, we decided that the local otter population probably needs to go on a diet-and-exercise routine. The brochure says "splake." It sounds to us like "put-and-take" trout stocking for the otters!

Although we did not see otters here, probably because they have the good sense to avoid the heat and blasting reflected light of a mid-summer's afternoon, we have seen them on several other rivers, lakes, and ponds in this area. River otters, large members of the weasel family, with a body length up to 30 inches and weighing up to 25 pounds, range coast to coast, from northern Alaska to Labrador, south to the tip of Florida, and across to Yuma, Arizona. In spite of this huge range, people rarely encounter this magnificent creature, mainly because it has grown increasingly rare. Development and commotion drive river otters away. They seem safe on South Pond, and we plan to return to look for them in the early morning or evening hours.

Cruising down the eastern shore, we spotted a doe and her spotted fawn at the water's edge, down for an afternoon drink. Ravens—almost always traveling in pairs, compared with the flocking behavior of closely related crows—croaked out their hoarse cries. A colony of ring-billed gulls, opportunists of the first order, no doubt also pleased by the otters' presence, patrolled the rocks looking for partially eaten rotting fish carcasses. A brood of common mergansers headed off into the reeds as we approached the north end, and two northern divers, the common loon, dove for fish as the sun started to dip down over the western horizon.

Reluctantly, we paddled back to the awaiting hill, past the rows of northern white cedar and other conifers that line the bank, gazing off at the distant hillsides of intermingled conifers and hardwoods. We look forward to our return to enjoy the splendid beauty of this wild place— and look once again for those big furry guys with fish breath.

Getting There

From the junction of Routes 30 and 28N in Long Lake, take Route 28N south toward Blue Mountain Lake. At 4.9 miles, turn off into the long pullout on the right. The trail to the pond is back along the highway toward Long Lake a few hundred feet. The steep trail down to the water about 250 feet away can be slippery when wet. Please do not leave your car at the trailhead; instead, move it back to the pullout after dropping off your boat and gear.

The Loon
Voice of the Northern Wilderness

No animal better symbolizes wilderness than the loon, whose haunting cry resonates through the night air on many of New York's northern lakes and ponds. The bird seems almost mystical, with its distinctive black-and-white plumage, daggerlike bill, and piercing red eyes. But like our remaining wilderness, the loon is threatened over much of its range. As recreational pressures on our lakes and ponds increase, the loon gets pushed farther away. We who share its waters bear the responsibility for protecting this wonderful bird.

Along with its status as a symbol of northern wilderness, the common loon, *Gavia immer*, is one of the most extraordinary birds you will ever encounter. A large diving bird that lives almost its entire life in the water, it visits land only to mate and lay eggs. Loons have a very difficult time on land because their legs, positioned quite far back on their bodies to aid in swimming, prevent them from walking—a fact that plays heavily in their threatened status in some areas.

Loons have adapted remarkably well to water. Unlike most birds, which have hollow bones, loons have solid bones, making it easier for them to dive to great depths. They also have internal air sacs, which they compress or expand to control how high they float in the water. By compressing this sac, a loon can submerge gradually (like a submarine) with barely a ripple or swim along with just its head above water.

Their heavy bodies and rearward legs make takeoff from the water difficult. A loon may require a quarter mile of open water to build up enough speed to lift off, and it may have to circle a small lake several times to build enough altitude to clear nearby hills or mountains. On occasion, a migrating loon will mistake a highway for a body of water and crash-land, injuring its feet. Unable to take off again, it will die unless brought to a large enough body of water. When migrating, a loon flies rapidly—up to 90 miles per hour—but cannot soar.

Loons generally mate for life and can live for 20 to 30 years. The female lays two eggs in early May, and both male and female, which are indistinguishable by the casual observer, take turns incubating the oblong moss green eggs. If the eggs are left unattended, the embryos can die in just half an hour. Because loons cannot walk on land, they always build their nests very close to shore—where a passing paddler can scare the birds away and a motorboat wake can flood the nest with cold water. Loons often nest on islands, where raccoons and skunks will be less likely to find and devour the eggs. On some lakes and ponds, you will see floating nesting platforms, built by concerned individuals or organizations to improve the

chances of nesting success. On reservoirs with varying water levels, these platforms take on special importance, because they rise and fall with the water level, reducing the likelihood of flooding or stranding a loon nest.

Loon chicks hatch fully covered in black down, and they usually enter the water a day after hatching. Young chicks may be seen riding on a parent's back, but they grow quickly on a diet of small fish and crustaceans. By two weeks of age, they have grown to half the size of the adult and can dive to relatively deep lake bottoms, covering more than 30 yards underwater. Loon chicks remain totally dependent on their parents, however, for about 8 weeks, and they do not fly until 10 to 12 weeks of age. After leaving the nest a day after hatching, loons do not return to land for three or four years—until they reach breeding age. The young mature on the sea, having followed their elders to saltwater wintering areas.

While loons are threatened or endangered in most states in the Northeast, they remain fairly plentiful in parts of the Adirondacks, though New York lists the species as one of "special concern." The last statewide survey of loons in 1984–85 by the New York Department of Environmental Conservation found a total of 157 breeding pairs with 197 chicks on 518 lakes. Including individual loons, 561 adults were counted. Of those lakes with breeding loons, 95 percent had only one pair, though a few lakes had more—notably Stillwater Reservoir with 15 pairs and Lows Lake with 6. By extrapolating the results to lakes that were not surveyed, the state estimates a total population of 800 to 1,000 adults and 220 to 270 breeding pairs.

Historically, loons occupied a much larger portion of the state than they do today. In 1824, the naturalist John James Audubon reported breeding loons on Cayuga Lake, and in the late 1800s they nested along the southern shore of Lake Ontario. Though long gone from these areas, New York's loon population seems to be fairly stable and, in fact, increasing slowly. According to Bob Miller of the New York DEC Division of Fish and Wildlife, a loon survey conducted between 1977 and 1979 found only 114 breeding pairs, though it may not have been a thorough survey. Also, the nesting success rate (the number of young raised per breeding pair) in New York has been higher than that observed in New Hampshire and Minnesota. Despite this generally good news, we should remain concerned about loons. As development encroaches on our lakes and as recreational use increases, recent population trends could well reverse.

Because loons react to disturbance when nesting, it is extremely important for paddlers to keep their distance and be aware of warning displays during the nesting season of early May through mid-July. If a nest fails, the loons may try up to two other times, though the later the chicks hatch, the lower their chances of survival. If you see a loon flapping its wings and making a racket during the nesting season, it probably has a nest or young chicks nearby. Paddle away from shore. Canoeists and kayakers can be a serious threat to nesting loons, because both loons and paddlers prefer shallower protected coves and inlets. If you see a nesting site marked with buoys or warning signs, as is done on some lakes and ponds, always respect those signs and keep your distance.

Loons have lived in this area longer than any other bird—an estimated 60 million years. Let's make sure this wonderful species remains protected so future generations may listen to its enchanting music on a still, moonlit night. For more information on loons, contact the New York State DEC, Division of Fish and Wildlife, Wildlife Resources Center, Delmar, NY 12054; 518-439-0198. You might also want to pick up a copy of the excellent book *The Loon: Voice of the Wilderness* by Joan Dunning (Yankee Books, Dublin, New Hampshire, 1985).

Forked Lake

Long Lake and Arietta

MAPS
> **New York Atlas:** Maps 86 and 87
> **USGS Quadrangle:** Forked Lake

INFORMATION
> **Area:** 1,248 acres; maximum depth: 74 feet
> **Prominent fish species:** Brook trout, largemouth bass, smallmouth bass
> **Camping:** Forked Lake Campground; 518-624-6646

On a calm day, Forked Lake (pronounced with two syllables: *fork*-ed) offers miles of wonderful shoreline paddling and exploration. But be forewarned: with its generally east-west orientation, Forked Lake can dish up treacherous waves on a windy day. The lake stretches over four miles east to west, with a two-mile section extending to the north.

Northern white cedars line much of Forked Lake's shoreline. White-tailed deer love cedar twigs, resulting in a conspicuous browse line marking the height deer can reach above the ground or ice to nibble the branches. White pine, red spruce, balsam fir, hemlock, red maple, sugar maple, yellow birch, paper birch, and beech round out the diverse mixed-hardwood-conifer forest surrounding the lake. Notice the dense stands of hobblebush that dominate the understory with their symmetrical pairs of big heart-shaped leaves. A variety of heaths—

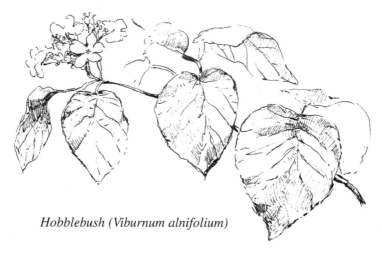

Hobblebush (Viburnum alnifolium)

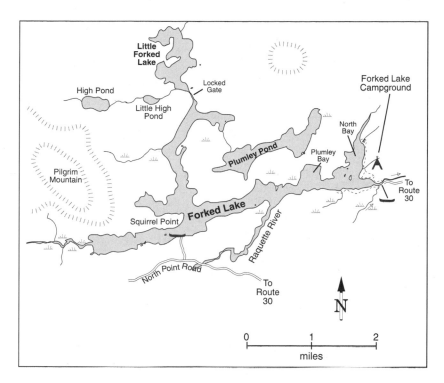

principally leatherleaf, blueberry, and sheep laurel—create a thick, generally impenetrable shoreline.

At the west end, where the lake narrows to a meandering inlet channel from Brandreth Lake, the shoreline becomes much boggier. Tamarack trees grow on the sphagnum hillocks, along with bog rosemary, pitcher plants, leatherleaf, and broad expanses of marsh grass. Thick floating vegetation clogs the shallow inlet, but you can work your way west for quite a ways—the effort will be well worth it! After paddling through the marsh for a mile or so, the channel narrows, hills gradually close in from the sides, a sandy bottom replaces the muck, and the current quickens. We carried above one beaver dam and were eventually stopped by bouldery quickwater.

As you paddle along, notice the towering white pines on the hill-sides north of the creek that rise up toward Pilgrim Mountain—at 2,785 feet, the tallest mountain in the immediate area. The boggy access and steep slopes probably protected this stand from logging in the 1800s. Now, this remnant patch of old-growth forest should remain for generations to enjoy. Individual trees are probably more than 150 feet tall and many hundreds of years old.

We paddled the northern fork of the lake, hoping to reach Little Forked Lake, but were blocked by a fence and locked gate. Most of the land around Forked Lake is owned by the Whitney family and public access restricted. This land was acquired in 1897 by William C. Whitney, the secretary of the navy and a relative of Eli Whitney. Though managed for timber by Whitney Industries, the 51,000 acres of Whitney Park (including 38 lakes and ponds) remain fairly pristine. This choice piece of wilderness has long been sought for inclusion in Adirondack Park, though New York State voters rejected in 1990 a bond measure that would have made funds available for purchase of this and other important parcels of land if and when they come on the market. Wilderness advocates hope someday to see this land become the heart of a proposed 400,000-acre Bob Marshall Great Wilderness, which would be the largest wilderness area in the East. Take some time to explore Forked Lake and see for yourself why this area simply must be protected—you owe it to your children and grandchildren!

We saw quite a few loons on Forked Lake, including one pair with a chick, great blue herons, common mergansers, kingfishers, and a great horned owl. On the south side of the lake, you can paddle up the Raquette River a ways toward Raquette Lake, but you will reach quickwater and rapids in less than a mile. The outlet of Forked Lake is at the far eastern tip near the boat ramp. Also at the eastern end of the lake is the Forked Lake Campground, which includes some island campsites, accessible only by canoe.

Getting There

From the village of Long Lake, where Routes 28N and 30 intersect, drive south on Routes 28N and 30 for 2.9 miles. Turn right onto North Point Road. Stay on North Point Road for another 2.9 miles, and turn right on the access road to Forked Lake Campground. You will reach the boat launch in 1.9 miles.

To reach the Whitney Park access on the south side of the lake farther west, where public boat access is also provided, continue west on North Point Road past the turnoff to Forked Lake Campground for another 5.6 miles (0.3 mile past the bridge over the Raquette River). Turn right onto a gravel road at the Canoe Carry sign, and you will reach the boat access in 0.4 mile.

Blue Mountain, Eagle, and Utowana Lakes and Marion River

Indian Lake

MAPS
  New York Atlas: Map 87
  USGS Quadrangles: Blue Mountain Lake and Raquette Lake
INFORMATION
  Blue Mountain Lake area: 1,334 acres
  Prominent fish species: Largemouth bass, smallmouth bass, northern pike, and stocked lake trout and landlocked salmon

Blue Mountain Lake

A sign at the public boat launch area at Blue Mountain Lake says Boat Speed Limit 45 mph, which is not very encouraging and is probably a good reason to avoid this lake on busy summer weekends. When we paddled here in September, few high-speed boats plied these waters, and we enjoyed the beauty of one of the most scenic locations in the Adirondacks.

Blue Mountain Lake, at an elevation of 1,790 feet, nestles among the High Peaks of the central Adirondacks, with Blue Mountain on the east stretching to more than 3,600 feet. Looking back from the west end of the lake, it becomes obvious how the mountain got its name: ringed with high-altitude conifers, the upper reaches of the peak always look dark, and even blue.

Scenic granite boulders and islands dot the lake, including Long Island, which contains a campsite owned and maintained by Eagle Nest Park. One cannot help but notice, especially on the western end of the lake, a conspicuous browse line on the northern white cedars that hang out over the water. Deer often yard up in cedar stands, and in this case they browse the shoreline cedars up to head height as they walk along the ice in winter.

Blue Mountain Lake holds a special place in the history of the Adirondacks. The lake environs served as the heart of the Adirondacks at the peak of its first wave of popularity. Luxury hotels and a full range of amenities greeted the rich and famous in the 1880s as they completed railroad and stagecoach excursions here from the cities to the east and south.

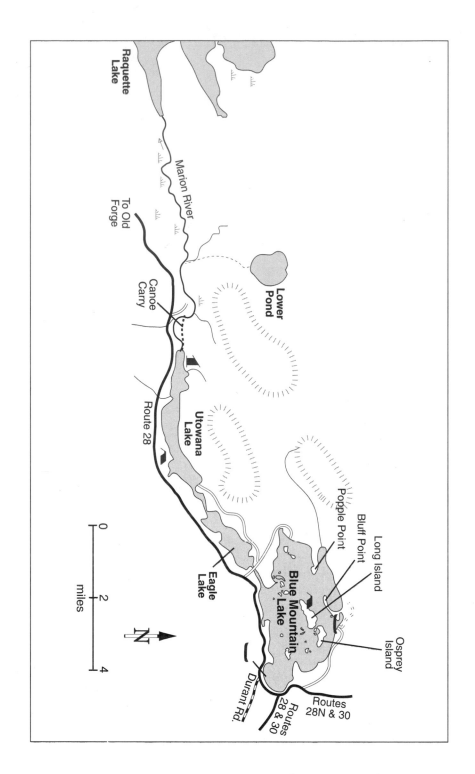

Raquette Lake

Marion River

To Old Forge

Canoe Carry

Lower Pond

Route 28

Utowana Lake

Popple Point

Bluff Point

Long Island

Osprey Island

Eagle Lake

Blue Mountain Lake

0

2

miles

4

N

Durant Rd.

Routes 28 & 30

Routes 28N & 30

The Prospect House here became the first hotel in the world to have electric lighting in every room! At this same hotel in August 1883, Verplanck Colvin first met with a commission to outline his vision of protecting the Adirondacks as a state park. Colvin, a lawyer by training, starting in 1872 spent several decades mapping and describing the Adirondack region. (Would that we could take the rest of the lawyers into the wilderness and leave them there. Look at the effect it had on Colvin!)

Thanks in large part to Colvin's efforts and vision, a law creating a state Forest Preserve was passed two years later, and in 1892, Adirondack Park came into being. Sadly, all of the grand hotels burned to the ground over the years, and what we see here today is probably closer to the original character than it was 100 years ago.

Except near the Blue Mountain Lake town site and on the northeast shore, little development intrudes on the shoreline. But in spite of the gorgeous setting and even with the huge expanse of boat-free water, we preferred to paddle on Eagle and Utowana Lakes—the rest of what some refer to as the Eckford Chain—and the Marion River for a variety of reasons. These latter waterways include more habitat diversity, including a small waterfall on Utowana Lake, extensive marshes, more aquatic plants, and a lot more wildlife. And they don't suffer nearly as much from wind. Even though islands block the wind in some locations, Blue Mountain Lake is still huge, and the wind can build up large waves. When we paddled here, the conditions on the smaller bodies of water were much more pleasant.

Eagle Lake

As you paddle into Eagle Lake, stay to the right, passing under the bridge to the north. The handmade stone bulwarks date to 1891, when William West Durant built the Pioneer Bridge in memory of his father, Dr. Thomas Clark Durant, conceiver, builder, vice president, and general manager of the first transcontinental railroad, the Union Pacific. The elder Mr. Durant also served as president and builder of the Adirondack Railroad.

Little development mars Eagle Lake. The Eagle Nest Park owns the lands surrounding Eagle Lake and most of Utowana Lake, preserving them from development. The north shore houses a summer artist colony. On our morning excursion, we paddled along with someone heading from Blue Mountain Lake to the artist colony on Eagle Lake. A kingfisher also accompanied us down the connecting waterway, and

The Thomas Clark Durant bridge at the entrance to Eagle Lake.

we watched black ducks dabble for aquatic plants, as crows called off
in the distance. Common mergansers fled before us as we paddled
through a canopy of cedar, hemlock, balsam fir, spruce, and very tall
white pine, along with occasional sugar maple, red maple, paper birch,
and yellow birch. As we neared the end of Eagle Lake, towering hemlocks appeared.

Utowana Lake

Resist the temptation to hurry through into Utowana Lake. The long
connector contains an extensive swamp with many side channels to
explore. Along with bog rosemary, sweet gale, alders, and other typical
bog vegetation, tall white pines and many large spruce cover the
islands. Red maple, sugar maple, and yellow birch grow here as well.
Ferns line the banks, and pickerelweed, water celery—with its long,
narrow leaves floating on the water's surface—and fragrant water lilies
grow in profusion in the shallows.

As you paddle out into Utowana Lake, stick to the left-hand,
southern shore. Watch for a small creek flowing into the lake from the
south, the entrance guarded by large patches of pickerelweed and a
grove of tamarack that give way to the balsam fir, yellow birch, striped
maple, red maple, and alder that line the banks. Paddle back up this

creek to a small waterfall that tumbles down over moss-covered granite boulders. Hemlocks drape out over the water to shade the falls, and ferns grow in clumps under the canopy. Look for pitcher plants in the marshy areas.

The Eagle Nest Park maintains a campsite on a point on the southern shore of Utowana Lake, just down from the creek access. Mussel shells litter the shore near the campsite, probably the work of foraging raccoons. Farther down the lake on the north shore, near the outlet, the state maintains a lean-to shelter. The marshy area right in front of the shelter provides habitat for an extensive patch of small pitcher plants.

Conifers seem to dominate the shore and hills surrounding Utowana Lake. Great, feathery tamaracks mix with red maple at the west end of Utowana, along with tall hemlock, a few white pine, spruce, yellow birch, and lots of balsam fir. A few mountain ash—not an ash at all but actually a member of the rose family—drip with large clusters of bright red berries in the fall. The marshes contain acres of fragrant water lilies, along with cattails and some pickerelweed.

These lakes provided excellent views of ring-billed gulls, loons, kingfishers, black ducks, common mergansers, and crows, while the marshes treated us to the sounds and sights of wood ducks, common yellowthroats, white-throated sparrows, yellow-rumped warblers, and great blue herons.

Marion River

A carry down the first few hundred feet of the Marion River begins at the end of Utowana Lake, taking you through a dense stand of balsam firs, interspersed with a few tall white pines and hemlocks. In contrast to the raucous calls of a group of flickers, white-breasted nuthatches called softly while we carried, fighting off the few remaining—but determined—mosquitoes.

At its beginnings at the small dam on Utowana Lake, the clear, shallow Marion River carves out a narrow meandering channel, lined with alders, ferns, cattails, and grasses, affording a relatively unobstructed view of the surrounding hillsides. Aquatic vegetation, including bur reed, pickerelweed, water celery, yellow pond lily, and fragrant water lily, chokes the marshy stream. Milkweed, sweet gale, swamp rose, and viburnum—with large clusters of dark purple berries— appear in clusters. We paddled over a couple of beaver dams, marked with many fresh cuttings.

Extensive marshes keep the conifers at bay as they sink their roots into the higher ground back from the water's edge. The pointed spires of tamarack and balsam fir, along with tall white pine and northern white cedar, mark the inexorable advancement of the higher ground as the marsh slowly fills in.

Many side channels lead off through the marsh, a wonderland filled with plants and wildlife, including many beautifully hued wood ducks, red-breasted mergansers, and several great blue herons. We watched a northern harrier as it hunted the marsh, tilting back and forth on motionless wings, ready to pounce on hapless rodents.

Spoiled by the wonders of the marsh, "civilization" intruded on our wilderness experience as we passed out of the river's mouth into Raquette Lake, with its noisy Jet-skis and shoreline development. Disappointed by the proximity of such threats to the marsh, we immediately turned around to retrace our steps back through nature's glory. The negligible current of the Marion River did not impede our progress, and the entire round-trip of 20 miles took one very long day in a sea kayak. You might want to arrange a pickup to make this a one-way trip, or camp en route.

The hardest part of the journey awaited us back at Blue Mountain Lake where the late afternoon wind had whipped the surface to a froth, providing a wet ride through ever-deepening troughs of whitecapped waves. With our cameras, binoculars, and field guides safely tucked away in watertight bags and with the knowledge that our life jackets would keep us afloat if we tipped, we plunged on through darkening skies that only enhanced the eerie beauty of the surrounding dark blue peaks. A long—but absolutely extraordinary—day, to be sure.

Getting There

From I-87, get off at Exit 23, the Warrensburg exit. Take Route 9 north, and turn left onto Route 28 north. Routes 28 and 30 join in Indian Lake and run together until they reach Blue Mountain Lake. At the stop sign in Blue Mountain Lake, turn left onto Route 28 as Routes 30 and 28N go north. From this junction, go 0.3 mile to the public boat access on the right. Park along the road, and carry your boat over the low fence down to the water.

From Long Lake village, take Routes 30 and 28N south to Blue Mountain Lake. After descending a long, steep hill in to Blue Mountain Lake, start measuring mileage as Routes 30 and 28 take off to the left. Continue south on Route 28 for 0.3 mile, as above.

Lake Durant and Rock Pond
Indian Lake

MAPS
> **New York Atlas:** Map 87
> **USGS Quadrangle:** Blue Mountain Lake

INFORMATION
> **Area:** 420 acres
> **Prominent fish species:** Smallmouth bass, northern pike, and
> stocked tiger muskellunge
> **Camping:** Lake Durant Campground; 518-352-7797

Although Routes 28 and 30 parallel the shore for about a mile, we
decided to include Lake Durant and the connected Rock Pond anyway
because of their scenic beauty, productivity, and their lowered suscep-
tibility to windy conditions—at least compared with nearby Blue
Mountain Lake. To get an appreciation of the Durant's beauty, stop at
the roadside rest area, and look out over the water at the distant hillsides. Hemlocks at the water's edge give way to mixed hardwoods that
cover the hillsides, with patches of darker conifers adding to their mul-

*Many types of aquatic vegetation crowd the surface of the shallows in Lake
Durant. In the fall, surrounding hillsides glow with red, yellow, and orange
leaves.*

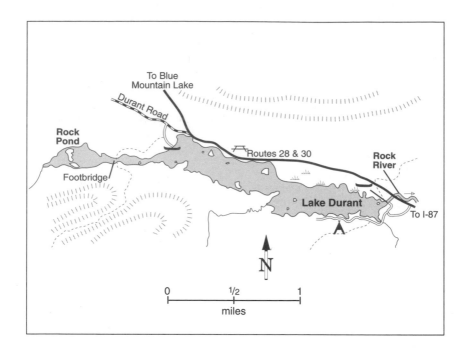

To Blue
Mountain Lake

Durant Road

Rock
Pond

Footbridge

Routes 28 & 30

Rock
River

Lake Durant

To I-87

N

0   ½   1

miles

tihued beauty. When we paddled here in the early fall, the hillsides
seemed painted with red, yellow, and orange against a dark green background of conifers.

Two official boat access points compete with several unofficial
access sites along the shores. If you stay at the Lake Durant Campground on the east end of the lake, you can put your boat in there. If
you want to avoid paying to launch, put in at the other maintained
access point off Durant Road at the west end of the lake.

The productivity of the lake draws people to its waters. Fishermen
come to catch trophy northern pike and smallmouth bass, their success
attested to by the many photographs on the bulletin board at the campground. This stands in stark contrast to events occurring in many other
lakes. Airborne acid rain spewed from tall smokestacks in the Ohio
River Valley rains down on Adirondack lakes, causing the slow death
of many. Sulfuric, hydrochloric, and nitric acids acidify them, lowering
pH to the point where aquatic organisms no longer reproduce, resulting
in barren, lifeless lakes. We should enjoy the primordial productivity of
Lake Durant and do what we can to protect it from the continued airborne assault from Midwestern pollution.

Carpets of aquatic vegetation cover the coves and shallows of
Lake Durant and Rock Pond. Fragrant water lily, pickerelweed, float-

ing heart, water celery, smartweed, water shield, cattails, and yellow pond lily seemingly compete for every inch of surface space in the shallows.

As you paddle west by a stand of beautiful balsam firs—with their pointed spires and upright purple cones—into the connector between Lake Durant and Rock Pond, many flattopped granite boulders greet you, clearly identifying how Rock Pond got its name. A low footbridge separates the two bodies of water. Part of the Blue Ridge Wilderness Area, Rock Pond enjoys a state prohibition on motors—who would want to motor there anyway with all the rocks? Two large islands add character and varied habitat to Rock Pond, a superb place to view wildlife early or late in the day among the rafts of aquatic vegetation.

We listened to the whistling wings of wood ducks as they leapt into the air upon our approach, black ducks bobbed nervously for aquatic plants, and several great blue herons stalked fish and frogs in the shallows, while kingfishers dove for minnows. White-throated sparrows called from the underbrush as we paddled here completely alone. If you tire from competition with motorboats and Jet-skis on many of the nearby lakes, enjoy instead the solitude provided by acres of aquatic vegetation on Lake Durant and Rock Pond.

Getting There

From the junction of Routes 28 and 30 in the village of Blue Mountain Lake, head east on Routes 28 and 30. Go 0.9 mile, watching for Durant Road turning sharply back to the right. Turn right onto Durant Road, and continue 0.2 mile. Turn left onto the dirt road, and go 0.2 mile to the boat access.

To get to Lake Durant Campground, continue east on Routes 28 and 30, watching for signs on the right. After turning into the campground, the boat launch is on the right, and the campground is to the left.

Indian Lake

Indian Lake and Lake Pleasant

MAPS
New York Atlas: Map 87
USGS Quadrangles: Blue Mountain Lake, Indian Lake, and Page Mountain

INFORMATION
Area: 4,365 acres; maximum depth: 85 feet
Prominent fish species: Smallmouth bass, northern pike, land-locked salmon, and lake trout
Camping: Indian Lake Islands State Campground; 518-648-5300. Lewey Lake State Campground; 518-648-5266.

Tired of camping cheek-to-jowl in noisy, crowded campgrounds? Indian Lake offers a peaceful alternative with widely separated campsites where you can listen to loons, barred owls, and whippoorwills calling at night, instead of to your neighboring campers' radio.

At 14 miles long, narrow and scenic, Indian Lake nestles among the sculpted cliffs and forested hillsides of the Adirondack peaks. Many people come to Indian Lake for weekend or weeklong camping. Consequently, we would probably avoid the lake on the busiest holiday weekends, even though the lake's great size can accommodate a lot of boat traffic. Under calm or modest wind conditions, the lake offers wonderful paddling opportunities, with many bays, inlets, protected coves, and islands to explore. However, when the wind blows out of the southwest or northeast—or strongly from any direction—the surrounding hillsides funnel the wind, raising whitecaps and two- to four-foot swells, making canoeing extremely hazardous.

This guide covers only the southern half of Indian Lake, because the northern half suffers much more from weather, development along the western shore, and motorboat traffic. The southern half of the lake has most of the campsites, with most accessible only by water. Each site has a picnic table and a fire grate. We mention some of the more scenic campsite locations below.

Paddling out from the boat access at the end of the western arm, note the bare cliffs under Snowy Mountain off to the left (north). This looks like a good spot for nesting peregrine falcons, and whenever you are in the Adirondacks, you should be on the lookout for these spectacular birds. Led by New York's Cornell Ornithology Laboratory, the

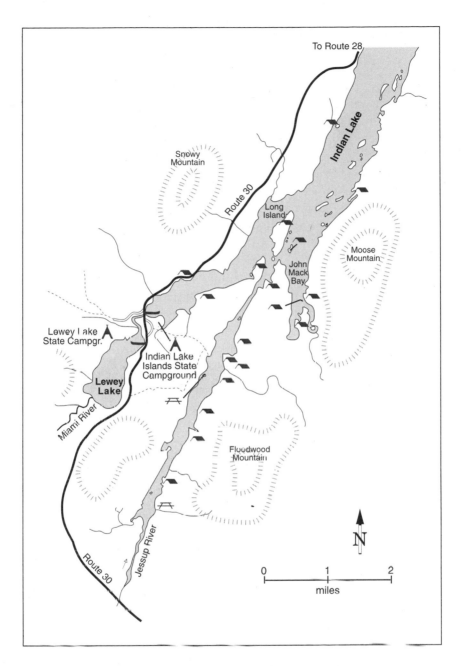

peregrine falcon has made a miraculous comeback from the brink of extinction. Because its diet consists almost exclusively of other birds, it eats way up on the food chain, where biocides get concentrated. Leaves sprayed with pesticides get eaten by insects, concentrating the poisons. Insectivorous birds eat the insects, in turn concentrating the poisons even more. When the peregrine eats bird after poison-laden bird, it gets a much higher dose than that intended for those original insects. Now that we no longer use the most deleterious pesticides—at least in this country (we still export these lethal poisons to the rest of the world to poison their avifauna)—peregrine falcons no longer suffer from disastrous eggshell thinning, which nearly wiped them out.

We were fortunate, indeed, to see one of these incredible birds swooping through the skies over the island just down from the entrance to the long, thin southwestern arm of Indian Lake. Peregrines soar high in the sky, swooping down on ducks and other birds at speeds up to an incredible 180 miles per hour. As it careens by its intended target, it rips open the bird with its talons, leaving a puff of feathers drifting slowly to the ground. We have seen this bird take waterfowl on the wing (its name in the time of Audubon was "duck hawk"), but its preferred prey in the cities is the ubiquitous pigeon.

They now nest on most of the large bridges leading to Manhattan and the other islands and on skyscrapers, as well as on cliffs in upstate New York. In 1994, 22 pairs fledged 35 young, showing that the peregrine continues on its recovery path. Keep your eyes open; if you are lucky, you may see one of these rare birds in action.

As you paddle out from the boat access, note the size of the deciduous trees lining the shore, with Adirondack peaks forming a scenic backdrop. Mature yellow and paper birches, sugar and red maples,

Sea kayaks offer a great way to explore New York's larger lakes, as John demonstrates on a cool October morning in the Adirondacks.

beech, and aspen, along with hemlock, balsam fir (particularly in wetter areas), spruce, and white and red pines cover the shoreline. Look for tall, conical balsam firs and hefty hemlocks lining the narrow channel at the entrance to the long southern arm. The usually quite clear water in this 85-foot-maximum-depth lake indicates low biological productivity.

In selecting a campsite, particularly in the early season, we would choose an exposed one, trading off some tent flapping at night with the need for an insect-reducing breeze during the day. The following campsites fill this need: 39 at the point separating the western and southwestern arms; 32 on the northern point of the small island on the east side of Long Island (lots of nice, large boulders gently sloping down to the water for lounging around; nice view up the lake, as well); 34 on the northern tip of Long Island; 28 on an island in John Mack Bay; 45 on a peninsula jutting out from the eastern shore about one-third of the way down the long southern arm.

Two nice picnic areas occur on the southern arm. The smaller one perches on an island along the right-hand shore, about two-fifths (two miles) of the way down. The second, larger one at the very end of the arm has three picnic tables, a grate, an outhouse, and a wide boat-landing area. Although it nestles back into a protected area that can suffer from mosquitoes, it boasts a beautiful series of cascading waterfalls flowing down a brook right in front of the picnic area and into a nice swimming area. This picturesque spot makes traveling all the way down the arm well worthwhile.

Continuing down the southern arm to its end, you encounter the meandering Jessup River flowing into the lake. In the spring, if you are willing to get out of your boat occasionally in shallow riffles and at beaver dams, you can paddle upstream all the way to the Route 30 bridge. This great wildlife-viewing area remains totally free of motorboat traffic.

Getting There

Take I-87 to the Routes 9 and 28 exit (Exit 23, Warrensburg); follow Route 28 to Route 30 south at the village of Indian Lake. Route 30 hugs the western shore of Indian Lake, and the boat access is at the south end of the lake at the Indian Lake Islands State Campground area. Alternatively, one can take Route 30 up from Amsterdam or Route 29 west out of Saratoga Springs—in which case you turn north onto Route 30 at Vail Mills. There is a small day-access fee that entitles you to launch your boat, in addition to camping fees.

The Lewey Lake State Campground is right across Route 30 from the boat access and campground entrance on Indian Lake.

Cedar River Flow

Lake Pleasant

MAPS
New York Atlas: Map 87
USGS Quadrangle: Indian Lake

INFORMATION
Area: 710 acres
Prominent fish species: Stocked brook trout

Cedar River Flow, too shallow and too remote to attract serious motor-boaters, remains one of the south-central Adirondacks' little-known treasures. Fed by cool, clear, mountain water flowing out of Cedar Lakes in the West Canada Lake Wilderness Area, the flow provides wilderness camping, paddling, and hiking opportunities, all of it above 2,100 feet elevation.

Accessible by a long drive down a gravel road, either from Inlet (23 miles) or from Indian Lake (14 miles), the flow will impress you with its wild, spectacular character. Although the flow extends only 3 miles south-southwest from Wakely Dam, many more miles of meandering streams and beaver meadows offer hours, or even days, of paddling pleasure.

A grove of aspens guards the entrance to the first cove on the right; farther back, spirelike balsam firs ring the shore. The shallow waters harbor, in addition to submerged rocks, tons of water shield, water celery, and a beaver lodge with a large stash of cuttings stored for the coming winter.

Returning to the main lake, we encountered piles of mussel shells, lots of paper birch, balsam fir, sugar maple, and masses of water shield, pondweed, bulrushes, and submerged rocks. Difficult to see in the dark water, rocks made frequent contact with our boat hull—a small price to pay for the privilege of paddling such pristine waters.

Buell Brook enters from the opposite (eastern) shore, about two-thirds of the way up the flow. The creek's mouth hides from view amid a sea of bulrushes. We paddled back up the shallow, sinewy, sandy-bottomed brook for about a mile, its depth varying from more than eight feet to just a few inches where sand and gravel deposits collect. Initially, the creek passes through a grassy marsh with Christmas-tree-perfect balsam fir spires scattered here and there. We expected instead to see tamaracks and black spruce, given the marshy conditions. Fallen red maple leaves swirled in the undulating, crystal-clear current during our

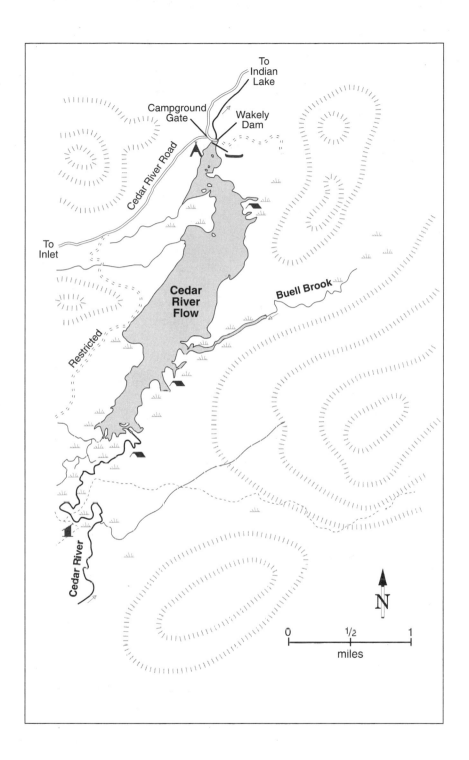

To
Indian
Lake

Campground
Gate

Wakely
Dam

Cedar River Road

To
Inlet

**Cedar
River
Flow**

Buell Brook

Restricted

Cedar River

N

0   1/2   1
miles

early October visit. Huge mats collected in the stream's eddies, reminding us, sadly, that we neared the end of the paddling season.

Reaching the south tip of the lake, we paddled up over several beaver dams to explore the marshes. Alders abound, along with typical marsh shrubbery, including sweet gale, leatherleaf, bur reed, and much more. Occasional stands of tamarack foreshadow the filling in of the marsh. We found that this area does not connect with Cedar River, which enters the flow on the southeast corner. Shortcuts will not get you to the river, as we found out after several attempts. Look for a thick line of alders and some trees, and head for where they end out in the lake. Follow the deep, broad channel, guarded by bulrushes, with downward-pointing underwater vegetation indicating the current's direction.

The meandering Cedar River flows clearly, the sun illuminating its sandy bottom. We paddled back up to the lean-to on the right shore; as we paddled a few hundred yards past the lean-to, the formerly barely noticeable current started to pick up, and we turned around reluctantly. As we paddled back under darkening skies, a beaver swam before us. After several meanders, it finally realized that we had paddled mere feet from its broad tail. It got even for the intrusion by splashing us with its flat, broad tail as it dove for cover.

We recommend early spring or late summer or fall paddling because of mosquito hatches from the swamps and blackflies from the river.

Getting There

From Indian Lake, take Routes 28 and 30 north. After about 2.0 miles, turn left onto Cedar River Road, across from the Cedar River Golf Course. Look for signs for the Moose River Recreation Area. Note your mileage here. In 2.1 miles, the Wakely Lodge Public Golf Course appears. At 9.1 miles, as White Plains Road turns off to the left, the pavement turns to dirt. The Cedar River gate at the campground and boat access are at 14.1 miles.

From the village of Inlet on Fourth Lake, travel east a few miles on Route 28 to Limekiln Road. Turn right onto Limekiln Road. After 2.0 miles, turn left onto a gravel road and register at the International Paper access control booth. Note your mileage here. In 4.6 miles, Moose River Recreation Area campsite #1 appears on the right; take the left fork. Campsite #2 is on the left; both are on the Red River. At 8.3 miles, turn left. The Cedar River gate at the campground and boat launch are at 21.4 miles.

Limekiln Lake
Inlet and Ohio

MAPS
   New York Atlas: Map 86
   USGS Quadrangle: Old Forge

INFORMATION
   Area: 446 acres; maximum depth: 72 feet
   Prominent fish species: Stocked brown trout and splake
   Camping: Limekiln Lake Campground; 315-357-4401

Our first exploration of Limekiln Lake began more than 30 years ago, when one of us paddled here as a boy. The lakeshore has changed some, but we were happy to see upon our return that state-owned lands surround most of the shore of Limekiln Lake, a rare jewel in the western Adirondacks high country. Limited private lands on the northeast corner suffer from a fair amount of development, so you will see a number of motorboats during the summer—far more than we recall from the 1960s. Even so, Limekiln Lake sees much less traffic than

A marshy stream flows through beaver meadows into the southeast corner of Limekiln Lake.

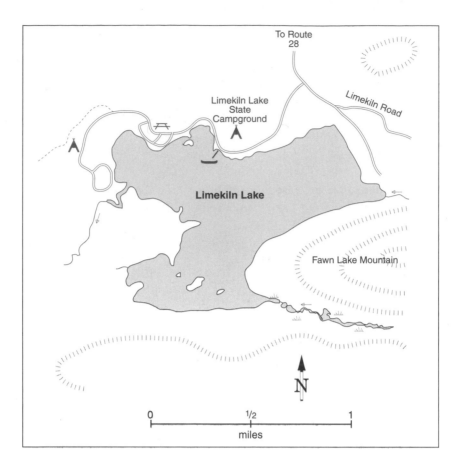

most of the rest of this very popular Fulton Chain vacation region. Closer to Old Forge, in the heart of the region, boat traffic increases dramatically, so that only Eighth Lake remains relatively undisturbed. Nick's Lake Campground just outside of Old Forge fills up each night of the summer, whereas Limekiln Lake Campground often does not.

In spite of the motorboat traffic, we feel that Limekiln Lake provides a quality quiet-water experience. Its high elevation (1,885 feet) and considerable depth make the waters oligotrophic, meaning very low biological productivity. The crystal-clear water allows you to peer into its depths and shows almost no evidence of tannic acid, which results from plant decay and turns the water yellowish brown.

Several other paddlers joined us out on the water; if you find yourself in this area without a boat, you can rent canoes from Payne's at the boat launch in the campground.

Coves, inlets, islands, and bays characterize this small lake, and we enjoyed exploring each of them, studying the fauna and flora. Forested hillsides surround Limekiln Lake, with some modest vertical relief. Studying the high tree-species diversity around the shore provides a diversion from wildlife watching; we found red and sugar maples, tamarack, balsam fir, black and red spruce, eastern hemlock, and white pine growing in profusion. Thick shrubbery dominates the understory.

In shallower waters, we found water shield, yellow pond lily, and other aquatic vegetation, but the dwarf fragrant water lilies provided a real surprise. Distinguishing characteristics of the two dominant species of white water lily include the following: fragrant water lily generally has purple undersides of leaves and purple sepals covering the upright closed flowers, while tuberous water lily has green undersides of leaves and green sepals covering the flowers. The diminutive deep purple leaves— measuring no more than two or so inches—of the water lilies in Limekiln Lake matched the minuscule flowers. We wondered whether the cold water of this high-altitude lake kept them from growing larger or whether this population has a genetic disposition to dwarfism.

Out on the main lake, loons dove for fish, and a family of common mergansers rested on a log, casting one wary eye at us as we paddled by. We suspect that the numerous black ducks hanging around the campground were looking for illegal handouts.

The small creek that flows into the southeast corner remains our favorite spot on the lake. As you paddle through the sinuous channel, note the large tamaracks starting to fill in the marsh. We paddled by sphagnum islands loaded with carnivorous pitcher plants and sundews, trying to cke out a little extra nitrogen from passing insects. You would have to travel widely to find a higher density of pitcher plants.

Balsam fir, black spruce, and yellow birch grow here, along with sheep laurel. Crush a leaf of one of the sweet gale plants that grow here in profusion, and note its aromatic odor. We lingered here for a long while, watching the bright colors of a male yellow warbler with its red streaking on the breast. We listened to hoarse "chick-a-dee-dee" calls of foraging boreal chickadees. We studied bankside flowers and watched the sun dip behind the western hills. Mesmerized by the reflected glow from still waters, we hated to leave this tranquil spot.

Getting There

From the village of Inlet at the head of Fourth Lake, travel east on Route 28 for about 0.8 mile to Limekiln Road on the right. Turn onto Limekiln Road, and go 1.7 miles to the turnoff to Limekiln Lake State Campground on the right. Launching a boat is free.

Eighth Lake (Fulton Chain)
Inlet

MAPS
New York Atlas: Map 86
USGS Quadrangle: Raquette Lake

INFORMATION
Area: 320 acres
Prominent fish species: Smallmouth bass
Camping: Eighth Lake State Campground; 315-354-4120

The Fulton Chain of eight lakes figures prominently in the early guide lore of the Adirondacks. While intrepid mid-nineteenth-century explorers plied these waters in elegant wooden guide boats, taking downstaters out into the wilds to fish and hunt, some modern explorers prefer floatplanes, high-speed boats, and Jet-skis, all of which dominate the first seven lakes of the chain.

The 90-mile guide-boat race from Old Forge to Saranac Lake draws overflow crowds as paddlers and rowers work their way up through the chain and over into Brown's Tract Inlet, which joins the Raquette River drainage. Among the Fulton Chain, only on Eighth Lake—whose shoreline is owned by the state—can paddlers escape the development and powerboating that characterize the rest of the chain.

The invasion of Jet-skis is more insidious than the invasion of Eurasian milfoil. These machines exist for one purpose: thrill seeking, as the operators jump wakes, drive 45 mph or faster, tow children on tubes at high speed, run over swimmers, crash into each other and into boats, intrude on the peace and calm, and inject oil into the gas, polluting the atmosphere. In proportion to their numbers, Jet-skis cause accidents and complaints about their behavior far more than other watercraft. In fact, recent Coast Guard boating accident statistics reveal that even though personal watercraft accounted for only 2 percent of all boats on the water in 1991, they accounted for 17 percent of boating accidents, including 26 fatalities. When will we wake up and ban these cursed machines, at least from small lakes, ponds, and rivers?

In comparison with the rest of the Fulton Chain, Eighth Lake is a pleasure to paddle. Nestled in a valley with hills all around, and lying in a north-south orientation, the lake suffers less from prevailing westerly winds. The relative calm of Eighth Lake stood in sharp contrast to

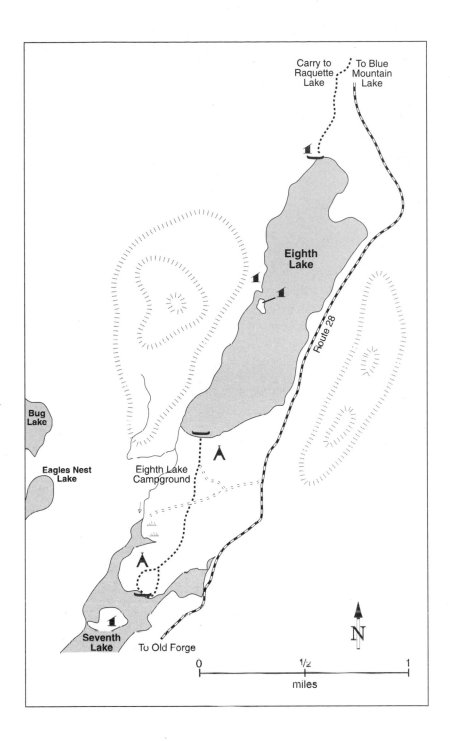

Carry to
Raquette
Lake

To Blue
Mountain
Lake

Eighth
Lake

Route 28

Bug
Lake

Eagles Nest
Lake

Eighth Lake
Campground

Seventh
Lake

To Old Forge

0   1/2   1
miles

N

A black bear peers at us from its resting place in the woods near Eighth Lake.

the wind-driven swells and whitecaps that dominated the surface of Seventh Lake when we paddled here in late August. We launched from the Eighth Lake State Campground, which also provides access into the north end of Seventh Lake.

Tame black ducks populate Eighth Lake, along with belted king-fishers, common mergansers, and common loons. The forested shores include northern white cedar, eastern hemlock, red maple, beech, yellow birch, striped maple, and tall white pines that tower over everything else. The sole island has white pine, paper birch, northern white cedar, and nice rock outcroppings for swimming and sunning. Three shelters, independent of the campground and available on a first-come basis, occur on the island, on the nearby shore, and on the northwest corner next to the canoe carry.

The clear water means low biological productivity, and without marshy areas, you may run out of areas to explore and vistas to enjoy. Because you cannot paddle the outlet of Eighth Lake, you have to carry about 0.8 mile through the campground to Seventh Lake if you are on a long-distance paddle or wish to observe Jet-ski frolics and seaplane takeoffs.

But if you wish for wilderness adventure, we would suggest instead that you paddle up Eighth Lake to the northwest corner and carry from there the mile and a quarter into Brown's Tract Inlet. This beautiful marshy stream meanders east just over two miles on its way to South Bay on Raquette Lake. From there we would paddle northeast, skirting the left side of Big Island, and up the Marion River toward Utowana, Eagle, and Blue Mountain Lakes (see Blue Mountain Lake section). Alternatively, you could paddle around to the right upon entering South Bay and on the east end paddle under Route 28 into the two-mile-long South Inlet, another marshy stream, reputedly one of the most gorgeous in the Adirondacks. You would see a lot more than tame black ducks while paddling through these marshlands, we assure you.

During the drought summer of 1995, when we paddled this area, the low-water conditions and lack of rain reduced food availability somewhat, causing wildlife to move about more than usual. While here, we saw a fairly large black bear whiling away the afternoon, back to a large tree, pretty much unconcerned by the presence of our cameras about 50 feet away.

While we did not see the abundant wildlife that you would likely see, for example, on the Marion River or North Branch of the Moose River, we did enjoy our only paddle on the Fulton Chain in the Eighth Lake valley along the historic Old Forge to Saranac Lake guide route. We felt part of history as we hiked the extremely well worn path to Brown's Tract Inlet. If you have time, we urge you to sample this history as well.

Getting There

Coming from the village of Blue Mountain Lake on Route 28, watch for the Eighth Lake sign; you can launch your boat from the pullout by this sign or drive into the campground 1.3 miles farther on the right on Route 28.

Coming from Eagle Bay, watch for the Seventh Lake fishing access. The Eighth Lake Campground turnoff is 1.9 miles farther up on the left.

Moss Lake
Webb

MAPS
   New York Atlas: Map 86
   USGS Quadrangle: Eagle Bay

INFORMATION
   Area: 130 acres
   Prominent fish species: No information available
   Camping permits: 518-369-3463

Moss Lake is simply gorgeous, nestled beneath the rolling, forested peaks that typify this part of the Adirondacks. With no development in sight, this is a far cry from the heavily developed and overused Fulton Chain lakes just to the south. Though very small, Moss Lake can provide a very pleasant few hours of paddling, hiking, and enjoying the fauna and flora.

We were surprised to see a pair of loons with chick during our visit, as it was late in the season—early October. Though nearly grown, we suspect the chick hatched from a second nesting, after the first

Alex paddles back up the brushy outlet of Moss Lake.

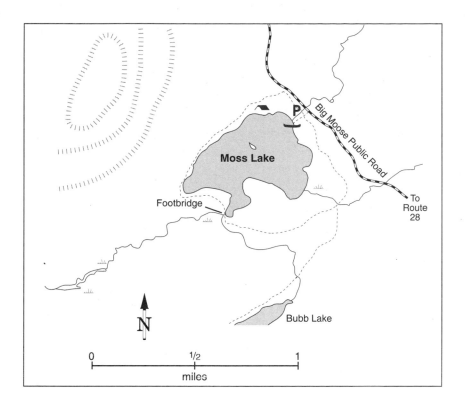

failed. Otherwise the adults would have migrated to the coast by this time. Loons nest very early, giving them an opportunity to lay a second pair of eggs if the first nesting fails. We suspect that they nest on the lake's sole island, where ospreys have also nested in recent years on a tall dead pine tree.

Moss Lake and some 600 acres of surrounding land were part of a large girls' camp from 1923 until 1972. The Moss Lake Camp for Girls spread along the lake's northern and eastern shores and provided a wide range of activities, including horseback riding, hiking, and canoeing. In 1973, Dr. George Longstaff, who developed and operated the camp, sold the property to The Nature Conservancy, which subsequently deeded the land to New York State to become part of the Adirondack Forest Preserve. During the period of 1974 to 1978, a group of Ganienkeh Mohawk Indians, who claimed title to the land, occupied the site, but this group eventually moved their settlement north to the Canadian border. In 1979, the Department of Environmental Conservation razed the remaining buildings to return the lake to its primeval condition.

A three-mile path extends all the way around the lake. This is the former camp's bridle path, built in 1924. Visitors use the trail during the winter months as a cross-country ski trail and in the summer for hiking. The trail meanders through mostly deciduous forest, dominated by sugar maple. We saw some massive yellow birch trees and one enormous cherry tree with its roots folding out over a large rock. A few large hemlock, spruce, and white pine added variety to the tree canopy. The understory was thick with hobblebush viburnum (*Viburnum alnifolium*), ferns, and clubmosses.

These trees form a backdrop to the water-loving shrubs right at the water's edge: leatherleaf, sweet gale, alder, and winterberry (a member of the holly family with bright red orange fall-ripening berries that are attached directly to the branches without stalks). During our fall visit, a few scattered mountain ash added an extra spot of brilliance to the autumn foliage.

At the south end of the lake, a footbridge crosses over the outlet stream. To explore below the bridge, you have to lift your canoe over. The sandy-bottomed channel meanders gently to the southwest through marshy vegetation. Fairly quickly beaver dams block your progress. We carried across a couple small dams but did not explore far. With a little effort, one might be able to go as much as a mile down this creek before running into quickwater—then again, around that next bend might be a stretch of rapids. . . .

There is a nice campsite on the north end of the lake, accessible by canoe or by trail. Camping is available by permit only (see above).

Getting There

In Eagle Bay, by Fourth Lake, turn north off Route 28 onto Big Moose Public Road. The Moss Lake trailhead and parking area are on the left 2.1 miles from Route 28. There is a short carry down to the water to launch a boat.

Stillwater Reservoir
Webb

MAPS
   New York Atlas: Maps 85 and 86
   USGS Quadrangles: Beaver River, Eagle Bay, Number Four, and
   Stillwater

INFORMATION
   Area: 6,230 acres; maximum depth: 32 feet; average depth: 6 feet
   Prominent fish species: Smallmouth bass and splake
   Camping: Campsite selection is by self-registry at the reservoir; it
   often fills by early afternoon.

The Beaver River flows west out of Lake Lila—a wonderful canoeing
spot—into Nehasane Lake, which is privately owned. From there it
flows down to Stillwater Reservoir, out into Moshier Lake, and then
into the series of lakes that comprise the Beaver River Canoe Route—
Beaver Lake, Soft Maple Reservoir, Effley Falls Pond, Elmer Falls
Pond, and Taylorville Pond. From there, it meanders another dozen
miles to its confluence with the Black River, which eventually flows
into Lake Ontario at Black River Bay.

   Along the river's heavily impounded route, many opportunities for
paddling appear, including at Stillwater Reservoir, by far the largest
body of water on the Beaver River. The reservoir's 117 miles of shoreline and 45 islands beckon boaters in large numbers. We observed in
our two trips to Stillwater that about equal numbers of paddlers and
motorboaters use the lake. In our rough survey, paddlers occupied more
than half of the 46 campsites sprinkled around the reservoir. Many
motorboaters visit this body of water just during the day to take advantage of the smallmouth bass fishing. Fortunately, the Jet-ski crowd has
not appeared in great numbers . . . yet.

   This long lake, with its east-west orientation, suffers greatly from
high winds blowing east off Lake Ontario. Even with 45 islands providing some shelter from the wind, Stillwater Reservoir can roll along
with huge waves and whitecaps. We strongly suggest that you paddle
here only when the weather forecast includes a stagnant high-pressure
cell. When the winds blow, paddle the nearby Beaver River Canoe
Route; when they blow strongly, paddle the more protected North
Branch of the Moose River at Old Forge.

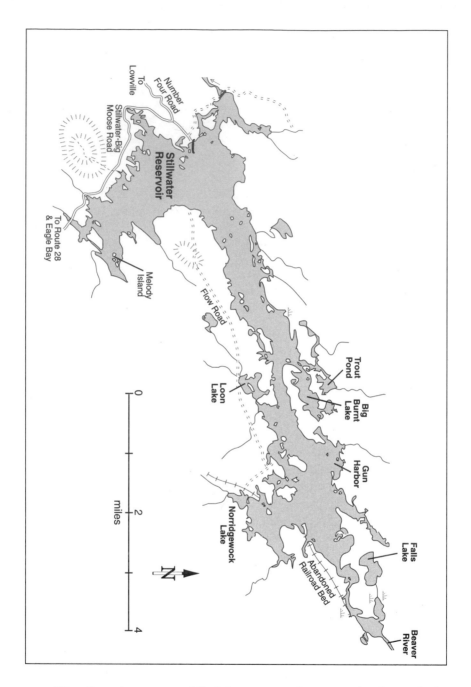

The first time we paddled here, a modest easterly flow of air kicked up two-foot swells, while the second time the lake lived up to its name with the surface barely rippling as arctic high pressure kept the winds at bay. The winds off Lake Ontario also carry a lot of moisture, and as the air cools in its ascent of the Adirondack Plateau, that air cannot hold as much moisture. Consequently, a lot of water gets wrung out along the western slopes, including at Stillwater Reservoir. Indeed, Stillwater also receives a huge amount of snow carried aloft by the winds over Lake Ontario; the record from the winter of 1971-1972 is 375 inches—more than 31 feet!

You can get away from most other boaters on Stillwater by paddling its connected lakes and bays. We paddled most of the shoreline, including a stretch of the Beaver River leading to Nehasane Lake. While paddling the east end of the lake, we met a solo paddler who had paddled from Stillwater to Lake Lila and back. He spent four hours of this trek walking his boat through shallows during the low-water year of 1995. We recommend that the adventuresome paddle this in one direction, from Lake Lila down to Stillwater. You cannot camp along the way at Nehasane Lake, as it is privately owned.

Our favorite locations on Stillwater include the Melody Island area in the southwest cove; Trout Pond along the north shore, with its sheltered coves; the deep, narrow, unnamed cove on the northeast; and Loon Lake along the southern shore, with its beautiful island for camping. We had to carry into Loon Lake, which you reach via a short, rocky stream that keeps out the motorized crowd.

A lesser yellowlegs runs along the shore. This large sandpiper is often seen in migration.

The fishing must be good on Stillwater, as evidenced by the huge number of loons. We counted them as we paddled the southern shore from the boat launch all the way to the mouth of the Beaver River: 34, including 4 young; we're sure we missed some along the north shore. The small number of young did not surprise us because, even with 117 miles of shoreline, the lake does not provide a lot of good nesting sites. First, nest sites must be free from human disturbance; second, fluctuating water levels drown nests or, more often, leave them stranded; third, they nest on mounds of grass or other vegetation. As the summer of 1995 proceeded, exposed rocky shorelines appeared, providing anything but ideal loon nesting habitat. Growing evidence also suggests that competition from unmated loons causes high infant mortality.

In our time here, we observed a lot of wildlife, including black duck, herring gull, raven, crow, great blue heron, lesser yellowlegs, spotted sandpiper, and dozens more bird species. We watched deer wander along the shore in many spots, but the biggest treat was to watch a flock of wild turkeys approach the shore either to get a drink or to pick up gravel to help grind their food—you might need gravel too if you ate a lot of whole acorns.

Back in the protected coves we studied yellow-flowered bladderwort—an aquatic carnivorous plant—and several species of water lily. Because most of the lakeshore does not include marshes, the swamp specialists do not appear in high numbers. Stillwater stands in marked contrast to our usual choice for paddling: swamps, marshes, bogs, and meandering, slow-flowing streams. The higher productivity of these latter types of habitat means more wildlife to view and plants to study. But we enjoyed paddling here where you can stretch your paddling muscles in a multiday trip. Stillwater provides many nooks and crannies to explore and is well worth the paddling effort—but keep your eye on that weather!

Getting There

From Lowville, take Number Four Road east for about 17 miles to Stillwater Road. Turn right onto Stillwater Road, and follow it all the way to the boat access (about 9 miles).

From Eagle Bay on Fourth Lake, take Route 1 (Big Moose Road) northwest for about 17 miles until it ends at Stillwater Road. Turn right onto Stillwater Road, and follow it for 0.5 mile to the boat access.

Beaver River Canoe Route
Croghan, Watson, and Webb

MAPS
  New York Atlas: Map 85
  USGS Quadrangles: Belfort, Number Four, and Stillwater

INFORMATION
  Area: N/A
  Prominent fish species: Smallmouth bass, northern pike, walleye, and stocked tiger muskellunge (Soft Maple Reservoir)
  Camping: Niagara-Mohawk provides a water-accessible campsite on the west end of Soft Maple Reservoir; prominent signs out on the water direct you to it. Information on Beaver River Canoe Route or camping; 800-NIAGARA (800-642-4272).

A series of connected reservoirs form the popular Beaver River Canoe Route, maintained by Niagara-Mohawk Power. You can travel this route, starting at Moshier Falls, paddling in succession east to west downstream through Beaver Lake, Soft Maple Reservoir, an unnamed reservoir, Effley Falls Pond, Elmer Falls Pond, and Taylorville Pond. Because of the dams, only in a few spots does current impede upstream progress, should you decide to paddle the route in both directions. During high-water conditions, fighting against the current in the Beaver River between Beaver Lake and Soft Maple Reservoir may prove difficult. Also, near the access point at the beginning of every reservoir, water rushes out of turbines in proportion to the power generated. At peak generation times, paddling against the current back up to the put-in spot may even be dangerous. Another consideration: on your return, all of the carries go straight uphill. We paddled this route in both directions and heartily recommend it as a one-way trip...downstream.

Beaver Lake

Beaver Lake is a study in contrasts. It starts at the power plant at Moshier Falls, travels through an ever-widening marsh, necks down as it enters the main lake—which has a fair amount of development—and then enters a long, beautiful stretch of the Beaver River, which in places has significant flow.

Just past the boat access at Moshier Falls we saw two adult loons, along with their nearly grown single offspring, in the pickerelweed and cattail-ringed marsh. If you have time, linger among the yellow pond lily, tuberous and fragrant water lily, and other aquatic plants that dot the huge swamp on the unpopulated southeast end. The extensive marshy areas that head off in all directions not only harbor a great deal of wildlife but they also represent the only examples of this habitat on the canoe route.

As you approach the main lake, stay to the right to avoid the houses and to enter the Beaver River as it flows north out of the lake. Paddling around the lake represents profitless enterprise; that is, unless you like to play the game of seeing who can spot the most different kinds of boats. We saw every watercraft imaginable, including canoe, kayak, pontoon boat, sailboat, outboard, inboard, stern drive, Jet-ski, bass boat, water-skier, floatplane, rowboat, paddleboat, and inner tube.

Fortunately, the next three and a half miles take you down a relatively unpopulated broad channel, past occasional islands, with scenic wooded hillsides all around. Watch for the eastern kingbird—a black-and-white flycatcher with terminal white tail-band—perched on streamside branches, waiting to pounce on passing insects. The narrow leaves of water celery point the way downstream as a belted kingfisher flies before you. Flocks of cedar waxwings, with their conspicuous crests, alternately catch flies and search for ripened berries.

Of the entire canoe route, this passage remains our favorite. For those with limited time, we recommend that you stick to Beaver Lake and the Beaver River.

Soft Maple Reservoir

After having paddled alone for the last hour, then completing the long, 0.8-mile carry into Soft Maple Reservoir, a pack of five Jet-skis greeted us within minutes of dipping our paddles in the reservoir. These two-strokers burn gas along with oil injected from a separate reservoir into the combustion chamber, producing not only a lot of noise but also a lot of smell. Operating a two-cycle engine for an hour can generate as much air pollution as driving a car halfway across the country!

Soft Maple Reservoir, arguably once the most scenic lake on this route, suffers greatly from summer home development and has become overrun with powerboats and Jet-skis. We paddled across it quickly. Unfortunately, Soft Maple has the only legal campsite on the route— on the western shore just to the left of the peninsula that defines the

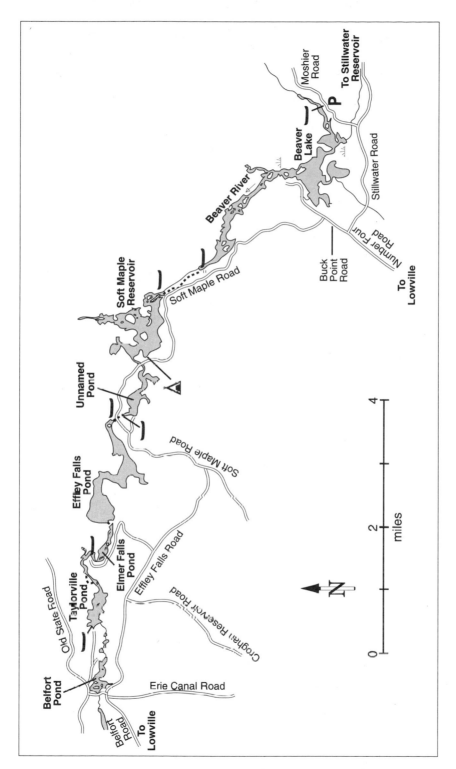

lake's outlet. Niagara-Mohawk signs on the peninsula point the way to the campsite and to the lake's outlet.

We slowed down after clearing the end of the peninsula to enjoy the yellow birches lining the shore at the outlet, which passes under a green iron bridge into an unnamed reservoir. On our return trip, as we paddled back through in the late afternoon, of all places we saw here our only beaver on the Beaver River. This lonely fellow stayed close to the power-plant at the lake's inlet, undoubtedly the area with the least human activity. It probably wandered here in the spring when parents drove away last year's brood to make way for the new kits. It probably recognized its poor choice 'long about Memorial Day.

Unnamed Reservoir

A very few well-kept, year-round houses greeted us as we paddled out onto this unnamed reservoir, peaceful and calm in comparison with our recent experience. Because no dam separates this body of water from Soft Maple, most people might count this as a continuation of the previous reservoir. We hope this book starts a movement to secede. The two bodies of water bear no resemblance.

The generally wooded shore, with branches hanging out over the water, reminded us to slow down, that we intended to study plants and wildlife rather than boat wakes and paddle whirlpools, that, as Gandhi said, "There is more to life than simply increasing its pace." Although no marsh existed to draw in wildlife, we lingered here, enjoying the peaceful surroundings, as two people on a Sunfish searched in vain for a breeze. On our return trip in the late afternoon, the glasslike water's surface reflected the sun's inexorable march down through the trees to the horizon.

At the western end of the lake on the left side of a narrow channel, the carry heads off briefly but steeply uphill, followed by a half-mile downhill to Effley Falls Pond.

Effley Falls Pond

Effley Falls Pond has some development but not nearly the traffic of Soft Maple Reservoir. We stopped to talk to other paddlers and to some swimmers. And we saw nary a motorboat, which was much to the liking of the four loons swimming about.

We observed late summer monarch butterflies sucking nectar from clumps of purple aster to provide fuel for flight. The monarch, *Danaus plexippus*—one of a very few long-distance migratory insects—summers from southeast Alaska to Newfoundland and south throughout the U.S. and Canada. It also ranges to Argentina, Hawaii, and many other locations throughout the world. Remarkably, each fall monarchs migrate by the millions to Michoacán in central Mexico, southern California, and south Florida. They overwinter as adults, mate in the late winter, and immediately begin their sometimes many-thousand-mile northward migration. What makes this mass migration so extraordinary is that most butterfly adults have life spans of only a few weeks. The heroic monarch hatches during the summer, grows through several caterpillar stages, pupates into an adult, flies from New York to central Mexico, hibernates among millions of other monarchs, mates, flies north to New York, lays its eggs, and dies!

Because all of the many millions of monarchs migrate, tracing their individual flight paths has not proved easy. By marking thousands of individuals in the Mexico highlands with wing tags, researchers then searched throughout the summer in the northern U.S. and Canada, hoping to recapture a few marked individuals. They found one in New York, and one that they marked in Toronto they later found in Mexico. Those overwintering in southern California migrate to the Great Basin and the Pacific Northwest.

What allows such a seemingly fragile species as the monarch to survive the rigors of two such journeys? Part of the answer lies in its larval diet of milkweed leaves. Plants with milky sap often indicate the presence of poison. Milkweed sap, the preferred food of monarch larvae, contains chemical compounds called cardiac glycosides—heart poisons such as calactin, calotropin, and calotoxin. Not all monarch larvae eat milkweed leaves, and not all milkweeds have cardiac glycosides, but of the monarchs examined in the Northeast, 90 percent had sequestered cardiac glycosides. Birds who try to eat the larvae or adults generally vomit and then refuse to eat any more of them. Monarchs rely on this food aversion to avoid predation on their long, slow flights. Flying at 12 mph, monarchs would be easy prey during the 250- to 300-hour flight from New York to Mexico. When we see late-season monarchs fueling up on flower nectar, we look at them in awe, knowing the long perilous journey that awaits them.

Elmer Falls Pond

We regret that Elmer Falls Pond, with no development whatsoever, is so small, just less than a mile in length. A slow early morning or late afternoon paddle should reward you with glimpses of wildlife. We paddled quietly up to a doe with two spotted fawns who had come down for a late-afternoon drink under the spreading boughs of an eastern hemlock. A female common merganser herded her flock of nine nearly mature young before us. The carry at the end goes over the right bank, steeply downhill into Taylorville Pond.

Taylorville Pond

Taylorville Pond, perhaps the nicest of the reservoirs, with its tree-lined grassy banks, fields of ferns under large, lacy green hemlocks, red maples hanging out over water, and majestic white pines, marks the end of the canoe route. The relatively narrow upper channel necks down as it spills out onto the main lake, followed by a gorgeous forested island. Past the island, a power line looms off in the distance, reminding paddlers not only of the impending end to the journey but also that this series of reservoirs exists to satisfy our insatiable urge for power. Paddling the final lake in our hand-powered craft, listening to the haunting calls of loons, the epitome of northern wilderness, we should all reflect on power usage in other areas of our lives. Do we drive fuel-efficient cars? Do we carpool? Do we take mass transit? What can we do to reduce our consumption of natural resources?

Although the character of the short drop into the main lake changes with water level, when we paddled here the drop was not more than a foot or so. But, coupled with the narrow banks, the water moved swiftly over the drop, forming whirlpools in the churning water below. Because we intended to turn around and paddle back to Beaver Lake, we had to negotiate this drop on our return. After a very futile effort at paddling back, we used discretion and carried to the left (north), hopping out onto a gigantic pink granite boulder, hiking back for a few hundred feet through a grove of hemlock, and relaunching in the slackened current of the widened channel.

We hated to leave this scenic spot with loon echoes bouncing off forested hillsides, nuthatches chattering softly from streamside, brilliant red cardinal flowers beckoning from the bank, and the sweet smell of balsam fir wafting in from the woods.

Getting There

To get to the Beaver River Canoe Route access on Beaver Lake from Lowville, take Number Four Road east for about 17.0 miles to Stillwater Road; turn right onto Stillwater Road, and follow it for 2.0 miles to Moshier Road. Turn left onto Moshier Road; the boat access is 0.6 mile down this road—parking lot on the right.

To drive here from Eagle Bay on Fourth Lake, take Route 1 (Big Moose Road) northwest for about 17.0 miles until it ends at Stillwater Road. Turn left onto Stillwater Road, and follow it for 5.8 miles to Moshier Road. Turn right onto Moshier Road, as above.

To get to the end of the canoe route at Taylorville Pond from Moshier Road, turn right onto Stillwater Road, and go 2.0 miles to a T. At this junction, Number Four Road goes left to Lowville; turn right at the T onto Buck Point Road, following signs for Beaver River Canoe Route. At the bottom of a hill in 0.5 mile, turn left onto a gravel road (Soft Maple Road) and start marking mileage. Drive by the eastern end of the carry from Beaver Lake to Soft Maple Reservoir at 2.5 miles (access road goes steeply downhill to right); western end of carry is at 3.3 miles (on right). Continue on, crossing the bridge separating Soft Maple and the unnamed reservoir at 5.0 miles. Pass the parking area on the eastern end of Effley Falls Pond at 6.1 miles. Turn right onto Effley Falls Road at 8.0 miles, just as Soft Maple Road turns to pavement. Effley Falls Road turns to pavement at 11.5 miles. A stop sign appears at the junction with Erie Canal Road at 12.3 miles. Turn right onto Erie Canal Road, cross two bridges over the outflow of Belfort Pond, and proceed to the stop sign at the junction with Old State Road at 12.6 miles. Turn right onto Old State Road, and turn diagonally right at 12.7 miles onto Taylorville Road. Stay left at the fork, and the launch parking area is at 13.7 miles.

To get to the end of the canoe route at Taylorville Pond from Lowville, take Route 812 to Croghan; when Route 812 goes left to cross the Raquette River, go straight onto Belfort Road. At the junction with Erie Canal Road, turn left, cross the bridge over the Beaver River, and turn right at the stop sign onto Old State Road, and follow the directions in the previous paragraph.

The Beaver
Resident Wetlands Engineer

The beaver, *Castor canadensis*, is one of the most fascinating and remarkable animals found in New York's lakes, ponds, and streams. Unlike almost any other animal except humans, beaver actively modify their environment. The sole representative of the family Castoridae, this 30- to 60-pound rodent—the largest rodent in North America—descends directly from a bear-sized ancestor that lived a million years ago.

Quiet-water paddlers frequently see beaver dams and lodges, especially when canoeing New York's more out-of-the-way lakes and ponds. This industrious mammal, a tireless worker, uses branches pruned from streamside alders or downed timber to construct dams and lodges. Beaver now work mostly under the cover of darkness, especially in areas suffering from large amounts of human traffic. In the wilds, where few humans tread, many beaver work away in broad daylight. We mention in our lake, pond, and stream descriptions where we have seen beaver abroad during the day.

Beaver build dams to raise the level of water in a stream or pond, providing the resident colony with access to trees growing farther away. The deeper water of their ponds also allows beaver to cache branches underwater for winter retrieval, even when a thick layer of ice covers their winter stores. They also dig small canals through marsh and meadow to transport branches from distant trees. Just as we find paddling a canoe easier than carrying it, beaver prefer swimming with a branch—taking advantage of water's buoyancy—than carrying it overland.

Studies show that the sound of flowing water guides beaver in their dam building—they jam sticks in the dam where they hear the gurgle of water. In one rather rude experiment, researchers played a tape of gurgling water; beaver responded by jamming sticks into locations that emanated sound, even though no water actually flowed there. Beaver dams can be very large, over 10 feet high and hundreds of feet long. The largest dam ever recorded, near the present town of Berlin, New Hampshire, spanned 4,000 feet and created a lake with 40 lodges!

Beaver dams benefit many other species. Their ponds provide important habitat for waterfowl, fish, moose, muskrat, and other animals. Plus, the dams provide flood control, minimize erosion along stream banks, increase aquifer recharge, and improve water quality, both by allowing silt to settle out and by providing biological filtration through aquatic plants. We credit beaver with creating much of America's best farmland by damming watercourses, thus allowing nutrient-rich silt to accumulate over many years. As the ponds fill in, meadows arise.

The beaver lodge includes an underwater entrance and usually two different platform levels: a main floor about four inches above the water level and a sleeping shelf another two inches higher. The beaver may construct the lodge in the center of a pond, totally surrounded by water, but more commonly the beaver sites it on the edge. Before the onset of winter, beaver cover much of the lodge with mud—which they carry on their broad tails while swimming—that freezes to provide an almost impenetrable fortress. The river otter—the only predator that can get in—can swim through the underwater entrance. Beaver leave the peak more permeable for ventilation.

Near the lodge, in deep water, beaver store up a winter's worth of branches in an underwater food cache. They jam the branches butt first into the pond-bottom mud to keep them under the ice. In the dead of winter, beaver swim out of their lodges under the ice and bring back branches to eat.

Beaver have adapted remarkably well to their unique aquatic lifestyle. They have two layers of fur: long silky guard hairs and a dense woolly underfur. By regularly grooming this fur with a special comblike split toenail and keeping it oiled, water seldom totally wets through to the beaver's skin. Their noses and ears have special valves that keep them stoppered shut when underwater, and special folds of skin in the mouth enable beaver to gnaw underwater and carry branches in their teeth without getting water down their throats. Their back feet have fully webbed toes to provide propulsion underwater, and their tails provide important rudder control, which helps beaver swim in a straight line when dragging a large branch. Both the respiratory and circulatory systems have adapted to underwater swimming and enable a beaver to stay underwater for up to 15 minutes, during which time it can swim a half mile! Finally, as with other rodents, their teeth grow constantly and keep sharp through use.

Beaver generally mate for life and maintain an extended family structure. Young stay with their parents for two years, so both yearlings and the current year's kits live with the two parents in the lodge. Females usually bear two—sometimes three—kits between April and June. Born fully furred with eyes open, they can walk and swim almost right away, though they rarely leave the lodge until at least a month of age. The yearlings and both parents assist in bringing food to the kits as well as with dam and lodge construction.

The demand for beaver pelts, more than any other factor, was responsible for the early exploration of North America. Trappers nearly exterminated them by the late 1800s. In New York State, only one known active beaver colony—plus a few scattered individuals—remained in 1904. Then began what certainly must be one of the most successful endangered species reintroduction programs ever.

The state released 6 beaver in 1904 in the Old Forge area of the Adirondacks. In 1906, they released another 25 animals imported from Yellowstone Park, and private landowners released 14 more on nearby private lands. By 1915, that tiny population had expanded to an estimated 15,000 to 20,000 animals. By 1924, the state opened a limited trapping season on beaver. In 1994, the Department of Environmental Conservation estimated the New York population to be 93,000 individuals in nearly 18,000 colonies.

As you paddle along the shoreline of lakes or quiet rivers, keep an eye out for telltale signs of beaver, including gnaw marks on trees, distinctive conical stumps of cut trees, canals leading off into the marsh, alder branches trimmed back along narrow passages, and well-worn paths leading away from the water's edge where the hardworking mammals have dragged more distant branches to the water.

We see beaver most often in the late evening or early morning. Paddle quietly toward a beaver lodge around dusk. Wait patiently, and you will likely see the animals emerge for evening feeding and perhaps construction work on a dam or lodge. When a beaver senses danger it slaps its tail on the water and dives with a loud "ker-chunk!" We hope that you will find that sound as exhilarating as we do.

Long Pond, Round Pond, and Oswegatchie River

Croghan

MAPS
> **New York Atlas:** Map 85
> **USGS Quadrangle:** Stillwater

INFORMATION
> **Area:** 134 acres; maximum depth: 72 feet
> **Prominent fish species:** Splake, brown trout, and brook trout
> **Books:** If you plan a longer paddle of the Oswegatchie River, purchase a copy of Paul Jamieson and Donald Morris's outstanding guidebook *Adirondack Canoe Waters: North Flow,* published by the Adirondack Mountain Club.

Long and Round Ponds, in holes left by retreating glaciers, form two wide spots in the West Branch of the Oswegatchie River. We include here these two ponds, along with an upstream portion of the Oswegatchie. You cannot paddle the river between the two ponds and the upstream section of river described here.

Long and Round Ponds

The Future Farmers of America maintain a camp on the northern shore of Long and Round Ponds and own the land surrounding these ponds. Fortunately, they allow the public to paddle through this area, in a cooperative agreement with the Department of Environmental Conservation. However, finding access is another matter. No obvious boat access exists at the camp, and No Parking signs line the roadside. With some difficulty, we did find an access point off Prentice Road.

Arriving the night before our paddle we camped nearby, dropped our sleeping bags on the ground, and listened to the haunting call of loons echoing off the hillsides. A barred owl called its "who-cooks-for-you, who-cooks-for-you" from the woods, and small animals scurried through the dense brush. Still, we had no problem drifting off, listening to the calls of the night.

We paddled here at first light, as mist drifted slowly across the water. We noticed a conspicuous browse line on the bankside hemlocks that dominate the south end of Long Pond. As we looked across the

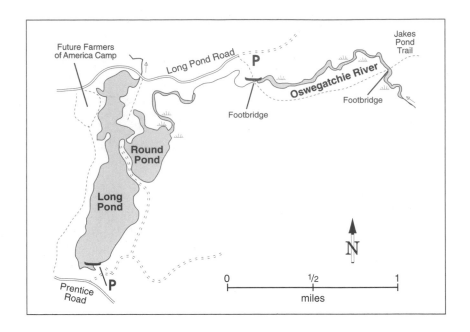

way, a deer ambled down for an early morning drink. The loons continued to call from up near the camp as we made our way north on the still water.

Although many tree species grow along the shore, nearly pure stands of some species grow in spots: eastern hemlock along the east shore of Long Pond and red pine, punctuated by an occasional tall white pine, along the peninsula separating the two ponds. The generally shrubby shoreline gives way to a carpet of needles farther back up under the pines. Out in the water, fragrant water lilies carpet the protected coves, along with minor amounts of pickerelweed, some pondweed, and a few large patches of water shield.

A ruffed grouse drummed on a log off in the woods, and two ravens practiced their aerial acrobatics over the pond. A flock of yellow-rumped warblers cast about for insects, and barn swallows skimmed over the pond's surface. Two common mergansers tried to hide from us among the reeds of a shallow cove, and a belted kingfisher announced our presence to the early risers at the camp with its rattling cry. We felt slightly guilty about causing such a ruckus but later retracted those feelings: Tuesday is mechanized day at FFA camp!

While some campers took turns spinning around the lake on water skis, others took 15-minute floatplane rides—over and over, all morning long. Surprisingly, this did not affect the resident loons as much as it did us. We paddled up the inlet for its navigable half mile to watch

Dew-covered spider web on the inlet to Round Pond.

the dew dry off the streamside spiderwebs. We listened to white-throated sparrows and catbirds call from the undergrowth, searched the waters for the beaver that own the lodge, studied purple elderberries, and then paddled back through tea-colored water to the boat access, under the pontoons of the floatplane and through the ski-boat wake.

Along the way, we investigated the outflow under the bridge on the north end of Long Pond. The current flows along here, as the river tumbles down over a rock-strewn streambed. We turned around because we sensed that paddling back up would be difficult at best.

Oswegatchie River

The contrast between these ponds and the upstream section of the Oswegatchie River stands out in our memory. Because you have to hike in to the river, few people paddle here among the tall tamaracks and pines that dot the extensive marshland. Between the widened upstream river and the entrance to Round Pond, the river passes under a foot-

Fragrant water lilies reflect early morning light from the rippled surface of Round Pond.

bridge and cascades down over beautiful waterfalls. But upstream from the last cascade, the river barely flows through sphagnum bogs that cover a flat plateau, and the paddling is superb. Because of the huge surrounding marsh that accumulates copious quantities of snow and water over the winter, water gets released slowly, maintaining paddlable levels, even during dry summers such as we found in 1995.

Brushy banks covered with alders, leatherleaf, sweet gale, and other streamside vegetation lead to mats of floating aquatic plants. We carried up over a beaver dam and paddled through another. You can paddle back in for about a mile and a half, eventually ending in an enormous beaver meadow and sphagnum bog that extends off into the distance. As you near the second Jakes Pond Trail footbridge, you have to walk your boat through the shallows during times of low water. We had to negotiate around the bald-faced hornet nest attached to the downstream side of the second Jakes Pond Trail bridge.

Because we did not paddle here in early June, we missed the azalea bloom mentioned in the *North Flow* guidebook. These showy flowers—in the heath family, along with rhododendron, mountain laurel, sheep laurel, blueberry, cranberry, and many other bog specialists—should enrich any paddling excursion.

Besides the beaver activity, expect to see beautiful wood ducks feeding on the abundant aquatic vegetation that laces the tea-colored water. Muskrats harvest grasses, and deer come to the water's edge to drink. Birds flit about in profusion, and moose will likely tramp these swamps again. In recent years, this largest member of the deer family has begun returning to New York after more than a hundred years' absence. A feeling of remoteness and peacefulness surrounds this extraordinary place. If you want wilderness, this is a good place to find it.

Getting There

From Lowville, take Route 812 north to Croghan; when Route 812 goes left to cross the Raquette River, go straight on Belfort Road. At the junction with Erie Canal Road, turn left, cross the bridge over the Beaver River, and turn right at the stop sign onto Long Pond Road.

To get to Long and Round Ponds, take this paved road for 4.4 miles to Prentice Road. Turn right onto Prentice Road as it angles off to the right. Go 4.3 miles down this road to a fork with a sign that says: Long Pond Cooperator Area, Fish and Wildlife Management, Owned by Future Farmers of America, Department of Environmental Conservation. As Prentice Road veers right, take the left fork downhill. Go slowly, as your turnoff to the left is in 0.1 mile; the access is 0.1 mile down the access road.

To get to the upstream section of the Oswegatchie River, return to the junction of Prentice Road and Long Pond Road. Turn right onto Long Pond Road. The first of three bridges over the river occurs 2.4 miles from the previous junction; go slowly on the dangerous curve here (speed limit 15 MPH). At 3.5 miles, the road turns to gravel at the second bridge. Enter the FFA camp at 4.9 miles, and cross the third bridge at 5.2 miles. Continue to the huge parking lot at the end of the road in 5.9 miles.

Most, if not all, of the cars in the lot belong to folks hiking the trail to Jakes Pond (4.3 miles) or visiting the nearby falls.

The boat launch is about 0.3 mile from the parking area along the Jakes Pond Trail. The newly relocated trailhead starts off downhill; after a short distance, the trail Ts. Take the left fork. You will hear the waterfall off to the right—it is worth visiting (look for a faint trail leading off to the right toward the roar).

Continue on the Jakes Pond Trail to the first footbridge; the put-in is on the far side on the left off some flat rocks.

Fish Creek to Oneida Lake
Vienna

MAPS

New York Atlas: Map 76

USGS Quadrangle: Sylvan Beach (note that Route 49 was relocated after the printing of this topographic map; refer to the New York Atlas)

INFORMATION

Length: Approximately 9 miles one way from the Route 49 bridge to Sylvan Beach on Lake Oneida; can paddle both directions at low water

Prominent fish species: Largemouth bass, smallmouth bass, and northern pike

Camping: Verona Beach State Park; 315-762-4463

We did not expect much when we put into Fish Creek in early October, even though a local kayaker told us we would enjoy paddling here. Sylvan Beach and its environs serve as a summer vacation mecca, drawing people from far and wide to the crowded shores of Oneida Lake. What we found on nearby Fish Creek was a wildlife haven, standing in sharp contrast with people-packed Sylvan Beach. We stress the importance of getting to the river at sunrise to maximize wildlife viewing. Also, resist the tendency to rush down the river—paddle the shoreline quietly looking for wildlife, trying to remain unobtrusive. Doing so will ensure seeing a wider variety and getting closer looks.

This section of the river flows through a broad, flat plain, cutting a wide swath itself. More than 100 feet in width, Fish Creek's shallow, clear waters reveal either a sand- or dead-tree-covered bottom. Grapevines and Virginia creeper drape over streamside vegetation that stands among the aspens, cottonwood, box elder, large flowing willows, sumac, and more. The layered canopy stretches for every available light ray to maximize photosynthesis; in one area an undergrowth of dwarf willow, a midstory of river birch, and an overstory of big-toothed aspen placed leaf surfaces in the sun from bank top to treetop. A beaver had nearly gnawed through the bases of some of the aspens, a favorite food of theirs.

As we paddled out at sunrise, the sun's early rays burned off the morning mist and the dew off shoreside plants as a white-tailed deer came down for an early morning drink. We listened to robins singing

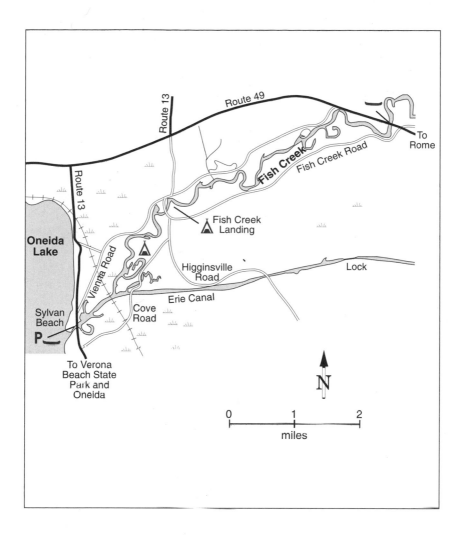

and blue jays squawking, and two black ducks leapt from the water at our approach. As we rounded the first bend on the very inside of the curve, we saw movement on the bank downstream. We quit paddling and drifted in the lazy current. A red fox pounced from tuft to tuft along the steep bank looking for mice, too intent on its pursuit to see us drifting toward a rendezvous. As it placed its forepaws on a log jammed against the bank, we arrived. It looked at us from 10 feet only for a moment before bounding up and over the bank in alarm.

As we curved to the left, wood ducks blasted out of the coves—in all we counted 10 taking off in this short stretch. The first of three great blue herons we would see took wing as well. A flock of about 40 Canada geese flew over, honking noisily as they began their southward migration to water that would remain open all winter. We stopped to look at a mixed foraging flock of more than 40 birds in an extensive grapevine thicket: we found song sparrows and white-throated sparrows near the ground, yellow-rumped warblers—the last warblers to migrate south—in the midstory, and chickadees and white-breasted nuthatches overhead, all trying to glean late-season insects and berries from the foliage.

As we drifted back out into the current, the first of two sharp-shinned hawks that we would see drifted across the waterway, and all became still in the grapevines. How could so many birds vanish so quickly? Evolution obviously favors those who become scarce when a major bird predator such as the sharpie appears. Across the way in a farmer's overgrazed field, a flock of red-winged blackbirds—the males' red epaulets barely visible in their fall plumage—foraged on the ground along with a herd of fat cows. Up in a dead tree among the sun-bleached branches, crows mobbed a stationary red-tailed hawk as another hawk circled on gathering thermals overhead. As we paddled over to the other side to get a closer look, two killdeer that we had not seen took to noisy flight. A greater yellowlegs, calling a descending "tew-tew-tew-tew-tew," ran along the shore as eastern bluebirds stood on fence posts watching for insects aroused by the rising sun.

Just after we passed a row of bank swallow holes in the soft steep bank—the swallows had long ago left for warmer climes still abuzz with insects—we heard a noisy chomping among the branches of a deadfall on the left bank. We drifted closer to see a young river otter munching away on a fish. Such manners! After a few minutes, deciding that we would not leave, it dove with its fish into the water behind the snag. A few moments later, it, its mother, and perhaps two siblings tried to sneak away upstream. After swimming about 15 feet away, the mother poked her head skyward to get a better look at us. If you have never seen this sight, you are in for a treat. The otter, with neck fully extended, thrusts its head abruptly up above the water's surface a full foot to look around, with no shoulders or arms in view, uttering a muffled snort as it clears its nose of water. What a bizarre sight!

While mourning doves perched on bare branches above, a belted kingfisher dove headlong into the water after a fish, emerging quickly to fly off to its perch. We spent some time trying to identify a flycatcher out on a limb. After a few puzzling moments, we decided that it was one we usually identify by song: the eastern wood pewee. It had two white wing bars, a gray breast, and did not bob its tail, all in contrast with the similar eastern phoebe, which we also saw.

As we neared Fish Creek Landing, where we would turn around to avoid the downstream development and motorboat traffic, the largest flock of common mergansers we have seen rested on stumps, logs, rocks, and the water of a protected cove. We counted 48 birds in our binoculars and turned around before the landing to avoid forcing them to fly off. Down here closer to the lake, ring-billed gulls flew over frequently.

We paddled back at a faster pace and saw only one new species, a rather tame green-backed heron that let us get within 20 feet before taking flight. As we paddled by a rope swing suspended from a willow branch, we reflected on the prodigious amount of wildlife we had seen and wondered about the protection of this wildlife paradise. The rope swing dangles from a fragile branch—willow branches shatter easily—but no more fragile than the habitat that harbors this wildlife. Clearly, shoreline development and tree clearing threaten this habitat.

Judging from the amount of downed timber, spring runoff topples streamside trees frequently along here. The roots of standing trees stabilize the banks, keeping the river from broadening and getting too shallow, and also provide habitat for fish, otter, mink, muskrat, and beaver. The narrow woods bordering houses and farmers' fields provide the only protection for this stream. We hope the people who enjoy nature's bounty here will seek protection of the shoreline. They might ask farmers not to cut trees within, say, 100 feet of the shore. They might convince residents not to subdivide their land and to plant trees along the bank. A cooperative effort could help ensure that this fragile habitat remains for future generations to enjoy.

Getting There

From Sylvan Beach on the east end of Lake Oneida, travel north on Route 13. Turn right onto Route 49 at the T. From this junction, Route 13 turns off north after 2.5 miles; continue straight on Route 49 for 3.7 more miles to the bridge over Fish Creek at the sign for City of Rome. Park well off the road on either side, just before the bridge.

If you wish to paddle Fish Creek in one direction, you can leave a car in Sylvan Beach at the public parking area on the lakefront. Take-out is on the right just downstream from the Route 13 bridge in Sylvan Beach. Or you could avoid most of the development and motorboats and pay to take out at one of the private campgrounds at Fish Creek Landing.

An alternative put-in exists at the Oswego Road bridge about 3 miles upstream.

Blackflies and Mosquitoes
Scourges of the North

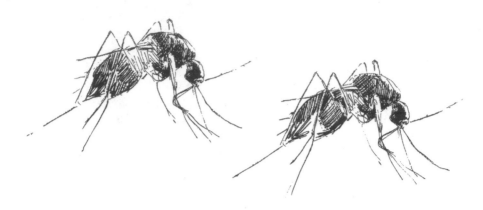

Anyone who has spent any time at all paddling or hiking in the Adirondacks knows these insects all too well. They can detract from outdoor fun throughout the summer and can make most of June virtually off-limits to outdoor recreation in northern parts of the state. So what are these little beasts that hover in clouds around your head, reducing you to a swollen, scratching, cursing basket case as you portage your canoe or attempt to tie a fly on your line? Though it won't take away any of the pain or itch, understanding these small insects may help you accept them as part of the ecosystem you so enjoy.

Blackflies
Blackflies belong to the family Simuldiidae ("little snub-nosed beings"), and most of the species of concern to us belong to the genus *Simulium*. Scientists have identified more than 1,500 species of blackflies worldwide, 300 in North America. Only 10 percent to 15 percent of blackfly species cause all the problems: sucking blood from humans or domestic animals.

In parts of northern North America, blackflies cause considerable losses to livestock—mostly weight loss because cattle do not eat well when tormented by the flies, but they actually kill cattle in some areas. In parts of Alberta, Canada, mortality rates from blackflies range from 1 percent to 4 percent. Researchers have collected as many as 10,000 feeding blackflies from a single cow!

Blackfly problems in North America, however, pale compared to problems in Africa and Central America, where the aptly named species *Simulium damnosum* has infected an estimated 20 million people with onchocerciasis, or river blindness (a disease caused by roundworms that are transmitted by the fly).

Blackflies begin their life cycle in streams and rivers. Adult females deposit eggs in the water, and the emerging larvae attach themselves to rocks, plants, and other surfaces in the current. Two tiny, fanlike structures sweep food particles into their mouths. In some streams the blackfly larvae become so dense that they form a slippery, mosslike mat. A several-hundred-foot stretch of a narrow stream can support more than a million larvae. In a river the population can be in the multibillions per mile.

After a period of days or weeks (depending on the species and available food), each larva builds a pupal case in which it metamorphoses into an adult blackfly. When ready to emerge, it splits the pupal case open and rides to the water's surface in a bubble of oxygen that had collected in the case.

Adult blackflies have one primary goal: to make more blackflies. The trouble begins when female blackflies seek the nourishing meal of blood they need to lay eggs. Only females bite (actu-ally more of a puncture-and-suck routine than a true bite); males lead a pacifist life, sipping nectar from flowers and searching for the "right" partner. Blackflies rely heavily on eyesight to find prey, so they are active almost exclusively during the daylight. Some blackflies fly more than fifty miles in search of blood meals.

No blackfly species sucks blood exclusively from humans. We are too new on the evolutionary chain to be a specific host to blackflies, which arose during the Jurassic period 180 million years ago. An estimated 30 to 45 blackfly species in North America feed on humans. There is one species (*Simulium euryadminiculum*) whose females feed only on loons.

Mosquitoes

Our other major insect nemesis of New York paddlers is the ubiquitous mosquito. Mosquitoes, members of the Culicidae family, number more than 3,400 species worldwide, including 170 in North America. Three-quarters of the mosquito species in the U.S. and Canada belong to three genera: *Aedes* (78 species), *Culex* (29 species), and *Anopheles* (16 species).

As with blackflies, mosquito larvae live an aquatic life. Unlike blackflies, though, most mosquitoes have adapted to *still* water. Whether on a quiet bog in the Adirondacks or a salt marsh on

Long Island, you can usually find mosquito larvae wriggling about during the spring and early summer months. If the spring has been wet, you can find *lots* of them. They eat algae and other organic matter they filter out of the water with brushlike appendages. Larvae go through a number of different molts as they grow and develop into pupae. Both larvae and pupae breathe through air tubes at the surface of the water.

Adult mosquitoes have short life spans. Most females live about a month, while males live only about a week. The high-pitched buzz of mosquitoes comes from beating their wings at about 1,000 beats per second. Females generate a higher-pitched whine than males, which helps the males locate mates. Males can be recognized with a hand lens by their much bushier antennae, which are used to locate females.

Both male and female mosquitoes feed on plant juices and nectars as their primary energy source, but females of most species also require a blood meal to fuel egg production. The habit of female mosquitoes to feed on blood—and especially *our* blood—has given this insect its deservedly nasty reputation.

As with blackflies, a mosquito does not really bite. Rather, she stabs through the victim's skin with six sharp *stylets* that form the center of the proboscis. Saliva flows into the puncture to keep the blood from coagulating while she sips it through her proboscis. The reaction most people have to mosquito bites—itching and swelling—is an allergic reaction to the saliva. Upon repeated exposure to mosquito bites, one gradually builds up resistance.

While really just a nuisance in New York, mosquitoes cause death and destruction in the tropics. Disease-carrying mosquitoes cause more human deaths than any other animal. They carry more than 100 different diseases, including malaria, yellow fever, encephalitis, filariasis, and dengue. The most destructive of these, malaria, kills about 1 million people a year, mostly children, and worldwide as many as 200 million people carry the disease.

Southern latitudes have far greater mosquito-species diversity (as many as 150 different species can be found in a square mile in some parts of the tropics), but the numbers of individual mosquitoes generally increase farther north. In the Arctic, there are fewer than a dozen species, but adults can be so thick they literally blacken the skies. In one experiment, several rugged (and, we suspect, intellectually challenged) Canadian researchers bared their torsos, arms, and legs to Arctic mosquitoes and reported as many as 9,000 bites per minute! At this rate of onslaught, an unprotected person could lose half of his or her blood in two hours.

So, you see, we really don't have it so bad in New York. Most of our mosquitoes do not carry deadly disease (though there have been occasional cases of a mosquito-borne encephalitis), and even in the Adirondacks in June, we've found that it's rare to get more than a thousand bites a minute....

Blackfly and Mosquito Control

Many different control strategies have been tried for blackflies and mosquitoes. For mosquito control, we drained thousands of square miles of salt marsh during the 1930s and 1940s by building long, straight drainage ditches—many of which are still visible. (As much as half of the wetland area in the U.S. has been lost during the last 200 years—partly for mosquito control and partly for development and agriculture.) Along with eliminating habitat, we have used thousands of tons of pesticides in the battle against these insects—mostly against mosquitoes. DDT was the chemical of choice for decades because of its supposed safety to humans and the environment—a claim that proved tragically untrue. Since the banning of DDT and other deadly chlorinated-hydrocarbon pesticides in 1973, osprey, bald eagles, peregrine falcons, and other important bird species have begun making a comeback in the Northeast.

Today, most attention focuses on biological control of these insects. Biological control relies on natural enemies of the pest: viruses, protozoa, bacteria, fungi, and parasites. The most successful control found has been a bacterium discovered in 1977 from samples of sand collected in the Negev Desert. This is *Bacillus thuringiensis* variety *israelensis,* generally known as Bti. Gardeners use another variety of this bacterium for controlling cabbage loopers, corn borers, and other garden pests, and foresters use it for gypsy moth control. Bti bacteria produce protein crystals that react with other chemicals in the insects' stomachs, producing a poison that kills the larvae. While Bti currently enjoys high success rates, some researchers are concerned that there will be hidden problems with this solution, just as there were with DDT.

Protecting Yourself from Biting Insects

One option is to stay out of the woods—buy a good book on paddling and read about it. While a bit extreme, this is not a bad solution during June, when clouds of blackflies and mosquitoes may stick in your mind as the most memorable part of an outing. Largely because of biting insects, in fact, our favorite times for canoeing in northern New York are in the autumn and in May—during that narrow window between ice-out and the blackfly hatch.

During all but the height of the blackfly season in June, however, there is no reason to let insects spoil your trip. In fact, because you are out on the water where there is often a breeze, bugs represent much less a problem for paddlers than for hikers. Proper clothing forms the most important line of defense against both blackflies and mosquitoes. During blackfly season, wear long-sleeved, tight-knit shirts with elastic cuffs. Turtlenecks work well as long as the material is thick enough and the weave tight enough that the flies cannot reach your skin through it. Wear long pants with elastic cuffs, or tuck your pants legs into oversized socks. Blackflies land on your clothing and search for openings—wrists, ankles, and necks are prime targets. If you have good protection at your neck, a mosquito-cloth head net works well, but with a collared shirt, blackflies will usually find a route in. Cotton gloves can be a big help, too.

Mosquitoes can penetrate soft clothing better than blackflies, so a more rugged material such as canvas works well for shirts and pants. Wearing two light shirts is also effective. Tight cuffs are not as important because mosquitoes usually fly directly to their dining table. With mosquito-cloth head nets, the key is to keep the mosquito cloth away from your skin—buy one with a metal band from which the cloth hangs. Make sure it has a drawstring or elastic; otherwise, mosquitoes inevitably find their way in.

Insect repellents generally repel mosquitoes better than blackflies. DEET (N,N-diethyl-meta-toluamide) remains the chemical of choice in the Adirondacks. Fortunately, one of our coauthors is a chemist and able to pronounce this chemical. Unfortunately, he also knows enough about its chemical structure to be concerned about potential toxicity to humans. Most of the repellents outdoorspeople swear by have DEET as the primary active ingredient; some are almost 100 percent DEET. Because DEET works by evaporating into the nearby air to clog insects' odor receptors, you have to keep slathering it on. While we admit to keeping some high-test DEET around when the bugs get really bad, we recommend clothing as the primary defensive strategy.

A relatively new repellent for blackflies that many claim to be highly effective is Avon Skin-So-Soft®. Applying a nontoxic skin softener instead of one of those toxic-sounding diethyl-type chemical concoctions sounds really great. We would be even more excited about it if it kept blackflies away. Maybe it does have some effect, maybe it even provides ironclad protection for some people, but we aren't convinced. Up in northern Maine—where the folks really know a lot about blackflies—at the height of blackfly season in mid-June, the repellent most locals use is smoke. Lots of it. Called smudge pots, or just smokes, the idea is to build a fire in a bucket or large can, then stuff green leaves in so it spews forth thick smoke. And you stand in that smoke. It seems to work beautifully, but after seeing these smokes in use all over the place (and enjoying their protection a few times), we can only wonder if there is an elevated incidence of emphysema and other respiratory ills among users. Also, we find they don't work well in canoes.

Is There Anything Good about Blackflies and Mosquitoes?

In reviewing all the problems with blackflies and mosquitoes, one wonders what might possibly be good about the little beasts. The answer lies in the role they play in aquatic ecosystems, where they provide a vital food source for a wide variety of animals. Many of our choice game fish rely on blackfly and mosquito larvae for at least a part of their diets. One study found that blackfly larvae comprise up to 25 percent of the brook trout diet. Even if blackfly and mosquito larvae do not provide a *direct* food source for our favorite game fish and waterfowl, chances are pretty good that the larvae form a vital part of the food chain upon which these animals rely. If we appreciate angling for brook trout, listening to the evening song of the loon, or watching the stately great blue heron, we should recognize that these species might not be here without blackflies and mosquitoes.

Not only that, but without these insect pests, every lake and pond in the Adirondacks might long ago have been sprinkled with vacation homes, and the solitude we so appreciate there might not exist. This is not to suggest, however, that we shouldn't slap the little devils with a vengeance, occasionally slather on the DEET, and do everything in our power to prevent ourselves from serving as walking smorgasbords for these guys—uh, gals. But we should recognize that, yes, even blackflies and mosquitoes have a place in the ecosystem.

Gifford Lake/West Branch Fish Creek
Amboy and Camden

MAPS

    New York Atlas: Map 76

    USGS Quadrangle: Westdale

INFORMATION

    Prominent fish species: Stocked brown trout and smallmouth bass

    Books: If you plan to run downstream sections of the East or West Branches of Fish Creek, purchase one or more of the following guidebooks: William P. Ehling, *Canoeing Central New York* (Backcountry); Mark Freeman, *Canoe Guide to Western and Central New York State* (Adirondack Mountain Club); Alec Proskine, *Adirondack Canoe Waters: South & West Flow* (Adirondack Mountain Club).

A popular one-way canoe route begins at the boat access on the downstream side of the dam on the West Branch of Fish Creek. Except for kayaker John Kowalski and a few friends from nearby Sylvan Beach and local fishermen, few people take advantage of the beautiful *upstream* paddling also available here. Above the dam, the West

Marshy areas abound at the entrance to Gifford Lake and in the many coves along the West Branch of Fish Creek.

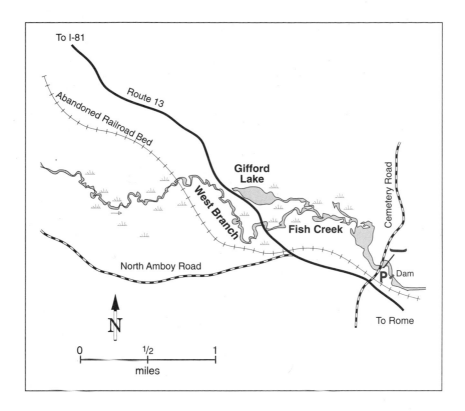

Branch meanders through forest and marsh, passes by the outlet of Gifford Lake, skims unobtrusively under Route 13, and heads upstream through brushy, wooded banks. Water celery and pondweed undulate back and forth, trailing in the lazy current.

After turning left at the put-in and heading upstream, you pass by a cluster of houses on the right. The next house on the right—actually a fishing camp—quite a way upstream marks the entrance to Gifford Lake. The last house we saw on the creek overlooks the water next to the Route 13 bridge. An old railroad grade several miles upstream where we turned around—although we could have gone farther—alludes to a time when civilization encroached more extensively on this wild little creek.

The creek meanders through an extensive marsh. Although tall hemlocks and silver maples line the right-hand shore occasionally, marshes and shrubs generally own the banks along this section of stream. The first side channel on the right penetrates well back into the woods, and tons of pondweed, pickerelweed, yellow pond lily, and underwater vegetation grow in the stagnant water. Two great blue herons patrolled the shallow water, ever watchful for their next meal of frogs or fish, while two kingfishers hovered in the air, waiting to dive headlong on unwary fish.

In most places, grasses, ferns, long-leaved *Rumex,* and shrubbery dominate the shoreline, while extensive marshes lead off in all directions. Clumps of arrowhead grow out from the bank, while pickerel-weed—growing singly—occurs in slightly deeper water. A large patch of iris, in and among the cattails, caught our eye, while in other places we noted that alders cover the banks.

The high biological productivity of this area makes it a paradise for bird-watchers and others interested in wildlife. We saw or heard great blue heron, kingfisher, robin, mourning dove, yellow-rumped warbler, yellow warbler, common yellowthroat, eastern phoebe, barn swallow, red-winged blackbird, grackle, osprey, eastern kingbird, song sparrow, rose-breasted grosbeak, and a flock of cedar waxwings. Although we did not see beaver, we did see lodges and lots of fresh alder cuttings. A muskrat, seemingly unconcerned by our presence, harvested grasses by the shore, and we witnessed a rare treat: a mink furtively fishing the shore, working stealthily along the bank, waiting to pounce on anything that moved.

Mink

Mink—like most other members of the weasel family—have very high metabolic rates; their elongated bodies give them a high surface-area-to-volume ratio, causing high heat loss for their size. This heat loss causes them to have voracious appetites. To satisfy such, they kill just about anything: fish, rodents, frogs, crayfish, birds, eggs, and your prized hen in the henhouse. Even though they usually weigh about two pounds, they easily can slay larger animals, giving them their "killer" reputation. The mink has an extraordinarily wide range, from Key West to arctic Alaska, from Labrador to central California. Given its huge appetite, and the need to kill a lot to fulfill it, mink never appear in large numbers in any habitat. So you're fortunate to see one, especially because they usually remain nocturnal.

To get to Gifford Lake, take the right-hand fork when you reach the fishing camp on the right, about a mile upstream from the boat access. One very well kept house and grounds occur on Gifford Lake. Although the lake sports a beautiful stand of hardwoods along its shores, its most interesting feature has to be the scenic creek that connects the lake with Fish Creek. A very narrow, meandering passageway leads through a wide expanse of marsh. Beaver cuttings along the way suggest that an early evening paddle here would be rewarding. Arrowhead crowds the channel, and you have to weave your way through fragrant water lilies and yellow pond lilies.

As we paddled back to the boat access in the waning afternoon sun, we marveled at the beauty of recently emerged, iridescent green damselflies with jet black wings that hovered over the drooping tips of streamside grasses.

Getting There

From Rome, head northwest on Route 69. At the stoplight in Camden, turn right onto Route 13, and note your mileage. In 5.0 miles, watch for a sign to Westdale followed by a crossroads as Route 13 curves to the left. At the crossroads, turn right onto Cemetery Road. The boat access is 0.1 mile down on the right. There is plenty of parking.

From Syracuse, take I-81 north to Route 104. Go east on Route 104 to Williamstown, and turn right onto Route 13 east. From this junction, it is 7.9 miles to Cemetery Road. Turn left onto Cemetery Road, and proceed 0.1 mile down to the boat access on the right.

Salmon River Reservoir
Orwell and Redfield

MAPS
  New York Atlas: Map 83 and 84
  USGS Quadrangles: Orwell and Redfield
INFORMATION
  Area: 3,200 acres
  Prominent fish species: Largemouth bass
  Camping: Campsites scattered about the lakeshore

The previous owner of Salmon River Reservoir, Niagara-Mohawk Power Corporation, used to restrict access to parts of the lake. The state recently purchased the reservoir, and now all reaches of the lake can be boated. Our two favorite areas of this little-used reservoir include the far west end, down through the cove southeast of the dam, and the far east end where the Salmon River flows into extensive marshes.

The state maintains three access points: one at the Redfield bridge on Route 17 near the east end and two within a mile of each other on the northwest shore off Route 2. When paddling the west end, we would use the Jackson Road access point closer to the dam, mainly because of wind problems. When we paddled out at sunup in late August, the surface barely rippled, but on our return at midmorning, the wind had started to roll waves down the lake in preparation for after-noon whitecaps.

This daily cycle of calm and wind happens for a reason. As the land mass heats up during the day, warm air rises, drawing in cooler, denser air off nearby Lake Ontario. Because of its generally east-west orientation, the reservoir suffers from high wind-driven waves from the west during the summer. By threading your way through the willow-clad islands near the Jackson Road boat access, then down the western shore to the cove past the dam, you can avoid the large waves that roll on through the main lake.

Alternatively, you could paddle the eastern end of the lake where the Route 17 bridge and a twisting channel through wooded shores block much of the wind. Indeed, the wildlife paradise on the lake's eastern end remains our favorite (see below).

At the western end, as we paddled down to the cove below Hall Island—really a peninsula—we watched gulls, loons, and crows and listened to chickadees and eastern wood pewees off in the woods. A belted kingfisher flew before us, leading us through stump-filled shallows, under a culvert, and out into a magnificent marsh. While we found a few campsites along Hall Island, we found none past the culvert. Aquatic plants—including Eurasian milfoil, yellow pond lily, pondweed, and water shield—choked the whole cove, dampening any swells from the freshening wind. As we paddled the shoreline, we noticed two large, but apparently inactive, beaver lodges. Had the inhabitants cut down all the nearby trees, eating themselves out of house and home?

Three great blue herons flew off at our approach, while a kingfisher stood its ground among the limbs of a dead tree out in the water. Paddling back up the shore through the clear water, as a brood of common mergansers rushed out of harm's way, we studied the shoreline trees, including red and white pine, ash, elm, sugar and red maple, box elder, eastern hemlock, birch, quaking and big-toothed aspen, cottonwood, apple, black and pin cherry, beech, yellow birch, and willow. Except for the hump that is Hall Island, the flat western landscape allows the water to creep up to the plateau's edge to spill through cataracts downstream to Lake Ontario.

While the lake remains popular with local fishermen, the Salmon River below the lower reservoir attracts thousands of fall anglers to fish the salmon runs. To accommodate river fishing, starting in late August, the power company starts to draw the reservoir down, eventually several feet, to maintain stream levels for the salmon run, making the reservoir a less pleasant place to paddle.

Making our way down to the eastern end of the reservoir, we passed under the Route 17 bridge and into a wildlife paradise. The entire northern shore, honeycombed with channels through small, willow-clad islands and patches of aquatic vegetation, provides habitat for myriad fauna and flora. As we paddled through the channel, a river otter paced us for a way, periodically bobbing up with a snort to look around, head high above the water, then diving in typical undulating otter fashion.

Feeding flocks of common mergansers, black ducks, and wood ducks scurried into the *Equisetum* and grasses as we approached. Two wood ducks bolted from a streamside tree as we rounded a bend, and a sharp-shinned hawk alternately flapped and glided across in front of us. This small hawk, a member of the accipiter group—along with Cooper's hawk and goshawk—preys mainly on other birds, which it chases down and plucks from the sky. The sharpie's small size, short rounded wings, and long tail give it an agility when flying through woods not shared with other hawks.

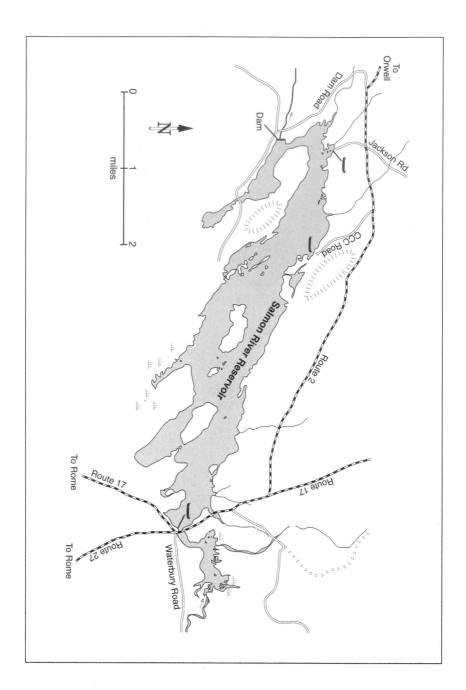

A much, much larger raptor soared on wide wings overhead: an immature bald eagle, dark brown with flecks of white on its tail and belly, cast its eagle eye on dead and dying suckers that littered the water. Our nation's symbol catches live fish, which it snares from the water's surface with powerful claws, but it more typically eats carrion, including dead suckers. We sometimes see eagles below hydropower plants, feasting on fish injured or killed by power-generating turbines.

As we paddled back by bushy basswoods, through islands of grass and willows, water celery indicated current direction. Upon reaching a shallow riffle, we drifted back down the Salmon River, following its flow into the reservoir, marveling at how close the pebbly bottom seemed in the crystal-clear water. Reentering the marsh, we found brilliant red cardinal flower in bloom near a beaver impoundment on a side channel. Smartweed, a member of the buckwheat family, with its leaves prostrate upon the water's surface, had sent up short bloom pikes with bright pink flowers measuring maybe an inch long. We spent hours looking at plants, animals, and birds in this huge wetland.

We paddled here alone until near the end, when a lone Jet-skier flew up the river from under the bridge. He took one look around and zoomed back down the reservoir. We who use this area should try to preserve the section upstream from the Redfield bridge as a motorless area. Apparently, when Niagara-Mohawk owned the reservoir, they did not allow the public into the upper marshlands. Given the huge concentration of wildlife—including bald eagle, sharp-shinned hawk, river otter, and many more less exotic species—we should try to protect their habitat from noisy, disruptive incursions.

Getting There

From I-81, get off at the Pulaski exit and travel east on Route 2. Start measuring mileage at the junction of Routes 2 and 22 in downtown Orwell. From there, the Jackson Road turnoff is 4.3 miles from Route 22. Turn right onto Jackson Road—leading to the west end of the reservoir—and reach the boat access in 0.4 mile.

The turnoff to the CCC Road boat access is 1.0 mile farther (5.3 miles from Route 22). Turn right onto CCC Road—initially paved, then gravel—and reach the boat access in 0.9 mile.

To reach the reservoir's east end, continue on past the CCC Road for 4.1 miles (9.4 miles from Route 22) to Route 17. Turn right onto Route 17, and travel 1.3 miles down to the Redfield bridge. The access point is across the bridge on the right.

From Rome, travel west on Route 69 to Route 13 in Camden. Proceed west on Route 13 to Route 17 north. Take Route 17 north to Redfield. Access is on the left, just before the Redfield bridge over Salmon River Reservoir.

Deer Creek Marsh
Richland

MAPS
New York Atlas: Map 83
USGS Quadrangle: Pulaski

INFORMATION
Prominent fish species: Largemouth bass, smallmouth bass, and
northern pike

Deer Creek meanders through one of the extensive marshes that line
the shores of eastern Lake Ontario. Fortunately, many of these marshes have protection from development by inclusion in six state parks or
wildlife management areas. Although the creek affords a view of only
a tiny portion of the Deer Creek Wildlife Management Area, we found
that the accessible area around the creek abounds with wildlife. True to
its name, a deer drank from the creek as we paddled along; upon spotting us, it crashed off through the thick cattails, waving its white tail at
us in annoyance.

Because Deer Creek remains unobtrusive—currently with no outlet to the lake—not many people boat here, compared with the heavy
fishing and recreational use of the Salmon River, just to the south.
Thus, the wildlife has not been forced to become nocturnal. When we
paddled here in June, we saw at least a dozen muskrats harvesting grass
in the late afternoon sun; one unconcerned fellow sat out in plain view
on the shore and watched us with a wary eye as we paddled by. On our
return trip we surprised a beaver cutting alder branches along the shore.
After staring at us for a few moments as we approached, it slid into the
water and glided by to get a better look at us. Satisfied that we did not
belong in its environs, it whacked the water vigorously, sending show-
ers into the air in front of us.

Numerous female snapping turtles—some certainly weighing 25
or 30 pounds—had climbed out onto the soft banks to lay eggs. As we
rounded a bend, we spotted one excavating a nest near the top of a huge
beaver lodge. Though we tried not to disturb her, she spotted us and,
amazingly, just let go and rolled like a rock, tumbling snout over tail
down the side of the lodge, ending with a large splash in the water.

Snapping turtles inhabit freshwater marshes and streams from
southern Canada to the Gulf Coast and from the Atlantic to the Rock-

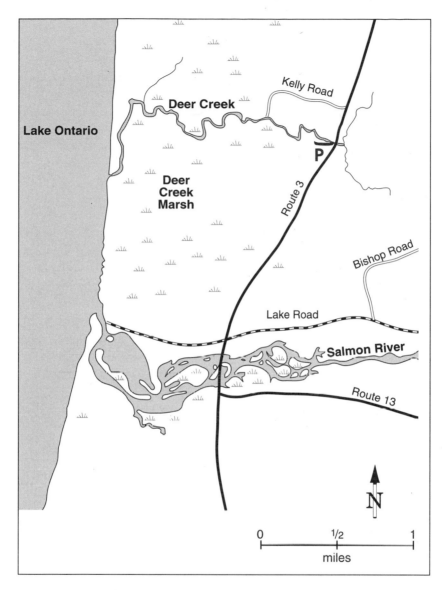

ies. They usually come up on land only to lay eggs; rarely do they bask on logs like other turtles. If you have ever confronted a big one on land—a huge one can reach 60 pounds—you probably know they act aggressively and will bite anything nearby. Their powerful bite can easily sever errant fingers. Surprisingly, they remain docile in the water; when stepped on, they just retract their heads into the shell. Indeed, some people hunt for them by walking barefoot in muddy areas, feeling with their toes for the saw-toothed rear edge of the carapace. Having found the nonlethal end, they reach down and yank the turtle out of the water by its long tail. We have no firsthand knowledge of this technique and should not be held responsible for any mishaps.

We also saw several great blue herons patiently stalking the shallows; at one point, we saw three of these majestic birds in the air at once. A veery called from the woods, while a rufous-sided towhee piped up from the brush. Marsh wrens, occasionally popping up into sight, sang melodiously from the reeds, while a female mallard with her brood of ducklings paddled back into the protection of the surrounding marsh. Red-winged blackbirds, by all odds the most common marsh bird, dangled from cattail stems as we slipped by.

Down by Lake Ontario, spotted sandpipers ran along the tall barrier dunes; a colony of bank swallows had carved nest cavities into the steeper sides of the dunes. Invading cottonwoods struggled to hold the dunes together, warding off erosion from rain and particularly from harsh winter winds off the lake. The "outlet" turned out to be an exposed sandbar—littered with the tiny dead shells of invading zebra mussels. These bars build up because winds from the west blow on most days across this shallow end of Lake Ontario, carrying along sand and the rest of the lake bottom. The sand deposits along the shore, choking off channels and building dunes. New channels get cut both by

A sandbar temporarily keeps Deer Creek from draining into Lake Ontario. Occasional storms alternately open and close access to the lake.

large storms off the lake and by inland runoff after major rains. We no longer wondered why no current flowed on Deer Creek.

The creek itself presents a study in contrasts. Alternately flowing by alders and oaks, through narrow then wide channels, by cattail swamps and coastal sand dunes, it provides a rich variety of habitats for plants, the basis of the food chain. Besides the alders and strong white oaks, we saw jewelweed with its delicate leaves, mighty hemlocks, clumps of yellow iris, and huge varieties of aquatic vegetation. This area and the other lakeshore parks and wildlife management areas contain the largest variety of water lilies in the U.S., including two species with white flowers and four varieties with yellow flowers.

Instead of paddling directly back to the boat access, we continued on upstream, passing under the Route 3 bridge. As we passed under, a raft of nesting barn swallows exploded out from under the bridge. We could paddle only a little way upstream, out into farm country, before the creek became impassable, but we did see a couple of broods of Canada geese and wood ducks above the bridge. As we paddled back down to the boat access in the waning sun, as it reflected on the placid water, we reflected on the huge amount of wildlife that we had seen in this incredibly biologically rich wildlife management area.

Getting There

From Watertown, go south on I-81 to the Route 13 exit in Pulaski. Go west on Route 13 until it ends at Route 3. Turn right, and go north on Route 3 for 1.8 miles. Turn left into the parking lot by the road by the sign for Deer Creek Wildlife Management Area. Hike the 125 yards down to the water.

From Rome, take Route 69 west; turn right onto Route 13 in Camden, and take it until it ends at Route 3. Continue as above.

Lakeview Wildlife Management Area—North and South Colwell Ponds, Goose Pond, Floodwood Pond, and Lakeview Pond

Ellisburg

MAPS
 New York Atlas: Map 83
 USGS Quadrangles: Ellisburg and Henderson
INFORMATION
 Prominent fish species: Largemouth bass and northern pike

Three access points allow paddlers to enter the Lakeview Wildlife Management Area on the south, the southeast, and the north. The southern boat launch provides access to South Colwell and North Colwell Ponds. The other two—one on South Sandy Creek and the other on Lakeview Pond—provide access to a series of interconnected creeks, sloughs, and ponds.

On your way to the South Colwell Pond boat access off Montario Point Road, stop at the lookout tower on the right, and enjoy the view out over the marsh. Most of the eastern shore of Lake Ontario harbored extensive wetlands. Although shortsighted humans drained some of these wetlands for agriculture and development, extensive pockets remain protected by a series of six state parks and wildlife management areas. The large expanse trailing off into the distance before you—Lakeview Wildlife Management Area—represents the largest of these remaining wetlands.

We paddled the Colwell Ponds in the middle of June, a perfect time for wildlife viewing. Because little water flows through these scenic ponds, they later become choked with aquatic vegetation. Trees cover the barrier dunes and narrow-leaved cattails ring the ponds, providing protected habitat for numerous white-tailed deer and multihued wood ducks. As we paddled the shoreline in the early morning, flocks of male wood ducks exploded from the cattails with their very unducklike cries, and deer crashed through the cattails after we interrupted their morning drink. In contrast, green-backed herons waited patiently over the water, suspended from low perches waiting to spear passing

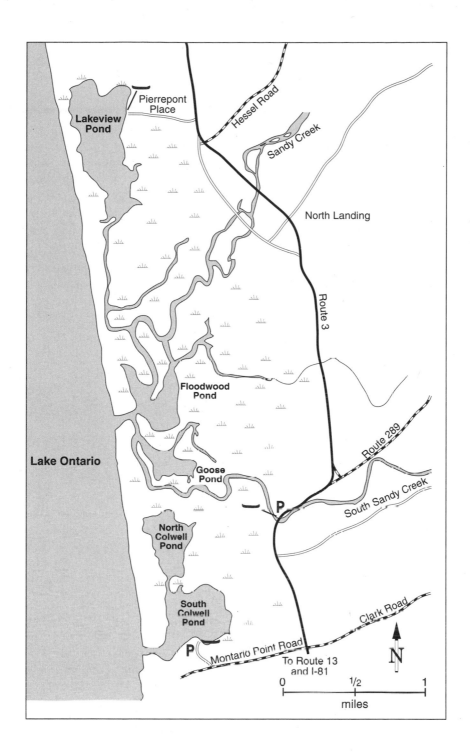

Lakeview Pond

Pierrepont
Place

Hessel Road

Sandy Creek

North Landing

Route 3

Floodwood
Pond

Lake Ontario

Goose
Pond

Route 289

South Sandy Creek

P

North
Colwell
Pond

South
Colwell
Pond

Clark Road

P

Montario Point Road

To Route 13
and I-81

N

0   1/2   1

miles

fish, and great blue herons stood stock-still out in the water, also waiting, but for somewhat larger passing fish.

Even in mid-June, aquatic plants crowded the water's surface, including an extensive patch of water crowfoot—a member of the buttercup family—with its small white flowers projecting just an inch or two above the water's surface. Note its submerged, threadlike leaves, evenly spaced along the stalk.

As we paddled out through a light morning mist hanging low over the water, a huge caddis fly hatch was on. Millions of tiny all-white flies flew erratically over the surface in some primordial mating ritual. As the sun rose into the sky, the caddis flies headed for the filtered light making its way through the tall trees. Caddis fly larvae build underwater structures of small twigs or stones and feed on microscopic underwater plants and animals that drift by. When they hatch into adults, they can be identified by their wings running the length of their bodies, folded over their backs like tents.

As we watched the terns, seemingly for an hour, we also watched the pond's surface change from early morning glasslike conditions to a wind-rippled surface. As the land heats up from the early morning sun, warm air rises. To replace the rising mass, cooler replacement air drifts in from Lake Ontario's surface, quietly at first, building in strength throughout the morning and early afternoon. Toward evening, along with the setting sun, the wind dies again and drifts toward calm.

Somewhat reluctantly, we left the terns and Colwell Ponds and headed to the South Sandy Creek boat access. With two cars, paddlers could travel from the north end of Lakeview Pond, down through Floodwood and Goose Ponds, and up South Sandy Creek to the boat access on Route 3. With winds out of the south, you might want to paddle this route in the opposite direction. With winds off Lake Ontario—the usual state of affairs—coastal dunes provide some protection from the wind and travel direction becomes less important.

If you wish solitude, we recommend you put in at South Sandy Creek access and paddle downstream into Goose Pond. Large willows and huge box elders crowd the water; several deadfalls—called structure by fishermen—in the water provide habitat for fish and turtles. We had no problem paddling around them. Surprisingly, we found a muskrat sitting out on one of these deadfalls, just watching us as we glided by.

Resist the temptation to paddle by Goose Pond, a wild, wonderful place to study aquatic plants and ducks in solitude. Yellow pond lily mats the surface, and clumps of very-narrow-leaved arrowhead poke up

A view from the lookout tower out over the flat coastal plain of the Lakeview Wildlife Management Area and Lake Ontario.

in clusters, while pickerelweed appears in patches. Cattails, with hidden marsh wrens singing their melodious songs, ring the pond. More black terns skimmed the marsh's surface, while ducks fed near the edges. Deer cautiously edged out to the water for a drink.

Floodwood Pond has more open water than Goose Pond, but it has its share of aquatic plants. As you paddle north out of Floodwood Pond, watch carefully for a narrow channel heading west that leads to Lakeview Pond. Yellow pond lilies cover this long, straight channel, providing outstanding habitat for pike, bass, turtles, and frogs.

We spent some time here trying to sort out the four resident species of yellow pond lily. We distinguished the two larger-flowered (1.5 to 2.5 inches wide), larger-leaved (8 to 15 inches long) species by how the leaf lobes leave the submerged stalk. In *Nuphar advena* the lobes spread from each other at about a 45-degree angle, while the lobes on *Nuphar variegatum* cross each other. *Nuphar microphyllum*, as its name suggests, has leaves less than 5 inches long and flowers less than an inch wide. The fourth species, *Nuphar rubrodiscum*, is the most difficult to identify; technically, it has leaves 5 to 8 inches long, flowers 1 to 1.5 inches wide, stigma with more than 10 rays (fewer than 10 in *N. microphyllum*), and leaf notch about half the length of the midrib (two-thirds in *N. microphyllum*). In practice, the last two species gave us fits; we're still not sure we've identified them correctly in some cases.

On your return from Lakeview Pond, you can turn left (northeast) onto Sandy Creek. We paddled up Sandy Creek to North Landing to the string of camps and houses on the island where the creek divides. Given the huge expanse of wetland wilderness waiting for exploration downstream, we decided to turn around. On the way back, watch for the relatively wide human-made connector that leads from Sandy Creek into the top of Floodwood Pond. When you get to the pilings at the end of the connector, a left turn (northeast) takes you up into the far reaches of the marsh, while a right turn (south-southwest) takes you back down toward Goose Pond.

We loved paddling this area, a true wildlife and plant paradise. Eventually we will return to sort out those *Nuphar* species.

Getting There

Take I-81 to the Pulaski exit, and turn right onto Route 13 west. When Route 13 ends in Port Ontario, turn right onto Route 3. Travel north on Route 3 for 10.0 miles to Montario Point Road, where Clark Road goes off to the right. Turn left onto Montario Point Road, and drive 0.7 mile. Turn right onto the South Colwell boat access road; the boat launch, in the midst of an open woodland with mowed grass, is 0.3 mile down this road.

From Watertown, take Route 3 south, watching for signs for Pierrepont Place (Lakeview Pond access), South Sandy Creek access, and Montario Point Road (Colwell Ponds access).

To get to the South Sandy Creek boat access from Colwell Ponds, go back out to Route 3. Turn left, and travel north on Route 3 for 1.1 miles; the boat access is on the left just after you cross the bridge.

To get to the Lakeview Pond access from South Sandy Creek, travel north on Route 3 for 3.3 miles to Pierrepont Place; the road is easy to miss. You'll know you're getting close when you cross the green iron bridge over Sandy Creek and pass Hessel Road going off right. Pierrepont Place is 0.2 mile past Hessel Road. Turn left onto Pierrepont Place; the boat access is 0.5 mile straight down this gravel road.

Black River Bay
Brownsville and Hounsfield

MAPS
>   **New York Atlas:** Maps 83 and 91
>   **USGS Quadrangles:** Dexter and Sackets Harbor

INFORMATION
>   **Prominent fish species:** Largemouth bass, smallmouth bass, and
>   northern pike
>   **Camping:** Black River Bay Campground; 315-639-3735

Black River Bay is a shallow, marshy wildlife paradise, protected as part of the Dexter Wildlife Management Area. The northernmost wildlife management area on Lake Ontario's eastern shore, Dexter harbors many plants and animals and few paddlers.

Supposedly, four boat launch points provide access to the bay. We launched from three of these—Black River Bay Campground, the southeast arm off Route 180, and Muskalonge Bay off Military Road—but did not check out the hand-carry access marked on the New York Atlas (Map 91) where Doane Road crosses the north arm.

We launched just after sunup from the campground on Black River, paddling southwest down toward the bay. After clearing the campground, we paddled by a few small islands with beautiful fractured rock formations, eventually leading out onto a huge bay with Lake Ontario in the background. We were totally unprepared for the unfolding sight. Shimmering water on the horizon made it impossible to judge distance over the glasslike surface that lay before us. Ripples created by Caspian terns diving on fish barely stirred the surface waters. Rarely do we confront a body of water this large under such calm conditions.

When we paddled here in late July, a high-pressure cell had stalled over the eastern Great Lakes, providing crystal-clear skies and, more importantly, absolutely windless conditions. In the summer, afternoon breezes blowing eastward off Lake Ontario can whip up formidable waves. Local fishermen told us that these waves often surge unimpeded right up Black River Bay, making boating treacherous. Under windy conditions, we strongly recommend sticking to the more protected Muskalonge Bay on the south.

Along the northern edge of Black River Bay, a northern water snake (*Nerodia sipedon*) swam along with us for a short distance before

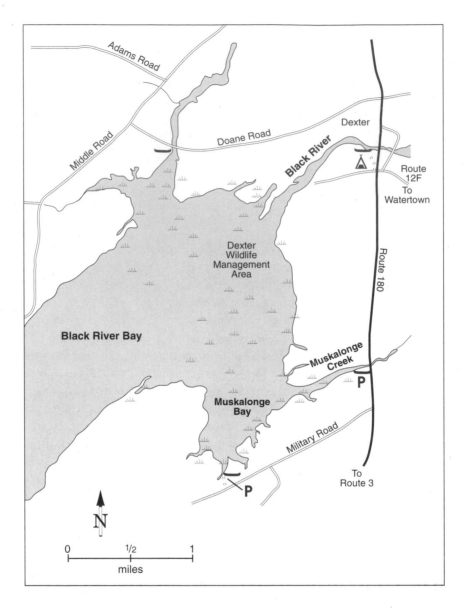

retreating into the cattails. Huge carp periodically startled us as they thrashed in the shallow, muddy water.

Much of the Muskalonge Bay, and particularly the southern end, contains intermittent dense stands of cattails that protect wildlife and paddlers from wind-driven waves. Here we found, literally, a dozen great blue herons fishing the shallows and several nesting black terns. When we got too close to one of the small cattail islands, three or four black terns dive-bombed us until we retreated quite a distance.

On the east end of the bay, cattail-covered islands give way to willow-clad shores. Here, among the trees, we listened to the "pee-o-wee" call of the eastern wood pewee, the whistled "peet-er, peet-er, peet-er" of tufted titmice, and the "bir-dee, bir-dee, bir-dee" song of the cardinal. Beaver had dined recently on felled willows. A crow-sized pileated woodpecker flew in undulating flight over the water in front of us, alighting in a dead tree. But the real attraction remained the marsh.

We found the diminutive yellow pond lily, *Nuphar microphyllum,* with leaves less than five inches long and flowers less than an inch across. And floating heart, *Nymphoides cordata,* an aquatic gentian with small heart-shaped leaves and small white flowers, choked the channel in protected areas. Acres of white and yellow water lilies, plants that don't grow in water deeper than four feet, confirmed the shallowness of the bay.

Clumps of arrowhead and yellow-flowered bladderwort, especially along Muskalonge Creek, added to the interesting plants to study. We watched as many as five great blue herons fishing at once, and ducks scurried into the cattails as we approached. Spotted sandpipers bobbed along the shore, and barn swallows skimmed the water's surface for a morning drink. We watched a cormorant trying to deal with a fish way too large to swallow, as marsh wrens serenaded us with their melodious songs off in the cattails. We spent most of the morning paddling the entire shoreline of the south end of the bay, and we believe that this protected area is a great place for quiet-water paddlers to study plants and wildlife.

Getting There

From Watertown, take Route 3 west to Route 180. Turn right (north) onto Route 180. In about 2 miles, Military Road goes off to the left. At this point you have a choice: take Military Road to the left for 1.3 miles to the boat access on the right, or continue on Route 180 north for 0.3 mile to the boat access on Muskalonge Creek on the left.

Also, you can launch at the Black River Bay Campground on the Black River, farther north just off Route 180. From Military Road, travel north on Route 180 for 1.9 miles to where Route 12F goes right. Instead of going right onto Route 12F, turn left. The campground entrance is just a few hundred feet down this road on the right.

Red Lake and Indian River
Theresa

MAPS
> **New York Atlas:** Map 92
> **USGS Quadrangles:** Muskellunge Lake and Redwood

INFORMATION
> **Area:** 359 acres; maximum depth: 47 feet
> **Prominent fish species:** Smallmouth bass, largemouth bass, northern pike
> **Camping:** Kring Point State Park; 315-482-2444

Red Lake, a fairly small, picturesque body of water, provides pleasant paddling plus access onto a quiet, winding section of the Indian River.

A great blue heron stood near the boat access where pickerelweed, bulrush, and grasses crowd the shoreline. Along much of the southeastern side of the lake, extensive cliffs extend upward from the water 100 feet or more. Many areas drip with polypody fern, lichens, and

Crimson cardinal flower in bloom along the banks of the Indian River.

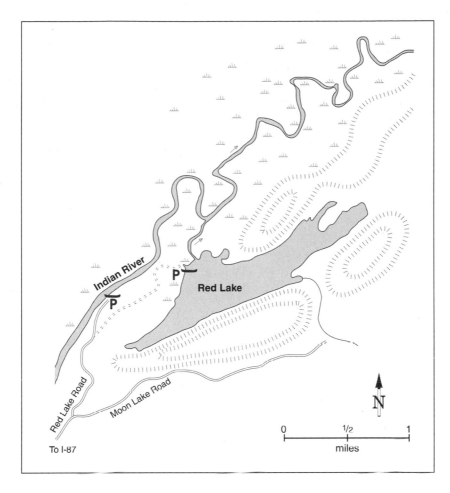

thick moss. On the more exposed cliff faces, look for delicate, lavender bell-like flowers of harebell, which has become established in the tiniest of cracks. The scarlet cardinal flower—always a favorite—grows in rocky soil closer to the water.

Where the banks are not too steep for vegetation to become take hold, you will see a diverse mix of conifer and deciduous trees—everything from northern white cedar to species usually found farther south, such as shagbark hickory and white oak. Hemlock, white pine, paper birch, basswood, white ash, silver maple, sugar maple, and red oak are also common. This area has high species diversity, because it represents a transition between the higher-elevation Adirondacks and the low-lying floodplains of the St. Lawrence River.

Just northwest of the boat access, Red Lake flows slowly through the outlet channel into Indian River. This broad, deep channel passes between a marsh and a small hill for a little less than a half mile to the river. Thick vegetation covers the banks, but surprisingly little floating vegetation occurs in the channel.

Indian River flows northeast toward Black Lake and the St. Lawrence River, but its channel meanders extensively. The minimal midsummer current makes paddling in both directions fairly easy. But in the spring and after heavy rainfalls, the water level rises quickly. Indian River and its tributaries drain a sizable portion of the western Adirondacks. When it rains steadily over the region, the river can rise a few feet in less than 24 hours. At high water, the river spreads out, providing access to bottomland, but the current makes it more dangerous and difficult, if not impossible, to paddle in both directions.

Thick aquatic vegetation lines the river. Pickerelweed dominates in most areas, with patches of arrowhead mixed in. Cardinal flower and swamp milkweed grow in abundance, along with buttonbush—with white spherical flower clusters and sycamore-like seedpods.

Along a five-mile stretch of river, we passed several beaver lodges, including a massive one with lots of cuttings. Mussel shells littered the bottom and shoreline. We saw red-tailed hawk, osprey, kingfisher, yellow warbler, common yellowthroat, white-throated sparrow, great blue heron, eastern phoebe, eastern wood pewee, red-winged blackbird, grackle, and ring-billed gull. Painted turtles sought a few rays of sunlight on a mostly overcast afternoon.

As we rounded a bend, a group of turkey vultures erupted into flight. They had been feeding on the bloated carcass of a huge snapping turtle. The vultures' broad wings wafted essence of long-dead turtle onto the river as we beat a hasty retreat from the malodors.

Getting There

Get off I-81 at Exit 49 and take Route 411 east toward Theresa (after crossing Route 37, Route 411 turns into Route 26). At the junction of Main Street and Commercial Street in Theresa, turn left onto Commercial Street (Route 26). Take Commercial Street out of downtown, and turn left onto Bridge Street. Cross the bridge over the Indian River almost immediately, and in 0.2 mile turn left off Bridge Street onto Red Lake Road (at the top of a hill). After 2.7 miles, turn left, staying on Red Lake Road, and continue another 0.9 mile. The road forks here, with the left fork reaching a boat access on the Indian River in 0.1 mile and the right fork bringing you to the Red Lake boat access in 1.0 mile (the road turns to dirt at this fork).

Crooked Creek
Alexandria and Hammond

MAPS
>   **New York Atlas:** Map 92
>   **USGS Quadrangles:** Chippewa Bay and Redwood

INFORMATION
>   **Prominent fish species:** Largemouth bass and northern pike
>   **Camping:** Kring Point State Park; 315-482-2444

Kring Point State Park, one of the first parks established on the St. Lawrence River back in 1898, offers one of the most scenic campgrounds in the Thousand Islands region and a wonderful base for exploring the streams and lakes in this region. Half of the 108 camping sites front on the water, and every site has a view of Goose Bay or the St. Lawrence. Because of its popularity, we strongly recommend that you make reservations.

More than 1,700 islands dot the St. Lawrence, luring fishermen from all over the East. Ironside Island—owned by The Nature Conservancy—in the waterway just north of the park provides a home for the largest great blue heron rookery on the river. Dozens of treetop nests—some measuring six feet wide and four feet deep—dot the island. We recommend that only seasoned paddlers venture out on the river, even under calm conditions, because of the truly huge wakes churned up by commercial vessels traveling the Great Lakes and by large pleasure craft.

Instead, we recommend that you turn your attention inland to some of the small streams and lakes in the region. One of our favorites is meandering Crooked Creek, which wends its way through extensive marshlands just on the other side of Route 12 from Kring Point State Park.

Three access points provide opportunities for trips of different lengths. We had two cars and decided to do a one-way trip downstream to Schermerhorn Landing. But first we put in at the Route 1 bridge and paddled upstream for just less than three miles, then paddled back downstream, under the Route 1 bridge, continuing on down to Chippewa Bay. We passed under the Route 12 bridge, which also has a boat access. If you take a leisurely trip, stopping to explore side channels or to study the plants and abundant wildlife, this trip will take most of a day.

Cattails become your constant companion on this trip, but many other plant species, both aquatic and terrestrial, crop up to keep things from getting boring. Pines appear beyond the marsh's fringe, along

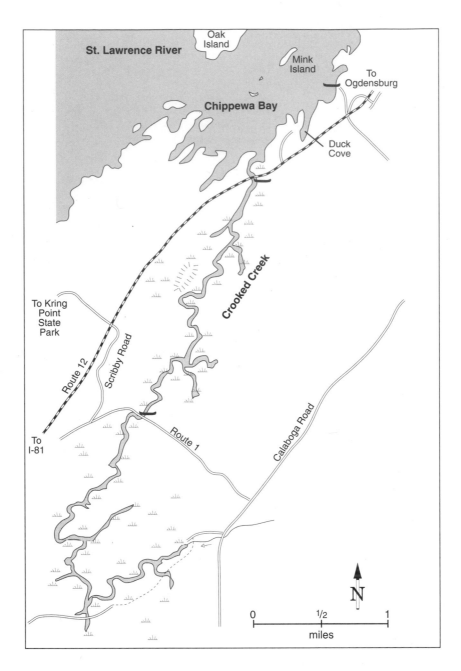

with large red oaks, but we focused more on the water.

We found huge patches of bryozoa, invertebrates in their own phylum (phyla include birds, mammals, reptiles, etc.). This bryozoan, in the genus *Pectinatella,* consists of huge, closely linked colonies of individuals called zooids. The zooids have protruding hairs, or cilia, that sweep the water to snare passing microscopic protozoans, algae, and diatoms. The slimy, gelatinous colonies look somewhat like translucent pineapples. We see bryozoa only infrequently, which is unfortunate because they are an indicator species. Their welcome presence points to pollution-free water.

Besides the ubiquitous cattails, we found rafts of yellow pond lily, lots of tuberous water lily, a fair amount of floating heart in the upper reaches, and frequent large patches of yellow-flowered bladderwort in the tea-colored water.

In one downstream section of the creek, tall cliffs and massive slabs of pinkish rock add dramatic variety to an otherwise marshy paddle. Some of these cliffs rise 50 or 60 feet above the water.

We watched a pair of red-tailed hawks circling lazily on afternoon thermals, rising skyward to get a better view of the surrounding fields. These rodent specialists have the widest range of all U.S. hawks, inhabiting every conceivable niche from desert to wet forest, sea level to mountaintops, coast to coast, and border to border.

We also looked for the typical marsh species, including large numbers of great blue heron, common yellowthroat, and the most abundant bird, the red-winged blackbird. We very much enjoyed our lazy trip down the creek, and because of our pleasant experience, we really didn't mind having to paddle the last little bit to Schermerhorn Landing out on crowded Chippewa Bay. If you plan a one-way trip ending at the landing, and if you get out onto a bay with wind-whipped waves, we strongly suggest that you paddle back upstream to the Route 12 bridge and walk the 1.4 miles to Schermerhorn Landing to retrieve your second vehicle.

Getting There

From Ogdensburg, travel south on Route 37. Take Route 12 when it splits off to the right. Take Route 12 south to the turnoff to Kring Point State Park. Either turn into the park, if you are camping, or turn left to get to the Route 1 boat access.

From the junction of Route 12 and the Kring Point State Park Road, here are the mileages: Route 12 bridge over Crooked Creek—1.6 miles north; Schermerhorn Landing turnoff—2.6 miles north on the left (the landing is 0.4 mile down this road; you may not park at the boat access but must leave your car back out near Route 12 in a designated parking area); Route 1 boat access—0.7 mile down Scribby Road directly across from the park road, then turn left onto Route 1, and go 0.2 mile to the bridge over Crooked Creek. There is limited parking along the road.

Coles Creek

Louisville and Waddington

MAPS
  New York Atlas: Map 99
  USGS Quadrangles: Chase Mills and Louisville

INFORMATION
  Area: 680 acres
  Prominent fish species: Warm-water species
  Camping: Coles Creek State Park; 315-388-5636

Coles Creek, flowing into the mighty St. Lawrence River, has the distinction of being the northernmost body of water in this guidebook. A large earthen dam at its outlet into the St. Lawrence backs up Coles Creek for several miles. The southern end of the impoundment has only truly tiny feeder creeks, which should make this body of water more a swamp than a flowage. Only about a mile away, the Grass River, which drains a major portion of the northwest Adirondacks, takes away much of the water in Coles Creek's environs. Having said this, the magnitude of the northward-flowing water under the bridges and culverts surprised us, especially in the drought year of 1995. Do major underwater springs feed this flowage?

Eurasian milfoil—an invading pest species that's clogging waterways all over the Northeast, crowding out native species—grows in profusion in the northern part of Coles Creek. Undoubtedly brought there by contaminated trailers and boats, it undoubtedly will spread rapidly throughout the waterway, especially during windstorms. However, we found only native fanwort in the southern parts of the impoundment. The three causeways that bisect the waterway have low culverts or low stone bridges, not high enough to paddle under. They also limit the action of wind-driven waves that might carry invading species under them. The surprising amount of current coming through these culverts from south to north also serves to keep milfoil from invading the southern portions. We will check back in a year or two to mark the progression down the waterway of this pesky invader.

Going up and over the two roads and the old railroad bed does not provide much of a challenge because the grades lie close to the water's surface. The several-mile-long waterway represents a real dichotomy: on the western shore, Canada geese and ring-billed gulls gambol in farmers' weedy fields, while the heavily wooded eastern shore with

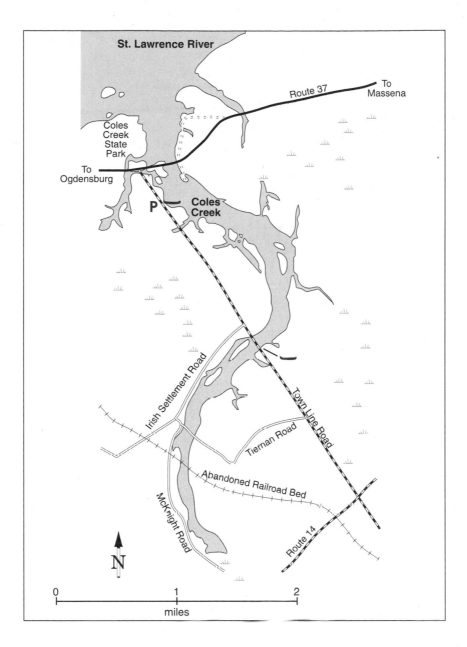

St. Lawrence River

To
Massena

Route 37

Coles
Creek
State
Park

To
Ogdensburg

P   Coles
Creek

Irish Settlement Road

Town Line Road

Tiernan Road

Abandoned Railroad Bed

McKnight Road

Route 14

N

0   1   2

miles

more-jagged inlets has a much wilder feel to it. A belted kingfisher guarded the entrance to a cove. Back in its depths, lacy green hemlock boughs bent low over the water, lending a primeval feeling of dark isolation. As we watched a painted turtle slide off a log into the stagnant, pea green water, a great blue heron startled us as it bolted skyward, squawking away; we spotted these magnificent predators in nearly every cove and in many shallow, marshy locations. In two coves, we watched white-tailed deer drinking at the water's edge.

Tree-species diversity provides another contrast between the north and south ends of Coles Creek. Most everywhere, deciduous trees dominate the landscape. On the north, cottonwood, big-toothed aspen, paper birch, American beech, yellow birch, black gum, ash, maple, and basswood dot the shoreline, while on the south, large conifers have made inroads into the hardwood dominance. Surprisingly, tamarack seems to be the biggest tree on the south end, with fair numbers of tall white pine and northern white cedar. When the southern understory isn't pine needles, it's ferns. Sumac surrounds the old railroad grade. Near the far southern shore, the water and surrounding land turn swampy, with large patches of cattails and more and more aquatic vegetation, including pondweed, yellow pond lily, bulrushes, and more. Bullfrogs called from the grassy shore and from among the lily pads.

We paddled back into every one of the many coves and around every island, finding great blue heron at every turn. Because of the depth of most of the coves, paddling the complete shoreline of Coles Creek presents quite a challenge for a daylong trip. As we emerged from the coves, the scene changed to common terns performing aerial acrobatics and yellowthroats singing in the underbrush. Loons dove for fish, and eastern wood pewees sang off in the woods. Some old beaver activity caused us to wonder why they disappeared. Will another colony move in soon to harvest the dominant hardwoods along the shore? Have conifers moved in on the southern part of the impoundment because of selective logging by beaver?

As we paddled back to the boat access, we noted another alien species starting its invasion: purple loosestrife. How soon will alien species crowd out our native species in these waters and shores? Only time will tell.

Getting There

From Ogdensburg, travel east on Route 37. Just after the entrance to Coles Creek State Park, turn right onto Town Line Road. The boat access is on the left, 0.3 mile down the road. If you continue down Town Line Road to where it bisects Coles Creek, there is a boat launch area on the far side of the causeway (this access is 1.8 miles from Route 37). From here, you can paddle south or north.

From Massena, travel west on Route 37 to the causeway over Coles Creek. Just past the marina on the right, turn left onto Town Line Road, and proceed as above.

Appendix A
Camping and Cabin Information
New York State Parks
New York State Forest Preserves

Addresses/Telephone Numbers for Information

Office of Parks, Recreation and Historic Preservation
Empire State Plaza
Albany, NY 12238
General Information on State Parks: 518-474-0456; TDD 518-486-1899
Campground and Cabin Reservations Only: 800-456-CAMP (2267);
   TDD 518-486-1899

Public Information and Publications Unit
New York State Department of Environmental Conservation
50 Wolf Road, Room 111
Albany, NY 12233-5253
General Information on DEC: 518-457-3521
Campground and Cabin Information Only: 518-457-2500

Listing of State Parks by Region

Office of Parks, Recreation and Historic Preservation
State Park Campgrounds

Allegany Region—716-354-9101

Allegany: Quaker	716-354-2182	Rt. 17, Exit 18, 11 mi. w. of Salamanca
Allegany: Red House	716-354-9121	Rt. 17, Exit 19, 7 mi. w. of Salamanca
Lake Erie	716-792-9214	Rt. 5, 7 mi. w. on Dunkirk

Central Region—315-492-1756

Bowman Lake	607-334-2718	off Rt. 220, 8 mi. w. of Oxford
Chenango Valley	607-648-5251	Rt. 369, 13 mi. n. of Binghamton

Chittenango Falls	315-655-9620	Rt. 13, 4 mi. n. of Cazenovia
Delta Lake	315-337-4670	Rt. 46, 6 mi. ne. of Rome
Gilbert Lake	607-432-2114	Rts. 205 & 51, 12 mi. nw. of Oneonta
Glimmerglass	607-547-8662	4 mi. s. of Rt. 20, E. Springfield
Green Lakes	315-637-6111	Rts. 290 & 5, 10 mi. e. of Syracuse
Hunts Pond	607-859-2249	off Rt. 8, 2 mi. n. of S. New Berlin
Oquaga Creek	607-467-4160	off Rt. 206, 11 mi. s. of Sidney
Pixley Falls	315-942-4713	Rt. 46, 6 mi. s. of Boonville
Selkirk Shores	315-298-5737	Rt. 3, 3 mi. w. of Pulaski
Verona Beach	315-762-4463	Rt. 13, 7 mi. nw. of Oneida

Finger Lakes Region—607-387-7041

Buttermilk Falls	607-273-5761	Rt. 13 s. of Ithaca
Cayuga Lake	315-568-5163	Rt. 89, 3 mi. e. of Seneca Falls
Fair Haven Beach	315-947-5205	Rt. 104A, 2 mi. n. of Fair Haven
Fillmore Glen	315-497-0130	Rt. 38, 1 mi. s. of Moravia
Keuka Lake	315-536-3666	Rt. 54A, 6 mi. w. of Penn Yan
Sampson	315-585-6392	Rt. 96A, 11 mi. s. of Geneva
Stony Brook	716-335-8111	Rt. 36, 3 mi. s. of Dansville
Taughannock	607-387-6739	Rt. 89, 8 mi. n. of Ithaca
Robert H. Treman	607-273-3440	Rt. 13, 5 mi. s. of Ithaca
Watkins Glen	607-535-4511	main entrance, village of Watkins Glen

Genesee Region—716-493-3600

Darien Lake	716-547-9242	Harlow Rd., Darien Center
Hamlin Beach	716-964-2462	Lake Ontario St. Parkway, 25 mi. w. of Rochester
Lakeside Beach	716-682-5246	Lake Ontario St. Parkway, 35 mi. w. of Rochester
Letchworth	716-493-3600	Rt. 36, Mt. Morris, I-390 Exit 7, or Rt. 19A, Castile

Long Island Region—516-669-1000

Heckscher	516-581-2100	Heckscher St. Parkway, E. Islip
Hither Hills	516-668-2461	Montauk Highway, Montauk
Wildwood	516-929-4314	N. Country Rd., Wading River

Niagara Frontier Region—716-278-1770

Evangola	716-549-1802	Rt. 5, 27 mi. sw. of Buffalo, Irving
Four Mile Campsite	716-745-3802	Rt. 18 or Robert Moses Parkway, 4 mi. e. of Youngstown
Golden Hill	716-795-3885	Lower Lake Rd , off Rt. 269, Barker

Palisades Region—914-786-2701

Harriman: Beaver Pond Campgrounds	914-947-2792	Gate Hill Rd., 5 mi. w. of Stony Point

Saratoga-Capital Region—518-584-2000

Moreau Lake	518-793-0511	Exit 17S off I-87, S. Glens Falls
Max V. Shaul	518-827-4711	Rt. 30, 5 mi. s. of Middleburgh
Thompson's Lake	518-872-1674	Rt. 157, 18 mi. sw. of Albany

Taconic Region—914-889-4100

Clarence Fahnestock	914-225-7207	Rt. 301, w. of Taconic Parkway
Lake Taghkanic	518-851-3631	Rt. 82 at Taconic Parkway, 11 mi. s. of Hudson
Margaret Lewis Norrie	914-889-4646	Rt. 9, 4 mi. n. of Hyde Park
Rudd Pond	518-789-3059	off Rt. 22, 2 mi. n. of Millerton
Taconic: Copake Falls	518-329-3993	east of Rt. 22, Copake Falls

Thousand Islands Region—315-482-2593

Burnham Point	315-654-2324	Rt. 12E, 4 mi. e. of Cape Vincent
Canoe–Picnic Point	315-654-2522	access by boat only, Grindstone Island
Cedar Island	315-654-2522	access by boat only, Cedar Island
Cedar Point	315-654-2522	Rt. 12E, 6 mi. w. of Clayton
Coles Creek	315-388-5636	Rt. 37, 4 mi. e. of Waddington
Cumberland Bay	518-563-5240	Rt. 314, 1 mi. e. of Plattsburgh
Dewolf Point	315-482-2012	I-81, Exit 51, 2 mi. n. of Alexandria Bay
Eel Weir	315-393-1138	Rt. 812, 7 mi. s. of Ogdensburg
Grass Point	315-686-4472	Rt. 12, 1 mi. w. of I-81, Alexandria Bay
Higley Flow	315-262-2880	Rt. 56, 2 mi. e. of S. Colton
Jacques Cartier	315-375-6371	Rt. 12, 3 mi. w. of Morristown
Keewaydin	315-482-3331	Rt. 12, 1 mi. w. of Alexandria Bay
Kring Point	315-482-2444	Rt. 12, 6 mi. e. of Alexandria Bay
Long Point	315-649-5258	Rt. 12E, 8 mi. w. of

		Three Mile Bay
Macomb Reservation	518-643-9952	off Rt. 22B, 2 mi. w. of Schuyler Falls
Mary Island	315-654-2522	access by boat only, Alexandria Bay
Robert Moses	315-769-8663	off Rt. 37, 3 mi. n. of Massena
Southwick Beach	315-846-5338	off Rt. 3, 2 mi. w. of Woodville
Wellesley Island	315-482-2722	I-81, Exit 51, 4 mi. w. of Alexandria Bay
Westcott Beach	315-646-2239	Rt. 3, 2 mi. w. of Sackets Harbor
Whetstone Gulf	315-376-6630	Rt. 26, 6 mi. s. of Lowville

Department of Environmental Conservation Forest Preserve Public Campgrounds

Warrensburg—518-623-3671

Eagle Point	518-494-2220	Rt. 9, 2 mi. n. of Pottersville
Hearthstone Point	518-668-5193	Rt. 9N, 2 mi. n. of Lake George Village
Lake George Battleground	518-668-3348	Rt. 9, 1/4 mi. s. of Lake George Village
Lake George Islands:		
Glen Island	518-644-9696	Bolton Landing
Long Island	518-656-9426	Cleverdale
Narrow Island	518-499-1288	Huletts Landing
Luzerne	518-696-2031	Rt. 9N, 8 mi. sw. of Lake George Village
Rogers Rock	518-585-6746	Rt. 9N, 3 mi. n. of Hague

Raybrook—518-897-1309

Ausable Point	518-561-7080	Rt. 9, 12 mi. s. of Plattsburgh
Buck Pond	518-891-3449	off Rt. 86, 6 mi. n. of Gabriels

Crown Point Reservation	518-597-3603	off Rt. 9N, 8 mi. n. of Crown Point
Fish Creek Pond	518-891-4560	Rt. 30, 12 mi. e. of Tupper Lake
Lake Eaton	518-624-2641	Rt. 30, 2 mi. w. of Long Lake
Lake Harris	518-582-2503	Rt. 28N, 3 mi. n. of Newcomb
Lincoln Pond	518-942-5292	Rt. 7, 6 mi. s. of Elizabethtown
Meacham Lake	518-483-5116	Rt. 30, 19 mi. n. of Clear Lake Jct.
Meadowbrook	518-891-4351	Rt. 86, 4 mi. e. of Saranac Lake
Paradox Lake	518-532-7451	Rt. 74, 2 mi. e. of Severance
Poke-O-Moonshine	518-834-9045	Rt. 9, 6 mi. s. of Keeseville
Putnam Pond	518-585-7280	off Rt. 74, 6 mi. w. of Ticonderoga
Rollins Pond	518-891-3239	Rt. 30, 12 mi. e. of Tupper Lake
Saranac Lake Islands	518-891-3170	Rt. 3, 5 mi. w. of Saranac Lake Village
Sharp Bridge	518-532-7538	Rt. 9, 15 mi. n. of Schroon Lake
Taylor Pond	518-647-5250	Silver Lake Rd., 9 mi. nw. of Au Sable Forks
Wilmington Notch	518-946-7172	Rt. 86, 3.5 mi. w. of Wilmington

Herkimer—315-866-6330

Alger Island	315-369-3224	Rt. 28, 8 mi. e. of Old Forge
Nicks Lake	315-369-3314	off Rt. 28, 1.5 mi. sw. of Old Forge

Canton—315-386-4546

Cranberry Lake	315-848-2315	off Rt. 3, 1.5 mi. s. of Cranberry Lake Village

Indian Lake—518-648-5616

Brown Tract Pond	315-354-4412	Rt. 28, 7 mi. e. of Eagle Bay
Eighth Lake	315-354-4120	Rt. 28, 5 mi. w. of Raquette Lake
Forked Lake	518-624-6646	off Rt. 30, 3 mi. w. of Deerland Village
Golden Beach	315-354-4230	Rt. 28, 3 mi. n. of Raquette Lake
Indian Lake Islands	518-648-5300	Rt. 30, 14 mi. n. of Speculator
Lake Durant	518-352-7797	Rt. 28, 3 mi. e. of Blue Mountain Lake
Lewey Lake	518-648-5266	Rt. 30, 14 mi. n. of Speculator
Limekiln Lake	315-357-4401	off Rt. 28, 3 mi. se. of Inlet
Tioga Point	315-354-4230	Raquette Lake

Northville—518-863-8216

Caroga Lake	518-835-4241	Rt. 29A, 9 mi. n. of Gloversville
Little Sand Point	518-548-7585	off Rt. 8, 3 mi. w. of Piseco
Moffitt Beach	518-548-7102	Rt. 8, 4 mi. w. of Speculator
Northampton Beach	518-863-6000	Rt. 30, 1.5 mi. s. of Northville
Point Comfort	518-548-7586	off Rt. 8, 4 mi. w. of Piseco
Poplar Point	518-548-8031	off Rt. 8, 2 mi. w. of Piseco
Sacandaga	518-924-4121	Rt. 30, 4 mi. s. of Wells

Schenectady—518-357-2234

Bear Spring Mountain	607-865-6989	off Rt. 206, 5 mi. se. of Walton
Devil's Tombstone	914-688-7160	Rt. 214, 4 mi. s. of Hunter
Little Pond	914-439-5480	off Rt. 17, 14 mi. nw. of Livingston Manor
North/South Lake	518-589-5058	off Rt. 23A, 3 mi. ne. of Haines Falls

New Paltz—914-256-3002

Beaverkill	914-439-4281	off Rt. 17, 7 mi. nw. of Livingston Manor
Kenneth L. Wilson	914-679-7020	off Rt. 28, 4 mi. e. of Mt. Tremper on Rt. 40
Mongaup Pond	914-439-4233	off Rt. 17, 3 mi. n. of DeBruce
Woodland Valley	914-688-6747	off Rt. 28, 6 mi. sw. of Phonecia

PASSPORTS & PASSES

Empire Passport: Provides yearlong vehicle entry to state parks and recreation areas. Purchase can be made at participating facilities or by mail from Office of Parks (address above).

Golden Park Program: Provides New York State residents 62 or older free entry weekdays, holidays excluded; simply show New York driver's license or Nondriver Identification Card.

Access Pass: Provides New York State residents with permanent disabilities free entry to state parks and recreation areas. Purchase can be made by mail from Office of Parks (address above).

About the Authors

Alex Wilson is a writer in Dummerston, Vermont. He is an avid canoeist and naturalist and has written two other quiet-water canoeing guides for the Appalachian Mountain Club: *AMC Quiet Water Canoe Guide: Massachusetts/Connecticut/Rhode Island* and *AMC Quiet Water Canoe Guide: New Hampshire/Vermont.* He is the editor and publisher of *Environmental Building News* and a widely published freelance writer on energy, building technology, and environmental issues for such magazines as *Architecture, Progressive Architecture, Journal of Light Construction, Fine Homebuilding, Popular Science, Home,* and *Consumers Digest.*

John Hayes is a professor of biochemistry and environmental science at Marlboro College in Marlboro, Vermont. He has canoed and kayaked in Minnesota's Boundary Waters Canoe Area, in Georgia's Okefenokee Swamp, in Florida's Everglades, as well as throughout the Northeast. When not in the classroom, he often leads natural history field trips to Central America, the Southwest deserts, the Rockies, and the Everglades.

About the Appalachian Mountain Club

The Appalachian Mountain Club pursues an active conservation agenda while encouraging responsible recreation. Our philosophy is that successful, long-term conservation depends on firsthand experience of the natural environment. AMC's 67,000 members pursue interests in hiking, canoeing, skiing, walking, rock climbing, bicycling, camping, kayaking, and backpacking, and—at the same time—help safeguard the environment.

Founded in 1876, the club has been at the forefront of the environmental protection movement. As cofounder of several leading New England environmental organizations, and as an active member working in coalition with these and many other groups, the AMC has successfully influenced legislation and public opinion.

Conservation

The most recent efforts in the AMC conservation program include river protection, Northern Forest Lands policy, Sterling Forest (NY) preservation, and support for the Clean Air Act. The AMC depends upon its active members and grassroots supporters to promote this conservation agenda.

Education

The AMC's education department offers members and the general public a wide range of workshops, from introductory camping to the intensive Mountain Leadership School taught on the trails of the White Mountains. In addition, volunteers in each chapter lead hundreds of outdoor activities and excursions and offer introductory instruction in backcountry sports.

Research

The AMC's research department focuses on the forces affecting the ecosystem, including ozone levels, acid rain and fog, climate change, rare flora and habitat protection, and air quality and visibility.

Trails Program

Another facet of the AMC is the trails program, which maintains more than 1,400 miles of trail (including 350 miles of the Appalachian Trail) and more than 50 shelters in the Northeast. Through a coordinated effort of volunteers, seasonal crews, and program staff, the AMC contributes more than 10,000 hours of public service work each summer in the area from Washington, D.C., to Maine.

In addition to supporting our work by becoming an AMC member, hikers can donate time as volunteers. The club offers four unique weekly volunteer base camps in New Hampshire, Maine, Massachusetts, and New York. We also sponsor 10-day service projects throughout the United States, Adopt-a-Trail programs, trails day events, trail skills workshops, and chapter and camp volunteer projects.

The AMC has a long-standing connection to Acadia National Park. Working in cooperation with the National Park Service and Friends of Acadia, the AMC Trails Program provides many opportunities to preserve the park's resources. These include half-day volunteer projects for guests at AMC's Echo Lake Camp, 10-day service projects, weeklong volunteer crews in the fall, and trails day events. For more information on these public-service volunteer opportunities, contact the AMC Trails Program, Pinkham Notch Visitor Center, P.O. Box 298, Gorham NH 03581; 603-466-2721.

Alpine Huts

The club operates eight alpine huts in the White Mountains that provide shelter, bunks and blankets, and hearty meals for hikers. Pinkham Notch Visitor Center, at the foot of Mt. Washington, is base camp to the adventurous and the ideal location for individuals and families new to outdoor recreation. Comfortable bunk rooms, mountain hospitality, and home-cooked, family-style meals make Pinkham Notch Visitor Center a fun and affordable choice for lodging. For reservations, call 603-466-2727.

Publications

At the AMC main office in Boston and at Pinkham Notch Visitor Center in New Hampshire, the bookstore and information center stock the entire line of AMC publications, as well as other trail and river guides, maps, reference materials, and the latest articles on conservation issues. Guidebooks and other AMC gifts are available by mail order (800-262-4455) or by writing AMC, P.O. Box 298, Gorham NH 03581. Also available from the bookstore or by subscription is *Appalachia,* the country's oldest mountaineering and conservation journal.

Alphabetical Listing of Lakes and Ponds